Global Power and Local Struggles in Developing Countries

Studies in Global Social History

VOLUME 47

Studies in the Social History of the Global South

Series Editors

Touraj Atabaki (*International Institute of Social History, Amsterdam, The Netherlands & Leiden University, The Netherlands*)
Rossana Barragán (*International Institute of Social History, Amsterdam, The Netherlands*)
Stefano Bellucci (*Leiden University, The Netherlands & International Institute of Social History, Amsterdam, The Netherlands*)

VOLUME 2

The titles published in this series are listed at *brill.com/shgs*

Global Power and Local Struggles in Developing Countries

Contemporary Perspectives on Europe and the People without History, by Eric R. Wolf at 40

Edited by

Paul Stacey

BRILL

LEIDEN | BOSTON

Cover illustration: Photo by Annie Spratt on Unsplash.

Library of Congress Cataloging-in-Publication Data

Names: Stacey, Paul (Professor of international development), editor.
Title: Global power and local struggles in developing countries : contemporary perspectives on : Europe and the people without history, by Eric R. Wolf at 40 / edited by Paul Stacey.
Description: Leiden ; Boston : Brill, [2023] | Series: Studies in global social history, 2590-3144 ; volume 47 | Includes bibliographical references and index. | Summary: "The volume challenges dominant narratives of progress with a rich range of investigations of local struggles from the Global south which are based on original ethnographic research. The chapters take a point of departure in ideas and concepts developed by the pioneering anthropologist Eric R. Wolf in 'Europe and the People Without History', and emphasize the relevance and usefulness of applying Wolf to contemporary contexts. As such, the collection contributes to knowledge of dynamic relationships between local agency in the Global south, and broader political and economic processes that make 'people without history.' This shows global power as both excluding local groups at the same time as conditioning local struggles and the forms that social organization takes"– Provided by publisher.
Identifiers: LCCN 2022040951 (print) | LCCN 2022040952 (ebook) | ISBN 9789004525481 (hardback) | ISBN 9789004527928 (ebook)
Subjects: LCSH: Developing countries–Social conditions. | Social movements–Developing countries. | Progress. | Wolf, Eric R., 1923-1999. Europe and the people without history. | Wolf, Eric R., 1923-1999–Influence.
Classification: LCC HN980 .G663 2023 (print) | LCC HN980 (ebook) | DDC 306.09172/4–dc23/eng/20221117
LC record available at https://lccn.loc.gov/2022040951
LC ebook record available at https://lccn.loc.gov/2022040952

Typeface for the Latin, Greek, and Cyrillic scripts: "Brill". See and download: brill.com/brill-typeface.

ISSN 2590-3144
ISBN 978-90-04-52548-1 (harback)
ISBN 978-90-04-52792-8 (e-book)

Copyright 2023 by Paul Stacey. Published by Koninklijke Brill NV, Leiden, The Netherlands.
Koninklijke Brill NV incorporates the imprints Brill, Brill Nijhoff, Brill Hotei, Brill Schöningh, Brill Fink, Brill mentis, Vandenhoeck & Ruprecht, Böhlau, V&R unipress and Wageningen Academic.
Koninklijke Brill NV reserves the right to protect this publication against unauthorized use. Requests for re-use and/or translations must be addressed to Koninklijke Brill NV via brill.com or copyright.com.

This book is printed on acid-free paper and produced in a sustainable manner.

Contents

Preface and Acknowledgements   VII
List of Figures and Tables   IX
Notes on Contributors   X

1 Global Power and Local Struggles in Developing Countries: An Introduction   1
   Paul Stacey

2 Commodifying the Countermovement: How Foreign Funding Turns Haitian Social Movements into Commodities   36
   Joshua Steckley, Nixon Boumba and Marylynn Steckley

3 A Brief History of Workers on the Move: Power in Puerto Rican Farm Labour Migration   59
   Ismael García Colón

4 Masking the Past, Legitimizing the Present: State-Making and Precariatization in the Agro-Industrial Landscape, Colombia   86
   Inge-Merete Hougaard

5 A Political Ecology of Fetishism in Brazil's 'Discovery Coast'
   Crisis, Socio-environmental Hybridization, and Historical Amnesia on the Frontiers of Global Liberalism   112
   Gustavo S. Azenha

6 Europe and the People without Class: The Example of Ghana   150
   Ioannis Kyriakakis

7 Impossible Histories, Power, and Exclusion in the Gold Coast and Ghana 1930–2020   172
   Paul Stacey

8 Persistent Connections and Exclusions in Mozambique: From Colonial Anxieties to Contemporary Discourses about the Environment   201
   Raquel Rodrigues Machaqueiro

9   Chinese Indonesian Identity at Work: Political Exclusion and Division of Labour in Indonesia   228
     Tirza van Bruggen

10   Global Competition and Local Advantages: The Agency of Samoan Factory Youth in an Untold History of the Automotive Supply Chain   254
     Masami Tsujita

Index   281

Preface and Acknowledgements

This anthology is the result of a three-year collaboration between the editor and the contributors located around the world. To start the ball rolling, I sent out a call for abstracts on the academic mailing lists 'Anthropology Matters', and 'Crit-Geog-Forum' in March 2019 asking for examples of contemporary 'People without History' in the Global South. The call also went out to colleagues, networks, affiliations, different university mailing lists, and selected presenters at the AAG (American Association of Geographers) annual meeting, held in Washington DC, 3–7 April 2019. The responses to these initial calls yielded more specific requests sent to selected contributors to develop their ideas into full-length papers. The contributions were selected based on four criteria: First, the abstracts had to focus on contemporary connections between local contexts in the Global South and global political or economic forces. Second, the papers should be based predominantly on ethnographic data collection and fieldwork undertaken in the Global South. Third, was an ambition for the collection to cover as wide a geographical and empirical spread as possible across different Global South contexts and, ideally, for the chapters to have historical contexts as well. Fourth, the contributors should comprise a gender mix of both junior and senior scholars and have representation from the Global South itself. The latter aimed at providing an opportunity to develop individual research profiles as well as to inspire interdisciplinary research into processes of local–global connectivity. What you have in your hands is the product of these endeavours – a collection of explanations of interlocking and dynamic processes of differentiation, crisis, struggle, capitalist expansion, and political development across the Global South today. The anthology is produced without any specific research funding, but special thanks go to the Institute for Social Science and Business, Roskilde University, for covering the costs of participation in the AAG conference, the language editing, and Open Source options. I would also like to thank Eric Komlavi Hahonou, Johan Fischer, Jacob Rasmussen, Karmen Tornius, Somdeep Sen, Lone Riisgaard, and Kirsten Mogensen, at International Development Studies, Roskilde University, for providing helpful input on an early draft of the introduction, Raramai Campbell for formatting the text, and Mike Kirkwood for the language editing. At Brill, thanks go to Stefano Bellucci for the initial encouragement to contact Brill, the review committee for approving and supporting the proposal, and Alessandra Giliberto for editorial support. All the contributors wish to thank the two anonymous reviewers for providing extremely helpful and constructive comments on the first draft.

Paul Stacey
International Development Studies, Roskilde University
2 June 2022

Figures and Tables

Figures

3.1 Farmworkers being recruited by an official of the Puerto Rico department of labor, circa 1950s. Courtesy of the records of the migration division, archives of the Puerto Rican Diaspora, Centro de Estudios Puertorriqueños, Hunter College, CUNY   70

3.2 Chartered flight with Puerto Rican migrant farm workers, circa 1948. Courtesy of the records of the migration division, archives of the Puerto Rican Diaspora, Centro de Estudios Puertorriqueños, Hunter College, CUNY   72

3.3 Puerto Rican migrant farmworkers disembarking in Buffalo, New York, circa 1948. Courtesy of the records of the migration division, archives of the Puerto Rican Diaspora, Centro de Estudios Puertorriqueños, Hunter College, CUNY   73

3.4 PRDL official Eulalio Torres greeting migrant farmworkers arriving in the United States, circa 1948. Courtesy of the records of the migration division, archives of the Puerto Rican Diaspora, Centro de Estudios Puertorriqueños, Hunter College, CUNY   75

3.5 Migrants working in the fields, circa 1948. Courtesy of the records of the migration division, archives of the Puerto Rican Diaspora, Centro de Estudios Puertorriqueños, Hunter College, CUNY   79

4.1 The omnipresent sugarcane plantation in Brisas del Frayle, Cauca Valley. Source: Author   87

4.2 Manual sugarcane cutters in the fields around Brisas del Frayle. Source: Ricardo León   104

7.1 Balaiwura, Obimpeh J. Mbimgadong I, 2009. Source: Author   188

8.1 Map of Mozambique with Zambézia area, adapted by the author. Source United Nations database   206

9.1 Chinese-Indonesian shopkeeper. Source: Author   240

Tables

6.1 Employment status of employed persons 15 years and older (Ghana Statistical Service, 2012: 10)   160

6.2 Economically active population (15 years and older) by occupation   162

6.3 Economically active population (15 years and older) by industry   163

6.4 Economically active population 15 years and older, by employment status   164

6.5 Distribution of occupations/economic activities in fieldwork village, April 2004 (Kyriakakis 2012)   167

Notes on Contributors

Gustavo S. Azenha
is Executive Director of Columbia University's Institute of Latin American Studies (ILAS) and Lecturer in the Department of Anthropology. Gustavo holds a PhD from Cornell University, where his training and research focused on environmental anthropology and political ecology. He specializes in development and socio-environmental politics in Brazil, directing his primary research efforts towards examining the historical and contemporary interrelations between environmental, indigenous, and economic development policies. More broadly, his interests and expertise are concerned with the politics of inequality and with the role of civil society and social movements in public policy dynamics. His research and professional experiences have included engagement with the politics of sustainable development, public health, and education and technology.

Nixon Boumba
is a social activist with over 18 years of experience in Haitian social movements and non-governmental organizations. Since the 2010 Haiti earthquake, Boumba has worked with anti-mining organizations, the land rights movement, the anti-corruption movement, LBGTQI+ campaigns, and the movement against the 'mega-projects' in the country. He has an MA in the Department of History from the Université d'État d'Haïti, in Port-au-Prince.

Tirza van Bruggen
has a PhD from the Institute for Food and Resource Economics, University of Copenhagen (2021). She holds a bachelor's degree in Cultural Anthropology and Development Studies from Radboud University Nijmegen and a master's degree in International Relations from the University of Groningen. Her research focuses on the dynamics of local politics and economy, the construction of identities, and the persistence of categorical inequalities in Southeast Asia. Her recently defended PhD thesis 'Fluid and Fixed: Chinese Indonesian Identity at Work' investigates the production of Chinese Indonesian identity through everyday social interactions around culture, occupation, taxes, and social geography.

Ismael García Colón
is a Professor of Anthropology at the College of Staten Island and The Graduate Centre, CUNY. He is a historical and political anthropologist with interests in

political economy and oral history. García Colón is the author of *Land Reform in Puerto Rico: Modernizing the Colonial State, 1941–1969* (2009). His current research explores the Puerto Rican experience in US farm labour and its relation to colonialism and immigration policies. He is the author of 'Confronting the Present: Migration in Sidney Mintz's Journal for The People of Puerto Rico' (*American Ethnologist*, 2017, 44, 3: 403–413), and *Colonial Migrants at the Heart of Empire* (University of California Press, 2020).

Inge-Merete Hougaard
is a postdoctoral fellow at Lund University Centre for Sustainability Studies, Sweden. She holds a PhD in Political Ecology from the Department of Food and Resource Economics, University of Copenhagen, Denmark. Her main research interests revolve around access and rights to land and resources, climate politics, landscape change, state making, and the politics of recognition. Currently, her research focuses on climate politics, exploring the promise of negative emissions for future carbon reductions. This chapter draws on her PhD research, where she investigated state-making, landscape change, recognition, and resource rights in Colombia as part of the ERC-project 'Rule and Rupture'.

Ioannis Kyriakakis
is an Adjunct Lecturer (Social Theory, Studies of European Culture) at the Hellenic Open University, and an Adjunct Lecturer (Economy of Culture) at the University of Peloponnese. He studied Political Science at Panteion University and Social Anthropology at University College London (MSc, PhD). He conducted fieldwork in England on English ethnicity, for his master's dissertation, as well as, in Southwestern Ghana, on religious pluralism and social differentiation for his PhD. He is concerned with global inequality, economic anthropology, and cultural economics. He has participated in research projects on cultural consumption and migration, published in international journals, and taught research methods at a Social Policy department (University of Peloponnese) and economic anthropology (Social University of Athens). He is currently teaching cultural economics at the Open University of Cyprus and Social Theory of the 20th century at the Hellenic Open University.

Raquel Rodrigues Machaqueiro
holds a PhD in anthropology from the George Washington University, Washington DC, where she is currently a postdoctoral researcher for the *Slave Wreck's Project*. Prior to that, she worked for eight years as a public-policy analyst for the Portuguese government on environmental and climate change issues. Informed by her experience in the policy world, her doctoral

thesis explores the creation of climate change policies in international arenas, and how these are then reinterpreted and implemented in Mozambique and Brazil, contributing to the expansion of transnational governance in domains other than the environment.

Paul Stacey
is an Associate Professor in International Development Studies at the Department of Social Sciences and Business, Roskilde University. His main research interests are historical and contemporary processes of exclusion, informal governance, and state building in the Global South. His PhD (2012) investigated social exclusion and state formation in Ghana, and post-doctoral research covered urban governance in one of West Africa's largest slums, Old Fadama in Ghana, resulting in *State of Slum: Precarity and Informal Governance at the Margins in Accra* (Stacey 2019). Current research projects focus on pastoralists' rights to land in contexts of climate change in Kenya (financed by the Danish Ministry of Foreign Affairs); the illegal extraction of gold and process of democratization in Ghana (financed by Independent Research Fund Denmark); and solutions and challenges to sustainable wastewater systems in urban Ghana (financed by the Danish Ministry of Foreign Affairs).

Joshua Steckley
is a PhD Candidate in the Department and Geography and Planning at the University of Toronto, with a specialization in Environmental Studies. His work focuses on the commodification of nature, international development, and informal economies in both the global North and South.

Marylynn Steckley
is an Assistant Professor in Global and International Studies at Carleton University in Ottawa. Her work is located in the field of political ecology, with a focus on peasant dispossession, struggles for change, and food sovereignty movements in Haiti.

Masami Tsujita
is Senior Lecturer in the Postgraduate Development Studies Programme, Centre for Samoan Studies at the National University of Samoa. Her research interests centre on development with a focus on transnational movement of people, capital, and company across Asia, the Pacific, and beyond. Her current research looks at the recent flow of South–South labour migration into Samoa and the Pacific. She is also working on a book on Yazaki Samoa, the Japanese-owned car parts factory, which operated in Samoa for 26 years.

CHAPTER 1

Global Power and Local Struggles in Developing Countries: An Introduction

Paul Stacey

This volume explains how global political and economic power influences local struggles and social organization in diverse sites in developing, or Global South, countries. It is inspired by the fortieth anniversary – 2022 – of the first publication of the seminal *Europe and the People without History* (EPWH) by Eric R. Wolf (Wolf 1982), while 2023 marks the centenary of Wolf's birth. The title '*Europe and the People without History*' immediately provokes. When published, it challenged dominant contemporary thought that history was only made by powerful Europeans and forced answers to questions like: How can people not have history? What people are we talking about? And what role do people without history play in the making of our own understandings and histories of the world? The phrase 'People without History' consequently serves to alert and chastise established understandings, which for Wolf were enacted and supported by generations of public officials, traders, opportunists, and scholars across the social sciences. This mixed group tended to share a view that people in peripheral lands – a long way away from their own perceived centres of civilization – simply did not contribute to global progress and were thus insignificant in world history. Moreover, such people were not only geographically peripheral but occupied overshadowed and lesser positions in evolutionary terms than those enjoyed by their Western counterparts – who, in turn, enjoyed the privilege of writing history from their own perspectives. The title thus directly challenged ideas of modernization and global development that remain popular today, of 'the West versus the Rest' and the 'North versus the South', where the West and North are understood as engines of global development, while the 'Rest' need to mimic the North/West developmental trajectory to reach desirable Northern or Western levels of 'progress'. A key aim of this volume is to challenge such perspectives with a range of original ethnographic investigations from the Global South, and to explain how local, national, and global political and economic development produces, and is dependent on, diverse groups of 'People without History'.

EPWH was a ground-breaking scholarly enterprise for many reasons, not least because it situated local contexts and the agency of people in peripheral countries, which today would be termed marginalized, developing-country, or Global South contexts, at the centre of a multi-sited anthropological and historical study of global processes (Hylland Eriksen 2010). Consequently, this volume situates localities of struggle and differentiation, and local forms of social organization and processes of 'People without History' into contemporary contexts of global political and economic development. The volume is not a *festschrift* for Wolf nor a decidedly anthropological investigation but selects different aspects of his rich theoretical and conceptual framings to support interdisciplinary explanations for the varied examples, which are mainly based on in-depth analysis of localized social change.[1] As such, the book aims to appeal to an audience not only of anthropologists and Wolf-aficionados, but also of students and researchers, practitioners, activists, and policy makers from other social science backgrounds, including international development studies, political economy, global studies, geography, cultural studies, political ecology, and history. This wider audience can use the book to develop critical insights into their own areas of work, deepen knowledge about processes of global development, inequality, and local struggles for rights, while all the while developing understandings of the usefulness of Wolf-based perspectives. It is in this vein that the introduction also serves to outline EPWH as well as other Wolfean works. At the same time, it is hoped that it will prove useful for readers without prior knowledge of Wolf's scholarship.

EPWH demolished a slew of dominant theoretical and conceptual understandings about global powers' impact on localized groups around the world and particularly perceptions of peripheral social and cultural organization as fixed, bounded, isolated, and homogeneous. In EPWH, Wolf explored an extensive historical period from about 1400 to 1900 to investigate a recognized conundrum. This was between, on the one hand, received wisdom about global homogeneity and drivers of progress as rooted in core countries, and on the other, widespread evidence of local differentiation and agency around the

---

1 We use 'Global' to cover the realities of power relations and the 'relational totality' of everyday social life extending beyond spatial interconnections, networks, and flows (Neveling and Steur 2018: 5). The term Global South broadly covers countries that share histories as former colonies; are categorized as developing economies or emerging industrial nations; are situated in the developing world, or that, previously, were categorized as Third World countries or in the periphery. The use of the term has increased together with acknowledgement of the complexity of relationships between development, continuity, change, structure, process, and agency. Its use is also related to recognition of unresolved colonial injustices around the world, and subaltern resistance to inequality and structural positioning in the capitalist system. For a useful overview of the concept of Global South, see Kalb and Steur 2015. For a discussion of the concept of globalization, see the introduction in Beynon and Dunkerley (eds).

world as shaped by historical relations between core countries and local actors in peripheral countries. The subsequent analysis elaborated on understandings of world systems that typically divided the world into core and peripheral countries and took the nation-state as a main unit of analysis (Wallenstein 1974).[2] Instead, it situated globalization processes at the centre of investigation and focused on variability and difference Although EPWH was well received, it is not without its faults.[3] Critical reviews pointed out, among other things, that it endeavoured to cover too much, geographically and historically; that the investigation fails to provide adequate voice to the numerous social groups named (Chirot 1984); that it theoretically affirms Eurocentric visions of modernity (Taussig 1989; McNeill 1984); and that the application and discussion of capitalist modes of production tend to centre on the economic domain and to disregard the role of the state and the political sphere (Abbink 1992, 97).[4]

The aims of this collection are not as bold as those of EPWH, but take as a point of departure some of the main issues it raised. As such, this collection is based on concrete, micro-historical cases drawing on extensive ethnographic fieldwork. Most chapters additionally frame the making of each case of 'People without History' in the context of state formation, politics, political development, and models of contemporary market-based growth, and provide voice to local actors. The rationale for limiting the book to the Global South reflects the research and disciplinary backgrounds and interests of the contributors, and the wish to develop new perspectives about marginalization processes in the Global South. The theoretical contribution of the anthology is therefore its foregrounding in original, in-depth empirical analysis of contrasting

---

2   For an elaboration of Immanuel Wallenstein's world system theory, see Robinson 2011. For a useful overview of development debates, see Edelman and Haugerud (2005), Chapter 6.
3   Following publication, EPWH attracted more than 20 – mainly positive – reviews in leading social science journals between 1983 and 1987. For a reappraisal of EPWH's positive legacy and influence, see Hämäläinen 2018, and particularly Schneider and Rapp 1995. For bibliographies, see Schneider and Rapp 1995; Wolf 2001. Many other writers refer to and discuss EPWH and Wolf's legacy, for example Asad 1987; Gould 1979; Marcus 2003; Hecht 2018; Susser 2016; Whitehead 2004; and Schneider and Rapp 1995. Critical reviews include Chirot (1984), who recognizes the book's originality but depicts the empirical material and narrative as 'full of mistakes', and the theoretical framework as 'seriously deficient'. Michael Taussig (1989) raised several objections, including that the book affirmed Eurocentric visions of capitalist modernity and exaggerated capitalist modes of production power, and which, among other issues raised were taken up in replies by Sidney Mintz and Eric Wolf (Mintz and Wolf 1989). Other critics point to an overt focus on material dimensions of periphery–core relations and a neglect of histories of ideas. See McGee and Warms 2013. Abbink (1992) provides a very useful elaboration of key points of critique against EPWH.
4   See also Asad (1987).

contemporary contexts of exclusion, mobilization, and crisis, all explained and discussed in relation to Wolf's theories and concepts.[5] As such, the collection offers a range of cases of shifting political and economic relationships across local, national, and global scales (Horner and Hulme 2019; Palmer 1990). Broadly, the volume aims to contribute to knowledge of these processes while revealing unseen and otherwise neglected dimensions of power within human agency and organization around the world – precisely those dimensions so often overshadowed and neglected by normative and overriding narratives of development (Saitta 2005).

For Wolf, power is fundamentally relational, concerns 'all relations among people', and where actors' positioning shapes their social settings 'so as to render some kinds of behaviour possible, while making others less possible or impossible' (Wolf 1990, 587). Positioning, agency, and manoeuvrability are accordingly conditioned not only by force and coercion but by language, discourse, and everyday interactions, and by their impact on thought, culture, ideas, and social life (Heyman 2003; Barrett, Stokholm, and Burke 2001; Weber 1978). Thus, the mobilization and organization of social groups, together with the language they use and forms of culture and identity they develop, are all manifestations of power in an open and unfinished process that is conditioned, enabled, and limited by broader forces (Hall et al. 2011; Procter 2004).

Several reviews of EPWH underscore a paradox between, on the one hand, the book's under-utilization, and on the other its substantial and sustained relevance for social sciences since its initial publication. One account states for example, that EPWH has 'irrevocably changed how we see and make sense of the world', and was 'strikingly timely and relevant', yet also concludes that we 'owe him [Wolf] another look' (Hämäläinen 2018). Another similarly states that the naturalization of EPWH into critical studies makes it 'almost impossible to assess' (Hecht 2018), while another notes that 'The more we read and re-read Eric Wolf, the more ahead of his time he seems ...' (Gledhill 2005, 37). Another response comments that 'Wolf's influence is too little acknowledged in most histories of agrarian studies' while noting that EPWH was an 'unparalleled work of theory and history' (Bernstein et al. 2018).[6] The consensus about the

---

5   For *historical* case studies based around Wolf's work, see Abbink and Vermeulen (eds) 1992. For a discussion of the development of peasant studies in which Wolf played a key role, see Bernstein et al. 2018.

6   There is a noticeable divergence between, on the one hand, the wide influence of EPWH and its contribution to critical studies, and, on the other, its actual citation history. In December 2021, for example, Google Scholar registered EPWH with some 11,300 citations. By contrast, '*The Invention of Tradition*' edited by Eric Hobsbawm and Terence Ranger (1983) had clocked

book's paradoxical legacy of underusage despite its considerable significance found echo in the foreword of the 2010 edition, where it is described as an 'unsurpassed survey of comparative global anthropology' despite the fact that Wolf's legacy is a 'large, untapped potential' (Hylland Eriksen 2010). With this ambivalence in mind, another humble aim of the present volume is to develop an awareness of the applicability and relevance of Wolf for investigations of contemporary local struggles against a backdrop of global connectivity.

The remainder of this introduction will provide an overview of *Europe and the People Without History*, followed by an outline of the main developments in Marxist anthropology over the last forty years. After this, I discuss contemporary developmental contexts in the Global north and Global South that produce different kinds of people without history. Finally, the structure of the book is detailed, including a summary of the empirical context in each chapter and how Wolf is utilized in each.

1 An Overview of EPWH

It is worth noting as a point of departure that EPWH resists summary due to its combination of theoretical ambition, historical depth, and geographical breadth. The emphasis is on many different social groups living outside different political and economic centres around and in Europe from about 1400 to 1900, and their diverse and changing relations with different cores. The investigation establishes the idea of the world as an interconnected whole made possible by the development of long-distance trade and the consolidation of political entities. In so doing, it exemplifies in detail global capitalistic expansion – with the circulation of commodities and development of labour relations – in the long-term historical trajectory of diverse core–periphery relations (Hecht 2018). In EPWH, Wolf accordingly 'developed an anthropologically grounded global history of capitalism' that rejected ideas of a medley of differentiated, fixed, and bounded societies dotted all over the world, whose role in history was theretofore often understood as independent from the developmental trajectories of 'core' countries (Neveling and Steur 2018, 6).

As a global historical anthropology EPWH subsequently traces how peripheral groups' labour and developing capitalist modes of production contributed to the development of core countries' political economies and helped shape the

---

over 32,000, the *'The Interpretation of Cultures'*, by Clifford Geertz (1973) nearly 82,000, and *'Imagined Communities'* by Benedict Anderson (1983) over 126,000 citations.

contours of a wider, modern, political, and economic world system. In a related way, Wolf demonstrates that processes of global integration and local connectivity produce social and cultural differentiation at local levels in the peripheral countries. Differentiation developed because local forms of organization met, challenged, adopted, and struggled with developing capitalist production methods in different ways. An unravelling of the diversity of local interests, resources, and power relations within and between different and changing groups of actors and across spatial levels therefore provides explanations for processes of social and cultural difference at local levels and the diversity of local–global interconnectedness. Wolf's investigation takes as a point of departure a deceptively simple and single research question posed early in the book. This contains a direct scholarly critique of contemporary social science methodologies and lays the ground for the ensuing comparative global anthropology: 'Why do we persist in turning dynamic, interconnected phenomena into static, disconnected things?' (Wolf 1982, 4). The question poses a recognized and long-standing challenge to Marxist anthropology and Marxist dialectical approaches more generally, of how to reconcile a common theoretical significance assigned to fixed structures when confronted with mounting empirical evidence of agency and change. Put another way, the challenge was how to 'imbue societal structure with motion' within the 'unfortunate rubric[s]' of Marxist anthropology (Gould 1979: 92–3). The ensuing investigation focuses on global connectivity between, on the one hand, the core powers of the Roman empire and Greek civilization, European powers, and non-European empires, and on the other, a considerable number of non-European groups and actors in peripheral areas. The latter are in various outposts, colonies, and trading sites and occupy a slew of positions such as merchants, middlemen, traders, producers, entrepreneurs, warriors, subjugated workers, peasants, and labourers. EPWH thus provides a panoramic, holistic, and Marx-inspired materialist investigation with a mass of empirical yet often brief examples of historical relationships, dynamics, and transformation processes.[7]

Wolf shows that peripheral-groups' social-cultural systems relate directly to the economic processes that generate surplus and commodities destined for the various and changing historical centres. Hence, Wolf's explanation that local forms of social and cultural organization are shaped by their interactions with much broader forces rejected the dominant social science understanding of fixity and isolation. Conceptually, Wolf developed three types of mode of

---

[7] Charles Tilly (2002) suggests that Wolf's anthropology was *Marxiant*, rather than Marxist. For Marcus, Wolf was a founder of American Marxist anthropology, publishing both 'Marxist, Marxian and crypto-Marxist' analysis from 1952 until 2001 (Marcus 2003).

production to explain historical contexts for local differentiation and global interconnectivity, and more broadly, dynamics between ideology and power (Hecht 2018). Through the 1970s Marx's concept of mode of production had anyway invoked major scholarly debate as anthropologists moved away from French structuralist accounts and applications that invariably offered teleological understandings and which categorized societies in terms of one specific mode of production or another. Countering this trend, Wolf in EPWH developed an open mode of production concept to undertake the anthropological inquiry and to situate societies' changing forms of organization around labour into broader contexts of uneven and contingent processes of global capitalism (Neveling and Steur 2018, 7). Subsequently, Wolf developed an anthropological usage of Marx's mode of production, eschewing assumptions of permanence and situating cultural phenomena in 'a specific, historically occurring set of social relations through which labour is deployed to wrest energy from nature by means of tools, skills, organization, and knowledge' (Wolf 1982, 91).[8] To avoid the connotations of fixity always present in Marxist 'superstructure' Wolf used instead terms such as 'vectors', 'fields', 'webs', 'weblike' and 'forces', which enabled understandings of change and contingency (Schneider and Rapp 1995, 4). Modes of production are (variously) *kin-ordered*, which is based on interpersonal relationships and obligations based around affinities including for example, age, gender, ethnicity, and marriage; *tributary*, where politico-military powers extract produce directly from producers; and *capitalist*, where, following Marx, unequal relationships of value develop as a result of the selling of labour by those without the means to control production and enjoy consumption, to those that enjoy the means to do so (Wolf 1982, 76). For Wolf, the modes of production comprise concepts that 'underlie, orient, and constrain' relations between man and the environment, and which form social, cultural, and socio-political relations, livelihoods, and labour mechanisms. Moreover, each mode constitutes a particular kind of unequal power and identifies how 'mutual interpenetration in a colonial and capitalist world formed and reformed specific social and cultural formations' (Bernstein et al. 2018, 698). Compared to earlier usage the open application of the concept enabled a better understanding of changes around the appropriation of labour, the production of class, and power relations. Similarly, the modes served as heuristic tools for explaining shifting social, political, and economic relations on local levels in the context of the broader production of ideas that justified such

---

8   For a much-discussed critique of Wolf's application of modes of production, see Asad 1987. For an overview of the mode of production debate more broadly, see Neveling and Steur 2018; Fogel 1988; Boesen 1979.

relations (Schneider and Rapp 1995, 8). The modes should then be understood as 'internally varied and dynamic, replete with [their] own engines of power and wealth accumulation, structures of social inequality, and ideological justifications' (McGee and Warms 2013, 942). And they are articulations of the extent of the commodification of land and labour at a given place and time, and as capitalist relations expand, and impact, on precapitalist forms of organisation. As strategic relationships of labour, the modes of production application subsequently challenged contemporary functionalist accounts explaining local social change in terms of environmental or demographic factors (Saitta 2005). It also contrasted with accounts which invariably assumed differences in social organization between localities as based in local determinants and idiosyncrasies (Nugent 2002). In earlier works (for example Wolf 1959), Wolf had already prepared the methodological ground for EPWH by rejecting environmental deterministic interpretations of local underdevelopment and pinpointing instead how deep historical and political-economic forces shape local cultural processes (Hecht 2018).

One contemporary reviewer described EPWH as 'a critique of anthropology [and an] anthropological critique of world history' (Cole 1985). This is because EPWH demonstrated the variability of historical processes, and the relativity of social and cultural trajectories that shape the peripheral groups' lives and forms of organization. By so doing, EPWH highlighted that recognition of the complexity of local differentiation amidst changing translocal forces demanded interdisciplinary research methodologies. Thus, EPWH established the idea of social and cultural organizational diversity and complexity as shaped by multiple, changing, and contemporaneous processes of contestation, consensus, crisis, and connectivity across spatial levels. It affirmed the idea of the world as an interconnected whole and the 'relational totality' which influences everyday social life (Neveling and Steur 2018; Hylland Eriksen 2010). Like earlier as well as later Wolf works, EPWH debunked received anthropological reasoning on numerous fronts by exposing fundamental weaknesses of essentialist, primitivistic, reductionist, atavistic, and relativistic methodologies, and dualist, deterministic, and reifying explanations. In a related way, EPWH exemplifies a scholarly shift away from traditions of evolutionism, exoticism, particularism, primordialism, romanticism, structural functionalism, subjectivism, and deconstruction (Laclau 1992; Dhawan 2018; Portis-Winner 2006). Not least, Wolf's EPWH situates history as central to anthropology – a stance which was widely denied by existing anthropological approaches – and demonstrates that explanations of context must consider both local and global components (Whitehead 2004).

2   Changing Perspectives for Marxist Anthropology since EPWH

The aim of this section is to outline shifts in Marxist anthropology since the writing of EPWH and together with the following section, it serves to contextualize the processes of development and struggle in focus in the empirical chapters. Although Marx focused predominantly on capitalist structure and not on paths towards social justice, a main thread running through Marxist anthropology from the late 1960s is the aim that scholarship contributes to social transformation and that scholars partake as active agents. In turn, this yielded critique aimed at the social role and obligations of anthropological inquiry itself. The pursuit of activist objectives was evident throughout Wolf's long career, during which a substantial scholarly production accompanied political engagement in, for example, anti-Vietnam War effort teach-ins and opposition to the use of anthropological field data utilized by the American state to achieve its war objectives in South-east Asia (Marcus and Menzies 2005).[9] Wolf played a key role in a generation of scholars around the late 1960s defined as enjoying the confidence to change society and producing scholarly work focused typically on Third World struggles in newly independent countries, for example in Sub-Saharan Africa. Together with active engagement there, there was widespread sympathy for campaigns of resistance and organized opposition to the numerous proxy wars and insurgency movements playing out at the time in different Central American countries as supported by the warring Cold War superpowers (Hecht 2018). Moreover, the social realities on the ground in far-flung locations provided Western-based scholars with empirical evidence to openly challenge received anthropological understandings of isolated social groups around the world (Neveling and Steur 2018). Still, the pursuit of justice and better futures for the many, ostensibly primitive groups also received critique for romanticizing and exoticizing these social groups and for lacking contextualization (Susser 2016). Through the 1970s these realizations spilled over to spark debate about anthropological inquiry, raising questions such as whether analysis should concentrate on the 'unravelling of the history of mankind' which alluded to a focus on fluid and indeterminate processes, or whether it should be a 'critique of [...] new forms of exploitation in the traditional bastions of capital' and which spoke more to structural explanations with connotations of fixity (Gould 1979, 93). Indeed, much Marxism-based analysis from the 1960s and 1970s soldiered on applying theoretically heavy explanations despite the increasing evidence to the contrary flowing in from

---

9   For bibliographies of Wolf's work see Schneider and Rapp 1995; Wolf 2001.

activist scholars' first-hand experiences (Gould 1979: 92). In turn, local actors' increased access to tertiary education in newly independent countries – which had been unavailable to parents or grandparents who may themselves have been objects of classical anthropological study a decade earlier – forced researchers to radically adjust how they studied and understood 'local' and 'traditional' forms of organization and culture (Marcus and Menzies 2005). Inevitably, such developments eroded both real and perceived boundaries between researchers and the individuals of study, as well as the received wisdom about the drivers of global growth and the roles and cultures of peripheral groups.

In Peasant Wars in the Twentieth Century (Wolf 1969), which is seen as a forerunner of EPWH, Wolf developed new ground by giving ascendancy to agency and process in specific developing country locations to explain the workings of broader forces, including the Cold War. In so doing, Wolf contributed significantly to the development of critical peasant studies and after EPWH to critical post-colonial and agrarian studies.[10] Wolf's work after EPWH continued to develop a realist epistemology and critiqued post-modern and post-colonial theorizations as ahistorical. The focus in *Peasant Wars* is on liberation struggles in countries as diverse as Mexico, Russia (Soviet Union), China, Vietnam, Algeria, and Cuba. This provided explanation of broader processes of peasant opposition to capitalism, showing that capitalist pressures shape peasant organization for justice and autonomy and influence national political trajectories (Hecht 2018; Wolf 1969; Susser 2016). Besides opposing rigid Marxist framings, the exposition marked a break from mainstream methodologies depicting localities as ahistorical backwaters populated by social groups with primitive traits structurally detached from wider political-economic forces (Gledhill 2005; Hecht 2018). Similarly, Peasant Wars contributed to the dissolution of assumed dichotomous relationships between forces 'internal and external' to given social groups, understandings of drivers of 'continuity and change'and explanations in terms of 'structures and events' (Burke 1992, 159). The methodological shift was from studies of 'traditions and their tribes' to the actual, complex, and changing social realities of lived lives (Moore 1978). Subsequently, Marxist analysis itself underwent various convolutions because

---

10 Wolf was a long-standing member of the *Journal of Peasant Studies* Editorial Advisory Board. After his death, an annual, International Eric Wolf Lecture series was established in Vienna, hosted jointly by the Austrian Academy of Sciences' Institute for Social Anthropology (ISA); the Linz University of Fine Arts' International Research Center for Cultural Studies (IFK); and the University of Vienna's Department of Social and Cultural Anthropology.

of the new insights and historical process: first, the earlier, rigid understandings of class, labour relations, and application of taxonomic modes of production were rejected. In their place came the so-called 'cultural' turn in studies of history and anthropology, which Wolf himself critiqued for 'analytical deforestation' due to an overt focus on culture at the expense of much else. This reflected Wolf's point of departure that 'all paradigms are mortal and likely to be superseded' and that there is a need to approach concepts and models with a professional suspicion (Gledhill 2005). Subsequent approaches developed conceptualizations of class beyond economic notions alone. This led to a return of sorts to previous understandings of dynamic relationships between class and culture as had been taken up by, for example, by E. P. Thompson, Raymond Williams, and Eric Hobsbawm (Kalb and Herman 2005).

The ending of the Cold War in 1991 and subsequent global shifts of power marked changes in the character of local political struggles around the world and ushered in increased scholarly recognition of the multi-level complexity of supposedly localized and isolated social struggles (Marcus and Menzies 2005; Hobsbawm, 1994). Numerous one-party states that were established after African countries had gained independence from colonial power started to collapse. Pressure for democracy increased, and multi-party politics spread. Many African, Latin American, and Asian nations also undertook ambitious programmes of local government reform as dimensions of a so-called third wave of democracy (Huntington 1991; Harvey 2001). Nevertheless, combinations of market-based growth models, as influenced by neo-classical economic theory, and liberal-democratic reforms did not convincingly reduce societal inequalities as otherwise envisaged (Fukuyama 1989). Rather, the end of the Cold War enabled the rise of neo-liberalism epitomized by the UK's Prime Minister Margaret Thatcher, and the USA's President Ronald Reagan from the early 1980s. For numerous Western countries this meant a dismantling of welfare state systems established in the post-World War II period; an ascendancy of economic methodological individualism; emphasis on market-based growth; the liberalization and privatization of state industries; the dismantling of Keynesian economic systems; and the weakening of organized labour.[11] For many countries in the Global South, neoliberalism meant the implementation of Economic Structural Adjustment Programmes, monetarism, and waves of

---

11 Neoliberalism is itself a slippery concept and often name-dropped fleetingly in popular, public, and academic usage and debate. Scholarly definitions range, in brief, from a subjective emancipatory project (Rose 1990); to a form of economic organization (Harvey 2005); to an all-encompassing governmentality (Foucault 2008). Here from Smith 2018: 248.

privatization and liberalization as conveyors of 'economy stability' that had very mixed results (Mohan 2009). In recent decades, moreover, the neoliberal turn in Western and Global north countries has influenced democratic crisis and new forms of struggle, with a general eroding of political ideologies and legitimacy. This has accompanied a rise in populist politics with shifts to the political right that, despite numerous economic crises around the world since 1990, seems to offer no realistic alternatives to capitalist expansionist logics and models of limited state intervention in markets that have gradually taken precedence over previous, state-driven forms of social development (McRobbie and Levitt 2000; Kalb 2015).[12] Consequently, there has been renewed attention in the Global north to the negative impacts of capitalism and market-driven growth with impacts on for example, living conditions, household debt, austerity, housing, employment, and education. One broad conclusion is that formal liberal-democracy and market-based growth models have not delivered on promises of societal stability, a trickling down of wealth, and more inclusive political and economic improvement (Stepan and Linz 2013; Standing 2011; Susser 2016; Graeber 2012). On a global level therefore, the conjunction of capitalistic expansion together with old and relatively new experiences with democracy and democratization has produced a whole new palette of 'People without History' and social groups without rights. This means that the need for critical studies is as relevant as ever.[13]

3 Contemporary Developmental Contexts for 'People without History'

Clearly, the developmental contours of the world today differ considerably from when Wolf set up to write EPWH in the late 1970s, and vastly so from the times lived by the excluded groups around the start of the period taken up in

---

12 Including for example, the international debt crisis from 1981–9; the East Asian crisis of 1997; the global financial crisis of 2008–9; the European sovereign debt crisis 2009–19.

13 Space limitations do not permit an assessment of the current state of Marxist anthropology or the many different contributions to the field. For a discussion of influential Marxist anthropologists over the last forty of so years and relations to Wolf's scholarship, see Marcus and Menzies 2005, and Schneider and Rapp 1995. Although new technology has undoubtedly increased scholars' ability to access empirical data over the last 40 years, there is also a recognition of new challenges that activist scholars face. For ethical challenges faced by anthropologists, for example, see Edelman and Haugerud 2005: 45. For discussions about (new) pressures on academic freedom see Carvalho and Downing 2010; Donlevy, Gereluk, and Brandon 2018; Enyedi 2018; Rhoades and Slaughter 2004.

EPWH, and where, in Hobbes's words, there was 'continual fear, and danger of violent death; and the life of man, solitary, poor, nasty, brutish, and short' (Hobbes 1651, I.XIII.9) Indeed, the processes of how power, politics, and capital interact and influence social life across local, national, and global scales appear increasingly complex, fluid, contrasting, and elusive, and clearly validate Wolf's presentation of the social world as a 'totality of interconnected processes' (Wolf 1982, 3). The aim of this section is therefore to provide a broad, yet necessarily limited, historical overview to situate local-global connectivity and the present day making of 'People without History' in the context of significant global and international developmental processes and capitalistic expansion since the writing of EPWH.

To start with a few examples, the recent Black Lives Matter (BLM) movement, founded in 2013 in the USA to counter institutionalized racism, and which gained further momentum and spread to other countries following the death of United States citizen George Floyd on 25 May 2020 under custodial violence inflicted by a Minneapolis police officer, has raised both public and scholarly attention about systemic race inequalities and exclusion. In turn, it has rallied civil mobilization against public meanings assigned to prominent Western historical political figures and resulted in the toppling and defacing of public statues.[14] Related action by the BLM calls into question how combinations of self-righteous and dominant national narratives and historiographies, and mass media depictions, smooth over past injustices; the relationships between political development and the marginalization of social groups; how the accumulation of extreme private, business, and corporate wealth elides any problematic origins and the human costs of such wealth; and highlights continuity and durability between historical and present-day race-based institutionalized inequalities (Beckett and Rockman 2016). Broadly, the BLM has publicly disclosed otherwise hidden relationships between oppression, capitalism, and inequality, and highlighted racism as a major and persistent social, institutional, and structural challenge in many Global north countries.

In the United Kingdom the so-called *Windrush* scandal exemplifies something similar with the political production of a 'problematic' group that was subsequently criminalized: a group of otherwise heterogeneous black individuals whose categorization as having an inferior legal status justified their deportation from the UK after many decades spent living and working there. The *Windrush* generation, named after the passenger ship on which migrants

---

14 Including the toppling of statues of Christopher Columbus, George Washington, and Thomas Jefferson, in the USA, Edward Colston in the UK, and King Leopold II in Belgium. See https://www.lifegate.com/black-lives-matter-statues (accessed 25 November 2021).

arrived in the UK from the Caribbean between 1948 and 1970, experienced that they had no residency rights and faced criminalization and subsequent deportation by the British government (Hewitt 2020). A similar campaign for citizenship rights in the UK developed in 2004 when the UK government denied status to retired Gurkha soldiers who, having served in the British armed forces, were denied residency. France likewise has experienced drawn-out struggles by soldiers of former colonies to gain rights after years of active service.[15] Meanwhile, histories of the plights of Sami in Northern Scandinavia and the Greenlandic people under different Danish governments in Greenland as well as in Denmark, call into question dominant narratives of Scandinavia as politically progressive and inclusive (Chatterjee 2021; Nygaard-Christensen and Bjerge 2021). Romani groups in Europe are more widely known as marginalized. Their contemporary struggle developed together with the construction of a 'Gypsy Question' in Nazi Germany; today they continue to contest for international recognition as 'a people without a country' and experience thinly veiled racist and Orientalist characterizations as fundamentally different to 'normal' Europeans (Richardson 2020; Jabeen 2020).

The long struggle of gypsies and Roma people in Europe reverberates moreover with the widespread, post-9/11 creeping criminalization and derogatory categorization of migrants, stateless persons, refugees, asylum seekers, and other more-or-less-distinct – and less distinctly tolerated – groups of people. Their categorical fate lies in the construction of understandings and definitions of them by others with greater power, for whom they emerge as inherently non-integrable. In other cases, categorizations are used as evidence of unreconcilable relationships between liberal democracy and the seeming unchanging cultural traditions of said groups (for example, the Muslim world). Narratives produce ideas of a migration and a refugee 'crisis' and of existential threats to European and national cultures. Yet they deny outright the role of migration and migrant labour in histories of capitalism, national economic development, and legitimize the suspension of inclusive rights (Wall et al. 2005; Trumpener 1992; Krzyżanowski, Triandafyllidou, and Wodak 2018). The discursive, popular, and legal construction of groups without rights feeds into broader processes that elide certain groups from the history books and popular imagination because they are inconvenient to dominant and politically produced narratives. In turn, the making of exclusive (and often binding) categories of people with disparate rights reproduces inequalities in new and more sophisticated forms, and with increasingly blurred lines as to who or what

---

15   See 'Gurkha vs government', *The Economist* 30 April 2009. https://www.economist.com/britain/2009/04/30/gurkhas-v-government (accessed 15 November 2021).

is accountable or responsible for such groups not enjoying rights. This takes place as rationalizing and objectifying political, administrative, and bureaucratic decision-making processes produce less worthy categories of people, who are subsequently moved socially, geographically, politically, and discursively to the margins of state formation. Hence, the expansion of the European Union has not necessarily reduced processes of exclusion within member countries, even though national idiosyncrasies related to inclusion and exclusion have become more streamlined across member states (Samers 1998). This is because processes of 'labelling' and categorizing constitute both domestic, national, and translocal power relations. So, the social categories themselves are objectified to enable the governance of practice and the reproduction of power and dominant ideas over time (Eyben and Moncrieffe 2007; Bourdieu 2005). And in turn, the construction of discourses around the social categories dissolves avenues of responsibility, fairness, and accountability.

The plight and historical trajectories of the above groups, as well as many others such as Uyghur, and Mongols in China; Palestinians in Israel and the occupied territories; and Rohingya in Myanmar, Aborigines in Australia, and native Indians in Brazil and the USA are of course very different – but they nevertheless share common experiences of marginalization and invisibilization as elements of state formation and power accumulation, and as subjects of propaganda which denies autonomous rights. In some cases, subjugation involves negating the history of a country, as well as a people, as with for example President Putin's depiction of Ukraine as a 'fake' country and as an inherent part of 'southwest' Russia (Applebaum 2022). Other examples of denying agency in both Global north and Global South countries are more clearly related to labour markets and capitalist modes of production. These include disparate groups of informal workers such as street vendors, factory workers, lorry and taxi drivers, seasonal fruit pickers, trafficked sex workers, gig economy workers, domestic servants, traveller communities, petty traders, artisanal miners, and residents of designated 'ghetto' areas, informal settlements, and slums (Stacey 2019). Conversely, the largely unrecognised contributions of female domestic work (including house-cleaning, and caring for elderly and children), reveals the long term, discursive production of a huge worker group across the world as outside of, and unrelated to, national economic growth, despite the obvious and immense contributions female domestic labour provides to all societies (Garbes 2022). Such 'groups' of people and categories of worker are invariably depicted with inferior traits, made 'invisible' and taken for granted, or provided with token recognition (Simonsen 2016). Some are relegated to 'social' history (as interesting but not important population elements).

Meanwhile, consumer-driven desires for commodities blinker consumer classes all over the world to processes of interconnectivity and the social lives of the actual people who assemble the commodities we all want and whose level of worker rights and recognition derive from corporate board strategies as influenced by the vagaries of market forces (Esposito and Pérez 2010). Hence, workers' life stories, histories, and roles in global economic development persistently lose out to the dominant, glossy media campaigns of household-name multinational and transnational conglomerates. Here, progress and success are explained in terms of unequalled technological ingenuity and unyielding entrepreneurial finesse (see Chapter 10). And here we see disjuncture between, on the one hand, the economic and financial imperatives of modern production forms to develop global interconnectedness, and on the other, the logic of corporate imperatives to discursively separate the market value of goods at the end of the supply chain, from their problematic origins and forms of production. In the meanwhile, popular, consumerist, and political narratives emphasize ever-increased participation in ever-more-competitive markets as prerequisites for national prosperity. This demonstrates the power of global capitalism to project itself as a source of social betterment, influence ideas of progress, and prioritize human wants over needs (Migone 2007). As such, one is immediately reminded of Wolf challenging presentations of national history as a series of incremental developments resulting in democratic societies and of history as a moral success story which elides the role of the disenfranchised. The contemporary making of 'People without History' then emerges from diverse combinations of political imperatives and capitalistic expansion, and necessarily involves a kind of historical amnesia that not only denies agency in the creation of essential 'inputs', but rests on societal acceptance of becoming blind to, and renouncing, the vulnerability of the social formations around production, to which globalizing modernity connects us (see Chapter 6).

The corollary is the denial of agency and rights of social groups despite their contributions through labour and their facilitating accumulation and capitalistic expansion. As such, the making of diverse 'People without History' continues unabated across all forms of political regime, and as conditioned by ever-sharper and contradictory process of social, economic, and political development. Indeed, that debates and struggles about rights and the social categories who should enjoy them are near-universal today, reveals how the rendering of people without rights and histories of their own is not only a by-product of global capitalism but is an inevitable condition for capitalist expansion and global interconnectedness. Related, the ballooning of civil society movements, charities, and NGOs across the world which advocate and define, defend, and claim rights for marginalized groups and increase political pressure for the implementation of progressive developmental norms (Grandia 2020; Lai 2011), is itself a symptom and 'indicator species' of the devastating effects neoliberalism has had over the last 40 or so years (see Chapter 2, this volume; Roy 2004). This speaks to the need to study processes of exclusion across spatial levels and political and economic contexts to 'understand exploitation [which] is important for understanding unjust reality because it opens possibilities for envisioning a just reality' (Chatterjee and Ahmed 2019, 367).

Combinations of newly acquired political and economic power, elite capture, and historical institutional and political positioning in global power structures (to name but a few drivers) have both hackneyed democratization and stymied broad-based social and economic improvements for the masses in countries as diverse as Brazil, India, Venezuela, Mozambique, and Russia. Numerous challenges to the relatively newly won political freedoms in the Global South are evident across different countries and have contributed to a faltering faith in 'third-wave' democratization theory in recent years (Stepan and Linz 2013; Neveling and Steur 2018). And the wavering experiences of Arab Spring movements for democratic reform that followed initial protests in Tunisia in 2010 have similarly cast doubt on the ability of multi-party elections, and social and progressive political movements, to bring about effective democracy. What of the social movements taken up by Wolf in *Peasant Wars* (Wolf 1969)? The revolutions in Cuba and Algeria seem now to have stalled indefinitely; China has transitioned to a centralized and non-consultative capitalist state; Russia, under the banner of United Russia, is a belligerent, authoritarian *de facto* one-party state; and Vietnam's ostensible transition to socialism with Đổi Mới is marked by extensive liberal-market-orientated reforms as directed by an authoritarian regime.

Over the last forty years, however, most developing countries *have* experienced sustained improvements across a wide range of human development indicators, including access to health services, standards of living, decreases in multi-dimensional poverty, increased income growth and access to education. And yet there is strong evidence, too, that social, political, and economic inequalities within many developing and developed countries have increased. Total global wealth today is concentrated in fewer and fewer pockets and there are increasing numbers of people needing humanitarian assistance (Piketty 2014; Standing 2011; Ourworlddata.org; OECD.org).[16]

---

16 At the time of writing the richest 1 percent of people in the world had accumulated more than double the wealth of some 6.9 billion others. See Oxfam: https://www.oxfam.org/en/5-shocking-facts-about-extreme-global-inequality-and-how-even-it.org. ReliefWeb writes that in 2021 one in 33 people around the world needed humanitarian assistance.

Parallel to such diverse and often contradictory processes played out both within and between Global north and Global South countries is the proliferation of simple narratives and descriptions of social organization and global development, to which Wolf took exception decades ago. Synchronic explanations assume and claim long-term convergence between all nations; media may depict 'Africa' as a wholesale problematic entity or even as a single country;[17] developmental unevenness, non-linear trajectories, and the divergent histories of individual countries are negated; the contributions of marginalized groups from the Global South to the political and economic development of the Global north are perfunctorily smoothed over or erased; evidence of developmental divergence is explained in terms of malfunctioning governance, failed states, and anomaly; 'culturalist' explanations with 'shared world visions' and 'based on collective traditions within a discrete social community' remain commonplace (Olivier de Sardan 2016); and deep-rooted myths about the positive effects of capitalism as broadly inclusive continue to provide legitimacy for the universalization of capitalist relations as *the* solution to the world's societal ills (Cole 1985; Smith 1986). Yet, as Wolf writes in the essay *Cycles of Violence* (Wolf 1987, 147): 'If capitalism has a special relation to the development of political freedom as we know it, it also exercises an extraordinary destabilizing power in its continuous search for higher profits and sustained capital accumulation'. Aspirations towards global economic and social homogeneity continue to situate the West as the model for the 'rest' to imitate, and narratives of development and inequality continue to take the nation-state as the unit of analysis (see Chapter 6). Despite widespread evidence to the contrary, therefore, we remain confronted and influenced by conventional and outdated ideas of linear development and homogeneity, where growth equates success, progress equates unabated economic expansion, and where democratization and capitalism are equal partners.

In the Global South relatively new bureaucratic forms of human categorization that deny or bestow rights and agency may merge with older, colonially based social categories that underpinned political structure (Stacey 2015). These include designations of people as natives, non-natives, citizens, subjects, migrants, foreigners, landless, casteless, or settlers; categories which, together with age, gender, ethnicity, religion, and social status, typically condition the

---

See https://reliefweb.int/sites/reliefweb.int/files/resources/GHO2021_EN.pdf. Accessed 19 November 2021.

17 For example: President Donald Trump's description of Haiti and African countries as 'shithole countries' in January 2018. For other examples of depictions of 'Africa' in popular media, see Mediaimpactproject.org/Africa-in-media.html.

everyday status that individuals or corporate social groups enjoy in a given polity, and which can easily override formal rights and political developmental objectives (see Chapter 3, this volume; Said 1978; Mamdani 1996; Boone and Duku 2012; Lund 2016; Stacey 2016; 2019). Thereby, struggles by excluded groups can involve the invention, reinvention, smudging, or affirming of versions of the past to legitimate the claims they lay in the present, to claim history for one's own group, and to render other versions inaccurate or unjust (Rabasa 2005; Hobsbawm and Ranger 2012). Processes of social mobilization may be influenced, moreover, by protection assigned to indigenous rights and self-determination by global organizations and NGOs. A case in point is the United Nations and the UN General Assembly Declaration on the Rights of Indigenous Peoples in 2007, which, together with the proliferation of social media, has both increased awareness of rights, claims of indigeneity, and influenced forms of mobilization across local, national, and global levels (Gagné 2015; Pelican 2013; Morton 2019). Still, it should be recognized that contemporary struggles for indigenous rights and the claiming of history based on global discourses and languages of rights have long roots (see Chapter 7).

Global political and economic development since the publication of EPWH has therefore provided for, and resulted in, an array of new and more complex ways by which 'People without History' are produced. An understanding of such processes demands consideration of the multifaceted changes in political and capital formation that locations have experienced historically and are presently undergoing. Shifts from national and state-driven forms of heavy industrial production to capitalist, neo-liberal, translocal, and post-Ford strategies, for example, have had substantial, diverse, and often negative implications for local work forces. In turn, excluded ethnic and social groups have both sought the retrieval of lost rights through political mobilization, learned how to use social media, and 'imagined', 'invented' and written histories of their own as part of the process of gaining access to education. The use of social media to define, promote, and defend collective rights moreover provides a reminder of the Hegelian perspective of the centrality of *writing* for social mobilization (Klein 1995). Further, whereas historically the destination for capital was typically labour and investment in the means of production in the Global north, more recent decades have witnessed an increased role of financial markets, financialization, and the availability of cheap money. This has had significant repercussions for land use changes and rural communities in the Global South. For example, widespread and new capital investments in land in the Global South enable the acquisition of large areas of land and lead to new forms of landlessness, alienation, expropriation, and dispossession (Borras et al 2012). This involves both local, national, and global stakeholders and defies explanations in terms of the North or West taking over land in the South (Adnan 2013; Borras et al. 2012; Wachira, Stacey, and Adela 2020). In turn, processes of finance-driven resource accumulation result in changes in land ownership from small-scale producers under customary land tenure systems with negotiated access to land, to more restrictive, exclusive, and expansive forms of private land ownership (see Chapter 4). Here, land may be controlled by assemblages of private and often obscure, unaccountable stakeholders (Joshi 2020; Zhang 2018; Harvey 1989), but may also involve local elders, leaders, and community members who find new avenues to benefit from formerly 'communal' land. Finance-based development is itself traceable to the financial crisis of 2008, which sparked investor interest in financing land and where, encouraged by rising commodity prices, investors sought land in the Global South to offset lower returns from financial markets (Fairbairn 2014). In a related development, the industrialization of large-scale agriculture and food production has increased the power of market-based agri-business, while market-based reforms have meant the withdrawal of the state from direct involvement in agricultural production (see Chapters 4, 5, and 8).

Market-based growth has thereby dissolved distinctions between economy and social life in rural areas and demanded the reshaping of local forms of organization around production methods and access to means of production, for example land (Schouten 2008). Furthermore, climate change mitigation efforts, ranging from conservation and protection of land masses to green energy transitions, reflect new extractive frontiers and drive new processes of violence and alienation (see Chapter 8 this volume; Allan, Lemaadel, and Lakhal 2021). Such vicissitudes have increased the availability of cheap food to urban areas and in much of the world but also rearranged relations between and within rural, land-based societies, between these and the state, as well as between localities of production, urban political environments, and global stakeholders (Stacey, Grant, and Oteng-Ababio 2021). As such, there are now new pressures on diverse rural communities of smallholders as they are incorporated into capitalist circuits of agricultural production and consumption (McMichael 2006; Hecht 2018; Hall et al. 2011; Vijayabaskar 2020).

The relatively new processes of producing people without history emerging from the increased role of finance and changing forms of capitalist production and exclusion are also conditioned by the historical compression of time and space, and the multiple and radical advances in technology in recent decades (Gross 1982; Harvey 1990). These have significantly reduced the transaction costs of travel, trade, communication, the production of information and knowledge, and market exchanges. Technology in combination with beneficial judicial and ideological developmental frameworks has created an enabling space for the ever-hungry movement of capital to occupy quickly. This often outmanoeuvres grassroots objections and democratic objectives in a seemingly ceaseless commodification of natural resources, land, labour, and organization (Chapter 2; Tsing 2003; Borg and Lund 2018; Smith 2018). Broadly, the opening and expansion of commodity frontiers in different locations all over the world demonstrates close relationships between an increased destruction of environmental and ecological systems, labour exploitation, and the globalization of capitalist production systems (Joseph 2019). Such processes exemplify the work of the *Capitalocene* and the '*age of capital*' where unabated destruction and accumulation, and 'putting Nature to work' organizes markets and production as a 'system of power, profit, and re/production in the web of life' (Moore 2017, 594–606). The corollary is often increased risk and uncertainty for already marginalized social groups of land-based producers, as ostensibly 'unused' lands come under the control of new global actors (Chapter 4). Diverse processes of commodification and alienation are manifest all over the Global South through extractivism, agrarian transformations towards cash-cropping, climate change adaptation and mitigation strategies, conservation and environmentalist drives, and infrastructural mega-projects. Thus, land use changes driven by finance and wider structures of economic power integrate local groups into broader power hierarchies over which they often have limited influence, and which contribute to spatial unevenness and social, cultural, economic, and political polarization. Subsequently, capitalism facilitates and acts as a proxy for the reproduction of uneven power relations in society and societal unevenness (Smith 2001; Tilly 2005). In this process, non-state forms of sovereignty may develop with a spatiality and influence that transcend the reach of nation-states and cause local material loss and alienation (Kalb 2015). Hence, in addition to James Scott's authoritative exploration (Scott 2010), of how and why states benefit from recording and ordering complex societies in the name of governance, there is a need to recognize how economic and capitalist power simplify complex and unpredictable social realities to reduce uncertainty and risk and to increase economic gains from investments (see Chapter 10). In other words, economic power directs and orders otherwise indeterminate social realities towards specific and planned institutionalization processes with the aim that local actors will follow concrete and predictable actions (Blundo 2015).

The stories of 'People without History' in focus in this volume exemplify some of the disparate processes sketched above in the Global South. Many tell of how social groups experience a reduction and erosion of their political and economic manoeuvrability as they continue to confront both historical institutions of political marginalization and as they adjust to increased immersion in economic and market-based power rationales (Hardt and Negri 2000). From the above, we see that the question posed by Wolf forty years ago at the start of EPWH (*Why do we persist in turning dynamic, interconnected phenomena into static, disconnected things?*) will certainly provide a different set of answers today, but the question itself has not only retained but increased its significance and relevance. The next section now outlines the empirical chapters and their developmental and Wolf-inspired contexts.

4 Structure of the Book, and Framing of the Chapters

The book comprises nine empirical chapters with micro-histories of struggle and local development employing Wolf's insights to explain broader, contemporary contexts of economic and political power. Overall, the aim is that the analysis of such micro-perspectives and quotidian experiences provide for what Wolf termed 'macroscopic history'. A common realization is that investigation of everyday lived lives and focused 'histories of the present' (Wolf's term) reveal otherwise hidden dimensions of agency to counter dominant explanations (Schneider 1995; Schneider and Rapp 1995, 6; Whitehead 2004). From Geertz, the chapters provide valid reminders of the methodological usefulness and significance of not to study villages or localities, but to study *in* a village or a locality (Geertz 1973, 22). One can add the imperative of studying *with* local people. Overall, the chapters demonstrate contrasting developmental trajectories that defy monochrome depictions of economic modernization and proclamations of a post-industrial, post-Ford, and post-material age inhabited by *homo economicus* and governed by democratic market forces (Kalb 2015). Most provide explanations of political relevance by making known the struggles that ordinary people face in their confrontations with unfavourable positioning in wider political and economic power configurations, and show local agency in defining the local political trajectories (Neveling and Steur 2018; MacLeavy, Fannin, and Larner 2021). Collectively, the chapters strive to overcome recognized limitations of anthropology and globalization literature by historicizing local experiences with global forces. Several contextualize analysis to consider the impact and workings of neoliberalism in given localities (Graeber 2002; Edelman and Haugerud 2005, 97) and incorporate the role of the state in analysis of struggle and relations between ideas, ideology, and power (Wolf, 1999). To paraphrase Marx, they provide insights not only into how man does not control the conditions under which history is made, but they also make known the conditions under which history is denied. Many chapters moreover provide original insights into anthropologies and processes of development as different forms of resistance (Mosse, 2004), and provide critical depictions and power-oriented perspectives of people's experiences of upheaval and uncertainty. Importantly the idea of fixed vertical hierarchies of power across spatial scales is rejected (Darian-Smith and McCarty 2017) as the volume brings together seemingly unrelated processes showing the 'universal pertinence of power variously manifested' around the world (Portis-Winner 2006).

The chapters take as a common point of departure investigations addressing broad questions related to the making of people without history today; How do contemporary dynamics of global political and economic organization shape local processes of social exclusion? Who are the present-day *People without History* and what role do they play in global forms of accumulation and production? And how do contemporary and historical economic and political power relations influence the production of local cultural and social norms?[18] Broadly, the contributions attest to the making of people without history today from combinations of two forces: struggles against unfavourable historical positioning in power relations which limit present-day avenues for social, political, and economic certainty; and destabilization and conditioning of social organization due to current imperatives of developing capitalism. The conjunctures of history and contemporary power mean that engrained processes of marginalization are often reproduced in new forms, which, in turn, give rise to new avenues and expressions of social struggle and organization as dimensions of political development and state formation (Escobar 1991; 1995; Stacey 2015). Empirically, the chapters cover processes in Latin America (Haiti, Puerto Rico, Colombia, Brazil); Sub-Saharan Africa (Ghana, Mozambique); Asia (Indonesia), and finally the Pacific Islands (Samoa) respectively.

In Chapter 2 Joshua Steckley, Nixon Boumba, and Marylynn Steckley examine post-disaster development in Haiti, where, following the devastating earthquake in 2010, billions of dollars of reconstruction funding flooded the domestic economy. They take a point of departure in Haiti's peasant movements of the 1980s, which were rooted in communal activism and ideals of rural populations as agents of change. This is traced to contemporary social movements and negative influences of developmental funding. The chapter examines from Polanyian perspectives how international funding results in the commodification of radical, rural-based social movements in the country in processes of 'counter-movement commodification'. This compellingly elaborates on Wolf's observation that social contestation is often a reaction to the forces of capitalism. It shows how countermovement itself adapts to and adopts capitalistic

---

18   These questions were posed in the original call for papers.

and commodifying forces by itself taking on characteristics of a commodity. Here, self-reliant peasant networks with vibrant community leaders experience division and competition through different funding requirements, project plans, pre-designated aid dollars, the introduction of salaries, and a subsequent blurring of distinctions between 'peasant movements' and 'local NGOs'. As such, the chapter illuminates how power influences local organization and processes of commodification, and acts to undermine prospects for collective resistance that have been central to Haitian history.

In Chapter 3 Ismael García Colón analyses the migration of Puerto Ricans to the United States from 1948 and how local, regional, and global power relations shape migrant farmworkers as colonial subjects within agriculture. This builds on Wolf's concept of structural power and elaborates on Wolf's first fieldwork experiences in Puerto Rico, including his considerations about conditions within both the sending and receiving states that make migration amenable. The chapter convincingly shows that Puerto Rican workers' experience of migration only partially reflect what Wolf hypothesized. This is because continental US growers resisted Puerto Rican workers because legislation meant they were difficult to deport. Hence, settlement was only made possible through state institutional designs that deployed, supported, directed, and shaped migration. The categorization of migrant farmworkers is showed to relate to dominant definitions of citizenship in terms of cultural and racial homogeneity as migrant workers' long-term experiences resonate with similar, open-border policies playing out elsewhere in the world today. Here, a capitalist mode of production demands a regular supply of dispensable labour but simultaneously negates migration's role in capitalist successes and national development. As such, the chapter argues convincingly that to understand Puerto Rican migration one needs to turn to Wolf's understandings of power, the role of government agencies and labour migration in capitalism, and the connections between local and global processes that demand a flexible work force while denying agency.

In Chapter 4 Inge-Merete Hougaard explores through a lens of historical political ecology the transformation of the landscape in the Cauca Valley, Colombia, from a *hacienda* economy to that of a sugarcane plantation and cash crop economy. It explains how the distribution and usage of land and resources for capitalist production, and legitimating processes of governing and controlling land and people, are based around discourses of 'empty space' and 'labour shortages', which develop together with counter-movements by disposed groups. The latter organize to overcome enslavement and forced labour bought about with the land encroachment and occupation by forming independent settlements, establishing labour unions, and striking. Hougaard consequently traces a dual process of contemporary agrarian transformation, capitalist forms of production, and dominant discourses that provide legitimacy for land use change, against the persistent negation of local actors' agency and their forms of organization to offset precariatization. In a Wolfean perspective the chapter draws attention to the production of 'People without History' as emanating both from the pursuit of purely economic and capitalistic objectives together with political and *patronage democratic* processes that shape broader dimensions of Colombian state formation.

In Chapter 5 Gustavo S. Azenha analyses dynamics of 'traditional' peoples' struggles over nature in the 'Discovery Coast' of Brazil in the context of historical as well as emergent processes, and in dialogue with anthropological value theory and political ecology. It draws on Wolf's work with its foregrounding of historicization, attention to global political and economic currents, and dialectic processes of connection and exclusion. Following Wolf, it emphasizes that global social forms are thoroughly transcultural articulations. Brazilian ruralities are consequently explained as socio-environmental hybridities as frontiers areas are shaped by global understandings of nature, humanity, and liberalism. The hybridities are both acknowledged and imagined through contradictory politics of revelation and concealment that obscure the histories and human subjectivities related to their creation. This demonstrates the interplay of heterogeneous social forms in moments of crisis and utilises Wolf's insights into crisis and differentiation in conversation with anthropological understandings of liminality and fetishism. One important result is forms of historical amnesia and affirmations of radical social difference. Hence, by approaching Brazil's 'traditional' peoples and the 'wild' spaces they inhabit as creative spaces in the shaping of contemporary frontiers, Azenha provides a rich and comprehensive understanding of the interplay between the expansion of global markets and the making of frontier people and places.

In Chapter 6 Ioannis Kyriakakis takes up the pertinent question of whether class theory is still relevant and operational for explaining the contemporary world structure. This returns to a key argument made by Wolf concerning the paucity of adopting the nation state as the unit of analysis and which is particularly relevant considering the predominantly transnational and global character of capitalism. Taking a point of departure in current global inequality, Kyriakakis investigates the methodological and theoretical implications of studying the world in terms of a unified conceptual space. It argues that an adoption of a global class system perspective or categorization would be beneficial because understandings of labour-related exploitation would not only be deeper and wider, but ultimately more realistic and aligned with the current workings of the global capitalistic system. The chapter utilizes data about occupation distribution and status from Ghana national statistics in combination with local understandings, experiences, and viewpoints to exemplify the making of a global underclass. This shows how the impact of the expansion of global capitalism lays bare our outdated yet persistent theoretical framings of class and class relations with the nation state as the focal point of analysis. The chapter subsequently provide a vivid reminder of how the production of knowledge about the world and our understandings of it reproduces unequal power relations.

In Chapter 7 Paul Stacey examines dynamics in the Gold Coast and Ghana between, on the one hand, the shaping of a local polity based on versions of tradition as asserted by colonial institutions, global organizations, and successive national governments, and, on the other, the production of 'alternative' versions by groups excluded from this process. Building on Wolf's understanding of power as orchestrating and conditioning social settings, influencing agency, and enabling and limiting societal organization, the chapter traces the exclusion and making of institutions around chieftaincy by the Nawuri from about 1930 to the present in East Gonja. Stacey follows how the excluded Nawuri develop social organization around ceremony, traditional leadership, and historical narratives to compete with their 'traditional' opponents, and shows how the group continue their struggle for recognition and a history of their own in the contemporary context of democratization. The Nawuri struggle is accordingly framed as a case of structural power in which 'the people who claim history as their own and the people to whom history has been denied emerge as participants in the same historical trajectory' (Wolf 1982). As such, the Nawuri are shown to continue to organize and struggle to thrive along ethnic lines in order to gain recognition from a system that long ago defined the group as unequal. This draws attention to how colonially established relations of unequal power are reproduced within new political developments, conditioning new crises, forms of organization, and differentiation along ethnic lines.

In Chapter 8, Raquel Rodrigues Machaqueiro investigates how internationally conceived efforts to address climate change in rural areas of Mozambique lead to the reproduction of colonially established processes of exclusion and rural marginalization. Solutions to the adverse impacts of climate change include conservation agriculture, the intensification of cashew production, and the industrial plantation of eucalyptus, plans that all carry the promise of local development. Yet the immersion of local sites within a larger system of agriculture that enables capitalistic expansion is convincingly shown to bear another product: a 'people to whom history has been denied'. The chapter subsequently interweaves ethnographic data from Mozambique with archival research about Portuguese colonial practices in the forestry sector, agrarian transformation, and marginalization. This provide for a multi-level and historical analysis of the political implications of developmental interventions as they are conceived internationally and implemented and experienced locally. Accordingly, the chapter builds on insights by Wolf to explain processes of global capitalist connectivity and social exclusion, showing how current developmental discourses and interventions legitimize a new political economy that perpetuates forms of colonially based capitalist accumulation and exclusion.

In Chapter 9 Tirza van Bruggen investigates historical and contemporary political and economic processes resulting in the overrepresentation of Chinese Indonesians in Indonesia in business, and their underrepresentation and social exclusion in politics – a phenomenon with a long history that has continued in new forms in the post-Suharto era of democratization after 1998. The chapter builds on Wolf's pioneering observation that contemporary social differentiation and inequality emerge from processes of global and local connectivity over time. Specifically, we see how the contemporary division of labour influences the making of, and knowledge about, social categories and exemplifies what Wolf terms a 'totality of interconnected processes' (Wolf 1982, 3). Bruggen traces the persistent exclusion of Chinese Indonesians from a combination of the historical organization of Indonesia's labour force by the Dutch to the social reproduction of naturalizing boundaries that discursively circumscribe social identities in the present-day labour market. Today, it is these which define who is appropriate for what job through processes of othering. With this, the chapter demonstrates how the historical and social construction of the division of labour limits the availability of occupational choices for Chinese Indonesians and denies political influence to this diverse group. Historical political rationalities are shown to have driven Chinese Indonesians into the economic sphere, and the process continues today with perceptions of mainland China's meddling in Indonesian affairs.

Last, but certainly not least, in Chapter 10 Masami Tsujita explores labour relationships between a powerful Japanese-owned multinational car parts supplier, the Yazaki Corporation, and its low-paid factory workers on the Pacific Island of Samoa. The chapter takes up key assertions in EPWH about the totality of interconnected global development processes, multidimensionality, and interdependencies with local forms of organization, and convincingly demonstrates dynamics between the making of a capitalist mode of production and local forms of socio-cultural organization. Yazaki opened a labour-intensive plant in Samoa in 1991 and was courted by the Samoan government with tax breaks and land concessions. The establishing of Yazaki occurred at a critical economic juncture for Samoa and played a key role in national development, with a total turnover of over 60,000 mainly rural Samoans out of a total country population of about 200,000. Yet in 2017 market-based logics forced the corporation to cease production and vacate Samoa. Tsujita's analysis of worker experiences and their agency contrasts sharply with structural perspectives and typical framings of low-paid factory workers as powerless victims of global capitalism and multinational corporations. Instead, and marking a key contribution to studies of relationships between core and peripheral economies, the chapter traces how, in diverse and ingenious ways, the Samoan workers used factory employment to expand choices in their lives and gain influence and leverage over the corporation, while taking advantage of the long working hours to develop social relations.

References

Abbink, Jan. 1992. "Epilogue." In *History and Culture: Essays on the work of Eric R. Wolf*, edited by Jan Abbink and Hans Vermeulen, 95–107. The Netherlands: Het Spinhuis.

Adnan, Shapan. 2013. "Land Grabs and Primitive Accumulation in Deltaic Bangladesh: Interactions Between Neoliberal Globalization, State Interventions, Power Relations and Peasant Resistance." *Journal of Peasant Studies* 40 (1): 87–128.

Allan, Joanna, Mahmoud Lemaadel, and Hamza Lakhal. 2021. "Oppressive Energy Politics in Africa's Last Colony: Energy, Subjectivities, and Resistance." *Antipode* 54: 44–63. https://doi.org/10.1111/anti.12765.

Anderson, Benedict. [1983] 1991. Imagined Communities: Reflections on the Origin and Spread of Nationalism. London, Verso.

Applebaum, Anne. 2022. "Ukraine and the Words that Lead to Mass Murder: First Comes the Dehumanization. Then Comes the Killing." *The Atlantic*, April 25, 2022.

Asad, Talal. 1987. "Are There Histories of Peoples without Europe? A Review Article." *Comparative Studies in Society and History* 29 (3): 594–607.

Barrett, Stanley, R., Sean Stokholm, and Jeanette Burke. 2001. "The Idea of Power and the Power of Ideas: A Review Essay." *American Anthropologist* 103 (2): 468–480.

Beckett, Sven, and Seth Rockman. 2016. Eds. *Slavery's Capitalism: A New History of American Economic Development*. University of Pennsylvania Press, USA.

Bernstein, Henry, Harriet Friedmann, Jan Douwe van der Ploeg, Teodor Shanin, and Ben White. 2018. "Forum: Fifty Years of Debate on Peasantries, 1966–2016." *The Journal of Peasant Studies* 45 (4): 689–714.

Beynon, John, and David Dunkerley. Eds. 2000. *Globalization: The Reader*. Routledge, USA.

Blundo, Giorgio. 2015. "'The King is Not a Kinsman': Multiple Accountabilities and Practical Norms in West African Bureaucracies." In *Real Governance and Practical*

Norms in Sub-Saharan Africa. The Game of the Rules, edited by Tom De Herdt, and Jean-Pierre Olivier de Sardan, 142–159. London, Routledge.

Boesen, Jannik. 1979. "On Peasantry and the 'Modes of Production' Debate." *Review of African Political Economy* 6 (15/16): 154–161.

Boone, Catherine, and Dennis Kwame Duku. 2012. "Ethnic Land Rights in Western Ghana: Stranger-Landlord Relations in the Democratic Era." *Development and Change* 43 (3): 671–93.

Borras, Saturnino M., Jennifer C. Franco, Sergio Gómez, Cristobal Kay, and Max Spoor. 2012. "Land Grabbing in Latin America and the Caribbean." *Journal of Peasant Studies* 39 (3–4): 845–872.

Borg Rasmussen, Mathias, and Christian Lund. 2018. "Reconfiguring Frontier Spaces: The Territorialization of Resource Control." *World Development* 101: 388–399.

Bourdieu, Pierre. 2005. *Outline of a Theory of Practice.* Cambridge University Press. UK.

Burke, Peter. 1992. *History and Social Theory.* Policy Press, UK.

Carvalho, Edward. J., and David. B Downing. Eds. 2010. *Academic Freedom in the Post-9/11 Era.* Palgrave Macmillan, New York.

Chatterjee, Ipsita, and Waquar Ahmed. 2019. "Dialectical Materialism: Marx's Method in Human Geography." *ACME An International Journal for Critical Geographies* 18 (2): 364–393.

Chatterjee, Pallavi. 2021. "Sweden's Troubled Relationship with the Indigenous Sámi Community." Human Rights Pulse. https://www.humanrightspulse.com/mastercontentblog?author=5fc9fe2d41142a3c4b437703. Accessed 10 May 2022.

Chirot, Daniel. 1984. "Reviewed Work: Europe and the People without History by Eric R. Wolf." *Journal of Social History* 18 (1): 119–24.

Cole, John W. 1985. "Reviewed Work: Europe and the People without History by Eric R. Wolf." *Theory and Society* 14 (1): 111–15.

Darian-Smith, Eve, and Philip C. McCarty. 2017. *The Global Turn Theories, Research Designs, and Methods for Global Studies.* University of California Press, Oakland, CA.

Dhawan, Nikita. 2018. "Marxist Critique of Post-colonialism." *Krisis. Journal for Contemporary Philosophy* 2. https://krisis.eu/marxist-critique-of-post-colonialism/.

Donlevy, James K., Dianne Gereluk, and Jim Brandon. 2018. "Trigger Warnings, Freedom of Speech, and Academic Freedom in Higher Education." *Education Law Journal* 28 (1):1–41.

Edelman, Marc, and Angelique Haugerud. Eds. 2005. *The Anthropology of Development and Globalization: From Classical Political Economy to Contemporary Neoliberalism.* Blackwell. UK.

Enyedi, Zsolt. 2018. "Democratic Backsliding and Academic Freedom in Hungary." *Perspectives on Politics* 16 (4): 1067–1074. doi:10.1017/S1537592718002165.

Escobar, Arturo. 1991. "Anthropology and the Development Encounter: The Making and Marketing of Development Anthropology." *American Ethnologist* 18 (4): 658–682.

Escobar, Arturo. 1995. *Encountering Development: The Making and Unmaking of the Third World*. Princeton: Princeton University Press, USA.

Esposito, Luigi, and Fernando Pérez. 2010. "The Global Addiction and Human Rights: Insatiable Consumerism, Neoliberalism, and Harm Reduction." *Perspectives on Global Development and Technology* 9 (1–2): 84–100.

Eyben, Rosalind, and Joy Moncrieffe. Eds. 2007. *The Power of Labelling: How People are Categorized and Why It Matters*. Routledge, UK.

Fairbairn, Madeleine. 2014. "'Like Gold with Yield': Evolving Intersections Between Farmland and Finance." *The Journal of Peasant Studies* 41 (5): 777–795.

Fogel, Joshua A. 1988. "The Debates over the Asiatic Mode of Production in Soviet Russia, China, and Japan." *American Historical Review* 93 (1): 56–79.

Foucault, Michel. 2008. *The Birth of Biopolitics: Lectures at the Collège de France 1978–1979*. G. Burchell, trans. New York: Palgrave MacMillan.

Gagné, Natacha. 2015. "Brave New Words: The Complexities and Possibilities of an 'Indigenous' Identity in Polynesia and New Caledonia." *The Contemporary Pacific* 27 (2): 371–402.

Fukuyama, Francis. 1989. "The End of History?" *The National Interest* 16: 3–18, Center for the National Interest.

Garbes, Angela. 2022. "The Devaluation of Care Work is by Design." *The Atlantic*. May 13.

Geertz, Clifford. 1973. *The Interpretation of Cultures*. Basic Books, New York.

Gledhill, John. 2005. "Some Histories are More Possible than Others: Structural Power, Big Pictures and the Goal of Explanation in the Anthropology of Eric Wolf." *Critique of Anthropology* 25 (1): 37–57.

Graeber, David. 2012. *Debt: The first 5000 years*. Penguin, UK.

Graeber, David. 2002. "The Anthropology of Globalization (with Notes on Neomedievalism, and End of the Chinese Model of the State)." *American Anthropologist* 104:1222–1227.

Grandia, Liza. 2020. "Back to the Future: The Autonomous Indigenous Communities of Petén, Guatemala." *Antipoda* 40:103–127.

Gross, David. 1982. "Time-Space Relations in Giddens' Social Theory." *Theory, Culture, and Society* 1 (2): 83–88.

Gould, Jeremy. 1979. Review of *Perspectives in Marxist Anthropology*, by Maurice Godelier, *Acta Sociologica* 22 (1): 90–93.

Hall, Derek, Philip Hirsch, and Tania Murry Li. 2011. "Introduction to Powers of Exclusion: Land Dilemmas in Southeast Asia, Singapore and Honolulu" National University of Singapore Press/University of Hawaii Press: 1–27.

Hämäläinen, Pekka. 2018. "Crooked Lines of Relevance: Europe and the People Without History", by Eric R. Wolf. *American Historical Review* 123 (3): 875–885.

Hardt, Michael, and Antonio Negri. 2000. *Empire*. Harvard University Press, USA.

Harvey, David. 2005. *A Brief History of Neoliberalism*. Oxford: Oxford University Press.

Harvey, David. 1990. *The Condition of Postmodernity: An Enquiry into the Origins of Cultural Change*. Cambridge, MA: Blackwell.

Harvey, David. 1989. *The Condition of Postmodernity*. London: Wiley.

Harvey, Neil. 2001. "Globalisation and Resistance in Post-cold war Mexico: Difference, Citizenship and Biodiversity Conflicts in Chiapas." *Third World Quarterly* 22 (6): 1045–1061.

Hecht, Susanna. 2018. "Europe and the People without History." *The Journal of Peasant Studies* 45 (1): 220–225.

Heyman, Josiah, McC. 2003. "The Inverse of Power." *Anthropological Theory* 3 (2): 139–156.

Hewitt, Guy. 2020. "The Windrush Scandal." *Caribbean Quarterly* 66 (1): 108–128.

Hobbes, Thomas. 1651. *Leviathan. Or the Matter, Form and Power of a Commonwealth, Ecclesiasticall and Civil*.

Hobsbawm, Eric. 1994. *The Age of Extremes: The Short Twentieth Century, 1914–1991*. London: Abacus.

Hobsbawm, Eric, and Terence Ranger. [1983] 2012. Eds. *The Invention of Tradition*. Cambridge University Press, UK.

Horner, Rory, and David Hulme. 2019. "From International to Global Development: New Geographies of 21st Century Development." *Development and Change* 50 (2): 347–378.

Huntington, Samuel P. 1991. "Democracy's Third Wave." *The Journal of Democracy* 2 (2).

Hylland Eriksen, Thomas. 2010. Foreword to the 2010 Edition of *Europe and the People Without History*, by Eric R. Wolf. University of California Press.

Jabeen, Firasat. 2020. "The Perpetuation of Colonial Legacy: Uncovering Internal Orientalism in the Form of English Supremacy in Pakistan." *Journal of Multilingual and Multicultural Development* 41 (5): 432–443.

Joseph, Sabrina. Ed. 2019. *Commodity Frontiers and Global Capitalist Expansion: Social, Ecological and Political Implications from the Nineteenth Century to the Present Day*. Palgrave Macmillan.

Joshi, Saba. 2020. "Contesting Land Grabs, Negotiating Statehood: The Politics of International Accountability Mechanisms and Land Disputes in Rural Cambodia." *Third World Quarterly* 41 (9): 1615–1633.

Kalb, Don. 2015. Forum: Anthropologists approach. "The New Capitalism: Class, Labor, Social Reproduction: Towards a Non-self Limiting Anthropology." *Suomen Antropologi: Journal of the Finnish Anthropological Society* 40 (2).

Kalb, Don. and Herman Tak. Eds. 2005. *Critical Junctions: Anthropology and History Beyond the Cultural Turn*. New York: Berghahn Books.

Kalb, Don, and Luisa Steur. 2015. 'Global South'. International Encyclopedia of the Social and Behavioural Sciences (Second Edition), edited by James D. Wright: 186–191.

Klein, Kerwin. L. 1995. "In Search of Narrative Mastery: Postmodernism and the People Without History." *History and Social Theory* 34 (4): 275–298.

Krzyżanowski, Michal, Anna Triandafyllidou, and Ruth Wodak. 2018. "The Mediatization and the Politicization of the 'Refugee Crisis' in Europe." *Journal of Immigrant and Refugee Studies* 16 (1–2): 1–14.

Laclau, Ernesto. 1992. "Universalism, Particularism, and the Question of Identity." *The Identity in Question* 61: 83–90.

Lai, On-Kwok. 2011. "Critical Engagements of NGOs for Global Human Rights Protection: A New Epoch of Cosmopolitanism for Larger Freedom?" *International Journal of Social Quality* 1 (2): 5–18.

Lund, Christian. 2016. "Rule and Rupture: State Formation Through the Production of Property and Citizenship." *Development and Change* 47 (6): 1199–1228.

MacLeavy, Julie, Maria Fannin, and Wendy Larner. 2021. "Feminism and Futurity: Geographies of Resistance, Resilience and Re-working." *Progress in Human Geography* 1–23.

McNeill, William, H. 1984. *The Journal of Interdisciplinary History* 14 (3): 660–62.

Mamdani, Mahmood. 1996. *Citizen and Subject. Contemporary Africa and the Legacy of Late Colonialism.* London: James Currey.

Marcus, Anthony. 2003. Ed. "Imaginary Worlds: The Last Years of Eric Wolf." *Social Anthropology* 11 (1): 78–94.

Marcus, Anthony, and Charles Menzies. 2005. "Towards a Class-Struggle Anthropology." *Anthropologica* 47 (1): 13–33.

McMichael, Philip. 2006. "Peasant Prospects in the Neoliberal Age." *New Political Economy* 11 (3): 407–418.

McGee, R. Jon, and Richard L. Warms. 2013. *Theory in Social and Cultural Anthropology: An Encyclopedia.* Sage Publications, Inc.

McRobbie, Kenneth, Karl P. Levitt. Eds. 2000. *Karl Polanyi in Vienna: The Contemporary Significance of The Great Transformation.* New York, London and Montreal: Black Rose Books.

Migone, Andrea. 2007. "Hedonistic Consumerism: Patterns of Consumption in Contemporary Capitalism." *Review of Radical Political Economics* 39 (2): 173–200.

Mintz, Sidney W., and Eric R. Wolf. 1989. "Relpy to Michael Taussig." Critique of Anthropology 9 (25): 25–31.

Mohan, Giles. 2009. "Structural Adjustment." In: R. Kitchin, and N. Thrift. Eds. *International Encyclopedia of Human Geography* 11: 1–9. Oxford, UK.

Moore, Jason W. 2017. "The Capitalocene, Part I: On the Nature and Origins of our Ecological Crisis." *The Journal of Peasant Studies* 44 (3): 594–630.

Moore, Sally Falk. 1978. *Law as Process: An Anthropological Approach.* International African Institute, LIT, James Currey.

Morton, Micah F. 2019. "From Hill Tribes to Indigenous Peoples: The Localization of a Global Movement in Thailand." *Journal of Southeast Asian Studies* 50 (1): 7–31.

Mosse, David. 2004. "Is Good Policy Unimplementable? Reflections on the Ethnography of Aid Policy and Practice." *Development and Change* 35 (4): 639–671.
Neveling, Patrick, and Luisa Steur. 2018. "Introduction: Marxian Anthropology Resurgent." *Focaal – Journal of Global and Historical Anthropology* 82: 1–15.
Nugent, David. 2002. "Review of Envisioning Power: Ideologies of Dominance and Crisis, by Eric R. Wolf." *American Ethnologist* 29 (1): 193–195.
Nygaard-Christensen, Maj, and Bagga Bjerge. 2021. "The Construction of 'Socially Marginalised Greenlanders' as a Target Group in Danish Welfare Policy and Practice". *Nordic Journal of Social Research* 12 (1):132–54.
Olivier de Sardan, Jean-Pierre. 2016. "For an Anthropology of Gaps, Discrepancies and Contradictions." *Antropologia* 3: 111–131.
Palmer, Bryan. D. 1990. *Descent into Discourse: The Reification of Language and the Writing of Social History*. Philadelphia: Temple University Press.
Pelican, Michaela. 2013. "Insights from Cameroon: Five years after the Declaration on the Rights of Indigenous Peoples." *Anthropology Today* 29 (3): 13–16.
Piketty, Thomas. 2014. *Capital in the Twenty-First Century*. Harvard University Press.
Portis-Winner, Irene. 2006. "Eric Wolf: A Semiotic Exploration of Power." *Sign Systems Studies* 34 (2): 339–356.
Procter, James. 2004. *Stuart Hall*. Routledge Critical Thinkers.
Rabasa, José. 2005. "On the History of the History of Peoples without History." *Humboldt Journal of Social Relations* 29 (1): 204–222.
Rhoades, Gary, and Sheila Slaughter. 2004. "Academic Capitalism in the New Economy: Challenges and Choices." *American Academic* 1 (1): 37–59.
Richardson, Kristina. L. 2020. "Invisible Strangers, or Ramani History Reconsidered." *History of the Present* 10 (2): 187–207.
Robinson, William. I. 2011. "Globalization and the Sociology of Immanuel Wallerstein: A Critical Appraisal." *International Sociology*. 26 (6): 723–745.
Rose, Nikolas. 1990. *Governing the Soul: The Shaping of the Private Self*. London: Routledge.
Roy, Arundhati. 2004. "Public Power in the Age of Empire: Arundhati Roy on War, Resistance and the Presidency." 23 August. *Democracynow.org*. Accessed February 24, 2022.
Said, Edward W. 1978. *Orientalism*. New York: Pantheon Books.
Saitta, Dean J. 2005. "Dialoguing with the Ghost of Marx: Modes of Production in Archaeological Theory." *Critique of Anthropology* 25 (1): 27–35.
Samers, Michael. 1998. "Immigration, 'Ethnic Minorities', and 'Social Exclusion' in the European Union: A Critical Perspective." *Geoforum* 29 (2): 123–144.
Schneider, Jane. 1995. "Introduction: The Analytic Strategies of Eric R. Wolf." In *Articulating Hidden Histories: Exploring the influence of Eric R. Wolf*. Edited by Jane Schneider and Rayna Rapp, 3–30. Berkeley: Univ. of California Press.

Schneider, Jane. and Rayna. Rapp. 1995. "Works by Eric R. Wolf." In *Articulating Hidden Histories: Exploring the influence of Eric R. Wolf.* Edited by Jane Schneider and Rayna Rapp, 351–356. Berkeley: Univ. of California Press.

Schouten, P. 2008. "David Harvey on the Geography of Capitalism, Understanding Cities as Polities and Shifting Imperialisms." *Theory Talks.* #20. www.theorytalks.org/2008/10/theory-talk-20-david-harvey.html. Accessed 18 July 2020.

Scott, James. 2010. *The Art of Not Being Governed: An Anarchist History of Upland Southeast Asia.* Yale Agrarian Studies Series.

Simonsen, Kristina B. 2016. "Ghetto-Society-Problem: A Discourse Analysis of Nationalist." *Studies in Ethnicity and Nationalism* 16 (1): 83–99.

Smith, Gavin. 2018. "Elusive relations." *Current Anthropology* 59 (1): 247–267.

Smith, Gavin. 1986. Review essay: "Anthropology and Underdevelopment." *Canad. Rev. Soc. and Anth.* 23 (3): 444–456.

Smith, Neil. 2001. "Geography of Uneven Development." In N.J Smelser, and P.B. Baltes. Eds. *International Encyclopedia of the Social and Behavioral Sciences.* Elsevier: 15958–15962.

Stacey, Paul, Richard Grant, and Martin Oteng-Ababio. 2021. "Food for Thought: Urban Market Planning and Entangled Governance in Accra, Ghana." *Habitat International* 115.

Stacey, Paul. 2019. *State of Slum: Precarity and Informal Governance at the Margins in Accra.* Zed Books.

Stacey, Paul. 2016. "Rethinking the Making and Unmaking of Traditional and Statutory Institutions in Post-Nkrumah Ghana." *African Studies Review* 59 (2): 209–230.

Stacey, Paul. 2015. "Political Structure and the Limits of Recognition and Representation in Ghana." *Development and Change* 46 (1): 25–47.

Standing, Guy. 2011. *The Precariat: The New Dangerous Class,* London: Bloomsbury Academic.

Stepan, Alfred, and Juan J. Lintz. 2013. "Democratization Theory and the 'Arab Spring'."*Journal of Democracy* 24 (2):15–30.

Susser, Ida. 2016. "Considering the Urban Commons: Anthropological Approaches to Social Movements." *Dialectical Anthropology* 40 (3): 183–198. The Fortieth Anniversary – Part Two.

Taussig, Michael. 1989. " History as Commodity." Critique of Anthropology 9 (1): 7– 23.

Tilly, Charles. 2005. *Identities, Boundaries and Social Ties.* Paradigm Publishers, Boulder, London. USA.

Tilly, Charles. 2002. Review of: *Pathways of Power: Building an Anthropology of the Modern World* by Eric R. Wolf, with Sydel Silverman. *Journal of Interdisciplinary History* 22 (3): 444–445.

Trumpener, Katie. 1992. "The Time of the Gypsies: A 'People without History' in the Narrative of the West." *Critical Inquiry* 18 (4): 843–884.

Tsing, Anna L. 2003. "Natural Resources and Capitalist Frontiers." *Economic and Political Weekly* 38 (48): 5100–5106.

Vijayabaskar, M. 2020. "Land Questions in the 21st Century Postcolony." *Journal of Agrarian Change* 20 (4): 682–689.

Wachira, Jackson, Paul Stacey, and Joanes Atela. 2020. "Large Scale Land Acquisitions and Pastoralists' Climate Change Adaptation in Kenya." RARE Working Paper, 2/2020, Roskilde University.

Wall, Thomas Carl, Peter Fitzpatrick, Erik Vogt, and Andreas Kalyvas. 2005. *Politics, Metaphysics, and Death: Essays on Giorgio Agamben's Homo Sace*. Duke University Press.

Wallerstein, Immanuel. 1974. *The Modern World-System I: Capitalist Agriculture and the Origins of the European World-Economy in the Sixteenth Century*. New York: Academic Press.

Weber, Max. 1978. *Economy and Society: An Outline of Interpretative Sociology*. Berkeley, CA: University of California Press.

Whitehead, Neil L. 2004. "Power, Culture, and History: The Legacies of Wolf, Sahlins, and Fabian." *Ethnohistory* 51 (1): 181–185.

Wolf, Eric R. 2001. *Pathways of Power: Building an Anthropology of the Modern World*. Berkeley: Univ. of California Press.

Wolf, Eric. R. 1999. *Envisioning Power: Ideologies of Dominance and Crisis*. Berkeley: University of California Press.

Wolf, Eric R. 1990. "Distinguished Lecture: Facing Power – Old Insights, New Questions." *American Anthropologist* New Series 92 (3): 586–596.

Wolf, Eric R. 1987. "Cycles of Violence: The Anthropology of War and Peace." In *Waymarks* edited by Kenneth Moore. Notre Dame: University of Notre Dame Press, 127–150.

Wolf, Eric. R. 1982. *Europe and the People Without History*. University of California Press.

Wolf, Eric. R. 1969. *Peasant Wars of the Twentieth Century*. New York: Harper Collins.

Wolf, Eric R. 1959. *Sons of the Shaking Earth: The People of Mexico and Guatemala*. Chicago: University of Chicago Press.

Zhang, Yunpeng. 2018. "Grabbing Land for Equitable Development? Reengineering Land Dispossession Through Securitising Land Development Rights in Chongqing." *Antipode* 50 (4): 1120–1140.

CHAPTER 2

Commodifying the Countermovement: How Foreign Funding Turns Haitian Social Movements into Commodities

Joshua Steckley, Nixon Boumba and Marylynn Steckley

1   Introduction

Haiti is infamously known as the 'Republic of NGOs' with 80 per cent of social services provided by non-governmental organizations (NGOs). The devastating 2010 earthquake further entrenched the NGO sector with a massive influx of $13 billion of international donations and bilateral aid; the US Ambassador to Haiti rightly exclaimed in then-classified diplomatic cables, 'The gold rush is on!' However, the influx of aid and loans – advertised with the slogan 'build back better' – resulted in few improvements compared to pre-earthquake Haiti. Haiti remains mired in poverty, with high unemployment, persistent inflation, parasitic state officials, extreme inequality, and a lack of rural investment and public infrastructure including access to health and education. The earthquake response has largely been viewed as a failure, with various activists, journalists, and scholars uncovering numerous problems surrounding corruption, sexual exploitation, ill-conceived policies, lack of transparency, and massive financial waste (Schuller 2012; Schuller and Morales 2012; Katz 2013; Bell 2013). Such critics argue that development aid should be redirected away from the large international NGOs – with their highly paid international staff, fleets of land cruisers, and generous per diems – and channelled to local communities and organizations that are better equipped with contextual knowledge to implement relief and development projects while simultaneously challenging the economic and social power structures at the root of inequality and poverty. In short, funds should support local, progressive, and radical organizations and movements firmly embedded within and accountable to their communities. But is this a fail-safe solution? In this chapter we build on long years of experience in Haiti to show how countermovement can take on the characteristics of a commodity being bought and sold in the marketplace of humanitarian relief and development projects. From a Wolfean perspective, we argue that broader forces and elements of commodification – particularly abstraction, privatization, valuation, and alienation – (re)constitute social movements at the grassroots level and highlight the importance of recognizing how and when commodifying forces begin to constitute a social movement in itself. Hence, our chapter critically explores the impact of foreign funding on progressive social movements in Haiti, and how funding inherently begins the process of commodification that reshapes the social relations within and amongst radical movements. We rely on Polanyi's (2001) concepts of 'fictious commodities' and the 'countermovement' to understand how capitalism attempts to dis-embed land, labour, and wealth from existing social relations and turn them into commodities for sale on the market. Wolf's work in *Europe and the People Without History* and *Peasant Wars of the 20th Century* implicitly and explicitly draws on Polanyi to understand how capital's imperative to extend commodity relations penetrates heterogeneous peripheral communities, transforming socio-ecological relations. Applying the theoretical and (methodological) insights developed by Polanyi and Wolf is useful today to identify how the general tendencies of capitalist incursions – particularly processes of commodification – are articulated into 'peripheral' communities in developing countries today. In so doing, this chapter pays specific attention to how resistance and rebellion are both instigated and subdued. In *Peasant Wars of the 20th Century*, Wolf is more Polanyian, arguing that what ties together social contestation – indeed, revolutions – is a reaction to capitalism's drive to dis-embed land, labour, and wealth from existing social relations, turning them into commodities for sale on the market.

Polanyi's and Wolf's insights have garnered renewed interest from theorists who see the rise of contemporary 'new social movements' as a Polanyian 'countermovement' to contemporary neoliberalism (Munck 2006; Levien and Paret 2012; Silva 2012). But what happens if we extend neoliberalism's commodifying tendencies to the countermovement itself? Our analysis examines how foreign funding for humanitarian and developmental assistance sparks a commodification process that shapes the constitution and operation of radical social movements in Haiti. In doing so, we ask a more fundamental question that moves beyond criticizing the structural inadequacies of NGOs: what happens when a reactive countermovement against capitalism's commodifying drives becomes a commodity itself?

Commodification is a pernicious process that can reconfigure the institutional structure and everyday activities of progressive movements. The heart of our argument is that the countermovement against capitalist incursions can itself be commodified and take on characteristics of a commodity being bought and sold in a market of relief and development projects. Our argument is not that NGOs merely act as a pacifying force during social unrest – what James Ferguson (1990) has called the 'anti-politics machine' – but that they are able to commodify social organizing itself. This has significant ramifications for the trajectory of movements, their objectives, their activities, and their relationships to constituent members. We begin the chapter with a discussion of Polanyi's conception of the countermovement, how Wolf applied this to peasants revolutions, and why it is relevant in the contemporary era of neoliberalism. We then define commodification and apply it to the context of development aid to see where our analysis aligns with and departs from past critiques of the so-called 'aid industrial complex'. In the final section of the chapter, we draw from examples in contemporary Haiti to highlight four interrelated elements of commodification – abstraction, privatization, valuation, and alienation – to identify how *countermovement commodification* reshapes progressive movements. We conclude by suggesting that social movements and their progressive donors[1] take seriously and explicitly identify the commodifying tendencies that are actively at work when financial resources change hands. To be clear, we are not advocating a full rejection of funding, or salaried positions; indeed, the dominance of market relations and the magnitude of foreign funding in a country like Haiti often necessitates wages and contracts with aid agencies as a livelihood strategy. Instead, it is a warning to evaluate the extent to which the commodity relations are affecting the aims and everyday activities of the countermovement and recognize how commodification will disembed local, radical movements from the contextual spatial-temporal social relations that gave rise to them in the first place.

---

1 The term 'NGO' encompasses a diversity of institutions with different political motivations, sources of funding, constituent bases, legal statures, and strategies for development. For our analysis, we focus specifically on the flow of funding between two groups of organizations. First, we refer to community-based organizations, grassroots organizations, progressive or radical movements, or local organizations as the formal or informal organizations of mostly smaller, regionally based social movements that *receive (or refuse to receive)* funding sources outside their constituent base. When such institutions contest capitalist incursions into their socio-ecological relations, we see them as part of the countermovement. In the second group, we use the terms 'donors', 'donor agencies', 'private foundations' 'government aid,' and 'progressively minded NGOs' to refer to those organizations that offer funds to these social movements. This includes a wide spectrum of organizations. They may be political, apolitical, faith-based, secular, self-financed through constitution donations, or dependent on government grants. What concerns us most in this chapter is not a typology of this second group of institutions, but rather that, in one way or another, they are the source of funds for those organizations named in the first group. We want to know what happens when such funding is directed towards those movements engaged in a countermovement.

2 Countermovement and the New Social Movements

Commodities for Polanyi are simply goods and services *produced for sale on the market* (Polyani 2001, 75). The simple definition has an extremely important implication; the motivating force that produces a commodity is not its usefulness, but rather its ability to generate a profit through market exchange. In turn, a functioning market economy requires such production for exchange to both increase the scope of commodity circulation (finding or creating new markets, usually through geographic expansion) and deepening commodification through the creation of new goods and services (Prudham 2009; 2007). The goal of the market economy, as Polanyi sees it, is for every single element of industry to 'be subjected to the supply and demand mechanism interacting with price' (Polanyi 2001, 75). The problem with this utopian vision, however, is that three important commodities of production are not actually *produced* for the market. *Land* is not produced for the market and must be transformed into the economic categories of 'property' and 'rent' to become commensurable. Nor is *labour*, which enters the market as wages, but is simply another name for human activity. And *money* has traditionally been a medium for exchange, as opposed to a commodity for sale in a market. As such, Polanyi calls these three conditional elements of production – land, labour, and money – 'fictitious commodities' because they are not actually produced for the purpose of market exchange. In earlier societies, he notes, the market was embedded within society to serve a social function. In a capitalist economy, however, the reverse occurs – society itself becomes embedded into the market to be traded as commodities, where 'the substance of society' becomes a mere 'accessory to the economic system' (Polanyi 2001, 75). This reversal has grave implications. In particular, the transformation of land and labour into commodities demolishes existing community social relations that had previously been the means for social reproduction. The commodification of land and labour is 'a short formula for the liquidation of every and any cultural institution in an organic society' (Polanyi 2001, 167).

For Polanyi, however, the capitalist drive to make all human activity and nature commensurable through supply and demand of the market is a pipe dream. Societies tend not to stand idly by while their material and cultural wealth – how they ensure survival – is stripped from them and sold as commodities. The so-called commodity called 'labour-power,' Polanyi notes, 'cannot be shoved about, used indiscriminately' (Polanyi 2001, 73). As such, the 'movement' toward a fully market economy that strives to affix a price tag to every person and thing simultaneously creates a reactive 'countermovement' that resists the commodifying drive. Wolf (1999) relies on Polanyi in his description of peasant wars of the twentieth century. The revolutions in Russia, Mexico, Algeria, China, Vietnam and Cuba were sparked by the incursion of capitalist relations into the countryside that distorted and destroyed societal norms, local markets, social relations, and property regimes: 'Thus, paradoxically, the very spread of the capitalist market principle also forced men to see defences against it ... In a sense, all our six cases can be seen as the outcome of such defensive reactions, coupled with a search for a new and more humane social order.' (Wolf 1999, 282). For Wolf, the revolutionary 'peasant wars' are intriguing precisely because the class of revolutionaries came not from the exploited proletarian protagonists as predicted by Marx, but from peasants struggling against forms of appropriation that threatened their very livelihoods.

The countermovement concept has gained more traction over the last several decades with the rise of neoliberalism that reasserted the primacy of the free-market exchange after decades of New Deal policies and Fordist labour regimes. In Western Europe and North America, class struggle during this post-war 'golden age' of capitalism pitted the industrial working class against capital, with the former making unprecedented gains. For the capitalist, this created an overaccumulation problem where capitalists had fewer and fewer avenues to generate profitable returns on their investment (Harvey 2005; Bello 2006). Beginning in the 1970s, the neoliberal project sought to re-establish capitalist class dominance through privatization, deregulation, loosening financial controls, and cutting social services. The ideological objective of neoliberalism was to unleash the free market as the supreme engine of economic growth and human prosperity. As Harvey (2005) notes, the economic growth attributed to the neoliberal era had less to do with increasing productivity or unleashing creative entrepreneurs and more to do with the appropriation and redistribution of assets – that is, a bottom-up redistribution through the appropriation, privatization, and commodification of public and commonly held wealth. Structural adjustment programmes in the developing countries in the 1980s and 1990s gutted social spending, loosened financial controls, mandated fire-sale privatization of public assets, and reduced protectionist trade policies, forcing small farmers to compete directly with capital-intensive and cheaper agricultural imports. Instead of accumulating capital through industrial production, wealth was generated by stripping populations of the resources that had sustained their livelihoods – agricultural production, land, common forests, access to waterways, and publicly owned assets and services. In turn, the contemporary flashpoints of class conflict moved outside of the industrial places of formal employment and into disparate locations across the world involving heterogeneous populations such as indigenous groups, women's groups, religious movements, peasant organizations, and landless peasants (Harvey 2003). These 'new social movements' are seen as contemporary countermovements that reject the utopian market logic that renders every aspect of social and ecological life commensurable to free market exchange (Levein 2007; Munck 2006; Munck 2004; Harvey 2003).

3 The Aid Industry

Arundhati Roy (2014) calls NGOs an 'indicator species' that signals the extent of damage caused by the neoliberal project: 'It's almost as though the greater the devastation caused by neoliberalism, the greater the outbreak of NGOs.' It is no coincidence that the massive social spending cuts dictated by lending institutions in the 1980s and 1990s in developing countries were carried out alongside the massive proliferation of NGOs. This is often referred to as the process of NGO-ization (Maniates 1990; Alvarez 2009) whereby popular movements, grassroots organizations, and community-based organizations are institutionalized into recipients of foreign aid and their funder's developmental prerogatives (Choudry and Kapoor 2013).

One of the more generous perspectives is that the multiplication of NGOs is a humanitarian response to privatization and the pruning of social services (Robinson 1997). As structural adjustment programmes forced developing countries to cut expenditure and sell state assets to repay international creditors, NGOs stepped in to fulfil previous functions performed by the state (Macdonald 2008). Reframed as a bottom-up approach to development, local actors and community-based organizations with foreign financial backing became the catalyst for development work in place of government (Sangeeta 2004). Other perspectives, however, see a more insidious process, whereby social movements are purposely co-opted and depoliticized to de-escalate potential class tensions. In his seminal book the *Anti-Politics Machine*, James Ferguson (1990) directly connects 'development' itself as an industry, a sweeping array of NGOs – along with aid workers and management staff – that seem particularly interested in small countries with seemingly little strategic or economic importance (Ferguson 1990, 7). As these NGOs infiltrate society, reactionary politics are subdued while aid interventions ignore structural and political power imbalances, instead fixating on more local, smaller-scale development projects such as drilling wells, building schools, and cleaning canals. Instead of militantly organizing their local constituents, social movements orient their activities to finding funding for these smaller projects: 'Many of the organizations that supported radical social change in the 1970s and 1980s have turned themselves into a professionalized aid sector' (Pearce 2010, 622). In this perspective, the increase of NGOs not only fills the gaps left by structural adjustment and neoliberal policies, but also placates those best positioned to resist it. Going a step further, Petras (1999) notes how deradicalized leaders, now salaried employees of the NGOs, 'directly compete with other social movements for influence among the poor, women, and the racially excluded'. In these cases, funding is a means to monitor, control, and undermine the organization's agenda by turning past radical organizers into future administrative consultants.

A more pernicious perspective is detected by Marxist and dependency theorists. Development discourse not only provides a band-aid fix that deradicalizes potential threats to power structures, but can be used to actively serve capitalist agendas. Here, foreign aid is a mechanism to exploit and 'reinforce the system which in the first place causes the poverty' (Lappé et al. 1980). Whether or not the lives of impoverished populations improve, is beside the point. Critical agrarian studies scholars, in particular, stress how the 'development industry' seeks to expand capitalism's reach and make inroads into the non-commodified realm of social reproduction and livelihoods by creating property markets (Carr 2006), profiting from conservation efforts (Kelly 2011), underwriting micro-financing initiatives (Roy 2010), or funding small-scale tropical commodity production (Steckley and Weis 2016). Development aid, in such cases, becomes a lubricant that facilitates avenues for capitalist accumulation (Hickel 2017; Kim and Gray 2016). Each of these interrelating perspectives are on full display in Haiti. Haiti is often called 'the Republic of NGOs' with more NGOs per capita than any other country (though the same is often said of India, and the claim is more dependent on what is classified as an NGO). Working in Haiti, we heard on several occasions that Haiti is the 'place where good development projects go to die.' The 2010 earthquake magnified these sentiments, with North American newspapers questioning the efficacy of international donations, asking 'Where did the money go?' (Ramachandran and Walz 2013). Journalists and scholars have identified an assortment of problems of post-earthquake NGO activities in Haiti: the lack of transparency and accountability (Katz 2013; Edmonds 2013); top-down institutional structures and objectives (Schuller 2012; O'Conner et al. 2014); aid dependency (Cunningham 2012); sexual abuse (Horton 2012); the redirection of aid money back to the donor country (Dietrich 2013); logistical disorganization (Zanotti 2010, Altay and Labonte 2014); biases against rural development funding (Shamsie 2011, Steckley and Weis 2016); and the bloated salaries and budgets of foreign aid workers, development grant writers, and international consultants (Katz 2013).

The common recommendation from these studies suggests aid money should be redirected towards more progressive organizations and grassroots 'social movements' consisting of locally run networks that seek to address the structural 'root causes' of social inequality and poverty (Edmonds 2013; Katz 2013; Zanotti 2010; Schuller 2012). The benefits of this locally based grassroots approach are self-evident. It puts financial control and decision-making power into the hands of populations who have the knowledge and palpable experience to address the immediate and structural challenges that keep them in poverty. But is this a sure-fire solution? What if much of the problem goes beyond the issues highlighted above; what if the problem is the funding itself?

If we are talking about an 'aid industry' then we need to specify what is 'industrial' about aid. This is more than simply demonstrating that certain groups such as the 'beltway bandits' – the consulting firms located within the Washington DC beltway that receive the lion's share of bilateral aid money (Alden et al. 2020) – are capable of profiting from Haiti's poverty. An *industry* presupposes production of certain commodities for sale on a market. What are the commodities that this industry produces, buys, and sells? We suggest that one of the commodities produced in the aid industry are radical organizations. Calls to fund 'local', 'grassroots', 'community-based' organizations often ignore the fact that they are, in some ways, calling for the commodification of the countermovement itself. The crux of our argument is therefore, not that these organizations are co-opted, or merely serve their imperial financiers. Indeed, much of the funding by progressive donors comes with explicit intents of decolonization, avoiding clientelism, and restructuring power imbalances specifically between organizations of global North and South. The more parsimonious explanation comes down to the use of money for payment of goods and services – that is, the buying and selling of commodities – and the subsequent ramifications of such payment on social relations within local contexts. What our chapter tries to show is that the exchange of money from donors to recipients – even for the most anti-colonial, anti-imperialist groups, and individuals – inherently treats social movements as commodities. A Wolfean framework allows us to examine how commodifying tendencies of the contemporary 'aid industry' reshape contemporary community resistance to the structural forces affecting people in 'peripheral' countries.

4 A Brief Note on Methodology

In his 1997 preface to *Europe and the People Without History*, Wolf argues that ethnography will be "needed to properly evaluate some unexamined romantic notions about the nature of human action in the world" (Wolf 2010, XXII–XXIII). In this chapter, we intend to apply this to the 'romantic notions' of development aid that funds 'bottom-up,' 'local,' 'grassroots' or even 'anticapitalist' organization and movements. Our notion of countermovement commodification is based on the individual and overlapping experiences of the chapter's three authors who have all worked directly for or in partnerships with a diversity of NGOs and funders, including governmental development organizations, medium-sized international NGOs, local urban-based movements, and both well- and ill-funded peasant organizations. Two of the authors spent six years both working and conducting ethnographic research in Haiti, and one has spent his entire adult live working directly for and in partnership with local Haitian movements and coalitions. This includes working with organizations we would classify as engaged in the countermovement. We do not use specific organizational names in this chapter as the objective is not to 'name and shame' organizations or plans, but to highlight the process of commodification that inherently affects each organization or social movement that receives donor funding.

5   On Commodification

Commodification is understood as a process that renders qualitatively different non-market goods equivalent in that they may be sold for the same monetary price (Castree 2003). This simple definition shows us how the process of commodification is not new and has existed in earlier historical epochs. Under capitalism, however, commodification and the reliance on commodities for survival become increasingly generalized across the world, where commodity production is motivated by exchange value (that is, profit) over use value. But what elements and processes are involved in commodification, and what impact do they have on dynamic social activity such as a radical movement contesting commodification itself?

We are certainly not the first to highlight the specific and deleterious effects of well-intentioned funding on radical social movements. In *The Revolution Will Not Be Funded* (INCITE! 2007) contributors note how corporate foundations and large donors deploy their financial leverage to assert control over 'activist energies' and redirect action toward more palatable activities that do not challenge oppressive structures. The general argument of the book suggests that objectives are better served when social movements are funded by their own constituents rather than by accepting the far greater sums of money offered by outsiders, and their case studies present a litany of accomplishments by social movements in diverse contexts that actively refused corporate or state funds (INCITE! 2007; see also Kohl-Arenas 2014). Other scholars/researchers such as James Petras and Henry Veltmeyer (2001) note similar problems when otherwise progressive international NGOs raise money for local partners in developing countries. These progressive donors, willing to fund activities that tackle the root causes of poverty and oppression, Petras says, use the local organization as a research project and are never around to 'stick their necks out' once the obligatory educational seminar has concluded (Petras 1999). They also 'co-opt the language of the left: "popular power", "empowerment", "gender equality", "sustainable development", "bottom-up leadership". The problem is that this language is linked to a framework of collaboration with donors and government agencies that subordinates practical activity to non-confrontational politics' (Petras 1997, 14). Krause (2014) explicitly evokes commodification in her work on NGO project design. She suggests that the projects themselves, and their putative 'beneficiaries' – the human beings whose lives are supposed to be improved – take on a commodity form, like pieces to be traded on a quasi-market of local NGOs and their benefactors. Her use of the commodity analytic extends the critique of NGOs beyond political deradicalization, or aid dependency, and puts the commodification process at the centre.

Like many of these commentaries, we have also seen in Haiti how funding fractures local organizations, prevents social mobilization, and creates animosity in the community that can lead to outright violence (burning buildings, destroying canals, smashing water lines). We can see when movement leaders get bogged down in administrative tasks or bounce from one funding agency to the next, constantly shapeshifting their objectives and, sometimes, their ideologies. We see how community activities (meetings, protests, workshops, communal workdays) become reliant on monetary stipends. The problem, we suggest, goes deeper than the political orientation of the donor agency, or who it decides to fund: it lies in the commodification process itself, which ties developmental objectives to global economic power. What is it about commodification that has the potential to wreak such havoc on otherwise progressive movements? We wish to highlight four interrelated elements of commodification – abstraction, privatization, valuation, and alienation – and use our experiences in the Haiti NGO world to demonstrate how the countermovement comes to be bought and sold like a commodity. In different ways, the four elements of commodification demonstrate how local developmental efforts must adapt to dominant norms about programming and accept economic conditioning if they wish to access funding and succeed. As such, the commodification process incorporates local forms of organization with broader logics of economic power.

6 Abstraction

For commodities to be exchanged they need to be commensurable. How is it possible to submit heterogeneous social movements in different places, addressing different issues, through different means under a common metric? When deciding to fund an organization, how does a well-intentioned, progressively minded donor compare, for example, a peasant movement occupying land with urban-based mothers struggling to challenge the prevailing mores of domestic abuse, or how do they compare building a vocational training school with planting a million trees? Much research has documented the practices necessary to turn a complex, unpredictable, organically constituted group of people into a formal organization that must write project plans and submit financial reports to state and non-state authorities alike. For Scott (1998) this is a process called making 'legible' or as Tania Li (2007) calls it 'rendering technical'. The objective is to recharacterize disparate and heterogeneous human and environmental landscapes through static and quantitative practices, which also make abstract individuals and communities more manageable, comparable, predictable, and accountable through maps, reports, statutes, budgets, contracts, surveys, salaries, and working hours. Accepting foreign funding, no matter how progressive or radical the receiving organization, requires an abstraction – something that allows the donor to make legible and commensurable a diversity of qualitatively distinct social activities and relationships. How is this done? For the sake of brevity, we focus on the logical framework within the project plan.

What was once a reactive, heterogeneous group of people, ideas, and activities must become codified into a 'logical framework'. The logical framework is meant to organize specific goals, outcomes, objectives, outputs, inputs, activities, available resources, indicators of change, and project budgets into a coherent project plan. There is an algorithmic character to the framework that takes complexity of social problems, human activity, and environments, and simplifies them into distinct technical problems that have an equally technical solution.[2] It is not easy to write a project plan with the appropriate algorithmic structure. NGOs claiming to take direction from their 'local partners' often must train such partners in writing these plans through weeklong conferences or seminars. In Haiti, over the past 20 years, it has become common to hear radio and television ads publicizing new post-secondary programmes and

---

[2] In our experience reading over a hundred logical frameworks, we have yet to see a project plan that acknowledges its incapacity to solve the problem it seeks to address!

diplomas in Project Management or NGO management. This has created a new class of project managers that have significant control in the NGO project market. In Haiti, there is often a budget line in project proposals labelled 'Project Developer'. This is usually a well-educated individual, likely educated in Port-au-Prince, who writes project proposals for organizations that may not have the 'skills' to properly abstract their visions and activities on paper. The project developer may get 5%–10% of the final project budget once funded – a very profitable venture for project budgets that run into hundreds of thousands, if not millions of dollars. With a project plan in hand, the donor agency now has a clear sense of where their money will be going and what to expect from the local organization through their 'results-based management' tools that can now compare the project across time and space. Krause (2014, 62) echoes this sentiment: 'projects can be treated as things that are potentially comparable to each other, and the wants in which they are in fact compared to each other when allocating scarce resources'.

Through this abstraction, it becomes less clear how, or even if the implementing organizations are connected to the community. Consider a 'pro-poor' project that one of the authors received from a progressive Haitian organization. The purpose of the pro-poor, pro-local food project was to distribute beans to farmers, which had been saved from farmers in other regions. The goal of the project was clearly articulated, and the logical framework impeccable. Project 'activities' were clearly defined, with the necessary 'inputs' outlined in the excel budget line. The 'activities' supported the 'outcomes' which in turn were measured through their 'indicators of change'. It was, in many ways, a donor's dream project. However, upon closer inspection, it was unclear whether the project developers had even been to the area of their intended intervention. The regions where the beans would be purchased were general in scope, and the project beneficiaries likewise were articulated in such vague terms (such as, lacking in potable water, low education attendances, engaged in small-scale agriculture) that the project described most rural Haitian communities. Upon asking around, we quickly found that no one had heard about the implementing organization, which had a perfectly good plan so thoroughly abstracted that the project plan could be implemented in nearly any community in the country. This example may be compared with another, less abstracted plan one of the authors received at a rural office. A peasant organization was requesting $5000. Their mountain road was prone to mudslides and had significantly eroded with the spring rains. The work to restore sections of the road was so urgent that they had already organized collective workdays, purchased food on loan, and over the course of weeks built a series of stone retaining walls to resist future eroding at critical points in the dirt road. Their project plan, written with pencil on a white piece of paper, wasn't really a plan at all; they were simply requesting $5000 to pay off some loans and cover the cost of transporting the rocks that were used to construct the wall. From the donor NGO's perspective, this project was useless because all the activities had already been completed and there were no articulated inputs or outputs. The budget was written in pencil, there were no receipts (the food was purchased from an open-air market vendor). There was no way to compute the community actions that had produced such a phenomenal result. It was not abstract, but very, very concrete.[3]

Whether for a small peasant organization, or an urban advocacy collective, the project plan strips the contextual specificity of social activity to render it as a commensurable commodity readily compared to other commodities qualitatively and quantitatively. Organizations engaged in social struggle, who seek funds in support of their counter-movement mobilization, are not spared from this abstracting process; this is the first step of counter-movement commodification.

7 Privatization

Privatization gives the exclusive right to an individual, corporation, or institution to use and dispose of the items listed in a legal title (Castree 2003). As mentioned above, since the neoliberal era, this has often meant a wide-scale transfer of public goods (land, social services, utilities) into private hands with the newfound right to profit (Harvey 2005). But how can a counter-movement be privatized? Put another way, who has the legal and exclusive right to use of and dispose of a local organization receiving funding? Who are the decision makers?

The rewards of a successful project can indeed be felt by the community: repaired canals, built schools, conserved seeds, or a change in agriculture policy. However, successful projects also lead to the procurement of additional grant money from donor agencies, whether governments, financial institution, philanthropists, or corporate foundations. The decisions around future projects and objectives are controlled not by the local project managers, animators, or community volunteers, but by the various 'country directors', 'regional officers' and other executives and board members of the funding organization

---

3 The project was eventually compensated after one of the authors rewrote the project (on a computer) and categorized the budget on an excel spreadsheet.

that extends distantly from the zone of intervention. The surpluses (the additional funding grants or fundraisers procured) are not the property of the local organization that created them, and the right to determine how to spend the surplus rests in the hands of the donor organization. This is a private claim on the counter-movement.

In Haiti, many of the pro-democracy movements and peasant organizations that were pushing for the ouster of dictator Jean-Claude Duvalier in the 1980s received funding from North American donors. At the time, the limited financial support aligned with many of the pro-democracy counter-movement objectives. The success of these counter-movements culminated in the election of Jean-Bertrand Aristide, a Catholic priest steeped in the liberation theology movement that had spread across Latin America and the Caribbean throughout the 1970s and 1980s. Aristide's tenure, however, was short-lived. Elected in 1990, he was overthrown in a military coup 8 months later. In 1994, Aristide agreed to a series of economic liberalizations in exchange for his return to Haiti with the backing of US marines. However, with the supposed return to democratic rule in 1995, funding to address related political and economic issues dried up. Struggles against privatizations, structural adjustment plans, and trade liberalizations were no longer attracting the attention of donors. Radical peasant organizations calling for agrarian reform, for example, had to shift their priorities or risk losing funders that had supported them in the past. The durability of these early radical pro-democratic organizations – some that continue to exist today – had less to do with their ability to mobilize constituents for radical social change, and more to do with their ability to placate their donors without straying too far from the dominant development orthodoxies.

How does this happen? There is a Haitian proverb that states, 'money makes the dog dance'. The donor agencies, regardless of size and scope, can make claims on what areas should be addressed. When a donor initiates a call for proposals, they have the power to specify an area of intervention as well as criteria that their local partners must fulfil. For radical local movements, this means they must decide whether to adjust their strategies and possibly restructure their organizations to meet such criteria. The fundability of radical local organizations depends on their ability to deftly respond to these criteria.

The point is not whether such criteria or areas of intervention are inherently detrimental to society. Indeed, funding criteria might require more accountability within a social movement and mandate quarterly elections for the local organization's executive committee. Or new objectives might stress gender equity in the development, implementation, and evolution of the project implementation. These could very well be laudable goals. For over a decade in Haiti, for example, large donors have specified the need for institutional gender equality and required a gender analysis of the proposed project outcome. How an organization responds to these criteria will influence its chances of funding.[4] The problem, however, is over decision-making power and claims on future activities that wrests control from social movements and sets limits to what issues and strategies can be pursued. The objectives are set by the donors, who in turn, are more concerned with the dominant, *a la mode*, trends in development literature – whether microfinance, capacity building, or conservation agriculture – and less responsive to the contextual social, ecological, economic, or political issues that local organizers have analysed. It is up to the counter-movements to restructure themselves to fit into these predetermined funding boxes.

This discussion of privatization – claims made on an asset – is in line with much of the academic literature that highlights how NGOs can act as a depoliticizing force. But it is deeper than this. Highlighting commodification shows how and why one actor (and not another) makes claims over a commodity. Private claims are made over the funds available to the local social movement whether the donor is radical or apolitical, big or small, faith-based or secular. A claim is placed on the development priorities, strategies, and activities, and it is up to the recipient organization to align – never vice versa. If the problem were solely about pernicious neo-colonial donors intent on pacifying radical organizations, the response would reasonably be to redirect funds to organizations with more emancipatory aims – that is, to fund the counter-movement. However helpful, this doesn't address the claims of ownership, or the decision-making power which increases control over the priorities of counter-movement actions.

8 Valuation

The value of a commodity is difficult to define. We can speak of intrinsic value, moral value, economic value, social value, or utility value. For Marx, under capitalism, value is the abstract socially necessary labour time embedded in the commodity (Marx 1990). Capitalists who produce a commodity employing labour more productively than their competitors will be able to charge less for an equivalent product. Less productive producers will not be able to compete in the market and will soon be extinct. In a competitive marketplace,

---

4   At the same time, with competition over limited funding opportunities, it is not difficult to exaggerate, manipulate, or fabricate a series of statutes or indicators that demonstrate an organization's eligibility.

producers are forced to find ways to increase labour productivity. What is the value of the counter-movement commodity and how is it determined? To begin, donors need to know what 'deliverables' or 'outcomes' are in the project plan. Put another, perhaps less forgiving way, the question is really 'what tangible results will the counter-movement labour produce with this specific amount of money; what is the movement's productivity in comparison to other counter-movement commodities? How many people will participate in the process, how many urban gardens will be established, how many youths will be trained, what policies will change, how many seeds will be saved and distributed? The value is determined by the productivity of labour under market pressure. If other movements can produce similar results with less cost – if their productivity outstrips their competitors – the value of the organization will adjust accordingly.

This has two main impacts. First, value is determined through competitive pressure that forces each social movement to increase its productivity. This does not mean local organizations cannot work together on various advocacy issues, campaigns, or specific development projects. Many funders might prefer to fund 'coalitions', 'platforms', or 'collectives' where social movement and grassroots organizations collaborate with one another on shared goals. Even in this instance, however, the commodification of social relations installs a competitive logic. Organizations may form a collective solely to receive funding and participate in the platform to secure at least a fraction of the funds, despite having no real interest in the platform's objectives. With more funding devoted to sexual discrimination, for example, it is not uncommon to have extremely homophobic organizations participating in coalitions promoting LGBTQ rights or seeing masochistic organizations sitting on a platform advancing the rights of women.

While working on a platform may limit the total amount of funds available to each organization, it also opens avenues for the local organization's future funding opportunities. The local organization can use its experience and completed activities as evidence of its value as an institution when seeking individual financing from a donor in the future. To better their image in front of the donor, certain coalition members might undermine other members of the platform or sew distrust amongst donor agencies over their local partners. This transforms the once-collaborative space into a competitive marketplace with each local organizer seeking to maximize its productivity. Second, the competition over funds determines the value of the social movement in a similar way to sub-contractor competition over contracts. Commodity production is subcontracted to organizations that can produce the most results with the fewest resources, without requiring the donor to get involved in the actual implementation of the project. The Ford Foundation doesn't know about egg production, but a peasant organization does. The Clinton Foundation doesn't know about mangos, but local farmers do. It is the responsibility of the subcontractor to minimize production costs and maximize outputs to out-compete the closest competitor. Local organizations often complain about funders increasing their total budget to complete more activities and count more beneficiaries, without sustaining a similar increase in operating expenses or additional human resources, or even having to acknowledge the added pressure on the community (which is simply asked to volunteer more time). As in any marketplace, the value of the counter-movement commodity will help the donor in making their purchasing decisions so as to assure a cost-effective, successful project. The more successful the projects, the more money can be raised. Put another way: 'Agencies raise funds to do projects, but they can also do projects to raise funds' (Krause, 2014, 70).

9 Alienation

Alienation, in the sense developed by Marx in his later writings, examines how the process of capitalist commodity production separates (both morally and physically) the labourer from the product. Under capitalist production, the concrete human activity that made the product or provided the service no longer has any power over the product, nor can workers make any claim on the value embedded within it (see 'privatization' above). The labourers lose control over their skills, abilities, relationships, and tools, and the production process is increasingly organized by the employer. The capitalist becomes instigator and organizer of production. What was once a creative, dynamic human being embedded in diverse social relations is transformed into a mere 'appendage of the machine', (Engels and Marx 2004) – stripped of the labour process, the product, and the value generated through the concrete labour. In this sense, funding not only abstracts heterogeneous places, people, and relationships into commensurable products through the production of the logical framework, but the loss of control through privatization and valuation alienates the actors, both physically and morally, separating them from the social context that instigated their participation in the countermovement in the first place. Wolf (1999, 280) describes multiple facets of 'alienation' in the context of capital incursions into twentieth-century peasant communities, but his detailed account runs parallel to our analysis of Haitian social movement leaders:

> The alienation of men from the process of production which had previously guaranteed their existence; their alienation from the product of their work which disappeared into the market only to return to them in the form of money; their alienation from themselves to the extent to which they now had to look upon their own capabilities as marketable commodities; their alienation from their fellow men who had become actual or potential competitors in the market; these are not only philosophical concepts; they depict real tendencies in the growth and spread of capitalism.

Throughout the 1980s, liberation theology swept through the Haitian countryside where small groups gathered for literacy lessons and popular education aimed at reflection on how to solve problems, resist dictatorial rule, and implement change through methods including community action. At the same time, new urban organizations were created to help coordinate, mobilize, and raise awareness amongst the more rural small groups of human rights, law, and socio-political policies. These urban institutions, known as *bouradè* or 'supporters', had the professional capacity to manage larger funds in support of local community organizations. Rooted in Paulo Freire's 'pedagogy of the oppressed', the *bouradè* would mentor smaller peasant groups, helping them to formalize their organizational structures, access various forms of training and popular education including space for political reflection, coordinating regional meetings and providing access to legal advice. In one sense, this support helped empower rural populations who had largely been excluded from political participation since independence. For a smallholding peasant farmer, local organizing and the support of *bouradè* created a self-determining path toward critical reflection and political engagement. Particularly active, intelligent, and charismatic peasants could quickly move through the ranks of the local peasant organization, possibly becoming an executive in their local chapter and representing their community at regional meetings. Often, such local leaders attract the attention of *bouradè* organizations, who may offer some form of employment, usually as an animator or community educator. As a salaried employee, this former peasant would begin attending conferences, meeting with international, regional directors of funding institutions, receiving an increased salary, travelling to developed countries, attending meetings in French and English (not Creole), accessing per diems, staying in hotels, and beginning to collect and submit receipts. However effective they were as organizers, these former local leaders slowly become detached from the community organizations of which they were members. They make the full transition from a vocal peasant engaged in struggle to an animator, educator, or project manager, living apart from their source community. They complete their social activities – collecting information, organizing activities, documenting expenses, writing reports – not in the community from which they came, but on behalf of the *bouradè* and the funding agencies, who assert increasing claims over their labour. Once small landholding peasants, they become firmly embedded in the NGO world.

Local organizations continue to complain that instead of reinforcing the capacity of their organizations in the same vein as the 1980s, the *bouradè* are extracting human resources from their communities. The onslaught of neoliberal policies, and the second ouster of Aristides in 2004, also threw these *bouradè* into a crisis of funding. They needed to justify their specific objectives and activities before their progressive funders. In response, the *bouradè* separated the Haitian territory amongst themselves, with each institution responsible for supporting a different geographical region. It is common, for example, for a single national peasant movement to fall under the informal jurisdiction of different *bouradè* (and their different funders), resulting in what some Haitian organizers have called a 'balkanization' of social organizing.

The post-earthquake funds also reoriented the *bouradè* towards relief work in place of critical reflection. Importantly, this generalized description is not to signal ill-intent on behalf of the peasant farmer, the *bouradè*, or even the progressive funding institution. Instead, it describes a logical progression of alienation in the countermovement. The commodification of their roles and their activities separates them from the social fabric from which they came and transforms what Polanyi calls the 'substance of society' into one of commodity exchange, paternalism, clientelism, and the ultimate dependence on the changing priorities of international development aid.

10   Conclusion

In the *Communist Manifesto*, Marx speaks of the homogenizing force of commodification that renders human beings 'trade-able' in the abstract: 'It has converted the physician, the lawyer, the priest, the poet, the man of science, into paid wage labourers' (Marx and Engels 2004). The commodification of the countermovement is thus not a unique phenomenon but the logical result of capitalist development where every service, action, or mobilization can be commensurable through a price. To Marx's list of occupations, we might add the peasant leader, the student activist, the humanitarian aid worker. Understanding the countermovement as commodity provides no simple answers for political change and we are not calling on Haitian organizations to reject funding full stop. Groups must organize, leaders must rise, fees be paid, buses taken, hostels rented, food purchased, and planes taken. The fact that movement exists within-but-against capitalism's commodifying drives means certain aspects of social movement require some form of financing. Indeed, the success of many organizations is because funding has been redirected to these grassroots organizations and we do not in any way mean to minimize such action.

But the debate over the role of NGOs cannot end there. Funding local organizations, however progressive or radical, is a form of commodification and both the donor and recipient must deal with the abstracting, privatizing, valorizing, and alienating elements that are bundled together with the exchange of money. Specifically, progressive or radical foreign donors whose intention is to increase the autonomy of local community organizations, who fund organizations with the explicit goal of political change at the structural level, might do well to look at what they are requiring of their partners and who decides how and on what funding is spent. Does the logical framework abstract social relations? Are there private claims being made on project successes? Is the funding driving competition between organizations, transforming them into productive sub-contractors? And to what extent are the project managers, accountants, animators, connected to, engaged with, or physically a part of the communities and environments which the funds seek to support?

Rethinking Wolf's *Peasant Wars of the 20th Century*, it might be a useful thought experiment to ponder how these revolutions would have unfolded if there were thousands of foreign donor agencies throwing millions of dollars at peasant groups trying to secure them as a 'local grassroots partner', 'increase their capacity' and make them 'self-sufficient' by means of, say, setting up a co-op to sell eggs to a local hotel? This chapter is not meant to chastise every NGO worker, nor are we ignorant of the fact that in many countries like Haiti, livelihoods are dependent on donor funding; indeed, each of us have relied on NGOs for employment, albeit in radically different ways and radically different social positions. The point, instead, is to recognize how and when the commodifying forces begin to constitute the movement itself. Commodification is a pernicious process that eats away at the social relations of countermovement in a piecemeal fashion – a new salary, a per diem, an additional output, a grant-writing seminar – until there is no social activity that can be completed without an associated budget line in an excel spreadsheet. Countermovements are called movements for a reason. They lack the institutional rigidity and permit open-ended, spontaneous modes of organizing with the capability to shape and be shaped by complex and ever-changing contexts. They should remain incommensurable, unexchangeable, and uncommodifiable.

References

Alden, Chris, Daniel Large, and Alvaro Mendez. 2020. "The Western Way of Development: A Critical Review." *New Development Assistance*, 19–38.

Altay, Nezih, and Melissa Labonte. "Challenges in Humanitarian Information Management and Exchange: Evidence from Haiti." *Disasters* 38(1) (2014): 50–72.

Alvarez, Sonia E. 2009. "Beyond NGO-ization?: Reflections from Latin America." *Development* 52(2): 175–184.

Bell, Beverly. 2013. *Fault Lines: Views Across Haiti's Divide*. Cornell University Press.

Bello, Walden. 2006. "The Capitalist Conjuncture: Over-accumulation, Financial Crises, and the Retreat from Globalisation." *Third World Quarterly* 27(8): 1345–1367.

Carr, David. 2006. "A Tale of Two Roads: Land Tenure, Poverty, and Politics on the Guatemalan Frontier." *Geoforum* 37(1): 94–103.

Castree, Noel. 2003. "Commodifying What Nature?" *Progress in Human Geography* 27(3): 273–297.

Choudry, Aziz, and Dip Kapoor. 2013. *NGOization: Complicity, Contradictions and Prospects*. Zed Books Ltd.

Cunningham, Oliver. 2012. "The Humanitarian Aid Regime in the Republic of NGOs: The Fallacy of 'Building Back Better'." *Journal of Advanced International Studies* (4): 101–126.

Dietrich, Simone. 2013. "Bypass or Engage? Explaining Donor Delivery Tactics in Foreign Aid Allocation," *International Studies Quarterly* 57 (4): 698–712.

Edmonds, Kevin. 2013. "Beyond good intentions: The structural limitations of NGOs in Haiti." *Critical Sociology* 39(3): 439–452.

Ferguson, James. 1990. *The Anti-Politics Machine: 'Development', Depoliticization and Bureaucratic Power in Lesotho*. Cambridge University Press.

Harvey, David. 2003. *The New Imperialism*. Oxford University Press.

Harvey, David. 2005. *A Brief History of Neoliberalism*. Oxford University Press, USA.

Hickel, Jason. 2017. *The Divide: A Brief Guide to Global Inequality and its Solutions*. Random House.

Horton, Lynn. 2012. "After the Earthquake: Gender Inequality and Transformation in Post-Disaster Haiti." *Gender Development* 20(2): 295–308.

INCITE! 2007. *The Revolution will not be Funded: Beyond the Non-profit Industrial Complex*. South End Press.

Katz, Jonathan. 2013. *The Big Truck that Went By: How the World Came to Save Haiti and Left Behind a Disaster*. St. Martin's Press.

Kelly, Alice. B. 2011. "Conservation Practice as Primitive Accumulation." *Journal of Peasant Studies* 38(4): 683–701.

Kim, Soyuen, and Kevin Gray. 2016. "Overseas Development Aid as Spatial Fix? Examining South Korea's Africa Policy." *Third World Quarterly* 37(4): 649–664.

Kohl-Arenas, Erica. 2014. "Will the Revolution be Funded? Resource Mobilization and the California Farm Worker Movement". *Social Movement Studies* 13(4): 482–498.

Krause, Monika. 2014. *The Good Project: Humanitarian Relief NGOs and the Fragmentation of Reason*. University of Chicago Press. Chicago.

Lappé, Frances Moore, Joseph Collins and David Kinley. 1980. "Aid as obstacle." *IDRC reports, v. 9, no. 2.*

Levien, Michael. 2007. "India's double-movement: Polanyi and the National Alliance of People's Movements." *Berkeley Journal of Sociology* 51: 119–149.

Levien, Michael and Marcel Paret. 2012. "A Second Double Movement? Polanyi and Shifting Global Opinions on Neoliberalism." *International Sociology* 27(6): 724–744.

Li, Tania M. 2007. *The Will to Improve: Governmentality, Development, and the Practice of Politics*. Duke University Press.

Macdonald, Terry. 2008. *Global Stakeholder Democracy: Power and Representation Beyond Liberal States*. Oxford: Oxford University Press.

Maniates, Michael. 1990. "Organizing for Rural Energy Development: Improved Cookstoves, Local Organization State in Gujarat." Phd diss., University of California.

Marx, Karl. 1990. *Capital, Vol. 1*. England: Penguin Classics.

Marx, Karl, and Fredrich Engels. 2004. *The Communist Manifesto*. Broadview Press.

Munck, Ronaldo. 2006. *Globalization and Contestation: The New Great Counter-Movement*. Routledge.

Munck, Ronaldo. 2004. "Globalization, Labor and the 'Polanyi Problem.'" *Labor History* 45(3): 251–269.

O'Connor, Amy, and Michelle Shumate., 2014. "Differences Among NGOs in the Business–NGO Cooperative Network." *Business & Society* 53(1): 105–133.

Pearce, Jenny. 2010. "Is social change fundable? NGOs and theories and practices of social change," *Development in Practice* 20(6): 621–635.

Petras, James., and Veltmeyer, Henry. 2001. *Globalization Unmasked: Imperialism in the 21st Century*. Zed Books.

Petras, James. 1999. "NGOs: In the Service of Imperialism." *Journal of Contemporary Asia* 29 (4): 429–440.

Petras, James. 1997. "Imperialism and NGOs in Latin America." *Monthly Review* 49(7): 10–18.

Polanyi, Karl. 2001. *The Great Transformation: The Political and Economic Origins of Our Time*. Beacon Press.

Prudham, Scott. 2009. "Commodification". In *A Companion to Environmental Geography*, edited by Castree, Noel, David Demeritt, Diana Liverman, and Bruce Rhoads, 123–142. Blackwell Publishing Ltd.

Prudham, Scott. 2007. "The Fictions of Autonomous Invention: Accumulation by Dispossession, Commodification and Life Patents in Canada." *Antipode* 39(3): 406–429.

Ramachandran, Vijaya, Julie Walz. 2013. "Haiti's Earthquake Generated a $9bn Response – where did the Money Go?" *The Guardian*. Online: https://www.theguardian.com/global-development/poverty-matters/2013/jan/14/haiti-earthquake-where-did-money-go.

Robinson, Mark. 1997. "Privatizing the Voluntary Sector: NGOs as Public Service Contractors." In *NGOs, States and Donors: Too Close for Comfort?* edited by Hulme, David, and Michael Edwards. New York: St. Martin's Press.

Roy, Ananya. 2010. *Poverty Capital: Microfinance and the Making of Development*. Routledge.

Roy, Arundhati. 2014. "The NGO-ization of Resistance." *Massalijin News*. http://massalijn.nl/new/the-ngo-ization-of-resistance/.

Sangeeta, Kamat. 2004. "The Privatization of Public Interest: Theorizing NGO Discourse in a Neoliberal Era." *Review of International Political Economy* 11(1): 155–176.

Schuller, Mark. 2012. *Killing with Kindness: Haiti, International Aid, and NGOs*. Rutgers University Press.

Schuller, Mark, and Pablo Morales. 2012. *Tectonic Shifts: Haiti Since the Earthquake*. Kumarian Press.

Scott, James. 1998. *Seeing Like a State: How Certain Schemes to Improve the Human Condition*. New Haven and London: Yale University Press.

Silva, Eduardo. 2012. "Exchange Rising? Karl Polanyi and Contentious Politics in Contemporary Latin America." *Latin American Politics and Society* 54(3): 1–32.

Shamsie, Yasmine. 2011. "Pro-poor Economic Development Aid to Haiti: Unintended Effects Arising from the Conflict-Development Nexus." *Journal of Peacebuilding & Development* 6(3): 32–44.

Steckley, Marylynn, and Tony Weis. 2016. "Peasant Balances, Neoliberalism, and the Stunted Growth of Non-traditional Agro-exports in Haiti." *Canadian Journal of Latin American and Caribbean Studies/Revue canadienne des études latino-américaines et caraïbes*, 41(1) : 1–22.

Wolf, Eric R. 1999. *Peasant Wars of the Twentieth Century*. University of Oklahoma Press.

Wolf, Eric R. 2010. *Europe and the People Without History*. University of Berkeley Press.

Zanotti, Laura. 2010. "Cacophonies of Aid, Failed State Building and NGOs in Haiti: Setting the Stage for Disaster, Envisioning the Future." *Third World Quarterly* 31(5): 755–771.

CHAPTER 3

A Brief History of Workers on the Move: Power in Puerto Rican Farm Labour Migration

Ismael García Colón

1   Introduction

This chapter analyses the migration of Puerto Ricans to the United States and the shaping of the migrant farmworker force as colonial subjects within agriculture by local, regional, and global power relations. Using Wolf's approach to the fields of power, history, and globalization, it covers important relationships between migration and labour, which Wolf himself admitted he left out in his own work on Puerto Rico. I argue that to understand Puerto Rican migration one needs to turn to Wolf's understandings of power, the role of labour migration in capitalism, the Puerto Rico farm labour programme, and the connections between processes happening in Puerto Rico and developments in the United States and around the globe. I use Wolf's insights from EPWH and his critique of his first publication and co-authored book, *The People of Puerto Rico* (Steward et al. 1956). My goal is to highlight Wolf's contributions – without overlooking their limitations – to the anthropology of labour migration by discussing his concepts of social fields and structural power, the role of government agencies in the development of labour migration, and the experiences of migrants. The case of Puerto Rican migrant farmworkers demonstrates the different strategies that capital interests and nation states use in mobilizing labour, the agency that migrants retain as they navigate this field of power, and the roles that colonialism, race, immigration policies, and citizenship play in the histories of Puerto Rican farm labour migration.

In the twenty-first century, Puerto Rico, an unincorporated US territory, is re-experiencing severe forms of precarity because of economic crisis, debt-restructuring austerity measures, neoliberal policies, and the devastation caused by Hurricane Maria. These developments are linked to Puerto Rico's political status as a US colony with limited self-rule. The United States invaded Puerto Rico in 1898, during the Spanish-American War; granted US citizenship to its inhabitants in 1917; and allowed circumscribed self-rule in 1952. The colonial problem of Puerto Rico became more evident in 2016, when the Obama administration imposed a financial control board with full authority over the local government's budget because of an unpayable debt of more than 72 billion dollars (Caraballo-Cueto and Lara 2018; Suárez-Gómez and García-Colón 2019).

In 1996, the US Congress's vote to eliminate Puerto Rico's federal tax-exemption incentives in the manufacturing sector, following a ten-year phase-out period, fostered the flight of transnational companies to other tax havens, undermining Puerto Rico's tax base and sources of employment (Caraballo-Cueto and Lara 2018). Consequently, since 2006, the territory has been undergoing an economic crisis that has decimated the construction and banking sectors, leading to austerity measures that resulted in a massive lay-off of government employees, the privatization of public services and corporations, and an increase in unemployment. These processes are the latest developments within a century-old history of US capitalist expansion, contraction, unevenness, and crisis in Puerto Rico. The disposability of Puerto Ricans in their homeland has impelled the migration of close to half a million people to the United States. At the same time, Puerto Ricans have become expendable for US employers in the low-wage and service jobs sectors because of rising nativism and the anti-immigrant climate, even though, as US citizens, Puerto Ricans are not immigrants.

Puerto Ricans not only migrate to settle permanently on the mainland, many return to Puerto Rico to seasonal and temporary jobs that trap them in circular migration. During the last decade, I have met airline workers, seasonal hotel employees, and farm labourers working in the US Northeast who keep their permanent residences in Puerto Rico. Many commute frequently between Puerto Rico and the continental United States. Indeed, labour recruitment in Puerto Rico has increased since the 2008 economic crisis. A case in point, chronicled in the *Boston Globe*, is Luis, Edgar, and Luz, who work in low-wage jobs for Broad Reach Healthcare, a rehabilitation and assisted living provider in Cape Cod, Massachusetts. Their employer attracted them and other workers by offering subsidized housing (Weisman 2019). Companies like Broad Reach Healthcare travel to Puerto Rico to recruit personnel because it is cheaper to hire Puerto Ricans because they are US citizens. Employers visit Puerto Rico, recruiting for jobs in nursing, public-school bilingual teaching, law enforcement, manufacturing, food processing, landscaping, and the hotel industry, among many other sectors. Employers' attraction to this new wave of Puerto Rican migrant labourers lies in their US citizenship within a climate of tightened immigration restrictions and in their willingness to work for low wages. Puerto Ricans' disposability in Puerto Rico and their expendability in the United States facilitates their availability in the US labour market.

The long history of labour migration from Puerto Rico to the continental United States enables these new waves of migration. As Eric R. Wolf aptly noted, 'Each migration involved the transfer to the new geographical location not only of manpower but also of services and resources. Each migratory wave generated, in turn, suppliers of services at the point of arrival, whether these were labour agents, merchants, lawyers, or players of percussion instruments. (1982, 362). Over many decades, Puerto Rican farm labour migration also developed an infrastructure of knowledge, services, and people that contemporary Puerto Ricans use when they migrate to the United States.

Next, the chapter examines Wolf's theoretical legacies and important contributions to migration studies in broadening our understanding of the impact of Puerto Rican farm labour migration to US farms on the history of twentieth-century capitalism. Wolf acknowledged the importance of migration in the history of capitalism. In *Europe and the People without History* (*EPWH*), he explains how capital deploys its power to mobilize multiple labour forces across vast geographical distances (1982, 361). His theoretical insights about power are also important to understanding migration in late capitalism. Puerto Rico, as a US colonial territory in the Caribbean, offers therefore a compelling case of Wolf's project to understand the formation of anthropological subjects within complex fields of power (Roseberry 1988). Puerto Rico was the first field site where Wolf conducted his dissertation research. His essay 'Facing Power', in *Pathways of Power* (2001), includes important observations about the role of migration and colonial institutions in the development of capitalism in Puerto Rico. His later works are still relevant to understanding how Puerto Ricans became subjects within the fields of power of the US empire.

I argue that to understand Puerto Rican migration one needs to turn to Wolf's understandings of power, the role of labour migration in capitalism, the Puerto Rico farm labour programme, and the connections between processes happening in Puerto Rico and developments in the United States and around the globe. I will discuss Wolf's concept of social fields and structural power, the role of government agencies in the development of labour migration, and the experiences of migrants. Using his insights from *EPWH* and his critique of his first publication and co-authored book, *The People of Puerto Rico* (Steward et al. 1956), I seek to explain the formation of a Puerto Rican migrant farm labour force in the United States during the twentieth century, and its relevance to a contemporary historical anthropology of labour migration. My goal is to highlight Wolf's contributions, together with their limitations, to the anthropology of labour migration. One of the limitations of his work is the narrow theorization of migration and mobility, and of how social fields of power are also migratory fields in which people manoeuvre to sustain their livelihoods. The case of Puerto Rican migrant farmworkers demonstrates the different entanglements that capital and states use to mobilize labour, as well as the migrants' agency as they navigate this field of power. Colonialism, race, immigration policies, and citizenship played important roles in the histories of Puerto Rican farm labour migration. My ethnographic fieldwork and archival research on migrant farmworkers and agricultural workers in Puerto Rico spans more than two decades, and in this essay I draw mostly on those historical records and interviews. In the next section, I will examine Wolf's theoretical insights into farm labour migration and follow with sections on the Puerto Rico farm labour programme and the experiences of Puerto Rican migrant farmworkers.

2   Migration and the People of Puerto Rico: Theoretical Insights

In the 1950s, when Wolf began his career, the anthropology of small-scale societies was still presenting its objects of study as isolated cultures. During the following decades, the ever-increasing migration from the Global South to the Atlantic north began to break apart models that reified cultures as isolated units of analysis. Migratory processes became important to demonstrate the interplay of local and global forces in historical processes. However, the anthropological tradition of peoples constituted as isolated cultures was still prevalent in the 1970s among anthropologists anchored in the old schools of thought amid the new interpretative approaches. Wolf sought to eliminate such representations from the anthropological project. He asserted that human aggregates designated by scholars as cultures and ethnicities are not bounded entities but, rather, fluid and permeable groupings connected to rather than insulated from the world (Wolf 1982).

Migration plays an important role in anthropological analyses, illuminating processes and relationships rather than fixed entities. Thus, EPWH engages with the histories and anthropologies of labour migration by examining the formation of working classes and their migration, and the role of ethnic segmentation in the development of capitalism. The book's last chapter, 'The New Laborers', and its section 'Labor on the Move' make an important contribution to understanding Puerto Rican farm labour migration by explaining how capitalism has shaped the movement of peoples across regions and continents. Wolf states that his analysis of rising labourers on the move was inspired in part by the new literature on migration that

> attempts to see it in international terms, as the result of political and economic changes in the 'sending' societies as well as of shifts in the

demand of labor on the part of the 'recipient' societies ... A successful attempt to apply the perspectives of the new approach to the particular case of Puerto Rico can be found in the volume by the History Task Force (1982, 424).

Wolf was referring to *Labour Migration under Capitalism*, an important work of historical political economy that examined the forces at home and abroad that shaped Puerto Rican migration to the United States in the twentieth century (History Task Force 1979). Like *Labor Migration under Capitalism*, EPWH concentrates on the history of capitalism as the history of the commodity form of labour power, particularly labour during the Industrial Revolution. Wolf also identifies the state and private efforts to mobilize people for factories, plantations, and mines as the 'structure of the situation', the field of force that shapes migrants' position in relation to other groups. When a migrant arrives in the host society, Wolf states, 'That placement determines which of his prior resources he can apply and which new ones he must acquire' (Wolf 1982, 362). Puerto Rican migrant farmworkers encountered the United States in small towns, labour camps, and fields in rural areas where they interacted with residents and other migrant workers. Their condition as colonial subjects and US citizens, and as gendered people of colour, placed them at the bottom of many of the rural communities into which they arrived (Wolf 2001, 366). Their encounter with life in the United States in relation to the unevenness of dispossession and unemployment in Puerto Rico cemented their migration within the US empire's field of force. Between the US invasion of Puerto Rico in 1898 and the mid-1940s, private and government labour recruiters took Puerto Ricans to Hawaii, Arizona, Cuba, St. Croix, the Panama Canal Zone, Mexico, Ecuador, Venezuela, and the US Southern states. The interconnection of local, regional, and global processes facilitated the formation of a migrant labour force when and where capitalism needed it, unbounded by great distances or politics (Wolf 1982, 361).

Puerto Rican migration to the continental United States became significant in the second half of the twentieth century, as Wolf's field work in Puerto Rico was beginning. In his mid-twenties, he was part of the Puerto Rico Project, directed by Julian Steward, his adviser at Columbia University, and sponsored by the University of Puerto Rico's Institute of Social Sciences. Under Steward's mentorship, the members of the project team, Elena Padilla, Sidney Mintz, Raymond Scheele, and Robert Manners, wrote their dissertations and various chapters of the book *The People of Puerto Rico* (TPPR) (Steward et al., 1956; Wolf 1978). The Puerto Rico Project studied the biggest island of the archipelago as a complex society composed of different ecological communities, each producing a specific agricultural commodity (coffee, tobacco, or sugar) for exportation, and of the elites of the territory (García-Colón 2017b; Heyman 2011; Silverman 2011).

The social, cultural, economic, and political fabric of Puerto Rico in the late 1940s was undergoing deep changes. The US federal government began to grant self-rule to Puerto Rico, facilitating policies of modernization and development. After suffering the effects of the Great Depression and the scarcities of the Second World War, Puerto Ricans increasingly sought better living conditions in the larger cities and in the United States. Local control of the Puerto Rican government was in hands of New Deal reformers and the technocrats of the Popular Democratic Party (Partido Popular Democrático, PPD). The government of Puerto Rico advocated for an anthropological study to facilitate implementation of the PPD's political programme. Following in the footsteps of the Rhodes-Livingston Institute in Africa, the Puerto Rico Project was able to secure funding from the Rockefeller Foundation, which collaborated with the University of Puerto Rico and Columbia University to advance the PPD's political programme. Under the guise of studying a 'complex society', the project became one of the first attempts to understand the connections of local communities to global capitalism.

Thus, Puerto Rico is one of the first places in the Global South where Wolf encountered a group of people experiencing an old and ongoing history of colonialism. The implicit Marxism of Wolf and Sidney Mintz in *The People of Puerto Rico* sought to understand community histories in terms of global historical processes, a radical break from studies that had wrongly depicted isolated and primitive small-scale societies (Roseberry 1978; 1988; 2002). *EPWH* echoes Wolf's fieldwork experiences in Puerto Rico (1982, 354–83). In analysing the project retrospectively, he makes important critiques of his previous work in *TPPR* that are key to understanding the long history of labour migration, the contribution of *TPPR* to anthropology, and his insights in *EPWH* (Wolf 2001, 38–48, 387–389). One of his important critiques of *TPPR* was 'its failure to take proper account of the rapidly intensifying migration to the nearby US mainland' (Wolf 2001, 387–8). He adds that

> we noted the beginnings of Puerto Rican migration to the mainland – surely the central fact of Puerto Rican life in the second part of the twentieth century – but we had no theoretical means for understanding it. Similarly, we had no way (could we have foreseen it?) to place this flow of labor from the island into the Northeast of the United States in relation to the changing relation of segments within the boundaries of the US mainland (2001, 47).

The arrival of Wolf and the other members of the TPPR team coincided with the enactment of intensive policies of population control (women's sterilization and men's migration) by the US colonial government of Puerto Rico. Since the late 1940s, Puerto Ricans had been increasingly migrating to the United States, mainly to New York City. Between 1940 and 1970, more than a quarter of the population of Puerto Rico migrated to the US Northeast (New York City, Philadelphia, and Boston) and the Midwest (Chicago and Cleveland) (Dietz 1986, 282–8). By 1947, the government of Puerto Rico had established a Farm Labour Program to facilitate employment in US agriculture. The case I present of Puerto Rican farm labour migration exemplifies Wolf's anthropology of global capitalism and labour relations but goes further by revealing who those migrants were and what they thought about their migration. The lived experiences of Puerto Rican migrant farmworkers provide the ethnographic details that Wolf's EPWH cannot provide.

Organized Puerto Rican farm labour migration began in 1899, one year after the United States invaded Puerto Rico, as policies of colonialism and imperialism integrated Puerto Ricans into the US labour market. As Wolf argues, capital found Puerto Ricans and other workers 'when and where it needed them, and migratory movements have carried labour power to market all across the globe' (1982, 361). In addition, cultural patterns were never an impediment for Puerto Ricans migrating long distances from the Atlantic to the Pacific United States (Wolf 1982, 361). In 1899, private labour agents recruited Puerto Ricans to work in the sugar cane plantations of Hawaii, after the Foran Act of 1885 restricted contract labour migration, mostly from China, and the labour organizing power of Japanese sugar cane workers prompted sugar planters to recruit Puerto Ricans (History Task Force 1982; Rosario Natal 2001). At the same time, the political ambiguity that Puerto Ricans posed for the policing of empire's boundaries led to the arrest of many migrants to the continental United States because immigration authorities considered them to be foreign aliens. This legal situation propelled the first US Supreme Court cases that defined the status of the islanders. In 1904, the US Supreme Court ruled that Puerto Ricans are nationals but not citizens of the United States, thereby allowing their free entrance into and movement within the continental United States. More than a decade later, in 1917, Congress passed the Jones Act, granting US citizenship to Puerto Ricans, further incorporating them into the farm labour market (Erman 2008; García-Colón 2017a, 139–42; 2020, 22–33).

US citizenship allowed the US Department of Labour to use a limited number of Puerto Ricans, among other groups, as labourers to reduce labour costs to US employers. In 1926, cotton growers in Arizona recruited Puerto Rican workers who, upon arrival, found that the living and working conditions promised and the wages offered were not true, prompting many to abandon the cotton plantations. Their citizenship, more than simply protecting them from abuses, endowed migrants with the mobility to flee inadequate situations and the right to be assisted by government officials. At the time of these events, the strong labour movement in Puerto Rico gave workers the knowledge to fight back, giving them a negative image among employers. Two years later, in 1928, during Congressional hearings on immigration from the western hemisphere, growers advocated in favour of Mexican *braceros* (guest workers), rejecting and strongly opposing the substitution of Puerto Rican and Filipino for Mexican workers. Government officials and employers began a campaign that 'held fast by constraints' Puerto Rican farm labour migration. The Great Depression eliminated any possibility for massive and organized migration from Puerto Rico to the United States, even when category-five hurricane San Felipe devastated the island (García-Colón 2017a, 142–4; 2020, 37–47; US House 1928, 187–90; Wolf 1982, 261).

World War II reopened mainland doors for the recruitment of Puerto Rican workers. Although unemployment and food scarcity in Puerto Rico increased because of the German submarine blockade in the Caribbean, the federal War Manpower Administration and War Food Administration opposed the hiring and transportation of Puerto Rican workers, acquiescing to the interests of employers who preferred deportable labour created by such guestworker programmes as the Mexican Bracero Program. As a result of the lobbying by Puerto Rico's governor, Rexford G. Tugwell, one of the most radical New Dealers, and officials in the federal Office of Territories, war-related industries and farms hired a limited number of Puerto Rican workers. After the war, as the scarcity of labour in the US Northeast became a problem, private labour agents began to recruit Puerto Rican workers to be placed on farms. Unscrupulous recruitment led to complaints by workers over wage loss, theft, and overcharging for room and board and airline tickets, to name a few of the many problems confronted by workers. As the regulation of labour markets was an important development promoted by New Deal policies, the government of Puerto Rico launched several investigations that led to the enactment of laws and the creation of agencies and programmes that fostered the migration of thousands of workers. In effect, the formation of a welfare state in the United States shaped colonial state formation in Puerto Rico (García-Colón 2017a, 144–5; 2020, 58–62; Maldonado 1979, 107–10).

EPWH points to capital as the force drawing workers to industrial manufacturing in Europe and the United States, to plantations in the Caribbean, and to South African mines. Wolf explains that the state deploys its power 'to support the regimes of work and labour discipline required' (Wolf 1982, 100).

In the case of Puerto Rico, the colonial government engaged in a project to develop the local economy by exporting its population, competing with other sources of migrant labour, and facilitating the control and discipline of workers necessary for US agrarian labour regimes. These Puerto Rican government efforts were aided by the Office of Territories, under the US Department of Interior, but officials at the US Department of Labour only accepted Puerto Rican migrant farmworkers reluctantly.

3   Social Fields, Institutions, and Structural Power

The study of the local connections to the global histories of capitalist development needs an approach to state formation that illustrates how ruling groups produce and reproduce their hegemony over subalterns through the interplay of coercion and consent. Processes of state formation are part of labour migration to US agriculture. *EPWH* considers policies of labour control and the barriers to migration, and how conditions in the sending countries facilitated migration, but without entering into the details of how agencies implement, enforce, and survey these policies. It is important to emphasize the roles of sending governments in the migration of their people. In the United States, procedures, regulations, and infrastructure for the deployment and allocation of a low-cost labour force in agriculture are essential state tools to sustain the production of food. Competing interests with different agendas shape the formulation and implementation of policies of labour control and migration. In the case of Puerto Rican workers, the government of Puerto Rico established the Farm Labour Program, under the Bureau of Employment and Migration (BEM), as part of its Department of Labour. Its goal was to regulate labour markets by controlling the flow of workers from areas of unemployment to areas with high demand for farm labour, that is, from Puerto Rico to the US mainland. However, the working and living conditions in the United States – together with the lack of steady employment, and unemployment, low wages, the cost of housing and food, and poor working conditions in Puerto Rico – produced a dual frame of reference for potential migrants, who could now evaluate the costs and benefits of migration by comparing conditions at home and abroad as they manoeuvred within the migratory field (Binford 2009).

Wolf's concept of structural power gives us an important analytical tool to explain migration from Puerto Rico to continental United States. In *EPWH*, he states that, 'The migrant's position is determined not so much by the migrant or his culture as by *the structure of the situation* in which he finds himself. Under the capitalist mode of production, this structure is created by the relation of capital to labour in its spatial and temporal operation, that is the structure of the labour market' (1982, 262, emphasis added). The structure of the situation is the field of power, social field, or field of force where subjects confront, manoeuvre, and resist when capital mobilizes and allocates their labour (Roseberry 1994). Wolf's analysis of the structure of the situation is developed in his article 'Facing power: old insights, new questions' (Wolf 2001), where he refers to it as the 'field of action' when explaining structural power or 'the relation of capital to labor'. Wolf defines structural power as, '[the] power that not only operates within the settings or domains but that also organizes and orchestrates the settings themselves, and that specifies the distribution and direction of energy flows' (Wolf 2001, 384). Power is socially constituted and socially constituting rather than the product of economic dynamics. Power shapes cultural practices and meanings, the formation of subjects and their way of life, and how capital mobilizes and distributes labour power. He adds that, 'Structural power shapes the social field of action in such a way as to render some kinds of behaviour possible, while making others less possible or impossible'. For Wolf, this is what Marx called 'the power of capital to harness and allocate labor power' (Wolf 2001, 384). Thus, migration is made possible by the institutions deployed by the state to foster, direct, and shape it. The Puerto Rico Department of Labour, with its Bureau of Employment and Migration (BEM), Migration Division (MD), and Farm Labour Programme, worked to facilitate jobs for Puerto Rican migrant workers in places far from home. Wolf considers that migration depends on both sending and receiving state constraints, and on governments allowing their subjects to migrate. But Puerto Rican workers' experience of migration only partially reflected what Wolf hypothesized, because mainland growers didn't readily accept Puerto Rican workers once they found them to be not easily deportable. In response, Puerto Rican government officials forced themselves into the structures of the federal government in charge of regulating labour demand and shortages, and in so doing the agencies of the government of Puerto Rico constituted social forces and depositories of human agency within the field of force (Schneider 1995, 4).

The BEM and the MD were products of New Deal efforts to intervene in and regulate the labour market. Another such creation was the Wagner-Peyser Act of 1933, which attempted to regulate the recruitment of labour from low to high areas of demand after officials observed that farmworkers often travelled to areas where they were not needed, lowering wages, and creating a burden in terms of housing and living conditions. The Wagner-Peyser Act established a mainland interstate employment service through which employers were required to post their job announcements. In turn, these orders were distributed to state employment offices where recruitment of the unemployed could take place. After the Second World War, Puerto Rican government officials confronted problems with private labour agents recruiting in Puerto Rico who were creating the same conditions that the Wagner-Peyser Act sought to eliminate on the mainland. Because the Wagner-Peyser Act didn't apply to Puerto Rico due to the territory's colonial status, officials tried to implement the Act's ideas while lobbying for Puerto Rico to be included in the federal-state employment exchange system (Galarza 1977; O'Leary and Eberts 2008, 1–4).

In 1946, after the Truman Administration gave the pro-New Deal PPD local control of the government by appointing Jesús T. Piñero, a PPD leader and Resident Commissioner of Puerto Rico in Washington, DC, as governor of Puerto Rico, the transformation initiated by New Deal labour reforms accelerated in Puerto Rico. Piñero appointed as Secretary of Labour Fernando Sierra Berdecía, who began to investigate allegations made by migrants against employers in 1947. The same year, following Sierra Berdecía's recommendations, the government of Puerto Rico enacted Public Law 89, which restricted labour contractors from recruiting in Puerto Rico without authorization from the Puerto Rico Department of Labour. The Puerto Rican government also created a farm labour programme, and, with the assistance of private labour contractors, the first contracted farmworkers migrated in the summer of 1947. In December 1947, the government of Puerto Rico enacted Public Law 25 establishing the Bureau of Employment and Migration (BEM) to oversee the flow of migration from Puerto Rico to the United States. The Secretary of Labour placed the Farm Labour Programme under the jurisdiction of the BEM (Lapp 1990, 173–4).

Assisted by officials of the US Office of Territories, Sierra Berdecía lobbied US-elected officials and growers to hire Puerto Rican workers. The government of Puerto Rico mobilized its allies in the US Congress, like Denis Chavez and Fred Crawford, to pressure officials at the US Department of Labour for the use of Puerto Rican contract workers in mainland agriculture. In 1949, Sierra Berdecía signed an agreement with Robert Goodwin, director of the US Employment Service, under which Puerto Rico became part of the federal-state employment exchange system. Puerto Ricans became domestic workers, giving them preference over guest workers. This meant that before any employer requested guest workers, they had to prove that no domestic workers were available in the United States and Puerto Rico. In 1950, Congress extended the Wagner-Peyser Act to Puerto Rico, providing federal funds for the BEM. The BEM transformed its offices in the United States into the Migration Division, in charge of implementing the policies of the Puerto Rico Department of Labour in the continental United States, including the Farm Labour Programme (García-Colón 2020, 73–5; Lapp 1990, 118–19, 174–6; USDL 1951).

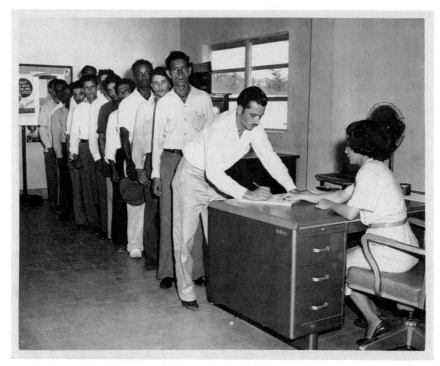

FIGURE 3.1　Farmworkers being recruited by an official of the Puerto Rico department of labor, circa 1950s.
COURTESY OF THE RECORDS OF THE MIGRATION DIVISION, ARCHIVES OF THE PUERTO RICAN DIASPORA, CENTRO DE ESTUDIOS PUERTORRIQUEÑOS, HUNTER COLLEGE, CUNY

In 1951, the government reorganized the BEM as the Bureau of Employment Security, and the MD became the representative of the Puerto Rico Department of Labour in the United States, with influence in the development of the Farm Labour Programme. It assisted the Department of Labour in negotiating and enforcing the contracts with farmers and their associations. The MD also provided the infrastructure needed for lobbying US-elected and civil service officials in the continental United States (Lapp 1990, 175).

The Puerto Rico Department of Labour, through the BEM, MD, and later the Bureau of Employment Security, arranged the hiring and transportation of migrant workers (See fig. 3.1). An important aspect of the Farm Labour Programme was the contract that regulated the relationship between farmers and migrants. As part of the contract, farmers and growers' associations and cooperatives charged workers for food, transportation, and airplane fares, deducting these costs from their pay checks. Sometimes, the government of Puerto Rico would cover the initial transportation costs, which would later be charged to workers and farmers. Some workers described their migration without referring to a contract, but to the fact that they paid for their own airplane tickets to migrate. In an interview in 2007, Norberto, a former sugar cane worker from Lajas, Puerto Rico, recalled his participation in the programme: 'You pay the ticket that they charge you for and you must fulfil the contract. I would fulfil it and fly back to Puerto Rico. The contract is for three, four, five months or more. I didn't like it'. The government also leased airplanes and pressured commercial airlines for a reduction in airfares (Stinson Fernández 1996, 124; See fig. 3.2). Contracts required employers to provide rent-free housing that met healthy standards of living and to guarantee 160 hours of work every four weeks and worker's compensation insurance. The Department of Labour also required employers to post a bond to assure their fulfilment of the contracts. In 1954, the Puerto Rico Department of Labour introduced health insurance financed by workers' contributions (Lapp 1990, 178–81; Nieves Falcón 1975, 134). With these measures, the government of Puerto Rico attempted to entice migrant workers, trying to make US agricultural work more attractive and to avoid problems and complaints by workers.

Government officials met migrants at the mainland airports and transported them to the farms. Artemio remembers arriving at Buffalo's airport in 1952 (See fig. 3.3). He told me that all the men were lined up by government officials and chosen by farmers. By the late 1950s, however, passenger manifests indicated to which farms migrants were allocated. From the airports, employers or MD officials took workers to the camps in buses. Workers were guaranteed 160 hours of work under the contract so that they could pay for their own airplane tickets. Government officials encouraged workers to stay on the mainland after the harvest, providing them with job placement services (Stinson Fernández 1996, 126–135).

The main destinations of migrant workers were New Jersey, New York, Connecticut, Massachusetts, Illinois, Pennsylvania, Ohio, and Florida. Other states that received Puerto Rican workers were Delaware, Maryland, Michigan, and Washington (Stinson Fernández 1996, 135). In the Northeast, Puerto Ricans replaced southern African Americans and West Indians in the fields. In places like southern New Jersey, Puerto Ricans became the bulk of the farm labour force, and this region became home to the Garden State Association, a cooperative of farmers that at its peak membership extended to Pennsylvania and western New York, and to the Glassboro camp, the largest farm labour camp in the Northeast. Norberto remembers arriving in Glassboro, New Jersey, during the late 1950s. He moved from labour camp to labour camp and back to Puerto Rico many times. He also travelled to labour camps in Florida. He indicated that, 'I arrived at the labour camp in Glassboro ... you will wait a week or two

FIGURE 3.2 Chartered flight with Puerto Rican migrant farm workers, circa 1948.
COURTESY OF THE RECORDS OF THE MIGRATION DIVISION, ARCHIVES OF THE PUERTO RICAN DIASPORA, CENTRO DE ESTUDIOS PUERTORRIQUEÑOS, HUNTER COLLEGE, CUNY

until [the farmers] come and pick people up to work in the farms. I stayed one or two months and went back to Puerto Rico …' Migrating from Puerto Rico's countryside to the rural Northeast became a common practice for thousands.

A BRIEF HISTORY OF WORKERS ON THE MOVE 73

The MD had an important presence in Puerto Rican communities, through its offices in New York City, Boston, Philadelphia, Camden, Hartford, Chicago, Cleveland, and throughout Puerto Rico. These offices oversaw the various

FIGURE 3.3 Puerto Rican migrant farmworkers disembarking in Buffalo, New York, circa 1948.
COURTESY OF THE RECORDS OF THE MIGRATION DIVISION, ARCHIVES OF THE PUERTO RICAN DIASPORA, CENTRO DE ESTUDIOS PUERTORRIQUEÑOS, HUNTER COLLEGE, CUNY

activities of the Farm Labour Programme, such as recruitment in Puerto Rico, transportation, contract negotiations, and resolution of problems with housing, employment, and health (See fig. 3.4). The MD offered farmworkers ESL classes and films and pamphlets with information on how to live in the continental United States and gain access to government assistance, identification services, job placement, and cultural programmes. It also provided support to community organizations helping workers. In Puerto Rico, the Department of Labour recruited workers through its regional offices, and the MD offices posted job openings and interviewed and hired workers (García-Colón 2020, 88). The vision of government officials was a planned and managed migration and settlement.

The Puerto Rico Department of Labour attempted to manage the migration of Puerto Ricans, particularly farm labour, but it was an impossible endeavour since US citizenship allowed Puerto Ricans to move to and among US jobs without legal barriers. For their part, mainland farmers continued to hire non-contract Puerto Rican workers, a practice that competed with the Farm Labour Program. At the same time, however, contract migrant farmworkers helped established ties between farmers and workers in Puerto Rico, minimizing non-contract migration. Families with children, however, migrated without contracts and lived in non-authorized labour camps (Migration Division 1963–1969). Guelo, who was a farmworker in Lancaster, Pennsylvania, until his early 80s, arrived initially under a contract but later migrated without one, and became a crew leader hiring workers from Puerto Rico; his wife cooked and washed clothes for migrant workers. Puerto Rican labour officials identified, fined, and prosecuted private recruiters to stop illegal hiring, but farmers still sent tickets and money with promises for employment to their former employees. However, like Guelo, many were never detected, particularly if they remained stateside and used their recruiting contacts back in Puerto Rico. Managing labour migration as a strategy to mobilize labour for capital remained an articulated state project rather than an achievement (Roseberry 1994, 365). Moreover, during the 1960s, an unexpected consequence of labour migration was the establishment of stateside Puerto Rican communities. As Wolf points out, labour migrations engendered other migrations of suppliers of services, 'creating an infrastructure of transport and communication, prerequisites for a further acceleration of capitalist development' (1982, 361–2).

Wolf's critique of the failure of TPPR to grasp the connections between the government of Puerto Rico and US institutions is an important one. The Puerto Rico Farm Labour Program was made possible by the ties of local

FIGURE 3.4　PRDL official Eulalio Torres greeting migrant farmworkers arriving in the United States, circa 1948.
COURTESY OF THE RECORDS OF THE MIGRATION DIVISION, ARCHIVES OF THE PUERTO RICAN DIASPORA, CENTRO DE ESTUDIOS PUERTORRIQUEÑOS, HUNTER COLLEGE, CUNY

government officials to federal agencies in Washington, DC, and by the integration of Puerto Ricans in the US labour market due to the extension and establishment of laws, funds, and agencies to operationalize such connections. However, as Wolf notes in *EPWH*, policies of labour control continue to be necessary to mobilize labour power (1982, 361). Applying Wolf's insights requires envisioning how migrant workers, government officials, and growers manoeuvred within a migratory field structured by citizenship, immigration, and guest worker policies that facilitated the migration of thousands of workers. However, *EPWH* does not provide an adequate analysis of the particularities and responses of colonial governments to the migration of their subjects outside the local colonial administrative jurisdiction. Thus, despite Wolf's critique of *TPPR*, *EPWH* still anchored Puerto Rico as a bounded entity (Wolf 2001), and its local connection to global history remained unexamined.

4   Puerto Ricans Migrating

One of the most important critiques of both TPPR and EPWH is that the social actors involved, the people without history, are obliterated from these histories. In EPWH, this obliteration occurs so Wolf can explain the global development of capitalism. In an article for a special issue on the twenty-five-year anniversary of TPPR, the Puerto Rican anthropologist Eduardo Seda Bonilla (1978), a former research assistant on the project, points out that one of the most important critiques of it behind doors was the question: 'Where are the people?' TPPR failed to describe ordinary Puerto Ricans and the significance of their lives. But his critique goes further: Seda Bonilla attacks how the project fits within the production of knowledge and the structures of power of academia in a colonial setting within the US empire. Indeed, most Puerto Rican anthropologists rejected the usefulness of TPPR and considered it a product of US colonialism in Puerto Rico (Asad 1973; Valdés Pizzini 2001). In EPWH, Wolf purported to answer the question of where the people are by representing human aggregates, like Puerto Ricans, as unbounded, without exotic boundaries, condemned to inequality and colonialism as 'the people without history' (1982, 6–7, 17–19). Wolf's project is grounded in ethnography of life histories and human agency, not a multivocal experiment but rather an agenda that demonstrates how individuals, communities, regions, and state formation are linked to global processes of capitalism.

Histories of Puerto Rican migration to the continental United States encompass more than a century of distinctive and ever-changing situations. The formation of Puerto Rican migrant farmworkers in stateside U.S. agriculture was and is still part of historical processes grounded in the context of specific and dynamic fields of power (Roseberry 1989, 9). For Wolf, the 'people without history' are the principal social actors of the 'processes unfolding, intertwining, spreading out, and dissipating over time' (Wolf 2001, 390). Therefore, histories of Puerto Rican farm labour migration are important in addressing how migrants encountered and manoeuvred within the fields of power. Precisely, Wolf's observations about TPPR emphasized the need to examine 'the complex interplay of hegemonic and subaltern cultural stances in the Puerto Rican situation' (2001, 389).

The Puerto Rico Farm Labour Programme emerged after the Second World War, when the government of Puerto Rico was carrying out projects of modernization consisting of massive industrialization, urbanization, land distribution, and population control through sterilization and migration, and the US federal government granted self-government by allowing Puerto Ricans to elect a governor and draft an insular constitution. Farm labour migration became a tool of state formation in which the colonial government sought to reproduce its hegemony by enticing and coercing Puerto Ricans into supporting this project. The hegemony of the ruling groups in Puerto Rico produced a common sense that allowed migrants to manoeuvre, talk about, and act upon a social field characterized by migration (Roseberry 1994). Thus, the government of Puerto Rico enabled Puerto Ricans to sell their labour power in a larger number of settings in the United States.

In Wolf's own words, the US colonial government of Puerto Rico had the 'clout to set up, clout to maintain, and clout to defend; and wielding that clout becomes a target for competition or alliance building, resistance, or accommodation' (Wolf 2001: 385). Government officials did not deal only with migrant workers; they also had to serve and be attentive to US elected officials, government representatives, farmers, agricultural cooperatives and association officials, inhabitants of rural communities, religious leaders, community organizers, and the families of migrants, among many others. To this end, the colonial state built an elaborate infrastructure for migration.

The protagonists of these histories were mostly men – landless agricultural workers or small farmers in Puerto Rico (See fig. 3.5). They worked on sugar, coffee, and tobacco plantations and farms on the coast and in the highlands of the island of Puerto Rico, and some came from the islands of Vieques and Culebra. Migrants, who ranged in age from 18 to 60 years old, had limited or no knowledge of English and many were illiterate in Spanish. Some migrants came from towns and cities, however, and Puerto Rican government officials complained that migrant workers with urban backgrounds caused problems because of their lack of agricultural skills and their unwillingness to perform heavy physical labour. Avelino, a Second World War veteran and landless agricultural worker, believed that he was going to work building irrigation systems but had to undertake harvesting asparagus, a painful, back-bending task. Brochures and flyers from the Puerto Rico Department of Labour emphasized that people without experience in agricultural work should not migrate (Vega 1966).

In my interviews, migrants always mention the fact that they were looking for better opportunities for their families and themselves. Economic hardship, especially industrial, manufacturing and land reform policies that decimated the sugar cane industry, left thousands of workers without jobs, forcing them to migrate (Ayala 1996). Government policies had increased public sector and manufacturing jobs, but these were insufficient, in part because the low wages and gender-specific jobs created by these programmes led to the hiring of more women than men. Men remained unemployed or underemployed, performing seasonal and occasional jobs in the service and agricultural sectors. For example, when I asked Norberto why he migrated, he indicated that, 'Because of my necessities ... then I went to look for a better environment ... I was a labourer, but I said to myself, good or bad one would die in the sugar cane, the only thing that I have is to go over there, to America, to look for another environment'. Others, like Avelino, could not find jobs because of their support for and political membership in the pro-independence movement and their political persecution by local authorities. In other cases, poverty and financial problems, combined with legal or family problems, impelled men to migrate (García-Colón 2020, 108–11).

Some migrants have been doing the same kind of work for more than 50 years, like Ramón, a 78-year-old seasonal farmworker in charge of recruiting workers, whom I visited in a labour camp in June 2013. I first met Ramón in the municipality of Cidra, in the eastern highlands of the island of Puerto Rico, in 2009. Coming from a landless family, he began to migrate seasonally in 1959. Since then, he has travelled to upstate New York, sometimes remaining for a couple of years. He worked simultaneously in factories and farms, with two or more work shifts a day. When he was not in upstate New York or with relatives in Philadelphia, Ramón lived with his wife in the basement of his father-in-law's house in Cidra, where he farmed a small plot of land. Ramón's children were born stateside, though they now live in Puerto Rico.

In the labour camp where he stayed, all the workers were from Cidra, Puerto Rico. When I visited the camp in 2013, the younger workers were in their late forties and had begun to migrate two years earlier. The economic crisis that began in 2006 decimated their jobs in the construction sector. They were teasing and joking around with Ramón about how he still works hard, never giving up, sometimes working for more than 12 hours a day. They told me that Ramón suffered a stroke a couple of years earlier and had undergone surgery the year before. Then, they laughed about Ramón's complaints about his body aches at bedtime. Ramón said that this would be his last trip because he is tired. The other workers made a gesture of disbelief. Two years later, Ramón finally retired and no longer travels to work in the harvest. Migration not only made the workers flexible in their mobility to find jobs but also offered them a temporary cushion to battle disinvestment, unemployment, and labour-busting in Puerto Rico. Many of the migrant workers were able to send money to their families for food, medicines, housing, or school; some, like Lalo, one of anthropologist Sidney Mintz's interviewees, were able to build houses in the neighbourhood of Jauca, in the municipality of Santa Isabel (1974). Mintz remarks that

> Though he [Lalo] continues to live in the United States, working and saving, he has been sending money to the barrio in expectation of coming

back some day. With the money a large lot was bought opposite [his uncle] Taso's house. On it there is a house which is a wealthy man's by Jauca standards. There are four bedrooms, a long living room, a kitchen with wiring for a stove and a refrigerator, and a shower. To have built the shower and kitchen as integral parts of the house is an unusual step, and suggests a change in the direction of United States culture.

MINTZ 1974, 273

As Puerto Rico became more urban, US patterns of consumption appeared, and seasonal farm labour migration became a way for many to sustain those patterns of consumption. For other migrants, seasonal migration gave an opportunity to purchase or establish stores. Avelino, who became a migrant farmworker when he could not find a job because of political persecution, was able to open a bar with the money saved during several migratory expeditions. Many migrant farmworkers were able to send their children to college

FIGURE 3.5   Migrants working in the fields, circa 1948.
COURTESY OF THE RECORDS OF THE MIGRATION DIVISION, ARCHIVES OF THE PUERTO RICAN DIASPORA, CENTRO DE ESTUDIOS PUERTORRIQUEÑOS, HUNTER COLLEGE, CUNY

or vocational high schools in the larger cities of Puerto Rico, such as San Juan, Ponce, or Mayaguez. Juan, a farmworker I interviewed in southern New Jersey, explained that he was able to pay for his daughters' university education. Overall, farm labour migration fed, dressed, and provided a roof to many families.

On the other hand, continuous seasonal farm labour migration relegated many families to a cycle dominated by structural inequalities. Farm work was and remains low-wage, non-union work. Many families escaping poverty suffered periods of unemployment and underemployment because of temporary jobs (see Griffith and Kissam 1995; Griffith and Valdés Pizzini 2002). Housing discrimination and lack of access to health care were some of the obstacles with which migrants had to deal. The labour camps that housed them also served as control mechanisms by keeping farmworkers outside the towns. Resistance to life in the camps was a constant problem that growers had to combat. In a report, Jorge Colón, an MD official, states that:

> In Owego I visited Raymond Walker's camp. This is the first employer in this area to have agricultural workers under contract from P.R. The original order was for 16 workers. Two of them left Kennedy airport after arriving from P.R. Names and addresses will be supplied to us by the employer in order that we may follow-up and if possible, collect the money lent to them for transportation. There are 12 workers in the camp, two disappeared overnight previous to my visit.
> COLÓN 1966

Farm work also made Puerto Ricans aware of other ethnic groups and immigrants as they encountered them in the farms, labour camps, fields, and small towns. Rafael describes his encounter with whites in New Jersey during the 1950s. He remarked,

> Listen, it was more peaceful around here because there weren't many Hispanics. The Italians I worked for treated me very well; they were good people. The Sicilians are generally good workers, and they are like us in many ways. There were never any problems with them. In those little towns there was a family of Padillas from Sabana Grande, and one of them had married a white woman. He had big problems with her family because they were white. But other than that, there were no real problems because there weren't many Puerto Ricans.

In an essay about *TPPR*, historian Juan A. Giusti-Cordero (2012) attempts to answer the famous critique of the project: 'Where are the people?' by tracing the families and communities mentioned in the ethnographic writing of Wolf and Sidney Mintz (Mintz 1951; Wolf 1951). He examines the municipality of Ciales, where Wolf worked, and the municipalities near Barrio Jauca in Santa Isabel, where Mintz interviewed workers. However, as I stated above, by 1948, when the fieldwork for *TPPR* was conducted, the first Puerto Rican migrant workers were already in the fields of New Jersey, New York, and Massachusetts. In his fieldnotes, Sidney Mintz notes many instances of the importance that migration was already playing in the lives of the peoples of Santa Isabel (see García-Colón 2017b). Workers from Santa Isabel, like Taso's nephew Lalo, were travelling to the United States as part of the Puerto Rico Farm Labour Programme. US farm jobs were shaping their lives in unexpected ways. It is in these fields that the global processes of labour mobilization and political power further structured the formation of Puerto Ricans as subjects and their identities in relation to Puerto Rico and the United States. Therefore, my answer to the question 'Where are the people?' is that they were always there and away, seasonally migrating and settling in the continental US.

5   Conclusion

The Wolfean project of an anthropology centred on historical political economy still has relevance for the efforts to decolonize anthropology. Wolf, as well as other anthropologists such as William Roseberry (1989), offered a perspective that illuminated the connections and social relations that we as humans engage in over time. For Wolf, anthropological inquiry involved history and explanation (Ghani 1995, 31–5). The goal was to understand historical processes in which people are active participants while shaping and being shaped by capitalism. Explanation of the consequences of historical processes did not involve seeking transhistorical laws; nor was it anchored in evolution and progress, nor in a multivocal experiment. For Puerto Rican labour migration, the lessons of this historical anthropology lie in uncovering the histories of the 'people without history' (Wolf 1982, x): of migrant farmworkers, like Artemio, Avelino, Guelo, Juan, Lalo, Norberto, Rafael, or Ramón, as agents, victims, and salient witnesses. This research agenda calls for an anthropology still based on historical realism (Smith 2014).

Historical realism means revealing how capitalist accumulation produced Puerto Rican migrant farmworkers. The forces of capitalism recruited these migrant workers from landless and small farming families in Puerto Rico, inserting them at the bottom of the social hierarchy of US rural communities. At the same time, Puerto Rican migrants changed these hierarchies through their very presence, even as they were, and still are, shaped by the growers, small farmers, government officials, and fellow US citizens who brought them to the mainland and need them to harvest their food. The forces of capitalism created long-lasting bonds and connections between the sending communities in Puerto Rico and the receiving communities in the United States. These forces continue to accentuate the diversity and segmentation of the migrant agricultural labour force in the United States. Colonial migration from Puerto Rico became part of the many and diverse diasporas at the centre of US empire. Puerto Rican farm labour migration illustrates the intricate, long, and continuous history of labour exploitation and dispossession. The world of labour migration is still very real in contemporary global capitalism, and the realities of migration affected and continue to affect what Puerto Rican migrants did and do; and what these farmworkers did and do affected, and still affects their world (Wolf 2001, 386). Nowadays, the ever-increasing migration of Puerto Ricans continues because of economic austerity measures, neoliberalism, and disinvestment. The magnitude of this migration reveals the relevance of Wolf's insights both about how power structures inequalities and how its ruling groups exercise such power while people struggle to make a living at home and abroad.

References

Asad, Talal. 1973. *Anthropology and the Colonial Encounter*. New York: Humanities Press.

Ayala, César. 1996. "The Decline of the Plantation Economy and the Puerto Rican Migration of the 1950s." *Latino Studies Journal* 7 (1): 62–90.

Binford, Arthur Leigh. 2009. "From Fields of Power to Fields of Sweat: The Dual Process of Constructing Mexican Agricultural Contract Workers in Canada and Mexico." *Third World Quarterly* 30 (3): 503–517.

Caraballo-Cueto, José and Juan Lara. 2018. "Deindustrialization and Unsustainable Debt in Middle-Income Countries: The Case of Puerto Rico." *Journal of Globalization and Development* 8 (2): 1–11.

Colón, Jorge. 1966. Progress Report on Projects to Raymond Walker and John Colloca, Oswego, N.Y., August 14, 1966. File 49. Box 1280. Director's Files, Administration, Migration Division, Centro Archives.

Dietz, James L. 1986. *Economic History of Puerto Rico: Institutional Change and Capitalist Development*. Princeton, NJ: Princeton University Press.

Erman, Sam. 2008. "Meanings of Citizenship in the U.S. Empire: Puerto Rico, Isabel Gonzalez, and the Supreme Court, 1898 to 1905." *Journal of American Ethnic History* 27 (4): 5–33.

García-Colón, Ismael. 2017a. "We like Mexican Laborers Better": Citizenship and Immigration Policies in the Formation of Puerto Rican Farm Labor in the United States. *CENTRO Journal* 29 (2): 134–171.

García-Colón, Ismael. 2017b. "Confronting the Present: Migration in Sidney Mintz's Journal for *The People of Puerto Rico*." *American Ethnologist* 44 (3): 403–413.

García-Colón, Ismael. 2020. *Colonial Migrants at the Heart of Empire: Puerto Rican Workers on U.S. Farms.* Oakland: University of California Press.

Galarza, Ernesto. 1977. *Farm Workers and Agri-Business in California, 1947–1960.* Notre Dame, IN: University of Notre Dame Press.

Ghani, Ashraf. 1995. "Writing a History of Power: An Examination of Eric R. Wolf's Anthropological Quest.". In *Articulating Hidden Histories: Exploring the Influence of Eric R. Wolf*, edited by Jane Schneider and Rayna Rapp, 31–48. Berkeley: University of California Press.

Giusti-Cordero, Juan A. 2012. "But Where Are 'The People'? Unfinished Agendas in The People of Puerto Rico." *Identities: Global Studies in Culture and Power* 18 (3): 203–217.

Griffith, David and Edward Kissam. 1995. *Working Poor: Farmworkers in the United States.* With Jerónimo Camposeco, Anna García, Max Pfeffer, David Runsten, and Manuel Valdés Pizzini. Philadelphia: Temple University Press.

Griffith, David, and Manuel Valdés Pizzini. 2002. *Fishers at Work, Workers at Sea: A Puerto Rican Journey through Labor and Refuge.* Philadelphia: Temple University Press.

Heyman, Josiah. 2011. "Eric R. Wolf." In *Oxford Bibliographies in Anthropology*, edited by John L. Jackson. New York: Oxford University Press.

History Task Force. Centro de Estudios Puertorriqueños. 1979. *Labor Migration under Capitalism: The Puerto Rican Experience.* New York: Monthly Review Press.

History Task Force. Centro de Estudios Puertorriqueños. 1982. *Sources for the Study of Puerto Rican Migration, 1879–1930.* New York: Research Foundation of the City University of New York.

Lapp, Michael. 1990. "Managing Migration: The Migration Division of Puerto Rico and Puerto Ricans in New York City, 1948–1968." Ph.D. dissertation, Johns Hopkins University.

Maldonado, Edwin. 1979. "Contract Labor and the Origins of Puerto Rican Communities in the United States." *International Migration Review* 13 (1): 103–21.

Migration Division. 1963–1969. File 10: Florida, undated, 1963-1969, Box 936, Subject and Resource Files, Farm Labor Program 1948–1993, Migration Division, Centro Archives.

Mintz, Sidney W. 1951. "Cañamelar: The Contemporary Culture of a Rural Puerto Rican Proletariat." PhD diss., Columbia University.

Mintz, Sidney W. 1974. *Worker in the Cane: A Puerto Rican Life History*. New York: W.W. Norton. First published 1960.

Nieves Falcón, Luis. 1975. *El emigrante puertorriqueño*. Río Piedras: Editorial Edil.

O'Leary, Christopher J., and Randall W. Eberts. 2008. *The Wagner-Peyser Act and U.S. Employment Service: Seventy-Five Years of Matching Job Seekers and Employers*. Report prepared for Center for Employment Security Education and Research, National Association of State Workforce Agencies. December 2008. http://research.upjohn.org/reports/29.

Rosario Natal, Carmelo. 2001. *Éxodo puertorriqueño: Las emigraciones al Caribe y Hawaii, 1900–1910*. Río Piedras, Puerto Rico: Editorial Edil.

Roseberry, William. 1978. "Historical Materialism and *The People of Puerto Rico*." *Revista/Review Interamericana* 8 (1): 26–36.

Roseberry, William. 1988. "Political Economy." *Annual Review of Anthropology* 17: 161–185.

Roseberry, William. 1989. *Anthropologies and Histories: Essays in Culture, History, and Political Economy*. New Brunswick, NJ: Rutgers University Press.

Roseberry, William. 1994. "Hegemony and the Language of Contention." In *Everyday Forms of State Formation: Revolution and the Negotiation of Rule in Modern Mexico*, edited by Gilbert M. Joseph and Daniel Nugent, 355–66. Durham, NC: Duke University Press.

Roseberry, William. 2002. "Political Economy in the United States." In *Culture, Economy, Power: Anthropology as Critique, Anthropology as Praxis*, edited by Winnie Lem and Belinda Leach, 59–72. Albany: State University of New York Press.

Schneider, Jane. 1995. "Introduction: The Analytic Strategies of Eric R. Wolf." In *Articulating Hidden Histories: Exploring the Influence of Eric R. Wolf*, edited by Jane Schneider and Rayna Rapp, 3–30. Berkeley: University of California Press.

Seda Bonilla, Eduardo. 1978. In "The Anthropology of the People of Puerto Rico," edited by Ronald J. Duncan, 65–75. Special section, *Revista/Review Interamericana* 8 (1).

Silverman, Sydel, ed. 2011. "The Puerto Rico Project." Special section, *Identities* 18 (3).

Smith, Gavin. A. 2014. *Intellectuals and (Counter-) Politics: Essays in Historical Realism*. New York: Berghahn.

Steward, Julian H., Robert A. Manners, Eric R. Wolf, Elena Padilla Seda, Sidney W. Mintz, and Raymond L. Scheele. 1956. *The People of Puerto Rico: A Study in Social Anthropology*. Urbana: University of Illinois Press.

Stinson Fernández, John H. 1996. "Hacia una antropología de la emigración planificada: El negociado de empleo y migración y el caso de Filadelfia." *Revista de ciencias sociales (nueva época)*, no. 1 (June): 112–55.

Suárez-Gómez, William and Ismael García-Colón. 2019. "Puerto Rico: Resistance in the World's Oldest Colony." *Focaal Blog*, September 11, www.focaalblog.com/2019/11/puerto-rico-resistance-in-the-worlds-oldest-colony.

U.S. Department of Labor (USDL). 1951. *Mobilizing Labor for Defense: A Summary of Significant Labor Developments in Time of Emergency, Thirty-ninth Annual Report of the Secretary of Labor for the Fiscal Year ending June 30, 1951.* Washington, DC: GPO.

U.S. House of Representatives. 1928. *Immigration from Countries of the Western Hemisphere hearings before the United States House Committee on Immigration and Naturalization,* 70th Cong., 1st Sess. Feb. 21, 24, 25, 27–29, Mar. 1, 2, 7, Apr. 5. Washington: U.S. GPO.

Valdés Pizzini, Manuel. 2001. "Dialogía y ruptura: La tradición etnográfica en la antropología aplicada en Puerto Rico, a partir de *The People of Puerto Rico.*" *Journal of Latin American Anthropology* 6 (2): 42–73.

Vega, Anthony. 1966. Memorandum to Joseph Monserrat, July 12. File 49, Box 1280, Director's Files, Administration, Migration Division, Centro Archives.

Weisman, Robert. 2019. "Care Worker Digs: A Nursing Home Owner on the Cape Offers Housing to His Employees." *Boston Globe*, November 11.

Wolf, Eric R. 1951. "Culture Change and Culture Stability in a Puerto Rican Coffee Community." Ph.D. diss., Columbia University.

Wolf, Eric R. 1978. "Remarks on *The People of Puerto Rico.*" *Revista/Review Interamericana* 8 (1): 17–25.

Wolf, Eric R. 1982. *Europe and the People Without History*. Berkeley: University of California Press.

Wolf, Eric R. 2001. *Pathways of Power: Building an Anthropology of the Modern World*. Berkeley: University of California Press.

CHAPTER 4

Masking the Past, Legitimizing the Present: State-Making and Precariatization in the Agro-Industrial Landscape, Colombia

Inge-Merete Hougaard

1   Introduction

In the flat plains of the Cauca Valley, midway between two of Colombia's mountain ranges, Cordillera Central and Cordillera Occidental, lies the village of Brisas del Frayle. The layout of the village is puzzling: squeezed in between sugarcane plantations, it stretches for a kilometre, comprising about 105 households patched closely together along one side of a dusty gravel road. Once an old national road connecting the towns Candelaria in the Cauca Valley region with Puerto Tejada in the Cauca region, the village is now nearly invisible from the main road. Yet, when interrogating the history of the present (Ghani 1995), the village tells the story of wider regional processes of colonial dispossession, state formation, and political and economic alliances in the construction of the agro-industrial landscape. Exploring this history reveals a different story alongside the dominant regional narrative of a successful sugarcane industry that continues to condition life in the village.[1] The plantations determine the arrangement of the houses, limit the installation of public infrastructure, and impact the villagers' health with smoke and pesticides from harvest fires and fumigation (see Figure 4.1). Nevertheless, it is not from the agro-industrial crop that the villagers draw their sustenance. Instead, they derive incomes from supplying the regional construction markets with manually extracted sand from the nearby river; from temporary employment in the regional poultry industry, and from seasonal migrant labour in the neighbouring regions' agro-industrial sectors (Hougaard 2019). Most of the villagers in Brisas del Frayle are excluded from the land that surrounds them and from the Cauca Valley's emblematic agro industry. They are both spectators to, and protagonists in, a global capitalist form of production, in which labour power is fragmented and

---

[1] This chapter has theoretical and analytical overlaps with a chapter in my PhD thesis (Hougaard, 2019).

relegated to precarious, temporary and uncertain conditions (Denning 2010; Li 2010; Millar 2014; Watts 2011).

In *Europe and the People without History* (EPWH), Wolf (1997) challenges the established narrative of history as a 'moral success story'. History, he argues, is often told as a series of incremental developments eventually leading to the democratic industrial societies of today. While dominant political and economic actors have had the privilege of telling history from their own perspective, other 'pasts' – those of the enslaved, the marginalized, the disenfranchised – are often suppressed or ignored, leaving large populations 'without history' (see also Reyes 2011; Trouillot 1995). Instead, Wolf argues that societal differentiation is shaped by local dynamics and global connections, in which a diversity of actors have played a central role in historical developments. Challenging the idea of the periphery as a homogeneous group without agency, set on the same universal developmental course as Western societies, Wolf invites a historicized ethnographic approach. He points to the importance of local contexts and the agency of diverse social groups – merchants, middlepersons, warriors, and workers – in forming historical trajectories and shaping diverging societal developments. Through conflicts, contestations, contacts, and collaborations, the so-called peripheries organized around and took part in different modes of production. Specifically, Wolf identifies three modes of production that are relevant for his historical analysis: *capitalist, tributary,* and *kin-ordered*, which respectively emphasize the exclusionary ownership of

FIGURE 4.1   The omnipresent sugarcane plantation in Brisas del Frayle, Cauca Valley.
SOURCE: AUTHOR

means of production and workers' need to sell their labour; the extraction of surplus by and through military and/or political power; and interpersonal and egalitarian relations structured by social obligations and community affinity (Wolf 1997: 75–100). He thus invites us to look beyond the nation state and interrogate how local societies have met, challenged and adapted to global processes of political and economic development.

At the same time, in understanding societal differentiation, the role of the state cannot be denied (Stacey, introduction this volume). One critique of EPWH is exactly that the focus on different modes of production tends to emphasize the economic sphere and draws less attention to the political sphere,and to the role of state-making in developmental processes (Abbink 1992; Asad 1987). Moreover, while Wolf's ideas indicate that marginalized groups are both at the centre and at the margin of the economy – because they are central for its functioning, but also relegated to precarity and easily disposable positions (see also Breman and Das 2000; Li 2010) – I argue that marginalized groups are also simultaneously at the centre and margin of the *political* (Butler 2015; Das and Poole 2004). As such, while marginalized groups are often excluded from political decision-making processes and the spheres of power where interventions affecting the lives and livelihoods are decided, their election votes are still central to the functioning and legitimization of what Simandjuntak (2012) calls 'patronage democracy'. Hence, political and economic interests at local, national, and global levels continue to depend on the marginalization of subaltern groups, and converge in the production of 'people without history'.

This chapter explores these dynamics in the context of the transformation of the fertile lands of the Cauca Valley into a sugarcane monoculture landscape. I unravel the construction of the dominant narrative of a successful agro industry, how it has been established and maintained, and what this has meant for the local people left out. Drawing on Wolf and EPWH, I therefore interrogate how conflicts and contestations, but also connections and collaborations have shaped the developments of the region, and how global forms of production have been met, resisted, and adapted to locally. The history of the Cauca Valley region has largely been told as a 'moral success story' of entrepreneurial 'pioneers' who have taken control of the 'empty land' and turned it into an economically successful sugarcane industry (see e.g. Bermúdez Escobar 1997; CVC 2004; Rojas Guerra 1983). In this narrative, the population residing in the valley prior to the colonial invasion and the people traded as enslaved labour in the transatlantic commerce are swiftly skipped; land appropriations, dispossessions, and social conflicts are erased; and subaltern groups are represented as 'people without history' (Mejía Prado 1993; Mina 1975; Wolf 1997).

I argue that an understanding of how dominant historical narratives were established and maintained requires attention to *discourses* and *landscape interventions*. This builds on and extends Wolf's (1997) historicized ethnographic understanding of how particular societal developments and forms of organization come about. Accordingly, I draw on historical political ecology, a field in which Wolf and EPWH have been acclaimed as frontrunners (Karlsson 2015). Historical political ecology investigates the power relations embedded in human–nature relations from a historical perspective (Offen 2004). In line with EPWH, I explore how landscapes are formed by social, economic, political, and biophysical processes – not in a gradual, linear progression, but in waves, altering between activity and relative stability (Renes 2015). Further, the chapter draws attention to the role of discourses and narratives in the depiction of human–nature relations. As social constructions, discourses, and narratives produce a certain social reality, they are mobilized to justify and reinforce power relations (Dunn and Neumann 2016; Foucault 2003). As argued by Wolf (1997), mainstream historical narratives are carried by dominant actors in society; they rationalize the distribution of land and labour, and shape understandings of current socio-natural relations (see also Christoffersen 2018). Hence, narratives and discourses serve both as a tool for *governing* the distribution of land and labour, and for *legitimizing* different forms of production, land appropriations, and historical dispossessions.

Further, historical political ecology points to the symbolic, governing, and naturalizing power of the landscape (Mitchell 2002). As illustrated by Wolf (1997), political and economic actors have throughout history built monuments, laid railroads, channelled waterways, and raised buildings, leaving traces in the landscape that can be read as symbols of power (see also Lansing 1991; Muir 2000).These landscape interventions work as instruments of power; railroads, highways, fences, dams, and dikes shape the landscape; order space; and govern the movement of people and resources (Mitchell 2002; Scott 1998). With time, these elements of authority and governance blend into the surrounding environment, and the engineered landscape becomes *naturalized*; it presents itself as independent of human intention, hiding the political and economic interests behind its construction (Mitchell 2002). Thus, the naturalizing power of the landscape masks past land appropriations and acts to erase local experiences of crisis while providing support for dominant historical narratives of progress to be readily accepted. Combined, naturalized landscapes and dominant historical narratives legitimize the current expansive-capitalist, agro-industrial production model, leave the present distribution of land and resources unquestioned, and limit land-based livelihood opportunities for local populations.

Thus, combining Wolf's historicised ethnographic approach and insights from EPWH with historical political ecology, this chapter explores how the sugarcane monoculture landscape of the Cauca Valley has come about, how the narrative of it as a 'moral success story' has been established and maintained through discourses and landscape interventions, and how the developmental process produces a 'People without History'. In line with Wolf's (1997) work, the chapter challenges the dominant narrative and explores the conflicts and contestations, connections and collaborations that have marked the history of the valley. It examines how the regional economic and political elites have narrated and shaped the landscape to serve their interests, while subaltern groups have contested, collaborated, and contributed to the regional economy and political development. In parallel, the chapter illustrates how the changing agrarian relations and developing capitalist mode of production, despite continuity and change, lead to a steady precariatization of the rural population.

Methodologically, the chapter is based on a review of written accounts of the regional history, as well as landscape observations, aerial photographs, a household survey (N = 102), and oral histories elicited through interviews and informal conversations. The research takes a point of departure in the village Brisas del Frayle, where I conducted ethnographic fieldwork for a total of ten months during 2016–18. This is complemented with data from other villages in the region, which I visited to triangulate data and to gain a comprehensive understanding of the wider regional developmental context.

The remaining part of the chapter is structured as follows. The next section explores the colonial dispossessions and the mode of production in the colonial and early republican era, illustrating the connections, collaborations, and contestations that led to the formation of a diversified small-scale peasantry. Afterwards, I investigate how the small-scale peasantry was gradually dismantled as nation-building and modernization projects paved the way for an emerging agro-industrial capitalist mode of production. In the following section I illustrate how high-modernist landscape interventions and elite alliances dispossessed the remaining peasantry to create a full-scale agro-industrial production model. Following this, I explore how the rural labour force has been squeezed off the land by selective discharging, migrant labour, mechanization, and tertiarization, and relegated to precarious conditions in the agro-industrial margins. The discussion reflects on the steady precariatization and the role of patronage relations in changing modes of production, before the conclusion rounds off by summarizing the role of discourses and landscape interventions in masking past dispossessions and legitimizing current rural inequalities.

2 Colonial Dispossession and Defiance

The narrative of the 'vacant, empty, unproductive land' has been used worldwide to justify land appropriations and dispossessions (Christoffersen 2018; Fields 2012; Moore 2005). The Spanish colonization of the Cauca Valley, which was a series of entries from 1538 onwards (Rappaport 1998), has retrospectively been explained by a similar mechanism. The eastern bank of the Cauca River was described as providing an 'almost unlimited availability of land for exploitation' and representing a "real 'agricultural frontier'" (Colmenares 1975, 24). While indigenous people of 'a considerable demographic density' (Colmenares 1975, 22) offered fierce opposition to the Spanish colonizers, they were often described as occupying the highlands or the western bank of the Cauca River, which is narrower and less fertile. Yet it is estimated that about 500,000 indigenous people lived in the Cauca Valley at the time of Spanish colonization (Mina 1975), and archaeologists have found indications of the presence of indigenous societies across the entire flat plains of the valley between 600 and 1500 AD covering an area up to 10,000 square kilometres (Rodríguez 1989). This challenges the framing of the region as 'empty' by the time of colonization: clearly, it had undergone various periods of stability and transformation (Renes 2015). Yet, told from the perspective of present-day elites (Wolf 1997), the discourse of the 'empty land' has been effective in overwriting this part of history and legitimizing colonial dispossession.

As Spanish colonizers during the sixteenth and early seventeenth centuries took possession over large stretches of land in the flat plains of the valley on the eastern shore of the Cauca River, indigenous societies were pushed up the mountain slopes on the western shore (Colmenares 1975). They were designated as *reducciones* (indigenous villages) and forced to labour for the colonial elites through the *encomienda* system.[2] Corresponding to Wolf's (1997) description of the tributary mode of production, their labour was either incorporated directly, as enslaved labour, or indirectly, as they were forced to produce food and pay tribute to the colonial elites (Colmenares 1975; Mina 1975; Rappaport 1998). Due to war, disease, and abuses by the *encomenderos*, the indigenous population diminished, and food production could not follow the increasing demand of the growing mining industry around Popayán. As the mining economy also needed considerable labour input, the colonizers started to import enslaved labour by the end of the sixteenth century, mainly from the

---

2 The labour of the colonized population was considered to belong to the Spanish monarch, who offered some labourers to individual colonizers, the *encomenderos*.

western coast of Africa. While the *latifundas*, covering the enormous land mass to the east of the Cauca River, had limited food production and were primarily used for cattle grazing and as signs of social status, the slavery-based *hacienda* started to appear as an economic unit towards the end of the seventeenth century and the beginning of the eighteenth. This development was partly driven by the entrepreneurial mining elites who saw an economic opportunity in framing the *latifundas* as 'unproductive'. This resonated with the Lockean logic of land for 'those who work it' (Fields 2012) and enabled appropriation of the land to start food production for mining sites (Colmenares 1975; Mejía Prado 1993). Enslaved African labourers became a central node of the regional economy: slavery-based *haciendas* supplied the mines with food in return for capital, metals, and more enslaved labourers. It was particularly the sugarcane-producing *haciendas*, each with its own *trapiche*[3] (sugarcane mill), that incorporated enslaved labour into their production. This merged tributary and capitalist modes of production through mercantile relations and exclusive ownership of the means of production (Wolf 1997). While other parts of the Americas shipped sugar to Europe as one of the 'colonial stimulants' and a luxury good (Wolf 1997, 149–51), sugar in the Cauca Valley in the seventeenth and eighteenth centuries was mainly consumed locally and regionally in the form of *panela* (sugar loaves) or alcohol for the mining sector (Rojas Guerra 1983). At this time, sugarcane was not yet a dominant or defining crop in the region, but one among various *hacienda* products, along with corn, beans, cotton, fruit trees, grains, vegetables and, above all, cattle.

By the end of the eighteenth century, the slavery-based *hacienda* system gradually started to crumble. This was partly due to a declining mining economy, and partly because enslaved labour escaped and formed independent settlements on the forest borders (Mina 1975; Valdivia Rojas 1992) not unlike the *palenques* known from the Caribbean region (Friedemann 1979), illustrating local contestations against the dominant political and economic elites (Wolf 1997). Concurrently, a range of different social arrangements of land and labour developed, still drawing on both the tributary and capitalist modes of production (Wolf 1997). First, a complex system of feudal tenancy arrangements emerged, where the tenants either worked on the *hacienda* or paid rent for a parcel of land on the landowner's property. In this way, the *hacendado* (*hacienda* owner) had access to labour but avoided paying a salary or other

---

3 A *trapiche* is a sugarcane mill from colonial times used to extract the juice from the cane, run either by horse or human power. The use of the term today refers to a traditional mill producing the non-centrifugated sugar called *panela*, in contrast to the agro-industrial *ingenio*, which produces centrifugated sugar and a range of other products.

expenses for the maintenance of labour power. Yet, *hacendados* complained about the 'scarcity of labour', and tenants had to ask for permission to work on neighbouring *haciendas*. To retain labour, *hacendados* offered the tenants protection in court cases and against other 'uncertainties of rural life' (Mejía Prado 1993; Mina 1975; Valdivia Rojas 1992), laying the foundation for later forms of patronage relations (Clapham 1982; Scott 1972).

In addition to tenancy, an independent peasantry started to form in the Cauca Valley during the late 1700s and early 1800s. Owners of medium-sized *haciendas* started to sell off their right to heritage, and poor whites, *mestizos*, Afro-descendants, and mulattos obtained small plots of land to cultivate. Some of the remaining *haciendas* still covered huge land extensions and only a fraction of the land was under cultivation.[4] Since absent landlords and random cattle ranching were not effective forms of land control, people started to occupy and settle on the outskirts of the *haciendas*, contesting the established land relations (Wolf 1997). Others formed independent settlements in wetland areas and next to roads, where they engaged in various productive activities such as cultivating plantain and fruit trees, fishing, hunting, and raising pigs using the swamps, bushes, and rivers nearby. Others, mainly craftspeople, settled in the *ejidos*, the common lands at the outskirts of cities, where they mounted their workshops, cultivated bananas and corn, and bred pigs and cattle (Colmenares 1975; Mejía Prado 1993; Valdivia Rojas 1992).

However, the political and economic elites were dissatisfied with the new heterogeneous social classes and utilized a discourse of a 'chronic lack of labour' to explain the limited production on the *haciendas*. Thus, elites endeavoured to capture labour in different ways: framing the population as 'lazy and unruly'; implementing vagrancy laws; and ordering people 'without known occupation' (meaning those who worked their own land) to be employed on the *haciendas* or in mines. They used health arguments, claiming that people should not live near the Cauca River due to the risk of flooding, typhus, and hepatitis, and encouraged work on the *haciendas* instead. Further, they implemented state-making elements such as taxation systems for using the transit roads to govern the population through landscape measures (Colmenares 1975; Mejía Prado 1993; Valdivia Rojas 1992), illustrating how political and economic interests converged to control landscapes and labour. However, the small-scale peasantry and people in the *ejidos* avoided the transit roads and instead carved

---

4   It is difficult to state the exact spatial extension of the haciendas, since boundaries were unclear and records only state the *price* of land (including labour, structures, and cattle) in the case of sales. Records suggest sales of land plots ranging from 4–30 ha, as well as land extensions up to 100–250 ha (Colmenares, 1975; Escorcia, 2011).

out their own roads and pathways, engaging in a form of 'counter-landscaping' and exercising 'weapons of the weak' (Scott 1985) to avoid the various coercive governing measures of the elites.

Hence, by the nineteenth century a diverse small-scale peasantry had gained a foothold in the region through tenancy arrangements and various forms of independent settlements (Colmenares 1975; Mejía Prado 1993; Mina 1975; Valdivia Rojas 1992). Despite resistance from the *hacendados*, slavery was officially abolished in 1851 – though, rather than a single event, this reflected a milestone in a century-long process of rebellion, escape, and self-freeing. Some *hacendados* still managed to hold on to the labour force through tenancy arrangements, and some peasants gathered in settlements around the chapels of the *haciendas* where they were guaranteed market access. Hence, during the second half of the nineteenth century small independent towns were gradually established in the Cauca Valley, and some of the current villages in the region still bear the names of former *haciendas*, such as Buchitolo, Cabuyal, Candelaria, and Jamundí. While the dominant elites during the colonial period and early republican era used the discourses of 'empty land' and 'lack of labour' as well as landscape measures such as road taxation to control labour, the subaltern population contested the dominant mode of production and formed a diversified and independent small-scale peasantry. Their story provides a different perspective on the regional history – a divergence from the moral success story told by the land-owning elites (Wolf 1997). At the same time, local and regional developments which shaped the system of land governance were key features of state-making processes just as much as they were the result of expanding national and international connections.

3   Towards a Capitalist Development Model

After the wars for independence – a series of battles in the period 1810–19 – Colombia was politically fragmented; rather than a nation, it was a union of various autonomous states, only partially responding to central government (LeGrand 1988; Rappaport 1998). During the wars, the country had accumulated enormous external debt, and plantation products were envisioned as the new export commodities that would recover the economy and unite the nation. Nation-building was, as in other Latin American countries (de la Cadena, 2005), constructed around the figure of the *mestizo* ('mixed') as the unifying national identity intended to overcome former divides and 'backward-looking' colonial classifications. Yet in Colombia the 'whiter' shades of the mix were ambiguously positioned as hierarchically superior (Wade 1993); thus, to 'whiten' the population, European migration was encouraged through travel subsidies and tax breaks (Appelbaum 1999; LeGrand 1988). The political fragmentation and economic regionalization had left the Cauca Valley region isolated, and it was framed as 'lazy' in comparison to the industrious regions of Antioquia and Medellín. This narrative was largely related to indigenous lands in the south of the region, but also aimed at the old landed elites who still controlled relatively large areas of what was still discursively framed as 'unproductive land' (Valdivia Rojas 1992). Hence – as an illustration of the local, national, and global connections (Wolf 1997) – the combination of a declining *hacienda* economy, a focus on agricultural exports, European migration, and the discourse of 'unproductive land' led in the second half of the nineteenth century to a liberalization of land laws and enabled (foreign) businesspeople and merchants to enter the property market.

One of these businesspeople was the politically and economically well-connected US consul Santiago Eder. After trying out different export crops, he established the sugarcane *ingenio*[5] Manuelita in 1864, and in 1901 he became the first to install an industrial sugar mill (Rojas Guerra 1983). In the following years sugarcane production expanded and, as technology improved, the sector developed the capitalist mode of production further. Around the turn of the century, the landed elites started fencing off the collective and individual peasant lands to absorb them into their production spheres (Rappaport 1998). Further, as many tenants did not have land titles, the *hacendados* could, with legal support, evict people from their lands to capture both land and labour (Mina 1975). In this way, the small-scale independent peasantry, which had formed during the eighteenth and nineteenth centuries, was increasingly dismantled, and former peasants became labourers in the growing sugarcane industry as the capitalist mode of production expanded (Wolf 1997).

This development was supported by a wider modernization discourse accompanied by investments in technology and infrastructure. Since 1872 Eder had advocated the construction of a railroad to the sea, but it was not until 1915 that the Cali–Buenaventura railroad was constructed. With the concurrent opening of the Panama Canal, the Cauca Valley now had direct access to the rest of Colombia as well as to markets in the USA and Europe. In addition, individual *ingenios* constructed their own networks of roads and railways connecting field and factory (Rojas Guerra 1983). As landscape interventions, railroads are symbols of authority and power; superimposed on previous ('backward')

---

5   While 'ingenio' means both 'wit, ingenuity' and 'company' in general, in the Cauca Valley the term is used particularly for sugarcane companies operating highly industrial production complexes (in contrast to the traditional *trapiches*).

landscape features, they reflect 'progress' and demonstrate a human domination over nature (Harvey and Knox 2015; Scott 1998). At one and the same time, they connect locations (Wolf 1997), govern the movement of people and resources (Mitchell 2002), and tell a new story about regional history and relevant actors in the landscape.

These landscape interventions were combined with investments in research and expert knowledge aimed at enhancing production methods. In 1927 an experimental agricultural research station was established in Palmira to get young people interested in the 'need to harness the resources of nature for the benefit of man' (Posada F. and Anderson Posada 1966, 56–7). Supported by national and international investments, Palmira over the next 50 years became a regional centre of international agricultural research (Valencia Llano and Acevedo Tarazona 2010).[6]

The Cauca Valley was indeed an ideal place for sugarcane cultivation: with more than six hours of daylight, an annual average temperature of 25 degrees centigrade, and a relative humidity of 76 per cent, the geographical and climatic conditions of the region could not be better for a crop so dependent on water and heat (Pérez et al. 2011). The favourable conditions meant that sugarcane had a permanent *zafra*, which means that the cane could be cultivated and cut all year round. This allowed for year-round harvesting and full utilization of the sugar-producing factory and transportation infrastructure, in turn requiring a constant supply of labour (Rojas Guerra 1983). Here, the railway to the sea served another purpose as it dealt a heavy blow to the self-supplying peasant economy. With the inflow of foreign capital, peasants started growing cash crops and became increasingly market-oriented in both production and consumption, illustrating the impact of global forms of production on local livelihoods (Wolf 1997). Many fell into debt through a putting-out system and gradually (re)turned to the large *haciendas* as wage workers (Mina 1975). Thus, during the second half of the nineteenth century and the first half of the twentieth, economic and political elites had joined forces to dispossess and proletarianize the small-scale peasantry, once again creating a 'people without history' (Wolf 1997). While global connections introduced new forms of production and relations between land and labour, state-making processes,

---

6 In the 1930s, the experimental farm developed into the Faculty of Agricultural Sciences of the National University of Colombia (Valencia Llano and Acevedo Tarazona, 2010), and since 1967 Palmira has been the seat of the International Centre for Tropical Agriculture (*Centro Internacional de Agricultura Tropical* – CIAT), initiated by the Rockefeller Foundation and part of the Consortium of International Agricultural Research Centres (CGIAR).

landscape interventions, and modernization discourses paved the way for the development of a capitalist agro-industrial production model.

4 High Modernist Dreams and Elite Alliances

By the second half of the twentieth century, the sugarcane industry had grown significantly in size. With Manuelita pioneering the sector, the *ingenios* Providencia and Riopaila started to produce centrifugated sugar in the 1920s, and from the 1930s to the 1970s nineteen new *ingenios* were established in the region (Rojas Guerra 1983). As a growing economic presence, industry increased its role in regional development and landscape management. In response to several droughts in the 1930s and 1940s, the economic and political elites united to introduce taxation and control the rights to rivers and irrigation canals (Mina 1975). They started developing a long-term planning vision for the region, including the construction of infrastructure for dam building, irrigation, and flood control (Posada F. and Anderson Posada, 1966). In 1954, this led to the establishment of the semi-public entity of the Regional Autonomous Corporation Valle del Cauca (*Corporación Autónoma Regional del Valle del Cauca* – CVC).[7] The CVC was modelled on the Tennessee Valley Authority (TVA) in the USA and was created by influential sugarcane entrepreneurs under advice from the president of the TVA, David Lilienthal, who also lent his name to the first programme of the CVC, the 'Plan Lilienthal'. Born out of the Great Depression, the TVA envisioned a comprehensive model of development inspired by high modernist thinking to transform the 'backward' region of the Tennessee Valley and bring its population 'into the 20th century' (Scott 2006, 18–19). Intent on securing the human domination of nature, high modernists assumed that engineering and population management could, expressing the authority of scientific knowledge, improve society almost to perfection.

Along the same lines, the CVC developed an ambitious development plan and a comprehensive portfolio for improving the human condition in the Cauca Valley (Posada F. and Anderson Posada, 1966). However, like the TVA

---

[7] Initially the CVC covered the area of the Cauca River basin, which includes land in the departments Cauca, Valle (del Cauca) and Caldas – therefore the acronym 'CVC' (CVC, 2004). With the establishment of the Regional Autonomous Corporations (*Corporaciones Autónomas Regionales* – CARs) at national level in 1993, the CVC kept its acronym, but its mandate was limited to the administrative unit of the Cauca Valley region.

(Scott 2006), the CVC development plan was soon co-opted by local elites; despite identifying small-scale peasants as 'those in need of development', the main programmes focused on large-scale engineering and landscaping projects including land reclamation, irrigation, and damming that would benefit the sugarcane industry. Even though an estimated 23 per cent of the 395,000 ha of flat land in the Cauca Valley was regularly inundated due to varying water levels in the wetlands, it was concluded that "the entire flat zone will need artificial drainage" (Posada F. and Anderson Posada, 1966, 87) and that 290,000 ha would need irrigation to counter the irregular rainfall. Flood control was to be achieved through dikes, river regularization and reservoir storage, which required the construction of five thermoelectric and hydroelectric powerplants (CVC 2004; Posada F. and Anderson Posada, 1966). Between the Cauca River and the regional capital, Cali, 5,000 ha were drained through the Agua Blanca project. The drainage was framed as a means to accommodate the increasing number of internally displaced persons (IDPs), victims of the internal conflict in the country, but it also allowed for the incorporation of vast areas of land, which had formerly been swampy and unsuited for sugarcane plantations, into agro-industrial production (Vélez-Torres 2012).[8]

The incorporation of wetlands and swampy areas was justified by framing these as 'unproductive' and 'wasted'. However, the lands were inhabited and served as production sites for a remaining small-scale peasantry who had built their livelihoods in the 'confluence of land and water' (Gagné and Rasmussen 2016). Periodic floods provided natural fertilization for the soil, which could be cultivated in dry periods, while the wetlands served as sites for hunting, wood gathering and fishing. The areas were rich in biodiversity and provided breeding grounds for various bird species that distributed seeds and guaranteed a genetic crop diversity (Vélez-Torres and Varela 2014). However, through land reclamation the sugarcane industry absorbed the collective lands and removed the productive basis of the multi-product peasants, who had to give up their individual lands to the sugarcane plantations. Likewise, the irrigation systems flooded low-lying peasant fields, destroyed harvests, and forced peasants to sell their lands to the *ingenios* (Mina 1975; Vélez-Torres and Varela 2014). In this way, the political and economic elites simultaneously created better conditions for sugarcane cultivation and erased the landscape features that tell the story of the multi-product peasantry, in effect producing 'people

---

8   See Vélez-Torres (2012) for the impact of the Agua Blanca Project and the construction of the Salvajína Dam on local livelihoods in the Cauca region.

without history'. As argued by Wolf (1997), controlling the flow of water has long been associated with 'the power of kings', state-making, and authority (see also Gagné and Rasmussen 2016; Lansing 1991). By damming, canalizing and irrigating, the *ingenios* managed to appropriate land, shape the landscape according to their production interests, and 'liberate' the rural population to labour within the capitalist production model of the sugarcane plantations. With continued representation in the CVC, the industry positioned itself as a powerful regional actor with the ability to shape and define the landscape in the name of a suitable regional historical narrative that illustrated the convergence of political and economic interests and legitimated the expansion of sugar as a capitalist endeavour.

The old, landed elite had initially opposed the sugarcane expansion, since the promotion of agro-industrial exports was linked to the discourse of the 'economic function of land'. Given the large tracts of 'unproductive' land on which their social status depended, the old, landed elites felt threatened by expropriation. However, the 1961 Agrarian Reform became, paradoxically, a point of reconciliation between the sugarcane entrepreneurs and the landed elites (Vélez-Torres et al. 2019). As the Colombian Institute for the Agrarian Reform (*Instituto Colombiano para la Reforma Agraria* – INCORA) gave the landed elites the choice between selling their lands for redistribution among landless peasants or planting sugarcane on their properties, they chose the latter. They adopted the modernization discourse and allied with the sugarcane entrepreneurs, arguing that agro-industrial export production would not be effective on small-scale farms but would require large-scale properties (Vélez-Torres et al. 2019). This did not only mean less land for redistribution through the land reform, but also that the existing and highly unequal land structure was maintained. Further, it ensured the *ingenios* a permanent source of land for sugarcane production, merging sector and region into one powerful unit. Indicative of how global events affect local contexts (Wolf 1997), the position of the Cauca Valley region as a sugarcane producer was further strengthened as the trade relations between USA and Cuba – a world-leading sugar producer – broke down, enhancing the region's access to international markets and increasing local political-economic dependency on the vagaries of global commodity fluctuations (Rojas Guerra 1983; Vélez-Torres et al. 2019).

Following the *hacienda-ingenio* alliance, the number of hectares under sugarcane cultivation in the region exploded, increasing from 32,000 ha in 1962 to almost 97,000 ha in 1974 (Vélez-Torres et al. 2019). The increase happened through land purchases, various forms of rental agreements, and through contract farming with independent suppliers.[9] The land concentration increased as remaining small-scale farmers had their crops destroyed by aerial pesticide fumigation on neighbouring sugarcane fields, and were forced to sell their lands or turn to sugarcane production themselves (Mina, 1975; Vélez-Torres and Varela, 2014; Hurtado and Vélez-Torres 2020). Further, sugarcane growers appropriated peasant land through 'intermediaries' who rented land from peasants with the promise of jobs and food production, but ended up cutting trees and preparing the land for sugarcane. While a few small-scale peasants resisted, the large majority adapted to the global processes (Wolf, 1997) and were incorporated into the agro-industrial production model.

The *hacienda-ingenio* alliance resulted in an increased separation between field and factory, where the *ingenios* focused on the sugar refining process and left cultivation to independent growers. Today, only 25 per cent of the sugarcane-cultivated land belongs to the *ingenios*, while the remaining 75 per cent is in the hands of sugarcane suppliers. These suppliers can be divided into two main groups: large-scale independent growers, often (absentee) landlords on former multiproduct *haciendas*, and small-scale producers – former multicrop peasants who have been forced to enter into contract-farming agreements with *ingenios*. The large-scale suppliers have established the Colombian Association of Sugarcane Producers and Providers (*Asociación Colombiana de Productores y Proveedores de Caña de Azúcar* – Procaña) to negotiate their interests in relation to the *ingenios*.[10] However, Procaña is an 'exclusive club' for wealthy landowners; with high membership fees, it effectively excludes small-scale producers, who stand alone when negotiating contractual relations with the *ingenios*.

One such small-scale producer is Doña Yellen in Brisas del Frayle, who, together with her brother and cousin, are the only villagers who own land for cultivation. Together with her daughter, Doña Yellen cultivates around 5 hectares of sugarcane, which is sold to the neighbouring *ingenio*. In Doña Yellen's supply agreement, the *ingenio* controls harvest and transport. They want a

---

9   Generally, three types of contracts can be identified: *compraventa*, in which the supplier does all the work, and the *ingenio* only collects the harvest; *semi-rental*, in which the provider produces and the *ingenio* oversees harvesting; and *rental*, in which the *ingenio* rents the land and manages the whole production. The contracts are typically of 5–10 years' duration. This roughly corresponds to the life cycle of a sugarcane plant, which can be cut 7–9 times with a growth period of 9–13 months, depending on the crop type, location, and production management.

10   The *ingenios* in turn have formed the Association of Sugarcane Cultivators of Colombia (*Asociación de Cultivadores de Caña de Azúcar de Colombia* – Asocaña).

constant flow of harvested sugarcane to the factory, and as they have various suppliers, they can choose when and where to harvest depending on how it suits their production plans. This leaves small-scale producers, like Doña Yellen, in a precarious situation; they may be forced to wait for more than 13 months for the harvesting of their sugarcane crops – and with it for payment, perhaps realizing a lower income as sucrose levels fall after full maturity. Without control over the production and harvesting schedule, small-scale contract farmers are left with very little decision-making power over the production on their land (Little and Watts 1994). Thus, the *ingenios* have developed a flexible production model with constant and immediate access to ripe sugarcane, while outsourcing the risk of harvest failures or other field responsibilities. Meanwhile, the small-scale producers are both pushed into marginalized positions *and* remain central to the economy (Breman and Das 2000); they have limited control over their lands, but, without them, the round-the-clock production of the sugarcane factories could not function. Hence, through high-modernist landscape interventions and elite alliances, political and economic actors have conditioned the landscape for sugarcane plantations. This has created a capitalist production model that serves elite interests while precaritizing the former peasantry, which, in turn, experiences limited manoeuvrability and ability to shape the conditions under which they produce.

5 Labour Regimes in the Agro-industrial Margin

While the *ingenios* by the 1960s and 1970s had constructed a flexible model of access to land, they still needed a considerable amount of labour in the fields. The division of labour was increasingly hierarchized between engineers and scientific-technical personnel in the factory and manual cutters and 'enrichers' (cane loaders) in the field (Rojas Guerra, 1983). Despite loss of land, the rural population was initially reluctant to engage with the *ingenios* due to the exploitative conditions (Mina, 1975), yet some took up labour on the plantations. The *ingenios* established entire plantation villages with a full range of services from education and health centres to police and prison facilities (Knight 1972), reinvigorating the social-engineering aspirations of high modernism (Scott 1998; 2006). Further, the *ingenios* created their own labour unions to negotiate conditions of work and establish themselves as protective agents (Knight 1972), introducing elements of social obligation into the capitalist mode of production. In this way, they combined high-modernist ideas with traditional patronage relations to retain and control labour for the agro-industrial production.

As the labour force grew, cane cutters started organizing in independent labour unions, claiming higher wages and compliance with the national labour law. Yet, both *ingenios* and the independent growers circumvented the law by rotating employees and selectively discharging active unionists. Further, the *ingenios* started to decentralize labour through increased use of sub-contractors, allowing an evasion of direct contact with the labour force, avoidance of paying social security, and ability to outsource the responsibility of labour to third parties (Knight 1972; Mina 1975). At the same time, the *ingenios* reinvigorated the discourse about the 'chronic shortage of labour' and sent *enganches* (literally 'hooks') to neighbouring regions of Cauca, Nariño, and Chocó in search of migrant labour. Here, the combination of internal conflict and capitalist expansion was displacing people from their farmsteads and served as a push-factor in the labour migration (Achinte 1999), illustrating how global and national events impact local contexts and production systems (Wolf 1997). By the mid-1960s, *enganches* were no longer needed; labour migration had become a self-sustaining mechanism as people enlisted on their own initiative or by invitation from a relative or friend already labouring in the industry (Knight 1972). Recruited into unfamiliar environments, migrant labourers are, Breman (1990) argues, easier to discipline; they make do with lower pay and can be used to put downward pressure on labour conditions and salaries. Migrant labourers in the sugarcane plantations were often not affiliated to the labour unions, and a constant influx of new labourers could thus ensure that wages remained low and conditions precarious. In addition, the *ingenios* increasingly turned towards mechanization of the sector, which reduced the demand for labour. Colombia had, as part of broader development programmes, obtained loans from the International Bank for Reconstruction and Development (IBRD) for the import of machines, and the *ingenios* could, through subsidies, buy tractors to replace field labour (Mina 1975). Hence, through the combination of migrant labour, subcontracting, and mechanization, the 'chronic shortage of labour' had finally been saturated, making the rural labour power in the Cauca Valley a 'surplus population' – one in excess of the needs of production and capitalist interests (Li 2010). While some migrant labourers returned to their home regions, others stayed and created small colonies with compatriots from their places of origin (Achinte 1999).

One of these migrant-based settlements is Brisas del Frayle. The village was formed in the late 1970s, when people started settling along what was then the main road between Candelaria in the Cauca Valley region and Puerto Tejada in the Cauca region. People came from the neighbouring regions, and many were displaced by a combination of internal conflict and capitalist expansion. Some people had lived a few years in Cali or Candelaria before they, through a relative or other connection, heard about the possibility of settling in Brisas del Frayle; the gradual settlement, bordering existing fields, explains the layout of the village with all houses located on one side of the road. Some of the first families came to work in the *haciendas* and small farms, which had a high demand for manual labour in the production of millet, corn, beans, cotton, fruit trees, and other food crops. Others came specifically to work in the growing sugarcane industry, which gradually absorbed the diversified *hacienda* production model. Yet mechanization and the continued migration led to an oversupply of labour, pushed down wages and working conditions, and created uncertainty of employment. Instead, the villagers started 'turning away' (Millar, 2014) and searched for other income sources in the agro-industrial margins, such as sand extraction and temporary employment in the regional poultry sector.

Despite mechanization, parts of the sugarcane industry are still sustained by the availability of cheap migrant labour and its necessity for the capitalist mode of production. While mechanical harvesting is widely used in the north of the region, manual labour is continually used in the south for harvesting and loading cane. One explanation for this is that the heavy machinery cannot function due to the soft and stony soil. However, the *ingenios* frame the use of manual labour as a social concern; the south of the region is marked by socio-economic challenges, and the *ingenios* argue that the use of manual cane cutters helps maintain jobs in an area. Moreover, I suggest, the use of manual labour can also be seen as a way to contain social protests in response to the many labour strikes that have marked the sector over decades (Knight 1972; Montoya Duque 2011; Sánchez Ángel 2008), and which illustrate that local populations have not been passive but have constantly contested and actively adapted to the changing relations of production (Wolf 1997).

Today, many of the manual cutters on the fields around Brisas del Frayle come from the neighbouring region, Cauca, and are subcontracted through so-called 'cooperatives' (see fig 4.2). These are an elaboration of earlier forms of subcontractor organization, with the cooperatives typically comprising about 50–90 cutters, and often with 2–3 cooperatives labouring in the same field at a time. In contrast to the conventional idea of cooperatives, the labourers do not own any productive facilities apart from their own bodies and labour power, and each labourer is paid on a piecework basis. In general, two types of cooperatives exist: those associated with the *ingenios* (though not directly part of the company) and the independent Cooperatives of

FIGURE 4.2   Manual sugarcane cutters in the fields around Brisas del Frayle.
SOURCE: RICARDO LEÓN

Associated Labour (*Cooperativas de Trabajo Asociado* – CTAS). In the cooperative associated with the *ingenios*, many people live in the labourers' quarters in the old hacienda buildings and continue to maintain some form of patronage relationship with the *ingenios*, thus contributing to the corporate social responsibility (CSR) image of the latter. In the CTAS, the labourers get their salaries and social services through the cooperative, and the *ingenios* avoid all matters with labourers such as insurance and social security (Montoya Duque, 2011). This places a significant part of the social security costs on the cane cutters themselves, and the CTAS seldom have the economic capacity to pay insurance and secure labour rights. While these different forms of production differ in terms of labour benefits and social security, they both build on the capitalist mode of production, while the cooperatives associated with the *ingenios* additionally draw in elements of social obligation and patronage relations (Clapham 1982; Scott 1972). This organization of production ensures the *ingenios* a constant and flexible access to land and labour. While they control a small part of the productive means through land ownership and associated labourers retained under neoliberal patronage relations, they enjoy the ability to access and control large swathes of land and labour through flexible contracts with independent suppliers and labour cooperatives, who are kept at bay and pressured to accept precarious conditions by the presence of surplus rural labour.

6   Discussion

The increasing precariatization of the agro-industrial sugarcane production, I argue, points to some important new developments since the publication of EPWH in 1982. While scholars argue that precarity is not a new phenomenon, scholarly attention given to 'surplus labour' and 'wageless life' (Denning 2010; Li 2010; Watts 2011) has gained new academic momentum in the wake of the increasing precariatization of the global labour force (Clifford 2012; Standing 2016; see also Chapter 6 this volume). The global trend towards short-term labour contracts, insecure conditions, and precarious employment is the defining condition for the rural population in the Cauca Valley as well: manual cane cutters are subcontracted through their own labour 'cooperatives' with little social security; small-scale contract farmers supply sugarcane on uncertain conditions without much control over land and production, and those who constitute 'surplus labour', like the villagers in Brisas del Frayle, seek temporary employment in the regional poultry industry, the neighbouring regions' agro-industrial sector, or gain an income through versatile independent livelihoods such as manual sand extraction. This precariatization enables the *ingenios* to draw on a flexible and available labour pool for their agro-industrial production model. In a broader perspective, the Cauca Valley exemplifies, therefore, how successfully economic and capitalist powers have formed a landscape that coerces people into uncertain labour conditions defined by the vagaries of market-based institutional logics.

Further, the simultaneous reconfiguration of patronage relations points to new political dynamics in relations of production that cannot be grasped fully through Wolf's (1997) three modes of production. As argued above, contemporary patronage relations build on a capitalist mode of production, but integrate local political elements such as protection, obligation, and reciprocity, even though these exist under highly unequal relations. Still, these can neither be understood through the kin-ordered nor the tributary mode of production but constitute a form of neoliberal patronage relations. While the villagers in Brisas del Frayle may 'step away' from exploitative conditions (Millar 2015) and build their livelihoods and community on notions of autonomy, dignity and recognition (Hougaard 2022), their livelihood strategies are still conditioned by capitalist structures and unequal relations. The patronage relations that condition these strategies are not only economic, but also political in form. Local political elites build relations with potential voters through promises (and, sometimes, deliverance) of jobs and services with the implicit expectations of election fidelity in return (Hougaard 2019). In this model of 'patronage democracy' (Simandjuntak 2012), subaltern groups are therefore not only situated at the centre and margins of the economy (Breman and Das 2000), but at the centre and margins of the political domain as well; they are marginalized in relation to decision-making processes, but are also central to the functioning and legitimization of the political system. Thus, in the neoliberal patronage democracy, political and economic interests converge in reproducing marginalized positions and 'people without history' as an element in a broader state formation process.

7 Conclusion

The history of the Cauca Valley is often told as a 'moral success story', of industrious pioneers who have managed to turn the 'empty lands' into a prosperous sugarcane industry. This chapter has challenged the dominant narrative and highlighted the role of subaltern groups as a 'people without history' in shaping the regional history. Drawing on Wolf's (1997) historicized ethnographic approach, it points to the long-term continuity and change of the connections and conflicts, contestations, and collaborations that have marked the rural transformation in the region. While Wolf's (1997) analytical framework helps understand societal developments, attention to discourses and landscape interventions provides additional weight to investigations of how the distribution of land and resources is governed and legitimized, and how dominant historical narratives are established and maintained. Throughout history, from the colonial dispossessions to the tertiarization of migrant labourers in agro-industrial production, the discourses of 'the empty, unproductive land' and 'scarcity of labour' have been utilized by political and economic elites to legitimize interventions, appropriate land and labour, and condition the developmental trajectory of the region. Meanwhile, they have used landscape interventions and infrastructure developments to govern the movement of people and resources and to cement themselves as authoritative actors in the landscape. With time, landscape interventions such as railroads, fences, dams, and dikes have morphed into the surrounding environment, and stand as naturalized ways of arranging the landscape, erasing the struggles that preceded them. Together, discourses and landscape interventions mask past dispossessions and legitimize the current landscape layout and relations of production.

Different production forms have been contested by subaltern groups. They have escaped enslavement and forced labour, trespassed on hacienda grounds, formed independent settlements, established labour unions, organized strikes, and occupied lands to settle in the margins of the agro-industrial landscape. However, the history of the Cauca Valley region and its changing modes of production also point to a steady precariatization of the rural population. Accompanied by reconfigured patronage relations, this positions the subaltern groups in the Cauca Valley at the centre and the margin of both the economy and of politics. While political and economic elites converge to reproduce marginalized positions, attention to global connection and local contexts reveals both the agency, struggle, and production of present-day 'people without history'.

Acknowledgements

Thanks to the villagers in Brisas del Frayle, El Tiple, Juanchito and El Hormiguero. Thanks to Irene Vélez-Torres, Christian Lund, Mattias Borg Rasmussen, Tirza van Bruggen, Paul Stacey and two anonymous reviewers. This chapter benefited from funding from the European Research Council (ERC), ERC Grant: State Formation Through the Local Production of Property and Citizenship (Ares (2015)2785650 – ERC-2014-AdG – 662770-Local State).

References

Abbink, Jan. 1992. "Epilogue." In *History & Culture – Essays on the Work of Eric R. Wolf*, edited by Jan Abbink and Hans Vermeulen, 95–105. Amsterdam: Het Spinhuis.

Achinte, Adolfo Albán. 1999. *Patianos Allá y Acá: Migraciones y Adaptaciones Culturales 1950–1997* [*Patianos Here and There: Migrations and Cultural Adaptations 1950–1997*]. Popayán: Fundación Pintáp Mawá.

Appelbaum, Nancy P. 1999. "Whitening the Region: Caucano Mediation and 'Antioqueño Colonization' in Nineteenth-Century Colombia." *The Hispanic American Historical Review* 79 (4): 631–67. https://doi.org/10.1215/00182168-79.4.631.

Asad, Talal. 1987. "Are There Histories of Peoples without Europe? A Review Article." *Comparative Studies in Society and History* 29 (3): 594–607.

Bermúdez Escobar, Isabel Cristina. 1997. "La Caña de Azúcar En El Valle Del Cauca [Sugarcane in the Cauca Valley]." *Credencial Historia* 92. https://www.banrepcultural.org/biblioteca-virtual/credencial-historia/numero-92/la-cana-de-azucar-en-el-valle-del-cauca.

Breman, Jan. 1990. *Labour Migration and Rural Transformation in Colonial Asia*. Amsterdam: Free University Press.

Breman, Jan, and Arvind Das. 2000. *Down and out. Labouring under Global Capitalism*. Oxford: Oxford University Press.

Butler, Judith. 2015. *Notes toward a Performative Theory of Assembly*. Cambridge, Massachussetts: Harvard University Press.

Christoffersen, Lisbet. 2018. "Amazonian Erasures: Landscape and Myth-Making in Lowland Bolivia." *Rural Landscapes: Society, Environment, History* 5: 1–19. https://doi.org/10.16993/rl.43.

Clapham, Christopher. 1982. "Clientelism and the State." In *Private Patronage and Public Power: Political Clientelism in the Modern State*, edited by Christopher Clapham, 1–35. London: Frances Pinter.

Clifford, James. 2012. "Feeling Historical." *Cultural Anthropology* 27 (3): 417–26. https://doi.org/10.1111/j.1548-1360.2012.01151.x.

Colmenares, Germán. 1975. *Cali: Terratenientes, Mineros y Comerciantes* [*Cali: Landowners, Miners and Merchants*]. Santiago de Cali: Universidad del Valle.

CVC. 2004. *Génesis y Desarrollo de una Visión de Progreso: CVC Cincuenta Años* [*Genesis and Development of a Vision of Progress: CVC Fifty Years*]. Santiago de Cali: Corporación Autónoma Regional Valle del Cauca (CVC).

Das, Veena, and Deborah Poole, eds. 2004. *Anthropology in the Margins of the State*. Santa Fe: School of American Research Press.

Denning, Michael. 2010. "Wageless Life." *New Left Review* 66: 79–98.

Dunn, Kevin C, and Iver B Neumann. 2016. *Undertaking Discourse Analysis for Social Research*. Ann Arbor: University of Michigan Press.

Escorcia, Jose. 2011. "Haciendas y Estructura Agraria En El Valle Del Cauca 1810–1850 [Haciendas and Agrarian Structure in the Cauca Valley 1810–1850]." *Anuario Colombiano de Historia Social y de La Cultura* 10: 119–38.

Fields, Gary. 2012. "'This Is Our Land': Collective Violence, Property Law, and Imagining the Geography of Palestine." *Journal of Cultural Geography* 29 (3): 267–91. https://doi.org/10.1080/08873631.2012.726430.

Foucault, Michel. 2003. *"Society Must Be Defended" Lectures at the Collège de France, 1975–76*. London: Penguin Press.

Friedemann, Nina S. de. 1979. *Ma Ngombe: Guerreros y Ganaderos En Palenque* [*Ma Ngombe: Warriors and Ranchers in Palenque*]. Bogotá: Carlos Valencia Editores.

Gagné, Karine, and Mattias Borg Rasmussen. 2016. "Introduction – An Amphibious Anthropology: The Production of Place at the Confluence of Land and Water." *Anthropologica* 58 (2): 135–49. https://doi.org/10.3138/anth.582.T00.EN.

Ghani, Ashraf. 1995. "Writing a History of Power: An Examination of Eric R. Wolf's Anthropological Quest." In *Articulating Hidden Histories: Exploring the Influence of Eric R. Wolf*, edited by Jane Schneider and Rayna Rapp, 31–48. Berkeley, Los Angeles, London: University of California Press.

Harvey, Penelope, and Hannah Knox. 2015. *Roads – An Anthropology of Infrastructure and Expertise*. Ithaca, N.Y.: Cornell University Press.

Hougaard, Inge-Merete. 2019. "Settled in Sand: State-Making, Recognition and Resource Rights in the Agro-Industrial Landscape." PhD diss., University of Copenhagen.

Hougaard, Inge-Merete. 2022. "Rural Precarity: Relational Autonomy, Ecological Dependence and Political Immobilisation in the Agro-industrial Margin." *Journal of Peasant Studies*. https://doi.org/10.1080/03066150.2022.2101097

Hurtado, Diana, and Irene Vélez-Torres. 2020. "Toxic Dispossession: On the Social Impacts of the Aerial Use of Glyphosate by the Sugarcane Agroindustry in Colombia." *Critical Criminology* 28 (4): 557–76. https://doi.org/10.1007/s10612-020-09531-3.

Karlsson, Bengt G. 2015. "Political Ecology: Anthropological Perspectives." In *International Encyclopedia of the Social & Behavioral Sciences*, edited by James D. Wright, 2nd ed., 350–55. Oxford: Elsevier. https://doi.org/10.1016/B978-0-08-097086-8.12215-9.

Knight, Rolf. 1972. *Sugar Plantations and Labor Patterns in the Cauca Valley, Colombia*. Toronto: University of Toronto.

la Cadena, Marisol de. 2005. "Are 'Mestizos' Hybrids? The Conceptual Politics of Andean Identities." *Journal of Latin American Studies* 37 (2): 259–84. https://doi.org/10.1017/S0022216X05009004.

Lansing, John Stephen. 1991. *Priests and Programmers: Technologies of Power in the Engineered Landscape of Bali*. Princeton: Princeton University Press.

LeGrand, Catherine C. 1988. *Colonización y Protesta Campesina En Colombia (1850–1950)* [*Colonisation and Peasant Protest in Colombia (1850–1950)*]. Bogotá: Universidad Nacional de Colombia.

Li, Tania Murray. 2010. "To Make Live or Let Die? Rural Dispossession and the Protection of Surplus Populations." *Antipode* 41 (S1): 66–93. https://doi.org/10.1002/9781444397352.ch4.

Little, Peter, and Michael J. Watts. 1994. *Living under Contract, Contract Farming and Agrarian Transformation in Sub-Saharan Africa*. Madison: University of Wisconsin Press.

Mejía Prado, Eduardo. 1993. *Origen del Campesino Vallecaucano: Siglo XVIII y Siglo XIX* [*Origin of the Vallecaucan Peasant: 18th and 19th Century*]. Santiago de Cali: Universidad del Valle.

Millar, Kathleen M. 2014. "The Precarious Present: Wageless Labor and Disrupted Life in Rio de Janeiro, Brazil." *Cultural Anthropology* 29 (1): 32–53. https://doi.org/10.14506/ca29.1.04.

Millar, Kathleen M. 2015. "The Tempo of Wageless Work: E. P. Thompson's Time-Sense at the Edges of Rio De Janeiro." *Focaal* 2015 (73): 28–40. https://doi.org/10.3167/fcl.2015.730103.

Mina, Mateo. 1975. *Esclavitud y Libertad En El Valle Del Rio Cauca* [*Slavery and Freedom in the Cauca River Valley*]. Bogotá: Fundación Rosca de Investigación y Acción Social.

Mitchell, William J. T. 2002. "Introduction." In *Landscape and Power*, edited by William J.T. WMitchell, 2nd ed., 1–4. Chicago: University of Chicago Press.

Montoya Duque, Gloria Inés. 2011. "El Paro de Corteros de Caña En El Valle Del Cauca – Colombia: Una Acción Colectiva de Cara Al Modelo Económico [Sugar Cane Cutters' Strike in the State of Valle Del Cauca – Colombia: A Collective Action in the Face of the Economic Model]." *Entramado* 7 (1): 104–13.

Moore, Donald S. 2005. *Suffering for Territory: Race, Place, and Power in Zimbabwe*. Durham: Duke University Press.

Muir, Richard. 2000. *The New Reading the Landscape: Fieldwork in Landscape History*. Exeter: University of Exeter Press.

Offen, Karl H. 2004. "Historical Political Ecology: An Introduction." *Historical Geography* 32: 19–42.

Pérez, Mario Alejandro, Miguel Ricardo Peña, and Paula Alvarez. 2011. "Agro-Industria Cañera y Uso de Agua: Análisis Crítico En El Contexto de Agrocombustibles En Colombia [Sugarcane Agro-Industry and Water Use: Critical Analysis in the Context of Agrofuels in Colombia]." *Ambiente & Sociedade* XIV (2): 153–78. https://doi.org/10.1590/S1414-753X2011000200011.

Posada F., Antonio J., and Jeanne Anderson Posada. 1966. *The CVC – Challenge to Underdevelopment and Traditionalism*. Bogotá: Ediciones Tercer Mundo.

Rappaport, Joanne. 1998. *The Politics of Memory: Native Historical Interpretation in the Colombian Andes*. Durham: Duke University Press.

Renes, Hans. 2015. "Historic Landscapes Without History? A Reconsideration of the Concept of Traditional Landscapes." *Rural Landscapes: Society, Environment, History* 2 (1): 1–11. https://doi.org/10.16993/rl.ae.

Reyes, Honorio Rivera. 2011. "Ethnic Representation in Colombian Textbooks." In *The Presented Past: Heritage, Museums and Education*, edited by Peter G. Stone and Brian L Molyneaux, 1st paperb, 398–407. New York: Routledge.

Rodríguez, Carlos Armando. 1989. "La Población Prehispánica Del Valle Medio Del Río Cauca Entre Los Siglos VII–XVI D.C [The Prehispanic Population in the Mid-Valley of the Cauca River between the 7th-16th Century A.D.]." *Boletín Museo Del Oro* 24: 72–89.

Rojas Guerra, José María. 1983. *Sociedad y Economía En El Valle Del Cauca – Tomo V: Empresarios y Tecnología En La Formación Del Sector Azucarero En Colombia 1860–1980 [Society and Economy in the Cauca Valley – Volume V: Entrepreneurs and Technology in the Formation of the Sugar (...)]*. Bogotá: Biblioteca Banco Popular.

Sánchez Ángel, Ricardo. 2008. "Las Iras Del Azúcar: La Huelga de 1976 En El Ingenio Riopaila [The Wrath of Sugar: The 1976 Riopaila Sugar Mill Strike]." *Historia Crítica* 35: 34–57.

Scott, James C. 1972. "Patron-Client Politics and Political Change in Southeast Asia." *The American Political Science Review* 66 (1): 91–113.

Scott, James C. 1985. *Weapons of the Weak: Everyday Forms of Peasant Resistance.* New Haven: Yale University Press.

Scott, James C. 1998. *Seeing Like a State: How Certain Schemes to Improve the Human Condition Have Failed.* New Haven: Yale University Press.

Scott, James C. 2006. "High Modernist Social Engineering: The Case of the Tennessee Valley Authority." In *Experiencing the State*, edited by Lloyd I. Rudolph and John Kurt Jacobsen, 3–52. New York: Oxford University Press.

Simandjuntak, Deasy. 2012. "Gifts and Promises: Patronage Democracy in a Decentralised Indonesia." *European Journal of East Asian Studies* 11 (1): 99–126. https://doi.org/10.1163/15700615-20120008.

Standing, Guy. 2016. *The Precariat: The New Dangerous Class.* London: Bloomsbury.

Trouillot, Michel-Rolph. 1995. *Silencing the Past: Power and the Production of History.* Boston: Beacon Press.

Valdivia Rojas, Luis. 1992. *Economía y Espacio: El Valle Del Cauca 1850 a 1950* [*Economy and Space: The Cauca Valley 1850 to 1950.* Santiago de Cali: Universidad del Valle.

Valencia Llano, Néstor Fabio, and Álvaro Acevedo Tarazona. 2010. "Origen de La Educación Agrícola Superior En El Valle Del Cauca, 1910–1934 [Origin of the Superior Agricultural Education in the Cauca Valley, 1910–1934]." *HiSTOReLo. Revista de Historia Regional y Local* 2 (3): 67–93. https://doi.org/10.15446/historelo.v2n3.12382.

Vélez-Torres, Irene. 2012. "Water Grabbing in the Cauca Basin: The Capitalist Exploitation of Water and Dispossession of Afro-Descendant Communities." *Water Alternatives* 5 (2): 431–49.

Vélez-Torres, Irene, and Daniel Varela. 2014. "Between the Paternalistic and the Neoliberal State: Dispossession and Resistance in Afro-Descendant Communities of the Upper Cauca, Colombia." *Latin American Perspectives* 41 (6): 9–26. https://doi.org/10.1177/0094582X14547515.

Vélez-Torres, Irene, Daniel Varela, Víctor Cobo-Medina, and Diana Hurtado. 2019. "Beyond Property: Rural Politics and Land-Use Change in the Colombian Sugarcane Landscape." *Journal of Agrarian Change* 19 (4): 690–710. https://doi.org/10.1111/joac.12332.

Wade, Peter. 1993. *Blackness and Race Mixture: The Dynamics of Racial Identity in Colombia.* Baltimore: Johns Hopkins University Press.

Watts, Michael J. 2011. "Planet of the Wageless." *Identities* 18 (1): 69–80. https://doi.org/10.1080/1070289X.2011.593433.

Wolf, Eric. 1997. *Europe and the People without History.* Reprint. Berkeley: University of California Press.

CHAPTER 5

A Political Ecology of Fetishism in Brazil's 'Discovery Coast'

Crisis, Socio-environmental Hybridization, and Historical Amnesia on the Frontiers of Global Liberalism

Gustavo S. Azenha

1   Introduction: towards a Symmetrical Historical Materialism

This chapter analyzes the recent dynamics of 'traditional' peoples' struggles over nature on the 'Discovery Coast' of Brazil and the novelty of emergent processes, while being mindful of historical continuities. Drawing on Eric R. Wolf's work – with its foregrounding of historicization, its attention to global political and economic currents, and the contradictory yet complementary process of connection and exclusion – in dialogue with anthropological value theory and political ecology, I critically explore the shifting terms of interdependence and social differentiation between 'traditional' peoples and global political and economic processes in Brazil. Following Wolf, this emphasizes that global social forms are, and have been, thoroughly transcultural articulations. Brazilian ruralities are marked by socio-environmental hybridities, while encounters with Brazilian frontiers have shaped global understandings of nature, humanity, and liberalism. While these hybridities are to some extent acknowledged, they are imagined through contradictory politics of revelation and concealment that selectively obscure the histories and human subjectivities imbricated in their creation. Drawing on Wolf's insights into crisis and differentiation, in conversation with anthropological understandings of liminality and fetishism, the investigation highlights how the interplay of heterogeneous social forms in moments of crisis is marked by an interconnected historical amnesia and the affirmation of radical social difference. Approaching Brazil's 'traditional' peoples and the 'wild' spaces they inhabit as creative nodes along the contemporary frontiers of global liberalism, the chapter seeks to contribute to understandings of frontier spaces and the expansion of global markets and liberal ideologies, encouraging a more finely textured reading of the interdependent and co-constitutive metabolism of subsistence and market economies.

Through a political ecology of indigenous communities in Brazil's 'Discovery Coast'[1] (the region around Porto Seguro, Bahia, the locale of Portuguese 'discovery' of Brazil), this chapter argues for a more finely textured understanding of the dynamic and hybrid character of socio-environmental engagements in rural communities. Underscoring the cultural hybridity and the ecological/economic hybridity of resource-use strategies, the chapter questions persistent assumptions of difference between the traditional and the modern that reinforce misleading distinctions between ways of being with nature, and foreclose possibilities of anthropological symmetry, which is vital to envisioning more sustainable and equitable resource use. These arguments seek to cultivate a reorientation of political ecology that better equips it for nurturing more sustainable and equitable resource use paradigms. Attenuating tendencies to emphasize historical rupture and radical difference is essential for fully appreciating the interdependency of global humanity (and nature) and developing more nuanced and productive understandings of uncertainty, vulnerability, and resilience.

Further, the chapter emphasizes the need for a more omnivorous and symmetrical political ecology that combines historical awareness, greater attentiveness to the values and aspirations of rural peoples, more empathetic and sophisticated appraisals of the workings of liberal agencies, and heightened critical reflexivity in the application of anthropological theories and practices. Such an omnivorous and symmetrical political ecology privileges a relational approach that emphasizes the plasticity of the interplay of socio-environmental forms, taking primary inspiration from the work of Wolf in dialogue with other scholars who engage with the concept of fetishism (e.g., Bruno Latour, David Graeber, Michael Taussig, and Rosalind Morris). This approach seeks to move beyond a conceptualization of socio-environmental difference that continues to encourage the simplification and marginalization of the values and expertise of 'traditional' peoples in the politics and practices of sustainable development, including their exclusion in the definitions and social taxonomies of growth, risk, uncertainty, vulnerability, and resilience.

---

[1] The term 'Discovery Coast' was developed by the Bahian state government for the purposes of tourism. It encompasses Porto Seguro and adjacent municipalities in which most Pataxó communities are situated.

2   Contemporary Pataxó Hybridities and Resilience

The Pataxó inhabit numerous settlements, villages, and towns along Brazil's 'Discovery Coast', with varying degrees of rurality, connections to markets, and land/resource rights. These comprise a loose and highly dynamic assemblage of communities linked through the circulation of goods, people, knowledge, and values. The communities engage in various spatially and seasonally dynamic resource-use strategies (e.g., agriculture, extractivism, craft production, and ecotourism) as they continuously acclimatize to changing political and economic trends, including:
- The ebb and flow of tourism money;
- Shifting agricultural markets;
- Aggressive land dispossession and concentration processes (primarily the result of real estate speculation tied to tourism and the rapid expansion of the eucalyptus forest plantation industry);
- Changing government social policies and programmes (e.g., conditional cash transfer programmes and rural pensions);
- Shifting conceptions of conservation policies (e.g., the supplanting of a focus on biodiversity with one on climate change);
- The reconfiguration of indigenous policies (including land rights policies, agricultural extension paradigms, and sustainable development projects).

With regard to indigenous policies, trends in recent decades towards administrative decentralization and fragmentation of the points of contact between indigenous peoples and government entities have yielded new constraints and opportunities for the pursuit of rights and the securing of public services. This has been accompanied by (and fostered) the development of novel local and extra-local political alliances and organizations. At the same time, the recent greening of development has shaped these emergent forms of political organization in important ways, with resource engagements coming to the fore of political and economic struggles in unprecedented ways. With heightened attention to biodiversity conservation and, more recently, climate change prevention and mitigation, there has been a greening of the rhetoric (and (sometimes the practices) of government agencies, civil society organizations, and private sector actors. As part and parcel of this phenomenon, Pataxó political struggles have become more self-consciously 'ecological', while new sorts of environmental subjectivities have emerged (such as engagement in ecotourism, reforestation, agroforestry, forest fire brigades, and environmental vigilance projects). In this context, there exist diverse articulations of Pataxó sustainability: heterogeneous projects of socio-environmental resilience compete with and complement each other internally, while also contesting or complementing the sustainable development paradigms of other notable regional actors (such as the forest plantation industry, the tourism industry, and international conservation organizations). This plays out as Pataxó seek to secure land rights and establish market and socio-political interdependencies that are compatible with their desired sense of autonomy and wellbeing.

These strategies of resilience are hybrid in multiple (and interrelated) senses: by virtue of their dynamic heterogeneity at individual, household, and community levels; but also in the sense that they are crafted from a complex synthesis of indigenous, Afro-Brazilian, and European values and ways of engaging with nature and markets. This latter cultural hybridity is an ongoing metabolic process that stretches back centuries as communities strove for resilience while navigating shifting social interdependencies at the margins of global economies. It permeates the socio-environmental hybridity of resource use in which a dynamic mix of extraction, cultivation, and labour reflects techniques and values of varied cultural provenance.

3   Connecting Past and Present: Historical Uncertainty and Resilience

Primary concerns in this chapter are the recent dynamics and transformations discussed above, but central is a historical (materialist) approach that recognizes the novelty of emergent processes, while being mindful of continuities and cautious about overstating the uniqueness of recent transformations. Like all rural communities, the Pataxó straddle multiple social, political, economic, and environmental worlds. This characterization is not solely valid for the contemporary moment: socio-environmental hybridity and dynamism have characterized Pataxó pursuits of subsistence, economic wellbeing, rights, and political agency since (at least) colonial times. Although the pronounced socio-environmental transformations of the late twentieth and early twenty-first centuries have brought new constraints and opportunities, as well as novel valuations of land, resources, and Pataxó subjectivities, there has been a symbiotic coexistence between agriculture, extractivism, and engagement in labour markets for centuries (albeit in highly variable configurations). Heterogeneous productive practices, marked by environmental and economic complementarities at individual, household, community, and regional scales, have long been the norm, along with cyclical and periodic mobility tied to socio-economic and environmental cycles. As is common for other frontier inhabitants, indigenous communities in southern Bahia have long been characterized by hybrid and adaptive systems of alternative sustainabilities, created and designed to thrive within situations of socio-environmental uncertainty. Environmental and climactic variabilities, shifting demands for – and valuations of – goods and labour, and unreliable state actors in a context of deeply 'differentiated citizenship', unequal land/resource rights, and uneven access to public services[2] – these have been perennial features of the rural that have necessitated and shaped past and present hybridities, along with shifting conceptions of socio-environmental resilience and interdependence.

This chapter explore this resilient acclimatization through the prism of Wolf's work. It starts with a brief primer of the theoretical orientations that undergird the approach adopted. I articulate an approach – a political ecology of fetishism – that rests upon Wolf's historical materialism while critically pushing it in new directions. The second section provides an overview of the socio-environmental history of the 'Discovery Coast'. Historical continuities and discontinuities are discussed, highlighting the endurance of forms of social and environmental unpredictability, and indigenous strategies and practices of resilient acclimatization.[3] In the concluding section, I revisit and deepen some of the initial theoretical considerations, arguing for the importance of attenuating tendencies to affirm radical discontinuity and difference, while heightening attention to the existential frictions beneath the surface of the politics of nature. I reason that a creative return to the concept of fetishism is vital to the conjuring of more inclusive and symmetrical forms of socio-environmental resilience more adequate to current global crises.

---

2 I borrow the idea of 'differentiated citizenship' from James Holston (2011: 337), who uses it to denote the differentiated 'distributions of rights, resources, powers, vulnerabilities, practices, identities, and so forth'.

3 The empirical research for this section is based on fieldwork, archival research, and secondary sources. Understanding of the recent history is based on fieldwork in the municipality of Porto Seguro (State of Bahia) in 2000–4 and in 2015 (consisting of interviews with representatives of Pataxó communities, environmental NGOs, indigenous rights NGOs, and government institutions), in combination with relevant anthropological literature, and indigenous and environmental policy documents. The longer-term historical background is based on published academic literature on the indigenous, environmental, and economic history of Brazil, and archival research conducted in 2017 at the Arquivo Público do Estado da Bahia in Salvador (Brazil) and the Arquivo Histórico Ultramarino in Lisbon (Portugal).

4 Theoretical Foundations: Global Metabolism, Historical Amnesia, Differentiation/Hybridization

The empirical concerns and analytical approach employed in this chapter follow the spirit of Wolf's *Europe and the People Without History*. The affinities with Wolf's influential work are manifold, including its foregrounding of global political economic currents, its concerns with historical erasure, and its linking of crisis and differentiation. More broadly, the chapter follows Wolf's lead in highlighting a productive dialogue between anthropology and history. Anthropological sensibilities are employed to understand the history of the hybridizing frontiers of modern liberal economies. Wolf's approach productively highlighted and explored the contradictory and intertwined processes of intensified interdependency and differentiation in globalizing political and economic development, adding flesh to dependency theory through introducing anthropological orientations and concerns, giving more attention to peripheral peoples and social formations, and underscoring their active participation and agency in both local and global processes (Wolf 2010, 22–23). While following in the spirit of dependency and world systems theories in its attention to global political economic currents and its preoccupations with power and inequality, Wolf's anthropological sensibilities yield a more dynamic and relational understanding of centres and peripheries, one that pays greater attention to the place of indigenous peoples in global processes, including their roles as victims, protagonists, and active agents in the articulation of local and global social formations. He employs a 'historically-oriented political economy' that takes account of 'the conjoint participation of Western and non-Western peoples' in global processes (Wolf 2010, xxv) and viewed humankind as a 'manifold, a totality of interconnected processes' (Wolf 2010, 3).

Wolf's understanding of the hybrid metabolism that characterizes globalization and asymmetrical development privileges what I would call historical amnesia, which is conceived as both cause and symptom of the absence of more relational understandings of global histories. By historical amnesia, I mean his critique of the tacit ethnocentric notion that 'primitive' peoples lack history and (creative) agency (and individuality). This notion of historical amnesia entails an erasure in the development of the West of 'primitive' agencies, whose labour, ideas, institutions, and materialities have shaped the history of Western modernity in more profound and sustained ways than typically acknowledged. 'Primitive' peoples, peasants, Third World countries, etc. are assumed to be trapped in tradition, and to be unchanging, inflexible, and irrational (Wolf 2010, 12–13). Tacit assumptions of their stasis and of their intellectual, moral, and economic stagnation, and the repression of the historicity of peripheral peoples, Wolf (2010, 18) argues, 'amounts to the erasure of 500 years of confrontation, killing, resurrection, and accommodation'. His work aims to recover the 'active histories' of primitive peoples, peasantries, labourers, and others typically rendered invisible or passive in accounts of history (Wolf 2010, xxvi), insightfully arguing that the presumed stasis of the others of the 'West' precludes relational understanding and analysis (Wolf 2010, 12–13). He affirms that attention to 'mutual interrelationships and interdependencies in space and time' is essential for cultural analysis (Wolf 2010, xx). A focus on interrelationships and on countering historical erasures are conjoined matters that are necessary for understanding the specificities of 'local' and 'global' cultures. Thus, historical amnesia involves not only an erasure of 'primitive' agencies, but also a disavowal of the pervasive hybridity that characterizes all social formations connected through globalizing modernity.

Wolf's understanding of the metabolism of globalization and its historical amnesia makes an important connection between crisis and differentiation (Wolf 2010, 296–309). He is concerned to highlight and explain the seemingly contradictory impulses of capitalism, marked by integration and unification, on the one hand, and differentiation and the production of heterogeneity on the other (Wolf 2010, xxiii). The preoccupation with differentiation is linked to his concern to recover the historical agency of peripheral peoples. He discusses varied 'sources of differentiation' under capitalism, including the frictive encounters and contaminating hybridization between capitalism and other modes of production in frontier zones (Wolf 2010, 303–7). The attention that Wolf places on crisis and differentiation is compelling for understanding sociocultural change, the interface between centres and peripheries, and their significance for the constitution of power and the creation and perpetuation of inequality. What is especially seductive about these discussions is the attention given to the role of crisis in processes of sociocultural, political, economic, technological, and environmental differentiation, and the understanding of differentiation, integration, homogenization, and diversification as unified processes. In my (more anthropologically symmetrical) reading, the relationship between crisis and differentiation underscored by Wolf and some of the nuances he attributes to this relationship are not unique to the dynamics of capitalism. This more universalist reading is one that productively dialogues with my understandings of the concept of fetishism, which brings me to the next point, and my main critique of Wolf.

5 Veiled Fetishism

Despite its explicit Marxian accent, notably absent in Wolf's work is the matter of fetishism. He has been critiqued for this and acknowledged it, admitting that he did not engage in 'the interesting, if problematic, concept of "commodity fetishism"' (Wolf 2010, xxii). It is a problematic term, to be sure, which carries a lot of baggage, but is nonetheless a valuable and indeed vital complement to Wolf's approach, with continued relevance and utility for political ecology, and for anthropology and social theory more broadly. To say that fetishism is absent in Wolf's work is somewhat inaccurate. EPWH is tacitly contaminated by the fetish concept, which is hinted at here and there, but it never rises to the surface. The fetishistic naturalization of power, for instance, is evident when he critically observes that history as a 'complex orchestration of antagonistic forces is celebrated instead as the unfolding of a timeless essence' (Wolf 2010, 5). Similarly, a veiled allusion to the fetish concept is apparent when he critiques the conversion of history into an ethnocentric, egocentric, and self-legitimating 'tale about the furtherance of virtue', and when he suggests that 'history is the working out of a moral purpose in time' in which 'those who lay claim to that purpose are by that fact the predilect agents of history' (Wolf 2010, 5). Fetishism also makes a timid appearance when Wolf, in discussing tributary 'modes of production', observes how power, domination, and inequality can be validated through inscribing them 'into the structure of the universe' and making claims to supernatural origin (Wolf 2010, 83). The title of his book is itself a veiled allusion to the fetishistic nature of ideology. His central concerns with historical amnesia and the shrouding of interconnections are clearly indebted to Marxian notions of alienation. Although Wolf is concerned with the erasure of interconnections (Wolf 2010, 4), he does not offer a fuller account of this process of 'myth making' in which the 'misleading' 'developmental scheme' of the West is created and rationalized. In short, the spectre of Marx's fetish concept clearly haunts Wolf's work but remains underdeveloped, in a manner that limits the force of his work.

The omission of an explicit engagement of fetishism is not a fatal flaw in EPWH, but it does dilute its force, by bypassing the theorization of the workings of power. How people are drawn into colonialism, capitalism, and other forms of power is treated somewhat matter-of-factly. Attention is recurrently given to matters of coercion and violence, without a finer-grained exploration of how authority imposes itself and seduces, matters which the myriad iterations of the fetish concept attempt to illuminate. In his explorations of how power maintains and regenerates itself, Wolf touches on a variety of matters that have figured within theorizations of the fetish concept, including coercion and violence, as well as dispossession, debt peonage, slavery, market discipline, appeals to consanguinity and affinity, control over the reproductive powers of women, and the invocation of supernatural entitlements. These observations provide some insight into processes of domination and social integration/differentiation, but gloss over the mechanics of subordination and fail to provide a more clearly articulated theorization of how power becomes instantiated, a fault which recourse to fetishism may help to rectify. The concealed and underdeveloped presence of fetishism in Wolf yields a historical materialism that largely lacks the 'socio-psychological' element that he points to and praises in Marx (from the contemporary vantage points of environmental studies and political ecology, the 'ecological' is also wanting in Wolf, as it was in Marx).

6   Towards a Political Ecology of Fetishism: Anthropological Value Theory

What do we mean by fetishism here? And how can it inform this hybridizing/differentiating global metabolism, marked by amnesia, that Wolf elegantly analyzes? My understanding of fetishism draws from Marxian anthropological value theory (most closely associated with Terry Turner and David Graeber). Value theory is kindred to Wolf's work, drawing upon many of the virtues of historical materialism discussed above. Value theory emphasizes processes of value production to understand social dynamics and overcome the conceptual impasses of opposing tendencies to focus on structure versus agency, or on materialism versus idealism. It does so by focusing its gaze on the mutual metabolism of materiality, human subjectivities, and value as a way towards conceptually reconciling the relationships between social structure and individual desire. It is premised on a view of productive labour as a creative and dynamic activity, through which people not only subsist and produce goods, but simultaneously produce individual and collective agencies, desires, and values, continuously articulating new conceptions and configurations of autonomy and collectivity (Turner 1986, 2003, 2008; Graeber 2001, 2005, 2013; Sangren and Boyer 2006). Among the virtues of value theory are its relational dynamism and its approach to integrating concerns with agency and structure. Its universalist impulses also help to overcome simplifying proclamations of difference and discontinuity. It is an approach that enables the pursuit of the sort of 'anthropological symmetry' (or 'symmetric anthropology') advocated by Bruno Latour (1991), which ultimately permits a more nuanced appreciation of cultural and epistemological difference and novelty.

I conceptualize my own take on anthropological value theory as a *political ecology of fetishism*, in which specific materialities mystify and legitimate interdependencies between subjectivities. While indebted to a Marxian heritage, this approach also embodies more recent intellectual currents, including practice-oriented approaches (e.g., Bourdieu 1977; Ortner 1984), phenomenological and ontological sensibilities (e.g., Holbraad et al. 2014; Viveiros de Castro 2004, 2011, 2019), and critiques of nature–culture dichotomies (e.g., Latour 1991; Descola and G. Pálsson 1996; Viveiros de Castro 1996), thereby yielding a more fluid and ecological understanding of subjectivity, materiality, value production, and the workings of power, in which fetishisms are understood as dynamic and unstable entities subject to ongoing processes of periodic and exceptional re-mystification. This fetishistic plasticity is envisioned as being catalysed by liminality, with crisis, violence, and trauma being the generative ground of fetishistic transformation.

7 Creative Deceptions

In my reading, fetishism is not a pathology restricted to selected groups of people (capitalists, for example), nor is it something that can be overcome or vanquished. It is a creative deception that is an integral part of human being/becoming, an existential imperative for engaging with our environments in meaningful ways. At a most basic level, I understand fetishism as (social) creativity – a point which Graeber (2001) repeatedly underscores. Fetishism is human creativity, the magical process by which we all imagine, express, and materialize meaning and value. It is a creativity, however, marked by (self and social) deception. Graeber (2001, 69) suggests that fetishism can be understood as the failure to recognize that one is producing value. Fetishism is not just creativity; it entails a failure to see creativity as such. It involves, to some extent, understanding acts of individual or collective creation as the mere reproduction of tradition (or as something external to human individual agency). Fetishistic deception is not simply a lie, however. As Graeber (2001, 60) argues, Marx's fetishism 'was less a theory of false consciousness than a theory of partial consciousness'. This partial consciousness involves not just a reflexive blindness regarding creativity. Its deceitfulness is multidimensional, including metaphysical deception, the artificial imagination of the boundaries and causal relations between beings. The creativity always involves a deceptive crafting of difference (including differentiation of self and environment, and the differentiation of social taxonomies). Marx's understanding of partial consciousness was particularly concerned with understanding the legitimation of inequality, with the 'naturalization' of asymmetrical social relations that are social in origin. Through the sorcery of fetishism, the creative choices of (certain classes of) humans are disguised as necessary, morally transcendent, or divine, via their deceptive displacement in commodities or other magical objects that symbolize and materialize this mystification. I distance myself somewhat from a Marxian understanding of fetishism as a simple 'naturalization' of the social, which rests on problematic oppositions between culturally specific definitions of 'nature' and 'culture', and 'subjects' and 'objects'. Rather than interpreting fetishism as an inversion of 'subjects' and 'objects', I see fetishism as the selective, relational, and asymmetrical/hierarchical accentuation of the subjectivity of specific subject/objects within assemblages of peoples, animals, plants, and other 'things'. Partial consciousness involves a more complex metaphysical creativity than a simple inversion of the 'social' and the 'natural'. This conception resonates with Latour's notion of 'factishes', understood as articulations that intermingle 'facticity' and 'ficticity' in the fabrication of truth and knowledge about the environments in which we engage (Latour 2010). Fetishism condenses fictitious/factitious fantasies of causal metaphysics that both conceal and reveal the workings of the beings that populate the worlds we inhabit and experience.

8 Violence and Self-Determination

Fetishism is not a thing, but a social process. An adequate understanding of fetishism must attend to the 'origins' of fetishes, which I locate in violence. Creative metaphysical deception finds intensified expression in moments of intersubjective contact and friction, the violent liminal spaces of frontiers and moments of crisis. It is worth emphasizing here that the very concept of fetishism materialized within frictive cross-cultural encounters in colonial frontiers (Pietz 1985, 1987, 1988; Morris 2017), emerging in a context of crises of value and the articulation of new social, political, and economic hybridities and interdependencies. The concept of fetishism that this chapter mobilizes places violence front and centre. I understand fetishism as a product of violence, forged through the acute violence of crisis and liminality, and sustained through 'slow violence' (as described by Nixon 2013). The fetish concept, as interpreted and mobilized in this chapter, not only links to the matter of crisis and differentiation discussed above. It also speaks to historical amnesia in important ways. Concealment, repression, and disavowal are vitally generative of fetishisms and their partial consciousness. Fetishism functions in the synchronization of heterogeneous social constellations. It symbolizes and materializes differentiation (and interdependency), sublating contradictions and (feebly) resolving crises, legitimating powerful actors and institutions, and rationalizing the subordination of others. Its powers of seduction involve a double movement of menace and containment of violence, as well as socially selective accentuation or erasure of agencies, histories, contingencies, interconnections, and determinations.

Physical violence is vital to understanding fetishism, but the conception of violence in this chapter encompasses a wider range of phenomena that allow violence to emerge in broader psychosocial, metaphysical, and existential terms, as threats to perceived capacities of self-determination. These can encompass phenomena that we bluntly classify as economic and environmental crises but go beyond these. Violence may be conceived as encounters with the extraordinary or encounters with (socio-environmental) alterity. This focus on violence, and the specific definition of violence as liminality entertained here, is important not only for understanding the contextual origins of fetishism, but the allure of fetishes, whose power resides precisely in their (illusory) promise of preserving or amplifying capacities for self-determination undermined by the spectre of violence.

At the core of the creative metaphysical deceptions of fetishism is the distortion and hierarchization of capacities for self-determination. Fetishism is an expression of resilient acclimatization, oriented by a will to preserve and/or enlarge powers of self-determination, which is manifested in encounters with existential violence. These encounters unsettle our contradictory distinctions between 'nature' and 'culture', 'self' and 'other', 'subject' and 'object', undermining the veracity and limits of our capacities for self-determination, which become embodied in fetishes that sublate these contradictions and redefine our sense of self-determination. These observations add important texture to our understandings of the origins and workings of the historical amnesia and the selective erasure of agencies that Wolf emphasizes in his analysis of global metabolism.

9   Unearthing Fetishism

Understanding the complexities of social integration/differentiation, benefits from a synthetic attention to crisis, violence, and historical amnesia, matters that are already unified within the fetish concept. Fetishism is a missing link in Wolf's anthropological historical materialism that offers a point of more potent synthesis of the somewhat fragmented virtues of Wolf's powerful work. Relatedly, Wolf's own disavowal of fetishism is arguably linked to his own fetishized distinction between capitalism and its others. As much as he unsettles entrenched distinctions between societies, he also maintains and erects boundaries between different modes of production that inhibit a more thorough appreciation for our shared and fully interdependent humanities. Despite critically mucking up the distinctions and boundaries between capitalist and non-capitalist societies, he ultimately emphasizes the exceptionalism of capitalism in a way that clouds a more thorough attempt at acknowledging our shared and interconnected humanity. Wolf's historical materialism brilliantly urges us to attend to the points of sociocultural contact and friction as shifting, contested, and fragile symbioses. The notion of a political ecology of fetishism aims to deepen our understanding of the fabrication of authority and workings of power in these symbioses, through explicitly linking crisis with fetishistic socio-environmental differentiation. Taking up fetishism in this manner provides a productive means to explore the tensions more deeply between creativity and constraint, resistance and domination, and agency and structure that are the ultimate focus of Wolf's intellectual project (and anthropology more generally).

The foregoing discussions provide a sketch of the conceptual approach that tacitly animates the political ecology of socio-environmental unpredictability and resilience along the Discovery Coast and beyond, and can serve as the foundation for an engagement with wider pertinent debates about precarity (e.g., Munck 2013; Millar 2017), the socio-environmental dynamics of frontier spaces (e.g., Rasmussen and Lund 2018; Campbell 2015); indigenous and rural resistance (e.g, Turner 1995, 1999; Martínez-Allier 1990; Pahnke et al. 2015; Hall et al. 2015; Hecht 2011, 2014), and environmental vulnerability/resilience (Fabinyi et al. 2014; Tsing, 2015). In the subsequent empirical analysis, this political ecology of fetishism manifests itself subconsciously in the details and phenomena to which this chapter turns its attentions (e.g., violence, creativity, social hybridization/differentiation, commodification of nature and labour, and self-determination), rather than being a formulation that overshadows the discussion (which, arguably, makes the author guilty of the same sins attributed to Wolf).

10   Historical and Contemporary Hybridities in the Discovery Coast Region: Crisis and Socio-environmental Transformation

It is beyond the scope of this chapter to provide a detailed political ecology of the Discovery Coast stretching back to colonial times. Instead, some brief observations of three historical moments – the late sixteenth century, the late eighteenth century, and the mid-twentieth century – that are marked by intensified socio-environmental transformation, that have been formative turning points in relation to indigenous policies, resource use and management, economic development models, and global interconnectivity, which are taken to be elements of a singular process of cultural change and value transformation. These are moments marked by violence and the emergence of new forms of fetishism and novel paradigms of social differentiation. They are moments of intensified cultural hybridization, and of social amnesia and marginalization. The historical review that follows privileges these liminal moments, not only because they have yielded lasting influences on social configurations and the landscape of the region, but also because each provides a privileged nexus for observing simultaneous processes of rupture and continuity in strategies and practices of socio-environmental resilience in the face of heightened uncertainty. In other words, they are strategically selected for their potential as microcosms for the underlying project of this chapter: rethinking political ecology in the context of contemporary crisis.

11 Early Colonial Period: Epidemic Crises and the Salvation of Wildness

In the late sixteenth century, epidemic outbreaks decimated the fledgling Portuguese colony, dependent on indigenous labour and expertise for dyewood extraction, sugarcane plantations, medicinals, and food provisioning.[4] In this moment, a novel administrative paradigm was established for integrating indigenous peoples and 'wild' nature into global markets. The perceived wildness of indigenous humanity and nature figured in the circumscription of indigenous agency to extractive sectors and spaces of the economy (and to a subservience to Jesuit paternalism in planned villages called *aldeias*).[5] In this context, a socio-environmental paradigm congealed in the Discovery Coast region that would largely persist until the end of the eighteenth century. The region remained one of the most 'wild' portions of coastal Brazil,[6]

---

4 Key texts that cover the history of the Pataxó include Agostinho (1972, 1974, 1980), Carvalho (1977, 2005), and Sampaio (2000). Paraíso (1991, 1994), and Vainfas (2005) cover important aspects of the colonial history of Indigenous people in southern Bahia.
5 Key works on environmental history of Brazil that inform this historical summary include Warren Dean's (1995) seminal work, as well as Schwartz (1985), Delson and Dickenson (1984), Miller (2000a, 2000b, 2003), and Pádua (2000, 2010, 2015).
6 For important critiques of the concept of 'wilderness' and its role in rendering the subjectivity of Indigenous people invisible see Diegues (1996) and Gomez-Pompa and Kaus (1992).

with a socio-environmental landscape characterized by an assemblage of forests, indigenous peoples, and missionary settlements, whose primary vocation in the colonial economy was the provisioning of extractive goods, including Brazil wood, the first important South American commodity for the Portuguese, which continued to be highly valued throughout colonial times. Indigenous communities inhabiting the region included autonomous settlements that ranged from more sedentary agriculture to nomadic hunter gatherer groups, as well as those in the missionary settlements. The boundaries between nomadic and sedentary groups appear to have been rather nebulous with seasonal movement between settlements and shifting settlement densities being commonplace. Indigenous peoples engaged in subsistence activities, as well as others directed towards trade, including manioc cultivation, logging of dyewood and other timbers, timber transport, harvesting of *drogas do sertão* ('backland drugs'),[7] and harvesting of estuarine food sources (i.e., crabs, molluscs, and fish), which yielded goods that were traded with missionaries, settlers, and soldiers.

Those within the *aldeia* system engaged in subsistence activities to support themselves and the missionaries. They also produced commercial goods, especially wood, wood products, and medicinals, with *aldeia* systems coming to occupy a unique and important niche within the colonial economy (Prieto 2011; Walker 2013) – one that was not only economically distinctive, but inherently unique spatially, environmentally, and socially. In addition to working in missionary settlements, indigenous peoples were subject to coerced labour and slavery. The Crown, the Church, and other elites of colonial civilization (merchants, for example) depended on the 'savage' peoples and places for their power and influence, despite the devaluation and invisibilization of indigenous labour, expertise, techniques, and technologies. In the *aldeia* system, indigenous peoples received certain rights and privileges, however circumscribed by their perceived wildness.[8] Indigenous peoples were granted humanity, rights, and even political agency even in the early colonial period. Similarly, their expert knowledge of plants, animals, and nature was also more widely acknowledged and valued than we tend to assume in hindsight. Importantly, during the early colonial period the boundaries between *aldeia* and non-*aldeia* Indians were ever porous. Permanent flight and temporary relocation of varying extents was common among *aldeia* Indians. Indigenous peoples engaged

---

7   A term to denote wild medicinals, that was also used as a general term for extractive goods, including timbers (but the term excluded brazilwood, at least as used by officials).

8   Both Metcalf (1999, 2005, 2014) and De Almeida (2014) explore the functioning of *aldeias*, with the latter providing valuable insights into the politics of land and resources.

in a continuous process of acclimatization to a dynamic, social, economic, and environmental matrix, in ways that sought resiliently to secure subsistence, wellbeing, safety, and a palatable balance between perceived autonomy from and dependency upon different colonial actors.[9]

12 Late Colonial Period: Enlightening Indigenous Nature and Culture

Between the mid-eighteenth and early nineteenth centuries, the socio-environmental paradigm established in the two centuries earlier underwent considerable changes, while maintaining important continuities. The late colonial era was a formative period for Brazil with regard to indigenous policies; conservation policies; conceptions of private property and economic liberalism; and the definition of Brazilian nationhood during a period of intensifying global interconnections. The era was marked by a considerable expansion of Brazilian shipbuilding and intensified crown interest in, and control of, the timber trade. Deforestation and its impacts on timber and fuel stocks and soil quality, as well as incipient concerns about links between deforestation and climate change, led to a more systematic articulation of conservation policies and institutions (that were highly contentious among plantation owners and those benefiting from the timber trade).[10] Reflecting broader trends in early modern science, official preoccupations with resource depletion were accompanied by intensified efforts to diversify colonial agricultural and extractive activities (which looked to indigenous expertise and techniques), impulses that also meshed with the pursuit of economic growth and competitiveness within global trade. Not coincidentally, at around the same time efforts intensified to civilize Indians and to transform them into agricultural and extractive labour. These civilizing efforts were refashioned, becoming more secularized and drawing on liberal principles and other emergent enlightenment ideals.[11]

---

9   For an insightful discussion of indigenous mobility in colonial Brazil see Roller (2014).
10 For discussion of the colonial history of forest policies and the timber industry see Morton (1978) and Miller (2000a, 2000b). In Miller (2000a) there is also valuable discussion of the role of indigenous labour and expertise in logging. For broader discussion of environmental history and the conservation concerns evident in late colonial Brazil see Dean (1995) and Delson and Dickenson (1984). Pádua (2000) provides an insightful analysis of late colonial conservation concerns and policies in the Portuguese empire, and their links to broader political, economic, and intellectual transformations.
11 Discussion on the shifts in indigenous policies, the Jesuit expulsion, and the secularization of indigenous administration in Brazil can be found in Cunha (2012), Roller (2014), Bieber (2014), and Langfur and De Resende (2014). For discussion of how these changes uniquely manifested within southern Bahia see Santos (2014), Cancela (2013), Barickman

The region of southern Bahia was one of the main foci of Indian 'domestication' efforts, logging activities, and conservation efforts.

The *aldeia* system became secularized with the expulsion of the Jesuits (1759) and with the creation of new royal policies (*Diretório dos Indios*), and local policies (*Instruções para o governo dos índio da Capitania de Porto Seguro*) for governing indigenous peoples and *aldeia* systems. These policies explicitly stimulated miscegenation and aimed for integration of indigenous peoples within Luso-Brazilian society. They also provided instructions to transform them into a sedentary agricultural peasantry, engaged in producing market goods, through measures defining *aldeia* land rights and detailed expectations regarding indigenous agricultural activities and their productivity (including specifications of crops and amounts of each crop), that sought to regiment their labour in economically productive ways, and to 'improve' the colonial economy.

The changes enabled predations on land holdings of indigenous peoples, increasingly coveted by the crown and private interests for their agricultural use and valuable timber stocks. In critiquing crown timber policies and defending their own land claims, private land holders even argued that areas inhabited by indigenous people should be the primary focus of crown timber operations, invoking in the same breath emergent liberal conceptions of private property rights and the notion that indigenous areas were wild, without demographic status, with land and resources free for the taking,[12] [13] (a contradictory and self-serving invocation of liberal principles often echoed in contemporary discussions of rural development, conservation, and 'traditional' resource rights). As elegantly analysed by Barickman (1995), oppositions between 'wild' and 'tame' Indians guided the differentiated and precarious granting of rights, with notions of degrees of wildness circumscribing the rights of 'tame' Indians and their value within rural political and economic structures.

As before, indigenous mobility was a constant, with flight from *aldeais* commonplace, and fluid seasonal, temporary, and permanent movement between different *aldeias*, autonomous indigenous settlements, mixed settlements, and plantations. The period was marked by intensified violence and

---

(1995), and Langfur (2005, 2006, 2014a, 2014b). Sommer (2014) provides invaluable insights into the changing political agency of indigenous peoples in late colonial Brazil.

[12] See Morton (1978), Miller (2000a), and Pádua (2000) for discussion of the backlash against crown conservation efforts.

[13] See Campbell (2015) for a more general overview of the evolution (and fluidity) of property systems, property logics, and property-making in Brazil.

extermination of indigenous peoples deemed to be 'wild', especially after 1808 following the relocation of the monarchical seat to Brazil and the official declaration of a 'Just War'. This proclamation sought to speed up efforts to domesticate Southern Bahia and other parts of Brazil (e.g., the Amazon), transforming and revaluating its forests into agricultural and extractive commodities. In the aftermath of the 'Just War' and up until the 1940s the Discovery Coast remained largely undeveloped, an anomaly for coastal Brazil. Indigenous resistance, combined with political transformations, changing economic and geographic priorities (for example, the coffee boom in the south-east), and changes to labour paradigms (for example, the abolition of slavery and the shift towards European immigrants), resulted in the petering out of the ambitious plans of the late colonial period to transform the landscape and economy of the Discovery Coast. In its wake there flourished a more modest transformation of the region into a site of cattle ranching, cacao cultivation, and extractive activities. In this period, some of the forest and agricultural products valued within local (and global) markets shifted, and the quantity and configuration of labour demands, and opportunities changed. But subsistence and market hybridity and seasonality remained consistent, as did seasonal, temporary, and permanent migration within the region and beyond. The *aldeia* system persisted for some time, with *aldeia* lands increasingly subject to predation and dissolution, through illegal measures and local political machinations. *Aldeia* Indians continued to engage in a mix of subsistence and market activities, including volunteer or coerced labour on cacao farms, on cattle ranches, in lumbering operations, and in other extractive activities. The boundaries between indigenous, *mestiço*, and Afro-Brazilian communities further blurred in this period, as novel land use practices and the abolition of slavery brought new immigrants to the region (Agostinho 1972, 1974; Sampaio 2000; Carvalho 1977). The region remained heavily forested up until the 1940s, being considered one of the most environmentally 'pristine' portions of Brazil's coast and its Mata Altântica (Atlantic Forests).

13 The Discovery Coast in the Anthropocene: Developing Nature and Culture

Around the mid-twentieth century, the region began to undergo a series of more radical socio-environmental transformations. Highway construction, informed by developmentalist mentalities, brought a wave of highly predatory logging, cattle ranching, and land speculation that swiftly transmuted most of the region's forests into pastureland within a few decades.[14] New immigrants came to the region, cities expanded, and new towns were established. Following this initial wave of deforestation, immigration, and economic change, in the final decades of the twentieth century the economy shifted towards tourism and eucalyptus plantations. With the changes of the mid- to late-twentieth century, indigenous and 'traditional' peoples were subject to a rapid process of dispossession (often accompanied by physical violence), which led to spatial reconfigurations of rural communities, alterations in subsistence activities, and changes in labour opportunities and engagements. At the same time, new forms of political subjectivity emerged, as indigenous and 'traditional' peoples sought to secure and defend rights to land, resources, and public services. There was a resurgence of indigenous communities, with the Federal government coming to officially acknowledge some communities and their land claims (as well as some of the land claims of landless peasants).[15] In the case of the Pataxó, their resurgence was precipitated by their dispossession by loggers, ranchers, *and* the National Park Service. The latter displaced communities for the establishment of the Monte Pascoal National Park, a monument to Brazil's 'discovery' and its natural bounty (created in the 1940s but only practically materialized starting in the 1960s). In the ensuing decades, the Pataxó and environmental agencies have endured a tense and at times violent relationship animated by competing land claims and valuations of nature.[16] In 1999, on the eve of the quincentennial celebration of Brazil's 'discovery', the Pataxó occupied the National Park, proclaiming themselves the rightful stewards of its land and resources. This was a critical socio-political and environmental juncture in Pataxó history that has been formative for them

---

14   For more on the rapid deforestation of the Atlantic Coastal Forest in the twentieth century see Dean (1995). Pádua (2015) provides useful discussion about distinct temporal patterns of deforestation of Atlantic forests and Amazon forest in the Anthropocene.

15   Increased acknowledgement of the rights of indigenous and 'traditional' peoples began in the waning years of the military dictatorship, especially after the establishment of the new constitution in 1988 and the subsequent strengthening of legal institutions and mechanisms for the pursuit of constitutional rights. Despite overall progress in the 1990s and 2000s, for many indigenous and 'traditional' peoples the realization of constitutional rights and other legislation falls far short of their promise and presumed intention. Hochstetler and Keck (2007) provide an excellent overview of the evolution of these environmental politics. For an overview of socio-environmental politics in the 2000s, with an emphasis on the gains and contradictions of the PT years, see de Castro (2014) and de Castro and Motta (2015).

16   For more on the history of Pataxó land rights struggles and tensions with environmental agencies, see Azenha (2005), Agostinho (1980), Carvalho (1977, 2009), and Sampaio (2000).

as citizens, political actors, and environmental activists. In the wake of the Pataxó counter-appropriation of the Park, a relatively more collaborative (yet still abrasive) relationship was established between the Pataxó, the Ministry of the Environment, and environmental NGOs through a variety of 'participatory' management projects animated by global discourses of biodiversity conservation, sustainable development and, increasingly, climate change prevention and mitigation.[17]

14   Contemporary Struggles over Nature

In parallel, over the last three decades, rural semi-subsistence communities have been caught up in struggles over land as the region's economy has shifted from cattle ranching and logging to monocultural fruit production, tourism, and eucalyptus production. Coastal portions of the region have witnessed an aggressive process of real estate speculation and development, while huge swathes of land further inland have been transmuted into eucalyptus plantations that have come to dominate the landscape (they supply pulp manufacturing factories that produce toilet paper and other export-oriented paper products). These have radically transformed rural communities in myriad ways. Markets for agricultural and extractive products have been altered substantially. Labour opportunities and seasonal dynamics have been transformed. These new (highly globalized) economies increased the value of lands and patterns of property ownership, pushing out rural communities through legal and extra-legal means (at times involving hired guns).

Tourism and eucalyptus production have also precipitated substantial environmental changes. There are intensified resource demands and increased pollution from tourism. Heightened energy demands from tourist towns and industry have been accompanied by hydroelectric dam construction, disturbing aquatic systems. Climate and hydrology have been modified by the eucalyptus forests. Many of these environmental changes are disruptive of the subsistence and market-oriented resource use of indigenous and 'traditional' peoples, with impacts on their agricultural and extractive activities that bring new forms of uncertainty and precarity. Importantly, tourism and the managed forest industry both depend directly on the environment and mobilize environmental discourses, framing their practices as aligned with the goals

---

[17]   The history of the occupation of the park and the ensuing politics of 'participatory' management are covered in Azenha (2005).

of biodiversity conservation, climate change control, and sustainable development. Their commitments to sustainable development (and those of the government policies that enable them) are articulated through fictitious/factitious narratives about nature and culture marked by omissions and erasures. Their discourses of economic growth, job creation, and sustainability are characterized by selective readings of environmental sustainability and by social taxonomies that marginalize the values, agency, and histories of the inhabitants of the region.

This brings us back to the Pataxó dynamics described at the start of this chapter, in which hybrid strategies – subsistence, market, and political – are employed as they seek to carve out a sense of autonomous resilience in a context marked by gross inequities in wealth, political and legal capital, and resource rights. In this context, too, neoliberal notions of property, economically productive labour, multiculturalism, and sustainable development have come to permeate struggles over nature. Neoliberalism has not, however, yielded a simple hegemony, as it intermingles (at global, national, and local levels) with older notions of developmentalism and traditional rural political and economic forms, yielding dynamics that are often a pale reflection of the idealized liberal free market. As in the past, conceptions of wildness continue to circumscribe the value of indigenous agency and their social, economic, and political subjectivities as they engage in struggles over land, nature, and livelihood. In the context of the growth of tourism and forest plantation industries described above, Pataxó efforts to create, protect, and expand official indigenous territories have been mired in protracted legal battles with elite actors who seek to undermine the legitimacy of their economic, historical, cultural, and environmental claims.

A central and unresolved element of Pataxó socio-environmental struggles has been their attempts to secure legal recognition of their territorial claims, a process that stretches back to the 1970s and which has resulted in the 2008 recommendation on the part of the Federal Indigenous Affairs Agency (FUNAI) to establish a Pataxó territory; however, the territory has yet to come to fruition – undermined by a lack of political will and the competing land claims of influential actors (including the Ministry of the Environment and land claimants in the forestry, tourism, and agribusiness industries). In these political struggles, the authenticity of the Pataxó and the legitimacy of their land and resource claims are continuously diminished, in ways that critically dialogue with notions of the 'ecologically noble savage' and draw upon other perennial tropes of 'savagery' (fickleness, laziness, backwardness, etc.) that have been long conjured up to rationalize violence, dispossession, the regimentation of productive labour, and the imposition of asymmetrical social, political, and economic interdependencies.

With the political and economic crisis of recent years in Brazil, the resurgence of a developmentalist logic towards rural nature and culture – one without regard for the equity and environmental concerns of sustainable development – has eroded the rights of 'traditional' peoples, through enabling and intensifying dispossession, dismantling forms of participatory governance, and delegitimating environmental regulations. This has involved the accentuation of discourses of wildness and an intensified historical amnesia that erases 'peripheral' agencies and socio-environmental interdependencies. In these processes of politico-economic struggle and differentiation, we see the material consequences of the sorts of forgetting that Wolf's critiques in his analysis of 'people without history'.

15 Historical Socio-environmental Continuities

Considering the above pivotal socio-environmental moments in the political ecology of the Discovery Coast, it is worth highlighting some key commonalities and continuities that link the past to the contemporary. In each of the (liminal) moments described we see a substantial re-valuation of peoples and nature, novel forms of socio-environmental differentiation precipitated by violence. They are marked by changing valuations of nature, the creation and reformulation of commodities (that is, fetishes), the reformulation of possessive regimes (and their social inequalities), and the articulation of novel taxonomies of labour. There are broadly similar processes in which expanding commodity frontiers precipitate liminal spaces that are generative of new fetishes, values, subjectivities, and terms of interconnectedness. These new creations are (asymmetrically) hybrid affairs, with commodities, notions of freedom, and political institutions being actively and reactively shaped by indigenous labour, expertise, and values (despite the elision of indigenous agency in colonial, academic, and popular accounts). European encounters with the human and ecological 'wildness' of Brazilian frontiers shaped, and continue to shape, 'global' understandings of nature, humanity, and liberalism.

These moments are also animated by misleading narratives of improvement and growth, with their elusive (and asymmetrical) promise of amplifying capacities for self-determination. There exists a continuity of liberatory discourses of progress tied to the shifting magical commodities of different eras. Despite surface differences, essentially similar Eurocentric discourses of progress are evident. From the early colonial discourses of spiritual salvation to the more secularized ones of economic improvement in the later colonial era, the mid-twentieth-century ones of development, and the more recent neoliberal ones of sustainable development, there is a deceptive appeal to a collective and transcendent moral order that holds the potential for amplifying self-determination. In other words, a similar political ecology of fetishism is evident in these different moments in which particular (hybrid) beings, 'things', and institutions become valorized and enchant heterogeneous peoples with the promise of an illusory liberatory empowerment rooted in metaphysical insufficiencies, thereby legitimating hierarchical social differences.

Besides these overarching ideological and metaphysical contours shaped by discourses of integration and betterment, there are many other continuities. Throughout these moments, we can see important continuities in the ways indigenous peoples were perceived and treated; the ways in which they acclimatized to shifting socio-material environments; and the ways in which they sought to exert a sense of self-determination. The following chart summarizes some recurrent features of indigenous being and integration in this region.

15.1   General Social Attributes
- High volume and frequency of mobility, and malleable social formations.
- Indigenous interdependence with global markets and political institutions (albeit peripheral and shifting).

15.2   Resource Management and Use
- Hybrid, diverse, and dynamic subsistence, and market engagements.
- Marked seasonality to agricultural and extractive activities.
- Subsistence centred around manioc agricultural systems.
- Market engagement via manioc flour, timber products, and other extractive goods.

15.3   Labour and Expertise
- Public and private demand for, and dependence upon, indigenous labour and expertise (for agriculture, extractive activities, construction, and security).
- Acknowledgement of the importance of indigenous labour and expertise, combined with devaluation and concealment of the extent of dependency.
- The existence of coerced labour and efforts to regiment indigenous forms of labour to be more 'productive'.
- Strong seasonality in labour demands/opportunities.

15.4 Socio-environmental Governance and the Politics of Difference

- Gaps between formal policies and actual practices (including social, labour, and environmental policies).
- 'Differentiated citizenship' and deep inequalities in access to rights, goods, and political influence.
- The official recognition of indigenous liberties, economic rights, and political agency, which in practice are nebulous and volatile.
- Assimilationist impulses tied to political and economic aspirations of government and other actors (animated by differentiated conceptions of subjectivity and productive agency).
- Dispossession and precarious indigenous dominion over land and resources, due to admixtures of discriminatory policies, chicanery, and violence.
- Discourses of wildness that rationalize dispossession and the exercise of violence.
- Conceptions of primitive alterity that underscore wildness, ignorance, fickleness, and sloth (perceived as circumscribing the social, economic, and political agencies of indigenous peoples).

16 Resilient Acclimatization and Hybridity

Throughout the history of this region, indigenous peoples have struggled with a process of integration marked by contested and asymmetrical terms of interdependence. This integration has been characterized by ongoing processes of socio-environmental differentiation, in which the dynamic articulation of social roles and relations goes together with processes of diversification in resource use and human intercourse with nature. This process of socio-environmental differentiation has been animated by frictive projects of resilient acclimatization of different actors, whose (tenuous) reconciliation is marked by asymmetrical powers to materialize competing projects of resilient acclimatization. Indigenous peoples in these different moments of history similarly have had to grapple with navigating desires for food and goods, land and resource access, markets in labour and goods, and the avoidance (or minimization) of coercion and violence. In reconciling these different desires and challenges, and in seeking to carve out a sense of autonomy, among the most important and recurrent attributes of indigenous strategies of resilient acclimatization are: 1) diversified resource use; 2) mobility; and 3) selectivity in social interdependencies.

Indigenous peoples have employed hybrid and highly dynamic subsistence and market engagement strategies, that defy their simple classification as agriculturalists, extractivists, and labourers. Diversified resource use, anchored by specific organisms that are particularly robust and resilient, has been a prominent strategy for sustainable existence. More specifically, manioc derivatives, wood-based products, estuarine resources, and the expertise to materialize them into valued forms, have been consistent elements of indigenous (and *mestiço*) ruralities. These have remained consistent pillars of frontier existence, sustaining indigenous communities and mediating their intercourse with wider Brazilian (and global) society, in a context of the shifting commodification of local nature. Importantly, manioc production, timber harvesting, and the harvesting of estuarine fauna are not isolated one-dimensional activities, but the most salient and valued elements of versatile, hybrid, and multifaceted systems of production/ management/harvesting that materialize a variety of valuable beings and things and are contingent on systemic environmental expertise. Understood in this way, manioc, timber, and estuarine fauna have been resilient assets for acclimatizing to the social, political, economic, and environmental indeterminacies that have characterized the contested spaces they have inhabited.

Hybridity is also manifest in mobility and the forms of social interdependencies. Mobility has also been a vital asset for resilient acclimatization to the socio-environmental vicissitudes of the Discovery Coast, past and present. It is a strategy that not only aims at securing resources that are seasonally and annually variable, but at reconciling impulses for a sense of autonomy with the desire for social interdependencies that are perceived as secure, fulfilling, and relatively symmetrical. Indigenous mobility and diversified resource use are tied to another main element in the repertoire of resilient acclimatization, the forging of strategic social interdependencies: that is, the development of selective and dynamic alliances and solidarities with other actors that have overlapping or allied interests and values (other indigenous ethnic groups, for example, missionaries, Afro-Brazilian and *mestiço* 'squatters', soldiers, environmentalists, tourism industry actors, and even plantation and ranch owners). Notably, these interdependencies serve as essential nodes in processes of transculturation and the articulation of innovative socio-environmental hybridities. Indigenous mobility, strategic social interdependencies, and their primary resource use preferences have been essential strategies for resilience in spaces that have, and continue to be marked by contested claims to indigenous territories and the flora, fauna, soils, and other biophysical resources therein, as well as contested claims to indigenous labour and expertise. Together, these three elements may be conceived of as complementary aspects of the pursuit of resilient socio-environmental interdependencies.

In underscoring indigenous strategies and practices of resilient acclimatization the motivation is not simply trying to point out and valorize indigenous resistance, but to draw attention to its socio-environmental nuances. It also aims to encourage a greening of our understanding of resistance, while problematizing the romanticization of both resistance and indigenous environmental knowledge. Indigenous (and other 'traditional' peoples) have a long and dynamic tradition of social and environmental sustainability, understood not within a romantic framework of perfectly calibrated, harmonious relationships between largely static traditions and a largely inert nature trapped in some sort of homeostatic regulation, but as eternally creative strategies for the resilient pursuit of subsistence, wellbeing, and a palatable balance between autonomy from, and interdependence with, wider social, political, economic, and environmental processes. It is a resilient acclimatization that is simultaneously and inseparably environmental, social, and existential. Subsistence resources and commodified agricultural/extractive goods are both similarly involved in the pursuit of a sense of self-determination, albeit tied to somewhat distinctive ideas of self-determination, and embedded in different imagined collective goods. But these are never entirely distinctive; they are involved within the creation of novel hybrid understandings of self-determination and transcendence (at local and global scales).

17 Discontinuities and the Exceptional Political Ecology of the Anthropocene

In emphasizing continuous, yet evolving, structural contours and 'traditions' of resilient acclimatization my point is not to trivialize difference and historical change, but to depart from a greater appreciation of similarities and continuities, essential for a mindful understanding of emergent challenges. The point is not to gloss over discontinuity and difference, but to decentre some of the habits critical scholarship has developed regarding the appraisal of discontinuity and difference. It is important that we encourage novel ways of recognizing, highlighting, and interpreting the emergent. Too often, the rhetoric of contemporary exceptionalism focuses our gaze on the wrong sorts of transformations, or exaggerates their significance, which distracts analysis from more productive critical reflections on the meaning and nature of recent environmental, social, and economic changes. Despite the foregoing emphasis on continuities, there are important ways in which the contemporary distinguishes itself from

the past. Since the mid-twentieth century, salient changes that are essential to understanding changing ruralities and forms of socio-environmental resilience in southern Bahia have included:
- Population growth and increased urbanization (including tourists, seasonal inhabitants who place novel and intensified resource demands).
- Acute intensification of deforestation and resource demands (for local and extra-local consumption).
- The specific admixture of natural resources demands and commodification.
- Relatively intensified levels of land concentration, and changing terms of the globalization of land ownership and concentration (although globalized land concentration is not itself novel).
- Transformations in the nature and forms of resolving land conflicts and 'conjuring property'[18] (but not necessarily a generalized intensification of conflicts and violence).
- More erratic patterns of climate change variability (which have arguably exacerbated the unpredictability of natural resource management, extractive activities, and agriculture).
- Unprecedented intensity and immediacy of interdependency with extra-local socio-economic and political currents (although global interdependency itself is arguably timeless).

In parallel with these socio-environmental transformations, political institutions and rights have changed, opening new possibilities for exerting political agency as well as hemming in others. Recent decades have been marked by articulations of 'insurgent citizenship' that have changed the socio-political dynamics of environmental governance and rural development.[19] More productive understandings of how these varied and complex trends are shaping emergent ruralities is enabled by an awareness of longer-term dynamics of hybrid forms of resilient acclimatization articulated by 'traditional' peoples and elite actors. A crucial point to underscore is that many or most of the more recent developments listed above can be seen as differences in degree rather than kind, accentuations, and elaborations of existing phenomena, rather than radical breaks with the past. An overemphasis on the Anthropocene, late capitalism, and/or neoliberalism as radical ruptures with the past, can obscure historical lessons and mystify our understandings of the emergent in deeply problematic ways.

---

18   I borrow this notion from Campbell (2015).
19   Hecht (2011, 203) usefully frames the critique of development as an articulation of 'insurgent citizenship'.

18 Revisiting the Political Ecology of Fetishism: beyond Radical Alterities

The analytical approach developed here is concerned with two related matters. One is the emphasis on radical historical rupture, which draws upon and reinforces a historical amnesia. The second, is the emphasis on radical difference. Both may be conceived as affirmations of radical alterity, one diachronic and the other synchronic. Although these may be regarded as distinct, they are ultimately related constructs. Wolf's work articulates this link between historical erasure and the erection of artificial boundaries that elide interdependencies, serving as the basis for his advocacy for a more relational perspective. Similarly, Latour (1991) has cogently argued that the 'great divide' of modernity also operates in the affirmation of epistemological difference in the present. Both variants of radical alterity simplify in ways that undermine more empathetic, symmetrical, and relational approaches to political ecology and environmental anthropology. By overstating or perverting cultural and epistemological alterity and misconstruing the exceptional uncertainties and other trends of the contemporary, the pursuit of a Latourian 'symmetrical anthropology' is inhibited, thereby instantiating and legitimating asymmetrical interdependencies. In the zeal to call attention to the profound socio-environmental injustices of the present, we often resort to alarmist and hyperbolic assessments that emphasize the exceptional dynamics of the present. These cloud our understandings of continuities and discontinuities, and the subtle textures of similitude and difference in the present, unsettling long-term thinking about uncertainty, vulnerability, and resilience, which is essential for imagining sustainable futures. Historical amnesia is conceptually and empirically connected to tendencies to emphasize radical difference in the social and environmental struggles of the contemporary world.

The approach taken in this chapter seeks to encourage novel ways to conceptualize frontier spaces that complicate our understandings of rural dialectics and the expansion of global capitalism and provide a more subtly textured reading of the shifting configurations of the state, the market, civil society, and rural communities. By attenuating radical alterities, this analysis aims to yield a nuanced attention to continuities *and* discontinuities, seeking to avoid overly simplistic claims about, and critiques of, the nature of neoliberalism and its impact and influence on indigenous, 'traditional', and other rural communities. This approach also aims to question and temper common oppositions between 'local' peoples and 'global' forces, such as those between particularity versus universality, stasis versus creativity/dynamism, traditionality versus liberalism, authenticity versus inauthenticity, resistance and power, communal ethos versus individualism, and holistic interdependence with nature versus alienation from nature.

My desires to attenuate these oppositions – and the simplistic romanticization and demonization in which they are ingrained – are not merely theoretical concerns. They are rooted in pragmatic considerations. These oppositions shape the valuation of rural expertise and taint the terms of epistemological contrast and integration in development policies and projects, affecting the goals of environmental initiatives and struggles over rights to land and resource use. The persistent notions of ecological nobility and precapitalist purity built into these oppositions are deeply problematic (Conklin and Graham 1995; Nadasdy 1999). For example, similar oppositions are mobilized in circumscribing the agency and value of 'peripheral' peoples (and nature) in rural development and sustainable development policies and practices, as this chapter has sought to demonstrate in its empirical analysis of the political ecology of the Discovery Coast. These oppositions can be especially thorny when it comes to *mestiço* and other non-indigenous rural actors – or indigenous actors whose authenticity is questioned, as is the case of the Pataxó – whose visible and palpable hybridity can come to signify inauthenticity and a sort of congenital complicity with the environmentally deleterious will of market forces and liberal ideologies, thereby devalorizing their expertise and agency within sustainable development. Importantly, these categories of people make up much of the rural poor in Brazil, Latin America, and globally.

Vitally, these oppositions also create mythologized understandings of neoliberalism and scientific rationalism that disguise their contradictions, inconsistencies, and hybridities. The common depictions of commodity fetishism and *homo economicus*, for example, do not quite capture the experience and exercise of contemporary liberal 'individualism' (in global 'peripheries' *and* 'centres'), which depart in good measure from their caricaturized versions in critical scholarship. These caricatures – and the immature anti-fetishism with which they are often connected – have demonstrated limited power to delegitimize or practically curtail resource hoarding, dispossession, land concentration, coercive and exploitative labour practices, and other forms of acute and slow socio-environmental violence. In Brazil, for example, there are indications that these have been reinvigorated in the last few years. The conventional scholarly and activist practice of unmasking and demystifying commodity and techno-scientific fetishisms appears to be a mere parlour game, without the requisite power to substantially transform the profound allure of the magical socio-environmental asymmetries they aspire to undo.

These depictions of neoliberalism and scientific rationalism are figments of anthropological myth making, entities that ultimately undermine the agency of 'primitive' others. Depicting indigenous and rural peoples as idealized foils to the figment of neoliberalism forged within academic imaginaries contributes to the undermining of their political agency and to prospects of sustainable development. These simplistic and stark distinctions reproduce romantic notions of incommensurability, inhibiting anthropological symmetry between the 'modern' and the 'primitive' in both scholarly literature and in contexts where development projects are conjured up and materialized.

The moral registers of the oppositions discussed may be somewhat distinct and seemingly at odds in scholarly and development contexts, but they share fundamental ideas about interdependence, hybridity, and self-determination. Although seemingly different, these are kindred creative deceptions, with similar metaphysical insufficiencies, that depend upon and mobilize similar notions of self-determination, and that are rooted in similar existential violence. Critiques of these oppositions should not be misconstrued as a facile critique of Western or Eurocentric binary thinking. Binary thinking is something both 'moderns' *and* 'primitives' do (and which I continue to fall back upon in this chapter). Binary thinking is a universal aspect of human faculties (it is fluid and unstable, and overlaps with other forms of categorization, yet contrastive rationality is part of our shared humanity). These oppositions are not creations of false consciousness, but of partial consciousness, which provide the scaffolding for more synthetic forms of magical deception to which we have alluded.

19 Fetishism, Global Environmental Crisis, and Resilient Acclimatization

The approach and arguments developed in this chapter seek to help shift the ways we conceptualize processes of value creation and the reproduction of politico-economic asymmetries in global frontiers, through articulating a political ecology that foregrounds a more radical and universalist understanding of interdependency. Viewing neoliberal agencies and 'traditional' peoples inhabiting global frontiers as relational subjectivities, as hybrid actors within global networks, obliges a fuller appreciation of their dialogical interdependencies. A fuller appreciation of the plasticity and porosity that has long characterized relations between global 'centres' and 'peripheries' – as Wolf's work has influentially insisted – and an appreciation of these as mutually constitutive of one another, part of a singular socio-ecological history, rather than a recent or sporadic encounter between strangers, may help to productively contest and reimagine prevailing conceptions of development. A more grounded, fluid, and relational understanding of peripheral and global political economies provides a more productive firmament for envisioning more sustainable and equitable futures.

The notion of fetishism mobilized in this chapter seeks to move beyond the impotent magic of conventional practices of unmasking and demystifying commodity and technoscientific fetishisms. In an article entitled 'Viscerality, faith, and scepticism: Another theory of magic', Michael Taussig articulates the notion of 'the skilled revelation of skilled concealment', which he describes as 'an art form dedicated to cheating', or 'contrived misperception' (Taussig 2016, 455). It is an idea that Taussig uses to interpret the power of shamanism, as well as ethnographic writing, but these ideas also seem compelling for thinking more generally about expertise, power, and inequality, and for reconsidering fetishism in more dynamic and relational terms. Although Taussig does not explicitly employ the language of fetishism in his discussion of the notion of 'the skilled revelation of skilled concealment', it seems to linger beneath the surface (like Wolf, he seems to have disavowed the term, yet remain tacitly enchanted by it). This notion seems to resonate productively with Latour's (2010) refashioning of fetishes as 'factishes', Graeber's (2005) emphasis on fetishism as social creativity, and Morris's (2017) foregrounding of disavowal in her dense and brilliant exegesis on the history, returns, and convoluted recursivity of fetishism. Synthesizing these ideas, I want to suggest that we can see affirmations of radical alterity, attempts to institute 'great divides', as prime examples of these socially creative practices that unify the artful concealment and shadowy revelation to which Taussig draws attention. The erasures and disfigurements of socio-environmental continuities and interdependencies are vital to the magic of liberalisms, from the redemptive charms of colonial civilization to the progressive promises of the economic and scientific technologies of late capitalism, to the enchanting emancipatory powers of critical scholarship. Perhaps making legible these kindred iterations of sorcery, more symmetrically revealing 'the skilled revelation of skilled concealment', can serve as sort of counter-magic to depoliticized and romantic ideas about sustainable development and the mythic individual subjectivities that sustain them.

The political ecology of fetishism mobilized in this chapter attempts to rethink and strengthen the critical power of fetishism by shifting its understanding of partial consciousness to the existential, by its (reflexive) attention to self-determination and existential violence. This chapter intimates a need to probe the frictive existential ecosystems lurking more deeply beneath the surface of the politics of nature. A political ecology of fetishism may serve to explore these existential frictions creatively and productively, and the role of fantasies of self-determination in fostering and undermining global resilience. The notion of resilient acclimatization has been suggested as a means of conceptualizing this interface between individual and collective politics, and between existential and environmental crisis. A creative return to the concept of fetishism, we suggest, is vital to the conjuring of forms of socio-environmental resilience more adequate to current global challenges.

Wolf's anthropologically oriented historical materialism – with its relational emphasis, its highlighting of interdependency, and its attention to crisis and differentiation – continues to provide an important conceptual template for anthropology, history, and political ecology. But his approach gains force through a return to fetishism, especially a conception of fetishism that is more ecological and existential than that articulated in much Marxian scholarship. It requires a more synthetic concept of fetishism – one that more successfully sublates the contradictions between 'nature' and 'culture', 'materialism' and 'idealism', 'objects' and 'subjects' in a vein imagined, but unsuccessfully realized in Marx's writings. This reformulated fetish concept also requires a deeper critical reflexivity regarding the nature of human being – of autonomy, contingency, and dependency. Perhaps we need to go beyond acknowledging that we are all equally historical agents, to also considering that we may all also be people without history. That is, it may not just be a matter of recovering the historical agency of our 'primitive' others but rethinking what is understood to be creative historical agency and its metaphysical and existential roots in the first place. A creative return to a fetishism – including a reflexive understanding of our fetish making – might be an indispensable and inevitable input to such a project.

A political ecology of fetishism provides a more nuanced understanding of the crisis and differentiation discussed by Wolf, and the complex dynamics of hybridization, erasure, subordination, and asymmetrical development. Emphasizing the role of violence in instantiating the deceptive enchantments of commodities, and the allure and authority of the wider political economic narratives in which they are embedded and realized, may provide a more potent sorcery with which to counter the misleading narratives of improvement and growth, with their elusive and asymmetrical promise of amplifying capacities for self-determination. The historical materialist approach utilized in this chapter – with its explicit attention to past moments of liminality and socio-environmental crisis as moments of change, continuity, and differentiation – might be especially productive for exploring the tangled complexity of the motivations, interactions, and histories that animate struggles over nature, and for rethinking sustainability, socio-environmental resilience, and interdependence as we strive to understand and acclimatize to the liminalities of current and future global crises.

To close, this chapter may be guilty of reproducing many of the flaws that critics have pointed out in Wolf's work (e.g., relapsing back upon the very problematic dualities it critiques; attempting to cover too much historical ground and obscuring its complexity; privileging the material and neglecting the history of ideas; and of providing little voice to the subaltern). Falling short of its theoretical ambitions and its striving for historical depth is partially attributable to space constraints, and to the limitations of historical records that require simplification and that marginalize peripheral agencies, ideas, and values. But, in part at least, I want to suggest that these flaws are artifacts of our ingrained fetishistic faculties, those artful schemes of revelation and concealment through which we deceive ourselves and others about human being and the socio-material nature of causal interconnections. But like Wolf's incantations, which provoked new ways to make sense of the world, perhaps these meditations can help conjure up novel and productive appreciations of our (creative and dynamic) global interdependencies, and fertilize transformative suspicions of prevailing myths of individuality and exceptionality.

References

Agostinho, Pedro. 1972. "Identidade e Situação dos Pataxó de Barra Velha, Bahia". Ms thesis, Federal University of Bahia.

Agostinho, Pedro. 1974. "Identificação étnica dos Pataxó de Barra Velha, Bahia". Lisboa, Instituto de Alta Cultura, *Junta de Investigações Científicas do Ultramar*: 393–400.

Agostinho, Pedro. 1980. "Bases Para o Estabelecimento da reserva Pataxó". *Revista de Antropologia* 23: 19–29.

Azenha, Gustavo S. 2005. "Conservation, Sustainable Development, and "Traditional" People: Pataxó Ethnoecology and Conservation Paradigms in Southern Bahia, Brazil". PhD diss., Cornell University.

Barickman, Bert J. 1995. "'Tame Indians','Wild Heathens', and Settlers in Southern Bahia in the Late Eighteenth and Early Nineteenth Centuries". *The Americas* 52(3): 325–368.

Bieber, Judy. 2014. "Cathechism and Capitalism: Imperial Indigenous Policy on a Brazilian Frontier, 1808–1845". In *Native Brazil: Beyond the Convert and the Cannibal, 1500–1900*, edited by Hal Langfur, 166–198. Albuquerque: University of New Mexico Press.

Bourdieu, Pierre. 1977. *Outline of a Theory of Practice*. Cambridge: Cambridge University Press.

Campbell, Jeremy. M. 2015. *Conjuring Property: Speculation and Environmental Futures in the Brazilian Amazon.* Seattle: University of Washington Press.

Cancela, Francisco. 2013. "Recepção e tradução do Diretório dos índios na antiga Capitania de Porto Seguro: uma análise das Instruções para o governo dos índios." *História Social* 2(25): 43–70.

Conklin, Beth A. and Laura R. Graham. 1995. "The Shifting Middle Ground: Amazonian Indians and Eco-politics". *American anthropologist*, 97(4): 695–710.

da Cunha, Manuela Carneiro. 2012. *Índios no Brasil: história, direitos e cidadania.* São Paulo: Editora Claro Enigma.

Dean, Warren. 1995. *With Broadax and Firebrand. The Destruction of the Brazilian Atlantic Forest.* Berkeley: University of California Press.

de Almeida, Maria Regina Celestino. 2014. "Land and Economic Resources of Indigenous *Aldeias* in Rio de Janeiro: Conflicts and Negotiations, Seventeenth to Nineteenth Centuries". In *Native Brazil: Beyond the Convert and the Cannibal, 1500–1900*, edited by Hal Langfur, 62–85. Albuquerque: University of New Mexico Press.

de Castro, Eduardo Viveiros. 2011. *The Inconstancy of the Indian Soul: The Encounter of Catholics and Cannibals in 16-century Brazil.* Chicago: University of Chicago Press.

de Castro, Eduardo Viveiros. 1996. "Images of Nature and Society in Amazonian Ethnology." *Annual review of Anthropology* 25(1): 179–200.

de Castro, Eduardo Viveiros. 2019. "Exchanging Perspectives: The Transformation of Objects into Subjects in Amerindian Ontologies". *Common knowledge*, 25(1–3): 21–42.

de Castro, Eduardo Viveiros. 2004. "Perspectival Anthropology and the Method of Controlled Equivocation". *Tipití: Journal of the Society for the Anthropology of Lowland South America*, 2(1): 3–22.

de Castro, Fábio. 2014. "Environmental Policies in the Lula Era: Accomplishments and Contradictions". In *Brazil Under the Workers' Party,* edited by Fábio Castro, Kees Koonings, and Marianne Wiesebron, 229–255. New York: Palgrave Macmillan.

de Castro, Fábio, and Renata Motta. 2015. "Environmental Politics under Dilma: Changing Relationships between the Civil society and the State'." In *LASA Forum* 46: 25–27.

de Carvalho, Maria Rosário. 2005. "Índios do sul e extremo-sul baianos: reprodução demográfica e relações." *Caderno CRH:* 18(43): 35–55.

de Carvalho, Maria Rosário. 1977. *Os Pataxó de Barra Velha: Seu Subsistema Economico.* Ms thesis, Federal University of Bahia.

de Carvalho, Maria Rosário. 2009. "O Monte Pascoal, os índios Pataxó e a luta pelo reconhecimento étnico". *Caderno CRH,* 22(57): 507–521.

Delson, Roberta M. and John Dickenson. 1984. "Conservation tendencies in colonial and imperial Brazil: An alternative perspective on human relationships to the land". *Environmental History Review,* 8(3): 270–283.

Descola, Philippe, and Gisli Pálsson, eds. 1996. *Nature and Society: Anthropological Perspectives*. New York: Routledge.

Diegues, Antonio Carlos. 1996. *O Mito Moderno da Natureza Intocada*. São Paulo: Editiora Hucitec Ltda.

Fabinyi, Michael, Louisa Evans, and Simon Foale. 2014. "Social-ecological systems, social diversity, and power: insights from anthropology and political ecology". *Ecology and Society*, 19(4): 28.

Gómez-Pompa, Arturo. and Andrea Kaus. 1992. "Taming the Wilderness Myth". *BioScience*, 42(4): 271–279.

Graeber, David. 2013. "It is value that brings universes into being". *HAU: Journal of Ethnographic Theory* 3(2): 219–243.

Graeber, David. 2005 "Fetishism as Social Creativity, or Fetishes are Gods in the Process of Construction." *Anthropological Theory* 5(4): 407–438.

Graeber, David. 2001. *Toward an Anthropological Theory of Value: The False Coin of our Own Dreams*. New York: Palgrave-Macmillan.

Hall, Ruth, Marc Edelman, Saturnino M. Borras Jr., Ben White, and Wendy Wolford. 2015. "Resistance, acquiescence or incorporation? An introduction to land grabbing and political reactions 'from below'". *Journal of Peasant Studies*, 42(3–4): 467–488.

Hecht, Susanna B. 2014. "Forests lost and found in tropical Latin America: the woodland 'green revolution'". *The Journal of Peasant Studies* 41(5): 877–909.

Hecht, Susanna B. 2011. "The new Amazon geographies: insurgent citizenship, "Amazon Nation" and the politics of environmentalisms". *Journal of Cultural Geography*, 28(1): 203–223.

Hochstetler, Kathryn and Margaret E. Keck. 2007. *Greening Brazil: Environmental Activism in State and Society*. Durham: Duke University Press.

Holbraad, Martin, Morten Axel Pedersen, and Eduardo Viveiros de Castro. 2014. "The politics of ontology: Anthropological positions". Theorizing the Contemporary, *Fieldsights*, January 13.

Holston, James. 2011. "Contesting privilege with right: the transformation of differentiated citizenship in Brazil." *Citizenship Studies* 15(3–4): 335–352.

Langfur, Hal. 2005. "Moved by terror: Frontier Violence as Cultural Exchange in Late-Colonial Brazil." *Ethnohistory* 52(2): 255–289.

Langfur, Hal. 2006. *The Forbidden Lands: Colonial Identity, Frontier Violence, and the Persistence of Brazil's Eastern Indians, 1750–1830*. Stanford: Stanford University Press.

Langfur, Hal. 2014a. "Recovering Brazil's Indigenous Past". In *Native Brazil: Beyond the Convert and the Cannibal, 1500–1900*, edited by Hal Langfur, 1–28. Albuquerque: University of New Mexico Press.

Langfur, Hal. 2014b. "Frontier/Fronteira: A Transnational Reframing of Brazil's Inland Colonization." *History Compass* 12(11): 843–852.

Langfur, Hal and Maria Leônia Chaves de Resende. 2014. "Indian autonomy and slavery in the forests and towns of colonial Minas Gerais". In *Native Brazil: Beyond the Convert and the Cannibal, 1500–1900*, edited by Hal Langfur, 132–165. Albuquerque: University of New Mexico Press.

Latour, Bruno. 2010. *On the Modern Cult of the Factish Gods*. Durham: Duke University Press.

Latour, Bruno. 1991. *We Have Never Been Modern*. Cambridge: Harvard university press.

Martínez-Allier, Javier. 1990. "Ecology and the Poor: A Neglected Dimension of Latin American History". *Journal of Latin American Studies* 28(3): 621–639.

Metcalf, Alcida C. 2014. "The Society of Jesus and the First Aldeias of Brazil". In *Native Brazil: Beyond the Convert and the Cannibal, 1500–1900*, edited by Hal Langfur, 29–61. Albuquerque: University of New Mexico Press.

Metcalf, Alcida C. 2005."The Entradas of Bahia of the Sixteenth Century." *The Americas* 61(3): 373–400.

Metcalf, Alcida C. 1999. "Millenarian Slaves? The Santidade de Jaguaripe and Slave Resistance in the Americas". *The American historical review* 104(5): 1531–1559.

Millar, Kathleen M. 2017. "Toward a critical politics of precarity." *Sociology Compass* 11(6): e12483.

Miller, Shawn William. 2000a. *Fruitless Trees: Portuguese Conservation and Brazil's Colonial Timber*. Stanford: Stanford University Press.

Miller, Shawn William. 2000b. "Merchant Shipbuilding in Late-Colonial Brazil: The evidence for a substantial private industry." *CLAHR: Colonial Latin American historical review* 9(1): 103–135.

Miller, Shawn William. 2003. "Stilt-Root Subsistence: Colonial Mangroves and Brazil's Landless Poor." *Hispanic American Historical Review* 83(2): 223–253.

Morris, Rosalind C. 2017. "After de Brosses: Fetishism, Translation, Comparativism, Critique." In *The Returns of Fetishism: Charles de Brosses and the Afterlives of an Idea*, edited by Rosalind C. Morris, 133–320. Chicago: University of Chicago Press.

Morton, F.W.O. 1978. "The Royal Timber Trade in Colonial Brasil." *Hispanic American Historical Review* 58(1): 41–61.

Munck, Ronaldo. 2013. "The Precariat: a view from the South." *Third World Quarterly* 34(5): 747–762.

Nadasdy, Paul. 1999. "The Politics of TEK: Power and the "Integration" of Knowledge." *Arctic Anthropology* 36(1–2): 1–18.

Nixon, Rob. 2013. *Slow Violence and the Environmentalism of the Poor*. Cambridge: Harvard University Press.

Ortner, Sherry B. 1984. "Theory in Anthropology since the Sixties." *Comparative Studies in Society and History* 26(1): 126–166.

Pádua, José Augusto. 2000. "'Annihilating Natural Productions': Nature's Economy, Colonial Crisis and the Origins of Brazilian Political Environmentalism (1786–1810)." *Environment and History*: 255–287.

Pádua, José Augusto. 2010. "European Colonialism and Tropical Forest Destruction in Brazil". In *Environmental History: As if Nature Existed*, edited by John Robert McNeill, José Augusto Pádua, and Mahesh Rangarajan, 130–148. New Dehli: Oxford University Press.

Pádua, José Augusto. 2015. "A Mata Atlântica e a Floresta Amazônica na construção do território brasileiro: estabelecendo um marco de análise." *Revista de História Regional* 20(2): 232–251.

Pahnke, Anthony, Rebecca Tarlau, and Wendy Wolford. 2015. "Understanding rural resistance: contemporary mobilization in the Brazilian countryside". *The Journal of Peasant Studies* 42: 1069–1085.

Paraíso, Maria Hilda Baqueiro. 1994. "De como se obter mão-de-obra indígena na Bahia entre os séculos XVI e XVIII". *Revista de História* (129–131): 179–208.

Paraíso, Maria Hilda Baqueiro. 1991. "Os Botocudos e sua trajetória histórica." In *História dos índios do Brasil*, edited by Manuela Carneiro da Cunha, 413–430. São Paulo: Companhia das Letras (FAPESP/SMC).

Pietz, William. 1985. "The Problem of the Fetish, I." *RES: Anthropology and Aesthetics* 9(1): 5–17.

Pietz, William. 1987. "The problem of the fetish, II: The origin of the fetish." *RES: Anthropology and Aesthetics* 13(1): 23–45.

Pietz, William. 1988. "The problem of the fetish, IIIa: Bosman's Guinea and the enlightenment theory of fetishism." *RES: Anthropology and Aesthetics* 16(1): 105–124.

Prieto, Andres. I. 2011. *Missionary Scientists: Jesuit Science in Spanish South America, 1570–1810*. Nashville: Vanderbilt University Press.

Rasmussen, Mattias Borg and Christian Lund. 2018. "Reconfiguring Frontier Spaces: The territorialization of resource control". *World Development* 101: 388–399.

Roller, Heather F. 2014. *Amazonian Routes: Indigenous Mobility and Colonial Communities in Northern Brazil*. Stanford: Stanford University Press.

Sampaio, José Augusto Laranjeiras. 2000. "Breve História da Presença Indígena no Extremo Sul Bahiano e a Questão do Território Pataxó de Monte Pascoal". In *Política Indigenista Leste e Nordeste Brasileiros*, edited by Marco Antonio do Espírito Santo. Brasília: FUNAIDEDOC.

Sommer, Barbara A. 2014. "The Amazonian Native Nobility in Late-Colonial Pará". In *Native Brazil: Beyond the Convert and the Cannibal, 1500–1900*, edited by Hal Langfur, 108–131. Albuquerque: University of New Mexico Press.

Santos, Fabricio Lyrio. 2014. "A "civilização dos índios" no século XVIII: da legislação pombalina ao "Plano" de Domingos Barreto." *Revista de História* 170: 233–260.

Sangren, Steve. and Dominic Boyer. 2006. "Introduction to Turner Special Issue". *Critique of Anthropology* 26(1): 5–13.

Schwartz, Stuart B. 1985. *Sugar Plantations in the Formation of Brazilian Society: Bahia, 1550–1835*. Cambridge: Cambridge University Press.

Taussig, Michael. 2016. "Viscerality, faith, and skepticism: Another theory of magic." *HAU: Journal of Ethnographic Theory* 6(3): 453–483.

Tsing, Anna. 2015. *The Mushroom at the End of the World: On the Possibility of Life in Capitalist Ruins*. Princeton: Princeton University Press.

Turner, Terence. 2008. "Marxian value theory: An anthropological perspective." *Anthropological Theory* 8, no. 1 (2008): 43–56.

Turner, Terence. 2003. "Class Projects, Social Consciousness, and the Contradictions of 'Globalization'". In *Globalization, the State, and Violence*, edited by Jonathan Friedman, 35–66. New York: Altamira.

Turner, Terence. 1986. "Production, Exploitation and Social Consciousness in the" Peripheral Situation"." *Social Analysis: The International Journal of Social and Cultural Practice* 19: 91–115.

Turner, Terence. 1995. "An Indigenous People's Struggle for Socially Equitable and Ecologically Sustainable Production: The Kayapó Revolt Against Extractivism." *Journal of Latin American Anthropology* 1(1): 98–121.

Turner, Terence. 1999. "Indigenous Rights, Environmental Protection, and the Struggle over Forest Resources in the Amazon: The Case of the Brazilian Kayapo". In *Earth, Air, Fire, Water: Humanistic Studies of the Environment*, edited by Jill Ker Conway, Kenneth Keniston, and Leo Marx, 145–169. Boston: University of Massachusetts Press.

Vainfas, Ronaldo. 2005. "From Indian Millenarianism to a Tropical Witches' Sabbath: Brazilian Sanctities in Jesuit Writings and Inquisitorial Sources." *Bulletin of Latin American Research* 24(2): 215–231.

Walker, Timothy D. 2013. "The Medicines Trade in the Portuguese Atlantic World: Acquisition and Dissemination of Healing Knowledge from Brazil (c. 1580–1800)." *Social history of medicine* 26(3): 403–431.

Wolf, Eric R. 2010 (1982). *Europe and the People without History*. Berkeley: University of California Press.

CHAPTER 6

Europe and the People without Class: The Example of Ghana

Ioannis Kyriakakis

1   Introduction

In his afterword in the classic 'Europe and the People without History', Wolf wrote:

> This book has asked what difference it would make to our understanding if we looked at the world as a whole, a totality, a system, instead of as a sum of self-contained societies and cultures; if we understood better how this totality developed over time; if we took seriously the admonition to think of human aggregates as 'inextricably involved with other aggregates, near and far, in web like, netlike connections' (Lesser 1961: 42). As we unravelled the chains of causes and effects at work in the lives of particular populations, we saw them extend beyond any one population to embrace the trajectories of others – all others.
> WOLF 2010: 385

The movement of history at the time of EPWH's publication looked to be heading to further integration and homogenization of different parts of the world, following Wolf's description of developments up to that time. However, the highly significant historical events of the fall of socialist regimes in the Soviet Union and Eastern Europe, the victory of neo-liberal capitalism, and the sweeping consequences of the cohesion of societies and communities in favour of capitalist markets – during the 1990s and onwards – gave the impression of a shattered and fragmented world. Despite the so-called process of globalization, launched by the liberalization of global trade and the domination of finance capital worldwide (Sklair 2002), it became evident that the speed with which different parts of the world followed this process was so radically diverse, that we could talk of different worlds, rather than of one world with just some systemic faults.

In this chapter I put forward two main ideas. The first is that we cannot maintain national frameworks as the basic research fields when enquiring into class theory in an era when class relationships are mainly transnational, and when current capitalism cannot be seen in any sense or perspective other than global. In this sense, Wolf's perspective on the historical validity of global processes is confirmed by developments on the ground. The second idea is that the strengthening of the global class system, although it does not change the nature of capitalist exploitation, forces the global working classes into two major transformations. First, exploitation becomes deeper and wider, with very low wages and longer working hours. Second, class consciousness and class struggle become extremely difficult for workers because their real patrons are thousands of miles away and because they live side by side with a substantial underclass, which is ready to replace them in their current workplace at any moment. The existence of a large population of generally unorganized underclasses living in conditions of extreme poverty is the hidden asset, so far unbeatable, of global capitalism. It pushes millions of people 'outside history' in a movement that reverses the shove applied by mature modernity in the 1960s and 1970s. In this chapter I attempt to shed light on the condition of current global inequality by investigating the methodological and theoretical tools we need in order to think of the current world as a unified conceptual space. In this attempt I draw on my ethnographic experience in Ghana, where I conducted extended doctoral fieldwork from 2003 to 2005. This is supplemented with data from Ghana's national statistics on occupational distribution and statuses of employment, which I use to exemplify a global underclass. Even though my research topic focused on religious pluralism, I soon realized that any attempt to draw conclusions from current social phenomena of any kind in Ghana was impossible without investigating the social and economic history of religious pluralism itself. Its prominent role in Ghana's history is seen in the transformation of labour relationships both during and after the colonial period. The study of the organization of labour is a main concern of Wolf in EPWH, where changes in labour relationships worldwide signify the domination of the capitalist mode of production outside the European continent. Nevertheless, changes in the composition of capital, as well as the relocation of industrial activities, along with the emergence of new information and communication technology in the post-1990s era, have deeply affected labour relationships since the writing of EPWH. In this regard Bauman (2001: 25) notes:

> The present day 'liquefied', 'flowing', dispersed, scattered and deregulated version of modernity does not portend divorce and a final break in communication, but it does augur a *disengagement* between capital and labour ... To an extent never achieved by the 'absentee landlords' of

yore, capital has cut itself loose from its dependency on labour through a new freedom of movement undreamt of in the past. Its reproduction and growth has become by and large independent of the duration of any particular local engagement with labour.

The main objective of this chapter is to shed light on the issue of social class within the conditions of liquid modernity, as described by Bauman, and under the perspective of a world system, as it was introduced by Wolf. I draw on Eric Olin Wright's distinction between class exploitation and non-exploitative oppression (see below) to show how a national/domestic perspective on labour relationships pertains to non-class oppression, and how a global perspective enables and reveals a deeper understanding of the class character of labour relationships in the contemporary world, especially with regard to the global periphery and Africa in particular.

I start with an examination of Marxian and Weberian frameworks regarding social class, continue with a short description of Eric Olin Wright's contribution, and then explain why it is valuable in attempting to regard class in a global perspective. I then examine the special conditions of labour in Ghana drawing on national statistics. Finally, I compare statistics with historical and ethnographic data, reaching the conclusion that new forms of capitalist exploitation make class theory not only relevant and operational within contemporary social science but also necessary, provided we employ a global perspective.

2 Similarities and Differences between Marxian and Weberian Frameworks

According to Wright (2000, 27–34), both Marxian and Weberian frameworks for studying social class focus on the relational character of social differentiation emanating from social structure built upon unequal relationships. This means that class positions are not just located side by side in an objective social taxonomy, or even rank, according to productive activities and services. On the contrary, it is their relationships which make productive activities and services possible in the first place. This relational character of social groupings (based on class, status, nation, gender, ethnicity, and race) is probably the foundation stone of sociology as a discipline itself. However, Marx and Weber differ in the emphasis they give to the crucial criterion of class belonging, and how they account for social differentiation altogether. Marx holds that this criterion is the famous 'one's relationship to the means of production', while for Weber what is crucial for placing individuals within social classes is the remarkably similar, or common, set of 'life chances' they must acquire, such as wealth, to pursue material interests (Wright 2000, 28). Although the two approaches are not mutually exclusive (one can claim that a favourable relationship to the means of production is a life chance in itself), they obviously lead to different methodological and theoretical priorities. A Marxian approach leads to prioritizing property and especially property (or deprivation of property) of the means of production, while Weberian approaches pay more attention to a range of social distinctions other than property, such as status, origin, profession, education, authority, culture, and prestige. There is no doubt that the Weberian perspective is much more inclusive, as well as, in a way, more operational, methodologically, for social research. If one asks oneself what differentiates oneself from others in a commonly accepted social ranking, the first thing one will think of is one's profession, then income and finally education, with regional and national origin following close. Few will immediately ask, 'What is my relationship to the means of production?'

Nevertheless, despite the advantages of the Weberian framework, in the sense that it is much closer to everyday social perceptions, the Marxian framework offers an unequalled opportunity not just to mirror social reality, but also to understand it in depth and change it. The dynamic potential of the Marxian principle of 'the means of production', although it does not accord that well with everyday experience, offers a unified framework for the entire range of social relationships regardless of one's own perception of them. This framework treats society as a system rather than a set of relationships that might, or might not, connect to each other. Therefore, the Marxian framework does not merely place groups and individuals in specific locations across the social hierarchy, but reveals the interconnections between these locations, claiming that the interconnections are more important than the locations themselves. In simpler words, Marxian thought does not merely reveal that the world is made of owners of capital and workers, and not even that capitalists merely exploit workers. Rather, it asserts that the workers are workers exactly because capitalists are capitalists and vice versa. Both positions are intertwined within a system of production that cannot work without them and especially without the nature of the relationships between them. Every change in the position of the one group affects the other, and nothing can change in one group's living conditions without a corresponding change within the living conditions of the opposite group. No worker's life can be improved without a capitalist giving up some luxuries! And capitalists cannot increase their profits unless some workers lose their wages, jobs, homes, and, in extreme cases, their very lives too. Of course, this is a very strong, almost absolute, set of assumptions about how class-oriented society works. It bears a vast explanatory power and can motivate huge support within and without academic circles, but unfortunately it is too abstract to withstand empirical testing. The problem is that there are so many intermediary groups and vague conditions in the social space between and beside these two basic classes. These are the so-called middle classes, as well as multiple conditions where class belonging is not clear-cut – such as people studying, young family members, artists and scientists, and service sector workers whose relationship to the means of production often remains very unclear.

It is in this instance that the Weberian framework is useful to facilitate research. Instead of categorizing people according to class, social scientists, theorists, students, politicians, and statisticians tend to use such indicators as income, occupations, forms of activity (employer, self-employed, employee), or educational qualifications, to interpret whether and how society leans towards social equality or inequality. The methodology may also act as a litmus test for a county's level of modernization and facilitates social research and data comparisons, but may also weaken the relational character of data and their connection to wider, theoretical perspectives. Most statisticians and statistical researchers follow this methodology (see for example, Savage et al., 2013, or visit any national statistics website around the globe) where profession and employment status (such as formal and informal) are the major criteria of social classification. Ownership is also used as a criterion but in the broad sense of total property (including houses and land) and not in the narrow sense of 'the means of production'. Entrepreneurs are typically framed as a unified category although differentiations between 'big' and 'small' are maintained. The idea is that people perform, share basic tendencies, and exert fundamental preferences according to their social and educational background. This enables categorizations in terms of the characteristics of big and small businesses, and key features of enjoying regular employment. Despite its operational validity and resemblance to 'real life' observations, the approach risks treating society as an aggregation of relatively independent locations and positions, which do not relate to each other, nor constitute a wider system, but which works towards their reproduction as they are categorized. The social dynamics of conflict, movement, and change (other words for 'dialectics') disappear in favour of 'accuracy', 'realism', and 'scientific objectivity'. Instead of treating social locations as directly affecting each other, one is led to imagine a world where a capitalist can increase profit exclusively through innovation, ingenuity, and shrewdness, without necessarily worsening the living conditions of workers. No matter whether it intends to do so or not, this tendency within social science and social statistical management contributes to the maintenance and reproduction of the current system of social hierarchy and exploitation – that is, the capitalist system.

This chapter argues that taking specific geographical regions and political entities like nation states as our units of study in isolation adds plausibility and validity to explanations of social differentiation in terms of income, education, profession, social status, and political participation within the specific regions. But if we take all countries and all regions, both North and South, as parts of one and the same global capitalist system, the Marxian framework of mutually interdependent global classes is the only one with explanatory strength and validity. The empirical basis of the argument lies in my fieldwork and the relevant secondary data supporting the fieldwork, which was conducted in southwestern Ghana back in 2004–5 and ongoing secondary research ever since.

3 Class in a Global Perspective

After the energy crisis of the 1970s, many manufacturing activities of global capitalism moved to the east and south-east of Asia. Drivers included the presence of a fair supporting network of infrastructure (road networks, rivers, trains, ports, communication lines, etc.), a vast reserve of cheap labour consisting of impoverished former peasants with cultural and work discipline appropriate for manufacture, increasing levels of political stability, and a bulk of governments and politicians who were eager to implement business-friendly measures and legislation that coerced peasants to enter wage-labour sectors (Hameiri and Jones 2020, 3–34). There is plenty of evidence (Gupta 1986, Okia 2012, 9–22) from the colonial past on how colonial governments pushed generations of peasants to enter wage labour (in mines, plantations, ports, and railways) by imposing small taxes, which subsistence farmers could not afford, and by encouraging migration. Post-colonial governments continued the trajectory in alignment with the needs of developing cash crop economies and mining industries. Although the forms that exploitation takes have changed considerably since the colonial period, the analogy between past and present, and between the West and the Global South, lies in the ability of economic power to direct marginalized groups into capitalist institutionalization processes.

According to Wright, not all unequal and oppressive relationships fall into the category of class exploitation. It is only the antithetical positions within productive activities (opposite relationships to the means of production) that form class relationships. As he writes: 'The crucial difference between exploitation and non-exploitative oppression is that, in an exploitative relation, the exploiter needs the exploited since the exploiter depends upon the effort of the exploited. In the case of non-exploitative oppression, the oppressors would be happy if the oppressed simply disappeared' (Wright 2000, 11).

The cases when the oppressed simply disappeared are not unknown in history. Genocides are good examples. The genocide of Native Americans by the white colonists exemplified neither that the strategy of the oppressors required an extended labour force, nor that the Native Americans were willing to offer it. Genocides do not therefore fall into class relationships, although they may be committed either to purge resistance, or to establish political domination. One difference worth discussing between class oppression and genocide is that of agency versus structure. From Marx, class oppression and its reproduction over time is grounded in structure while genocide, although also grounded in structure, is perhaps more based on agency – take, for example, the decisions of the Third Reich. So, although both class-based relationships and genocide spur oppression and misery, their dynamics and reasons for being are different (Wright 2000, 12). Class oppression arguably demands stable and well-established institutions that support a supply and organization of labour. On the other hand, oppression that is not based on class distinctions could typically concern unstable and uneven social and productive relationships. However, as we shall see below, there is an indirect link between oppression based on political, ethnic, or other kinds of agency and that based around class structure. Especially in parts of Africa as well as other fringes of the Global South, capitalistic expansion falters and manufacturing firms experience declining interest in investment due, for example, to very poor or absent infrastructure, political and economic structural inequalities, unstable political and social conditions, and the existence of a heterogeneous, undisciplined, and poorly educated labour force.

Nevertheless, there are zones where the Global north and multinationals express very strong interest in, for example, extractive industries (mining, oil and gas, timber) and in the production of agricultural raw materials. In these zones capitalist multinationals are particularly interested in consolidating beneficial and productive relationships with local and state authorities. In the Ghana case their interest typically seeks out state officials, various regulatory institutions, and local chiefs – because these are the power sources that control land access, and because securing access to land with a clear legal basis for extractive concessions is generally more important than establishing viable relations with a labour force, which, anyway, is in adequate supply. In Ghana, selected semi-skilled and unskilled workers are needed for mines, while timber and agricultural production is typically supplied through local brokers who deal with local loggers and farmers themselves. Therefore, the demand for *direct* employment of local workers by multinationals is restricted (Chukwuemeka et al. 2011). The area in Western Ghana where I conducted my fieldwork was a gold-mining area. Many of my friends and informants had worked in the gold mine, owned by an Australian company, which leased the land for peanuts. Compensations paid for destroying farms were also extremely low. Locals were not trusted to undertake skilled work and were hired for US$1.5 a day as unskilled labour. Most drillers and other skilled workers were Ukrainians hired by the mining company and transferred directly to Ghana to work exclusively in the mine.

Ghana is used as an example of employment conditions because of the direct experiences gained during fieldwork and because characteristics of economic life there are to be found all over sub-Saharan Africa. Overall, the number of local workers hired by multinationals in Ghana is relatively small – consisting, for example, of the skilled and unskilled workers hired locally by capitalist firms in chemical and plastics industrial production (Aryeetey and Baah-Boateng 2007, 2016). However, much of the economically active population is engaged in two major categories of economic activity with a low level of formal regulation: small-scale farming and petty trading. Still, the existence of a very complex land-rights system in Ghana does not allow statistics to distinguish definitively between large- and small-scale farmers (Blocher 2006, Amanor and Ubink 2008, 10–26). What is clear, however, is that Ghana experiences a steady seasonal flow of migrant workers towards cocoa, cashew nuts, palm oil, rubber, and copra plantations. These cash crops are the most important, with cocoa providing 18 percent of Ghana's total exports (worldstopexports.com 2020). Unstable and insecure land rights however (see below) and the almost exclusive dependence of small-scale export farmers on the fluctuations of international trade, mean that a large number are *indirectly* related and heavily influenced by trade and market decisions taken thousands of miles away at the centres of cocoa, nuts, and palm-oil transactions. A long history of colonial intervention in cocoa production many decades ago led to a deliberate underdevelopment of farming technology, land-rights regimes, and levels of infrastructure. This aimed to keep production costs low and favour local and international brokers and traders (Kyriakakis 2012). On the other hand, petty trade is a vast, marginal, and informal activity and the preserve of millions of people comprising the 'underclasses' in Ghana – and found all over sub-Saharan Africa as well. This heterogeneous group is dominated by people who for diverse reasons cannot access established and formalized economic and political structures and experience marginalization from avenues to betterment. Although it is not evident at a first glance, one can reasonably claim that the very logic of this class structure creates and reproduces a large underclass and socially marginalized population, rendered essentially dispensable and invisible to both local economic elites and their overseas patrons, the Western multinationals in the Global north. This is especially the case in Africa, where dominant forms of production such as large-scale farming and mining are typically characterized by flexible seasonal, local, and liquid relations of labour. What is more important for Ghana's economy and society is to retain and develop export markets for foreign currency and to finance the state from export tariffs and levies. Gold is the major export commodity, providing 50 percent of total export value, followed by crude oil (21.5 percent) cocoa products (13 percent), and cashew and other nuts (2 percent) (https://oec.world/en/prof ile/country/gha, 2019). However, since much gold mining narrowly relates to the exclusive operations of large-scale extracting multinationals, and because cocoa production relates to international firms in Europe and America, control over production and trade is exerted by global capitalists. Local elites play the role of brokers and intermediate agents serving the interests of multinational companies, which enjoy the ability to determine conditions of production and avenues of wealth distribution. Financial dependence on foreign support and external trade makes the political elites (politicians and chiefs) relatively indifferent to popular support, while corruption and favouritism prevail due to weak democratic control, accountability, and transparency (Frimpong-Ansah 1991; Amundsen 2019,1–28; Asante and Khisa 2019, 29–51).

The narrow basis of an economy directed exclusively to export trade is reflected in a general underdevelopment, lack, and sometimes absence of basic infrastructure: quality roads and bridges in remote areas, connections to power networks for 30–40 percent of the country, health and education facilities, sewage and sanitation networks, hygienic waste disposal sites, telephone landlines, and so many other things including justice and quality policing (Foster and Pushak 2011). Restricted areas and fringes serving export trade infrastructure may enjoy high levels of amenities, but these are the exceptions that verify the general rule (Fuseini, Yaro and Yiran 2017). The weakest groups within this system are constantly exposed to the risk of fatal diseases, with no effective social welfare protection and no chance of organizing collective resistance. Therefore, we can talk about an *indirect,* or else 'non-exploitative' oppression in the sense of Olin-Wright's term and as discussed above. However, since a basic driver for this situation is the capitalistic system itself and the hunger for profit and expansion of global multinationals, we can also speak credibly of an international organization of labour in favour of the expansion of a global capitalist class. Global capitalists (also a very heterogeneous group) are typically located in core countries far away from the actual sites of extraction and exploitation. Local political and economic elites and brokers meanwhile comprise a global middle class in the context of the global organization of labour. As discussed below, the global middle classes enjoy precious privileges including ability to freely travel abroad and access to amenities from which underclass segments are excluded. Further, it is typical that the Ghana underclass does not come into direct contact with the global capitalist class, even though the system of 'non-exploitative' oppression is based on the latter's ability to influence international prices of agricultural products such as cocoa, coffee, palm oil, etc. On this basis, large swathes of otherwise diverse workers in Africa constitute a burgeoning global underclass comprising informal petty-traders, illegal miners, unemployed or underemployed youth, small-scale subsistence farmers, and seasonal agricultural workers.

4 Can We Talk of a Working Class or Classes in Africa?

Apart from the global division of labour and proliferous neo-colonial exploitation and oppression, can we talk of class at the domestic and national level? Are African countries structured according to class difference, class struggle and class exploitation? Or is the concept of class an exclusively Western invention, describing solely particular industrial historical experiences? Jean Copans claimed long ago that in Africa citizens' relationship to the state is much more important than the relationship to the means of production. He writes: 'The exportation of concepts, forged exclusively from European realities, is no speculative and innocent enterprise. It was made possible, and afterwards maintained, through all those processes of domination and exploitation which have linked the south and the north for the last 500 years' (Copans 1985, 25).

The most misleading and hypocritical concept exported from the West to Africa has been that of 'development'. The ideology of development had it that African countries should emulate the Western industrial countries by taking the same steps they took throughout the previous two centuries, in order, some day, to reach the current level of economic, social, technological and political advancement. Perhaps this is one of the greatest deceits in human history, since whilst theorists of development made such claims, many global political and economic developments have served to keep African countries (except for South Africa) in a seemingly permanent process of broad, structural stagnation and underdevelopment, pockmarked only with isolated successes and growth. Ghana had substantive experience of deliberate underdevelopment, where the British colonial authority halted the commercialization of land and maintained the customary law of chiefs and clan heads, who retained power to allocate community land to commoner farmers (Howard-Hassman 1980;

Grier 1981, 1987, 1993). The corollary was the reproduction of chief-based land control, the proliferation of subsistence farmers, a low level of land-based productivity, and the creation of a migrant work force. The average productivity of cocoa beans per hectare in Ghana today is about 400 kg per hectare, while in Cote d' Ivoire and Indonesia it is 1.4 and 1 tonnes per hectare respectively (Asamoah and Owusu-Ansah, 2017, 4). The majority of farmers continue to manage (but do not own) 2–4 hectares of cocoa farms, while 72 per cent do not possess any legal document proving their formal title to the land (Asamoah and Owusu-Ansah 2017, 2, 4). In the following I now detail the categorization of workers in Ghana by the Ghana Statistical Service and discuss what this can tell us about the existence of a class society.

Table 6.1's data clearly show a large percentage of self-employed persons in Ghana, indicating the two major occupations, namely farming and petty trading. What is of great importance is the proportion of people working under formal and informal conditions, with 86 percent of economically active people identified as working in the informal private sector. This percentage spreads along all categories of Table 6.1. However, it also contributes to a great extent to the high percentage of the 'self-employed' (Ghana Statistical Service 2012, 11). In Tables 6.2, 6.3, and 6.4 we find statistical data on occupation distribution, as well as the economic activities and specific industry distribution involved, along with the distribution of employment status. However, the data are somewhat contradictory because in the category 'agricultural, forestry and fishery

TABLE 6.1 Employment status of employed persons 15 years and older (Ghana Statistical Service, 2012: 10)

	Male	Female
Worker category		
Employee	25.3	11.4
Self-employed	60	69.4
Casual worker	2.8	1.3
Contributing family worker	8.7	14.2
Apprentice	2.5	2.9
Domestic employee	0.6	0.7
Other	0.2	0.1

Note: The Ghana statistical service 2010 census was published in 2012.

workers' (the largest column), smallholders are included because, as we have said, they are not formal landowners and therefore cannot be taken as either 'managers' or 'professionals', which are the categories under which entrepreneurs are typically found. Yet, in the 'self-employment' status, they are also included, as they are in fact self-employed. The same statistical discrepancy occurs in the presentation of petty traders, the vast majority of whom are informal workers. They are not really owners of capital or self-employed, but usually indebted to a wholesale merchant, food seller, or street vendor (Obeng-Odoom 2011). In one statistical category, however, they appear as 'self-employed'; in another as service workers; and in yet another as wholesale and retail traders. All three categorizations are correct, but all depends on the angle from which these petty traders are observed. As statistician Monica Threlfall (2002) notes, pure statistical data in isolated categories may easily mislead or even contradict similar data of related categories (of other regions/countries) if we do not pay attention to the 'denominators', that is, the wider groups of the population to which these people supposedly belong. Returning to the main question of this section, whether we can speak of a 'working class' in Sub-Saharan Africa, one can see that the usual criteria of social classification according to employment are blurred and uncertain. The category of 'employees', which usually refers to working classes, is particularly undersized. Nevertheless, other data indicate otherwise.

From Table 6.2, one can conclude that the working class in Ghana is over 85 percent of the economically active population (agricultural workers 41.2%, + service workers 21.3% + retail workers 15.2 + machine operators 6, Elementary workers 5 = 88.2). However, when one looks at Table 6.4, the working class seems to shrink to between 22 and 23 percent (employee: 18.2 + casual worker 2.0 + Apprentice 2.7 + domestic employee 0.2 = 23.1). Although both images are true according to the angle of view one employs, as said, considering income, property rights, and the precarious conditions of existence of farmers and petty traders, one would place most working people in Ghana in the working classes – that is, all the classes that are deprived of the ownership of the means of production. However, this is not a sufficient condition for labelling Ghana a class-divided society. Such a society requires also a socially and economically distinct bourgeoisie – that is, owners of the means of production who derive their profits from the direct exploitation of the labour of the working classes. Despite the development of domestic industries of plastics, chemicals, food-processing, and textiles (the latter now vanishing, see below), some manufacturing, and some plants of spare-parts for computers and laptops with mainly Chinese support (Cheru and Obi 2010; Alemayehu 2017), the number of actors which can be categorized reasonably as the domestic bourgeoisie is quite

TABLE 6.2 Economically active population (15 years and older) by occupation

Economically active population (15 years and older) by occupation	%	Number
Managers	2.5	263,191
Professionals	5.3	559,455
Technicians & associate professionals	1.8	193,821
Clerical support workers	1.5	153,375
Service & sales workers	21.3	2,227,441
Skilled agricultural, forestry & fishery workers	41.2	4,319,237
Craft & related trades workers	15.2	1,594,378
Plant & machine & assembly operators	5.0	518,873
Elementary occupations	6.0	631,247
Other occupations	0.2	18,267
Total	100	10,479,485

GHANA STATISTICAL SERVICE 2012, P. 74

small. Out of the 4.9 per cent of employers in Table 6.4, more than 60 per cent employ 1–9 employees, while state firms take the lion's share of large enterprises (Ghana Statistical Service , 2015). Thus one can credibly claim that the privileged classes in Ghana are not the owners of factories and large firms but the diverse holders of strategic social, political, and economic positions such as customary authorities, state officials, and high-ranking civil-administrative personnel, public officials, and private business actors. These represent the national entrepreneurial elite which deals with the foreign multinationals, who are the real grand investors and directors of Ghana's economy (Anazodo and Nzewi 2011; Mendes et al. 2014).

During the last two decades, Ghana (especially the major cities of Accra and Kumasi) has also developed a large and powerful middle class of homeowners, entrepreneurs, business actors, academics, professionals, and the like. Growth rates in Ghana after 2009 are impressive (on average 5–7% annually) but the structural composition of economic growth seems to favour the aggrandizement of the middle classes instead of increasing the number of bourgeoisie or improving the lot of working classes (Shimeles and Ncube 2015). The economy seems to be based on three pillars: (1) Investment by 'migrant' Ghanaians who live in or return from Europe and the US; (2) Export agriculture and gold-mining industries, as well as a significant post-2009 contribution

TABLE 6.3   Economically active population (15 years and older) by industry

Economically active population (15 years and older) by industry	%	Number
Agriculture, forestry, and fishing	41.5	4,435723
Mining and quarrying	1.1	115,394
Manufacturing	10,8	1,135,612
Electricity, gas stream, and air conditioning supply	0.2	16,237
Water supply, sewage waste management, and remediation activities	0.2	24,996
Construction	3.1	321,360
Wholesale and retail: repair of motor vehicles and motorcycles	18.9	1,981,290
Transportation and storage	3.5	371,461
Accommodation and food service activities	5.5	574,671
Information and communication	0.4	43,600
Financial and insurance activities	0.7	72,666
Real estate activities	0.0	4,562
Professional scientific and technical activities	0.9	96,223
Administrative and support service activities	0.7	68,218
Public administration, defence, compulsory social security	1.5	154,559
Education	3.9	409,694
Human health and social work activities	1.2	125,254
Arts entertainment and recreation	0.6	57,997
Other service activities	4.5	476,722
Activities of households as employers: undifferentiated goods- and service-producing activities of households for own use	0.8	80,287
Activities of extraterritorial organizations and bodies	0.0	2,959
Total	100	10,479,485

GHANA STATISTICAL SERVICE 2012, P. 75

to the economy from oil and gas extraction (Abudu and Sai 2020). Returning Ghanaians from Europe and the US invest in services (transport, real estate, and retail industry), while the predominance of mining industries and agriculture in the economy favours seasonal and unskilled domestic labour, with

TABLE 6.4   Economically active population 15 years and older, by employment status

Economically active population 15 years and older, by employment status	%	Number
Employee	18.2	1,904,039
Self-employed without employees	60.0	6,282,509
Self-employed with employees	4.9	509,061
Casual worker	2.0	210,087
Contributing family worker	11.5	1,206,935
Apprentice	2.7	282,618
Domestic employee (House-help)	0.6	66,570
Other	0.2	17,666

GHANA STATISTICAL SERVICE, 2012, P. 78

skilled labour usually coming from abroad, as discussed above. Manufacturing, except for petroleum by-products, has not made substantial progress despite the growth rates of the wider economy (Addo 2017). Some sectors (like the food processing industry) have grown, and others (like the textile industry) have declined or even vanished (Amankwah-Amoah 2015). Therefore, most workforces in Ghana comprise a combination of poor, marginalized, labourers with experience limited to small-scale, non-mechanized farms, or petty trading with uncertain conditions. A huge proportion of workers are unregistered and unmeasured by statistics – such as the unemployed or underemployed, or those engaged in seasonal labour (see next section).

These conditions are highly desirable from the perspective of the global multinational firms, who are thus relieved of serious competition from an organized national bourgeoisie. A vast pool of very cheap and flexible labour is at their disposal in selected profitable sectors like mining, agriculture, and logging (Sears et al. 2001). In conclusion, African countries and societies are not class-divided in narrow Marxian terms, despite the vast inequalities within them (see also Emery 2018). But they are subjected to the domination of a diverse class of global capitalists in an economic sense, and dominated by domestic elites in a political, social, and economic sense. That is why the Weberian perspective appears appropriate for studying the economic organization of Ghanaian society, where major economic exploiters are situated thousands of miles away from sites of production. The same is true of the (post-) industrial North. Everybody looks middle-class, since the real working and underclasses are thousands of miles away.

5 The Ethnography: Living Conditions of the Working Classes in Africa

When I was doing my fieldwork in south-western Ghana back in 2004–5 (Kyriakakis 2010) – searching for the connection between social differentiation and religious affiliation (the topic of my PhD) – I reached a dead-end in my endeavour to find links through interviews and life histories, and decided to conduct a survey with the help of local friends and assistants. I was living in a village of approximately 1,700 inhabitants, 5 km from the Atlantic coast in a gold-mining region. Most people were farmers, cultivating coconut trees in what had been a wild forest region, but occasional legal and illegal mining was also very popular – especially among young males.

The distribution of occupations in the village of my fieldwork is shown in Table 6.5. Immediately, one can see striking similarities to the national statistics. The relatively large number of 'students' and 'unemployed' (more than double the national average) hid the fact that gold mining was not merely occasional but also illegal. An illegal mine was established near the village on stool (that is, communal) land which, a few years later, the local chief, along with state officials, would lease to an Australian gold-mining multinational. Therefore, it was not possible for anyone to declare on the questionnaire, 'I am an illegal miner'.

What caught my interest most at the time was the level of social inequality, since the assumption of the research was that religious preference related to social status. A lot of demographic questions were included in the survey, and, in the end, a full demographic profile of the village came out of an endeavour that aimed to elicit information on social differentiation and inequality. One of the survey questions was: (a) *If we divide the village residents into three categories, into which category would you place yourself? Upper? Middle? Or Lower?* (b) *Due to your condition regarding money? Land ownership/property? Housing? Origin? Education? Profession? Age? Gender? Marital status? Other?* In the first part of the question, although a majority of 547 (52 percent) placed themselves in the middle stratum (as expected for a rural area), another very significant 375 (36%) regarded themselves as lower stratum and only 102 (10%) said they were from the upper stratum; 19 respondents (2%) did not reply to the question. Regarding the second part, the most popular criterion for placing oneself in a social hierarchy was by far 'profession' (275, 27%), with education level (199, 19%) and money/wealth? (189, 18%) placing second and third. The ownership of land and other properties came fifth, with just 78 responses (7%). Therefore, the respondents to my questionnaire were certainly Weberian! Fieldwork findings supported the argument that most working people, especially the youth, engage with seasonal, illegal, or informal labour and thus escape statistical registration as either workers or unemployed. Many of my informants declared their status as Senior Secondary School (SSS) students, although they were, in fact, illegal miners, having stopped schooling, with the hope of going back to school sometime in the future.

The most important issue for villagers was regular income and access to cash, because after the implementation of IMF-supported economic structural adjustment programmes in Ghana from 1983, a whole range of services became based on market logics. Education and school fees were introduced, health and national insurance contributions and medical payments became financially burdensome (Gifford 1998, Hutchful 2002). Local farmers sold their crops to a local coconut-oil processing factory, but pests and diseases were a constant threat, and in the absence of state extension services money was also needed to cover the costs of fertilizer and pesticide, and as security against farming risks. In the village, residents experienced a lack of running water, roads and bridges, telephone landlines, public toilet facilities, the presence of a medical doctor – while a badly maintained power network resulted in daily power disruptions that lasted for hours. Some 50 percent of the villagers were illiterate and only 25 percent could speak fair English, which is the official language of the state – and thus had difficulty in contacting state agencies for support.

Some of the demographic data gathered provides significant insights into the social fabric of the village and the everyday struggle. Almost half of the girls between 16 and 20 years old were single mothers; almost half of couples were divorced; most children lived with only one of their parents or with grandparents; a quarter of local men were temporarily living elsewhere, either working or seeking employment. These figures show that families and households had literally disintegrated. National data provided for similar evidence across Ghana, where, for example, only 5 percent of solid and 10 percent of liquid household waste was disposed of hygienically in 2010! The rest went into open gutters and open waste sites beside slums, houses, and markets. (Ghana Statistical Service 2012, 84, 88–91). Ten years later the numbers have not improved significantly: Only 10 percent of solid waste and 20 percent of liquid waste were safely disposed of in 2020, in a country that experienced substantial economic growth and annual GDP increases from 2010 to 2020 (Lissah et al. 2021, Statista 2020b). In some sectors, however, vast improvements have been made during recent years. Internet usage has increased from 28 percent of the population in 2017 to 50 percent in 2021, and up considerably from 7 percent at the time of my fieldwork! Among the current (50 percent) internet users, 97 percent use smart phones (Statista 2017–2021; Statista 2020a). These numbers show how 'development' in Ghana has been a highly selective enterprise, hitting diverse segments of the population in vastly different ways. Smart-phone technology

TABLE 6.5 Distribution of occupations/economic activities in fieldwork village, April 2004 (Kyriakakis 2012)

Occupation	Number	%
Farmers	340	32.5
Teachers	43	4
Craftsmen: (carpenters, electricians, masons, mechanics, smiths, drivers)	49	4.7
Craftswomen: (seamstresses, hairdressers)	24	2.5
Shopkeepers/Entrepreneurs	14	1.5
Workers and Apprentices	32	3
Food Sellers (all women)	47	4.5
Market Women and Petty Traders	151	14.4
Miners	10	0.9
Students	193	18.5
Unemployed	140	13.5
Total	*1043*	*100*

looks like a good case for new middle-class consumerism, but in fact enhances and favours the global producers of such products rather than local economies. Therefore, the living conditions of the middle and upper classes, who can afford internet connection in areas with proper sanitation, differ vastly from those of the lower classes, without regular employment or income, who reside in unhealthy conditions deprived of basic goods, services, and infrastructure.

6   Conclusion

In this chapter I have attempted to show that class analysis and class theory are highly operational within social science and can contribute to Wolf's argument that we need to investigate and understand the world as a unitary system – though we also need to consider carefully significant changes that have occurred in the world during the last four decades. Not only Weberian but also Marxian perspectives on class remain valid today – though we need to follow the development of means of production, the global division of labour, and the new forms of global capitalist domination to be able to see this validity clearly. To restrict research and theoretical elaborations within the borders of the countries of the Global north – without considering what is happening in the rest of the world – may turn out to be an ideological, and by no means an academic choice, one that in the final analysis serves the system of global capitalist domination. Concerning the character of contemporary global capitalism, Wolf's analysis presented 40 years ago in EPWH retains much of its validity, since his major methodological tool for evaluating historical social formations and the organization of labour provides explanation for current developments as well.

However, recent neoliberal deregulation and related global (re)organization of labour also make other descriptions of society, such as Bauman's depiction of bleak post-modernity, equally relevant (Bauman 1997, 2004). Categories such as outcasts, wasted lives, strangers, pariahs, and vagabonds provided convincing descriptions of populations who in Marxist analysis would be expected to join the working classes. Still, this has not occurred, and the workings of global capitalism continue to produce new forms of people without history who are invisible to national records. A striking case of this condition occurred in the village of my fieldwork. When I was there in 2005, more than 300 young men were occasionally occupied in illegal goldmining. After 2011 an Australian multinational leased the land and established a legal goldmine in the same area. With their new equipment they needed only 40–50 semi-skilled and unskilled workers, whereas the skilled drillers were imported directly from overseas. Besides, a significant amount of farmland was destroyed to build their goldmine, leaving dozens of farmers and their families landless. Wage labour for the few meant unemployment and devastation for the many, and this seems to be a spiral movement towards people with history but without class in twenty-first century global capitalism.

References

Addo, Eric Osei. 2017. The impact of manufactoring industries on Ghana's economy, in *International Journal of Research Studies in Management*, vol. 6, No 2, pp. 73–94.

Abudu, Herman and Rockson Sai. 2020. Examining prospects and challenges of Ghana's petroleum industry: A systematic review, in *Energy Reports*, vol. 6 (2020), pp. 841–858.

Amankwah-Amoah, Joseph. 2015. Explaining declining industries in developing countries: The case of textiles and apparel in Ghana, in *Competition and Change*, vol. 19 (1), pp. 19–35.

Anazodo, Rosemary and Hope Nzewi. 2011. African Underdevelopment and the Multinationals- A Political Commentary, in *Journal of Sustainable development*, vol. 4, No 4, pp. 101–109.

Alemayehu, Mariam G. 2017. The Chinese Neo-Colonialism in Africa. *Pambazuka News* 7-9-2017. https://www.pambazuka.org/global-south/chinese-neocolonialism-africa, accessed 9-1-2019.

Amanor, Kojo and Janine Ubink. 2008. Contesting land and custom in Ghana: Introduction in Kojo Amanor and Janine Ubink, *Contesting Land and Custom in Ghana*. Leiden University Press, pp. 9–26.

Amudsen, Inge. 2019. Extractive and power-preserving political corruption in Africa, in Inge Amudsen, *Political Corruption in Africa*. Cheltenham UK, Northampton MA USA: Edward Elgar Publications, pp. 1–28.

Aryeetey, Ernst and William Baah-Boateng. 2007. Growth, Investment and Employment in Ghana. *Policy Integration Department-International Labour Office*. Geneva March 2007.

Aryeetey, Ernst and William Baah-Boateng. 2016. Ghana needs a new strategy to create new jobs and reduce inequality. *The Conversation*. 5 March 2016. https://theconversation.com/ghana-needs-a-new-strategy-to-create-decent-jobs-and-reduce-inequality-55179 accessed 20 September 2020.

Asamoah, Mercy and Franc, Owusu-Ansah. 2017. Report on Land Tenure and Cocoa Production in Ghana. Accra and Washington DC: A CRIG/WCF Collaborative Survey, February 2017.

Asante, Kofi Takyi and Moses Kisha. 2019. Political corruption and the limits of anti-corruption activism in Ghana, in Inge Amudsen, *Political Corruption in Africa*. Cheltenham UK, Northampton MA USA: Edward Elgar Publications, pp. 29–51.

Bauman, Zygmunt. 1997. *Postmodernity and its Discontents*. New York: New York University Press.

Bauman, Zygmunt. 2001. *The Individualized Society*. Cambridge, Malden MA: Polity Press.

Bauman, Zygmunt. 2004. *Wasted Lives. Modernity and its outcasts*. Cambridge, Malden MA: Polity Press.

Blocher, Joseph. 2006. Building on Custom: Land Tenure Policy and Economic Development in Ghana, *9 Yale Hum. Rts. and Dev. L.J.* (2006). Available at: https://digitalcommons.law.yale.edu/yhrdlj/vol9/iss1/5. Accessed 22-09-2020.

Cheru, Fantu and Cyril Obi. 2010. *The Rise of China and India in Africa. Challenges, Opportunities and Critical Interventions*. London, New York: Zed Books.

Chukwuemeka, Emma and Anazodo, Rosemary and Nzewi, Hope. 2011. African Underdevelopment and the Multinationals- A political Commentary, in *Journal of Sustainable Development*, Vol. 4, No. 4, doi:10.5539/jsd.v4n4p101.

Copans, Jean. 1985. The Marxist conception of class: political and theoretical elaboration in the African and Africanist context, *Review of African Political Economy*, 12 (32): 25–38, DOI: 10.1080/03056248508703612. Accessed 18-10-2018.

Emery, Alan. 2018. Class and Race Domination and Transformation in South Africa, in *Critical Sociology* 34 (3) 409–431.

Foster, Vivien and Natalyia Pushak. 2011. Ghana's Infrastructure, A Continental Perspective. *Policy Research Working Paper 5600*. The World Bank. Africa Region. Sustainable Development Department. March 2011.

Frimpong-Ansah, Jonathan H. 1991. *The Vampire State in Africa. The Political Economy of Decline in Ghana*. London: James Currey, Trenton NJ.: Africa World Press.

Fuseini, Issahaka, Joseph Yaro and Gerald Yiran. 2017. City Profile, Tamale Ghana, in *Cities 60*, 2017: pp. 64–74. https://www.researchgate.net/deref/http%3A%2F%2Fdx.doi.org%2F10.1016%2Fj.cities.2016.07.010, Accessed 21-09-2020.

Ghana Statistical Service. 2012. *2010 Population and Housing Census. Summary Report of final results*. Accra: Ghana Statistical Service, May 2012.

Ghana Statistical Service. 2015. *Integrated Business Establishment Survey. National Employment Report*. Accra: Ghana Statistical Service, September 2015.

Gifford, Paul. 1998. *African Christianity: its public role*. Bloomington Indiana: Indiana University Press.

Grier, Beverly. 1981. Underdevelopment, Modes of Production and the State in Colonial Ghana, *African Studies Review*, Vol. 24, No 1: 21–47.

Grier, Beverly. 1987. Contradiction, Crisis and Class Conflict: The State and Capitalist Development in Ghana Prior to 1948, in *Studies in Power and Class in Africa*, 27–49. Oxford: Oxford University Press.

Grier, Beverly. 1993. Pawns, Porters and Petty Traders: Women in the Transition to Export Agriculture in Ghana, in *Pawnship in Africa*, edited by Paul E. Lovejoy and Toyin Falola, 159–183. Boulder: Westview Press.

Gupta, Ranajit Das. 1986. "From Peasants and Tribesmen to Plantation Workers: Colonial Captialism, Reproduction of Labour Power and Proletarianisation in North East India, 1850s to 1947." *Economic and Political Weekly* 21, no. 4 (1986): PE2–E10. Accessed September 20, 2020. http://www.jstor.org/stable/4375248.

Hameiri, Shahar and Lee Jones. 2020. Theorising Political Economy in Southeast Asia, in Toby Carroll, Shahar Hameiri and Lee Jones (eds.) *The Political Economy of Southeast Asia*. Palgrave Macmillan, pp. 3–34.

Howard (-Hassman), Rhoda 1980. Formation and stratification of the peasantry in colonial Ghana, *Journal of Peasant Studies*, vol. 8, No 1: 61–80.

Hutchful, Eboe. 2002. *Ghana's Adjustment Experience: The Paradox of Reform*. Geneva: United Nations Research Institute for Social Development in association with Oxford: James Carrey, Portsmouth NH: Heinemann and Accra: Woeli Publishing Services.

Kyriakakis, Ioannis. 2010. *Christian Pluralism and Social Differentiation in an Nzema Village in Southwestern Ghana*. Doctoral Thesis, University of London.

Kyriakakis, Ioannis. 2012. "Free Market", Society and Capitalism in the Ex-Colonies: The Case of Ghana. *International Journal of Anthropology*. Vol. 27 n. 3:167–181.

Lesser, Alexander 1961. Social Fields and the Evolution of Society, in *Southwestern Journal of Anthropology*, 17: 40–48.

Mendes, Ana Paula, Mario Bertella and Rudolph Teixeira. 2014. Industrialization in Sub-Saharan Africa and import substitution policy, in *Brazilian Journal of Political Economy*, vol. 34 (1), pp. 120–138.

Obeng-Odoom, Franklin. 2011. Informal Sector in Ghana Under Siege, in *Journal of Developing Societies*, Vol. 27, Issue 3–4, pp. 355–392.

Okia, Opolot. 2012. *Communal Labor in Colonial Kenya*. New York: Palgrave Macmillan.

Shimeles, Abebe and Mthuli Ncube. 2015. The Making of the Middle-Class in Africa: Evidence from DHS Data, *The Journal of Development Studies*, 51:2, 178–193, DOI: 10.1080/00220388.2014.968137

Savage, Mike, Fiona Devine, Niall Cunningham, Mark Taylor, Yaojun Li, Johs. Hjellbrekke, Brigitte Le Roux, Sam Friedman and Andrew Miles. 2013. A New Model of Social Class: Findings from the BBC's Great British Class Survey Experiment. Published online 2 April 2013, *Sociology*. DOI: 10.1177/0038038513481128. Accessed: 18-12-2018.

Sears, Robin, Liliana Davalos and Goncalo Ferraz. 2001. Missing the Forest for the Profits: The Role of Multinational Corporations in the International Forest Regime, in *The Journal of Environment and Development*, Vol. 10, No. 4, pp. 345–364.

Sklair, Leslie. 2002. *Globalization, Capitalism and its Alternatives*. Oxford, New York: Oxford University Press.

Statista 2017–2021. Statista Ghana Internet Penetration 2017–2021. https://www.statista.com/statistics/1171435/internet-penetration-rate-ghana/ Accessed 13/02/2022.

Statista 2020a. Statista Ghana ownership rate of selected digital devices 2020. https://www.statista.com/statistics/1171486/ownership-rate-of-selected-digital-devices-in-ghana/ Accessed 13/02/2022.

Statista 2020b. Ranking of the population share having access to at least basic sanitation in Africa by country 2020. statista.com/forecasts/1167669/access-to-basic-sanitation-in-africa-by-country. Accessed 10.05.2022.

Threlfall, Monica 2002. Labour Market Statistics, in *Radical Statistics*, Issue 88, pp. 22–34. https://www.radstats.org.uk/no088/Threlfall88.pdf accessed 20-09-2020.

Wolf, Eric R. 2010[1982]. *Europe and the People without History*. Berkeley, Los Angeles, London: University of California Press.

Wright Olin, Eric. 2000. *Class Counts. Students edition*. Cambridge, New York, Melbourne: Cambridge University Press.

CHAPTER 7

Impossible Histories, Power, and Exclusion in the Gold Coast and Ghana 1930–2020

Paul Stacey

> In the rough and tumble of social interaction, groups are known to exploit the ambiguities of inherited forms, to impart new evaluations or valencies to them, to borrow forms more expressive of their interests, to create wholly new forms in answer to changed circumstances ... "A culture" is thus better seen as a series of processes that construct, reconstruct, and dismantle cultural materials in response to identifiable determinants.
>
> WOLF 1982, 387[1]

⋯

> That the [Nawuri] case has been shown to be fictitious does not disprove the forces of tradition.
>
> Colonial Officer Dixon (DIXON, para. 66, 1955)

⋮

1   Introduction

Wolf emphasizes the making of cultural forms and related social organization as an inherently messy and relational process shaped by combinations of broader forces, local ingenuity, changes in circumstances, and the positionality of diverse actors: notions of fixed and bounded groups are altogether negated. In contrast, the second quote alludes to colonial ideas of African social organization as held together by eternally fixed traditions and is used to justify the dismissal of Nawuri claims of autonomy. The colonial assertion was important

---

[1] Also in Schneider and Schneider 2004: 502.

© PAUL STACEY, 2023 | DOI:10.1163/9789004527928_008
This is an open access chapter distributed under the terms of the CC BY-NC-ND 4.0 license.

and forceful because state formation and local authority in this part of Ghana was based on versions of the past that had no place for Nawuri agency; any Nawuri claim to the contrary faced systemic rejection. This chapter examines the dynamic relationships between, on the one hand, power initially vested by the British colonial authority in particular versions of tradition based on local polities governed by ethnically defined chiefs, and, on the other, the production of 'alternative' versions of traditional chief-based authority, and the making of an ethno-political group – the Nawuri – who were excluded from the process. This provides insights into relational features of power as producing opposing social categories and cultures through a contested historical process where groups borrow, exploit, and invest new meanings in inherited categories to reduce uncertainty and maximize ability to influence and gain from local development. In a Wolfean perspective we see how Nawuri historical usage and subsequent social mobilization as an excluded group was influenced by translocal power relations and colonial understandings of African tradition as fixed and bounded. The significance of categories established under colonial influence is also relevant for understanding present-day social organization, where cultural expressions relate to the deeper and older organizational and ideologically charged forces and produce understandings of tradition to lay claims to new opportunities in the present that arise from Ghana's democratization. As such, the chapter unravels 'the articulation between the microphysics of politics and the macro-physics of the state' (Ghani 1995, 33).[2]

Today, ethnic identification, the promotion of a unique history and culture with ties to specific lands, and institutions of chieftaincy are all significant markers of countless groups all over Ghana. Such markers reproduce popular perceptions of society as organized around loosely connected yet distinct cultural groups that have existed since time immemorial and whose development is somehow separate from modern political developments. In contrast, this chapter endeavours to explain the making of such cultural traits as an open-ended and contested historical process which, in the case of the Nawuri, emerged following exclusion from the colonial state and through efforts to define themselves as autonomous and equal to others. Today, the group remains disadvantaged and unrecognized, and continues its struggle to gain autonomy. Consequently, the group continues unsuccessfully to wrestle itself

---

2 The title of this chapter was inspired by the article: '*Some histories are more possible than others:* Structural power, big pictures and the goal of explanation in the anthropology of Eric Wolf', by John Gledhill (2005). This chapter is based on doctoral research kindly financed by the Consultative Research Committee for Development Research (FFU), under DANIDA (Danish International Development Agency). Project nr. 926-RUC.

from an unfavourable positioning in histories of the area that were written by others long ago in the colonial period to underpin local governance (Stacey 2015). The formal institutionalization of Nawuri exclusion by key actors, state institutions, and formal state law means therefore that from a state perspective Nawuri history and traditions are 'impossible', and state formation has demanded that they constitute a people without history.

This chapter, then, is a story of a group formed as they create for themselves their own history, institutional forms, and traditions from the ambiguities they experience as they are edited out of area history by more powerful forces, including the British administering authority and the UN Trusteeship Council in the colonial period, and successive Ghanaian governments after Ghana's independence in 1957. To set the scene, the following section describes a recent Nawuri cultural celebration. This is followed by a discussion of Wolf's concept of structural power that informs the analysis, and an overview of the data collection and methods. Next, Nawuri struggles covering three historical periods of crisis are presented and discussed. The chapter closes by drawing the main points together in a conclusion, highlighting the continued significance of 'tradition' as established in the 1930s and exemplifying Wolf's concept of structural power.

2   A Nawuri Celebration of Uniqueness

At dawn on Christmas Eve 2019, a large group of volunteers lined up in Kpandai, Ghana and started to sweep the length of the dusty, partly tarred and potholed main road with short brooms of coarse grass.[3] The early start avoided the coming heat of the sun as the three-hour sweep helped to prepare for a six-day festival. This was to welcome Nawuri on their return from all corners of the traditional homeland and to commemorate a new institution, the NPA (Nawuri Professionals Association). The NPA aims to harness unity, expertise, and experience amongst a diaspora Nawuri community and promote a unique cultural heritage. Festival activities included a well-attended 'Unity Walk' with 'Saaru' traditional dancers and drumming. Traditional dignitaries led the walk accompanied by two women carrying large saucepans of chicken cooked with maize and palm oil. Three other women chanted while carefully sprinkling the food on the ground from East to West, and from South to North to pacify evil spirits, purify the land, and invite Nawuri deities to feast. In another

---

[3]   Special thanks to Ben Asunki for collecting data about the ceremony.

libation ceremony attended by chiefs adorned with colourful traditional regalia and representing different Nawuri villages, a ram and a white cock were sacrificed to appease Nawuri ancestors and land deities, and to grant Nawuri a new beginning devoid of all harm. The chiefs were flanked by enthusiastic Nawuri youth dancing to different 'Baya' traditional dances and coming from the different chiefly villages in Nawuri lands: Kitare, Nkanchina, Bladjai, Balai, Kabonwule, Dodoia, Kpandai, and Katiejeli. Ghanaian national media in the form of Tv3, UTV, and Home Base TV filmed the spectacle. In the following days activities included readings of Nawuri history, presentations of Nawuri belief systems, speeches with appeals to increase recognition given to Nawuri Queen mothers, and a hotly contested Nawuri proverb competition. During the festival representatives from each traditional area performed their own customary warrior dance with contrasting styles of drumming, colour, and choreography as markers of uniqueness. Youth from Kitare danced 'Kaake'; Nkanchina youth danced 'Kalei', Kpandai youth danced 'Sukuudai', Balai youth danced 'Gangaan', Kabonwule youth danced 'Kakpancha', and Katiejeli youth danced 'Ijii', which is exclusively for women. On 28 December a grand durbar was well attended and led by the chiefs and elders.

Invited guests including local government officials, parliamentarians, and religious heads, who were all seated together, many of them dressed colourfully. Here, the Okyeame (chief linguist) of the KpandaiWura (Chief of Kpandai) offered libation. The invited guests and dignitaries made speeches for fund-raising programmes such as the launch of a youth scholarship scheme for up-and-coming Nawuri professionals. Speeches calling for ethnic unity and mutual respect were given by representatives of other ethnic youth associations in the area, including Konkomba, Kotokeli, Ewe, and Nchumuru. Prior to each speech a powerful Nawuri appellation, 'Kamanchor Kabuja', was chanted. After the speeches Nawuri women of the witch hunter's cult 'Alijii' or 'Okule' performed another traditional dance. One Nawuri onlooker described how 'the durbar was indeed historic, colourful, sensational, memorable and an unforgettable event that would forever linger in the minds of all Nawuri and other ethnic groups at large on our land'. A church service attended by a large congregation dressed wholly in white rounded off the festival on Sunday 29 December.

The numerous activities and enactments of Nawuri ritual, ceremony, and ancient traditions provided ample opportunities for interaction between villagers and dignitaries, affirming ideas of Nawuri culture in the popular imagination and its inherent uniqueness among other ethnic groups. The customs built bridges between imageries of an ancient, non-secular past and the secular ambitions of the present; between ideas of Nawuri as a corporate body and the relative autonomy and complexity of each Nawuri sub-clan. The displays projected a powerful image of Nawuri as having unique traits, an essence that declared what it is to be Nawuri while defining who belonged to the group and who did not (Schneider and Schneider 2004). For any observer it was difficult not to be overwhelmed by the reverence enacted, while for outsiders the displays of culture were purely incomprehensible, fascinating, and obscure – as was wholly intended.

3   Grasping Power

How can we comprehend such displays of tradition and culture from a power perspective? One starting point is to recognize power as a notoriously slippery concept where, on the one hand, it is often central in explanations for societal change, yet, on the other, is often ill-defined, used in the abstract as either a catch-all or as a singular unexplained force, or understood as an ideological charge (Hall et al. 2011). In EPWH, and especially in later works, Wolf established an open and comparative approach to power, which theretofore was a concept most routinely encountered in Universalist philosophy (Portis-Winner 2006).[4] In brief, Wolf distinguished four modalities of power: (1) embodied or inherent as an individual attribute or capability; (2) the ability to impose one's will on others; (3) tactical or organizational control by groups over settings or contexts in which people interact; and (4) structural power, as the ability to organize the settings themselves through, for example, ideology – so defining the political economy (Wolf 1990; McGee and Warms 2013).[5] For Wolf, a general characteristic of power is as a quotidian feature of 'all relations among people', and as derived from positions in structural power, itself defined as the ability to organize social settings, and which 'shapes the social field of action so as to render some kinds of behaviour possible, while making others less possible or impossible' (Wolf 1990, 587). This resonates with Bourdieu, for whom 'The degree of autonomy of a certain field is measured by its ability to reject external determinants and obey only the specific logic of the field' (Bourdieu 1993, 38–9).[6] In EPWH, a principal argument is the interdependence and changing

---

[4] Geertz 1973 however is a pre-EPWH example of power conceptualized to explain how traditional ideas around culture influence the political character of contemporary organization. Here from Barrett et al 2001.
[5] The concept of power was developed by Wolf after EPWH in, for example, *Envisioning Power: Ideologies of Dominance and Crisis* (Wolf 1999).
[6] Despite the similarity for Bourdieu a main concern is governmentality, while for Wolf it is the political economy.

temporal and spatial relationships between power, ideas, and social relations (Barrett et al. 2001). Hence, Wolf's approach to the power of culture is to trace and relate social life and traditions to histories of unequal relations and the workings of discourse, as opposed to basing investigation around notions of group commonalities or differences (Wolf 2001; McGee and Warms 2013). For Wolf, power is fundamentally *relational* and extends beyond typical Weberian perspectives in terms of the exercise of force and coercion (Heyman 2003; Barrett et al. 2001; Weber 1978). Social groups' development of a language of mobilization, their organization, and the forms that culture and identity take are therefore manifestations of power, as are the ways they confront, form alliances, and collude with other forces in an open and unfinished process (Hall et al. 2011; Procter 2004). Wolf's conceptualization of power subsequently also considers social groups' ability to bring about intended effects, the shaping of surrounding conditions of indeterminacy, and the unintended outcomes within a social field (Moore 1978; Heyman 2003; Russell 1938). Structural power is also elusive and processual, as it 'makes, maintains, and erodes' social and cultural relations (Wolf 2001, 386; Heyman 2003, 140). The 'making' aspect resonates meanwhile with E. P. Thompson, who rejected structural functionalism and exemplifies the impact of power in terms of social fields that 'make' and 'unmake' categories such as class out of disparate groups of people, endeavouring (successfully and unsuccessfully) to adjust contrasting heritages into new social orders.[7]

The Wolfean idea of power as a force field causing differing and multiple outcomes is common today, where, for example, 'forms of dominance, contention and resistance may develop, as well as certain regularities and forms of ordering', and where organizing practices are the result not of 'a common understanding or normative agreement', but of 'the forces at play within the field' (Nuijten 2003, 12). Consequently, it is how individuals and social groups position themselves in structural power that conditions social and cultural organizational possibilities.[8] Indeed, for Wolf, the relationships between structural power, actual forms of organization (social, socio-political, or cultural), and modes of production are so significant that structural power is only perceptible after a clean break from the forms of organization in which it occurs (Heyman 2003, 140). This means that power is often not immediately observable, noticeable, or tangible although ethnographic methods allow for the

---

[7] The 'making' from E.P. Thompson as in *'The Making of the English Working Class'.* Thompson 1982.
[8] For brevity culture is taken to mean 'shared understandings and their representations in language, objects, and practices', Tilly 2005, 96.

observation of both its intended and concrete effects, and its unintended and unfinished outcomes (Smith 2018; Heyman 2003). The epistemological point of departure of a mutually constitutive relation between culture and power marked Wolf's distance from contemporary anthropology which, with its keen focus on deciphering meanings, invariably negated either the power of culture, or the culture of power.[9] The centrality of wider power relations as well as the role of history in making culture is also evident in Bourdieu and Foucault, for whom the universalizing and ubiquitous forms that power takes, and which impact on consciousness, demand investigation from multiple perspectives; and where, like Wolf, 'a society without power can only be an abstraction' (Foucault 1982, 791).[10]

Wolf's conceptualization of power bridges Foucault's focus – its impact on consciousness, omnipresence, and indeterminacy – with that of Marx, where power is manifest in the shaping of the political economy and particularly the organization of labour (Portis-Winner 2006). By Wolf, the history of Nawuri is consequently explained in his chapter as that of a 'people without history' emerging from an unfavourable positioning in structural power, which shapes the social setting, the organization of the group, and where 'both the people who claim history as their own and the people to whom history has been denied emerge as participants in the same historical trajectory' (Wolf 1982: 23). As such, the cultural festival described above and the assertions of unique history should be understood in the context of Nawuri efforts to shape the broader political developmental trajectory of the polity in which they live, though this has defined them as unequal, and conditions the forms that their social organization takes, and shows how 'complex historical processes produce differentiated sociocultural forms over time in any given location' (Schneider and Schneider 2004: 501).

The key methodological points of departure for this chapter, then, are to approach power as an open process with both intended and unintended effects on social organization (Procter 2004), in which, to paraphrase Sally Falk Moore, the focus on *process* provides a flag under which structural

---

[9] This research focus on societal schisms and crisis reflects a Marx epistemology that reveals otherwise hidden and contradictory societal conditions, together with the power relations behind.

[10] In *Envisioning Power* ... (1999) Wolf establishes a distance from both Foucault and Bourdieu by undertaking anthropological case studies and formulating grand theory, based on the comparison of concrete manifestations of power in three very different temporal and spatial empirical settings: the Kwakiuti, the Aztecs, and National Socialist Germany.

explanations are dismissed (Moore 1978, xix), and where representations of social organization and related institutions are approached as claims rather than facts (Lund 2007).

4   Methods

The empirical data for this chapter are based on six months of ethnographic fieldwork and archival research in Ghana over three visits from July 2008 to February 2010 (Stacey 2012). This has been followed up by online and telephone communication and written documentation received from Nawuri residents. Data collection focused on the usage and instrumentalization of tradition by different stakeholders, and the meanings and significance given to Nawuri institutions of chieftaincy, both in everyday life and in formal state law over the period from 1930 to the present. One key area was how processes of recognition and non-recognition impacted on the ability of the Nawuri to benefit from a range of valuable resources (Ribot and Peluso 2009). For this chapter, the empirical data of the Nawuri struggle are interpreted anew with Wolfean perspectives to unravel the workings of structural power 'that not only operates within settings or domains but [...] also organizes and orchestrates the settings themselves' (Wolf 1999).[11] For example, the data are interpreted to explore how structural power conditioned the making of unequal relations and social categories, determined the ability to control land, labour, and people, defined access to positions of authority in state institutions and ability to determine employment opportunities, influenced the ability of groups to enjoy public funding for traditional institutions, and enabled both the collection and distribution of land rents and tax revenues, and how local organization and mobilization were shaped.[12] The following empirical sections of the chapter are divided into three periods marking crisis and differentiation: The first covers the institutionalization of tradition from about 1930 to 1957 and covers Nawuri experiences in the colonial period from the implementation of

---

11   Here from Barrett et al 2001.
12   The archival research was undertaken at Northern Region of Ghana Public Records, Tamale, Northern Region, Ghana (NRG). A notable informant was J. Mbimgadong (Nana Obimpeh ca 1930–2013), a central Nawuri figure for at least sixty years. Obimpeh spoke to the UN General Assembly in 1952 for the Togoland Congress, was voted in as MP for Kpandai with the National Alliance of Liberals in the short-lived return to parliamentary election in 1969, and was Chief of Balai in the Nawuri traditional area (Balaiwura) for nearly thirty years. Another key informant is Nana Atorsah II, present day Kpandaiwura, and son of Nana Atorsah I (*ca.* 1920–72).

the system of indirect rule by the British administering authority, to Ghana's attainment of independence. The second covers a decade-long period of political instability in Ghana that overlapped with a local and drawn-out Nawuri-initiated dispute over chieftaincy from the late 1960s to the mid-1970s. Finally, the last period covers the emerging democratization of Ghana from the 1990s (which saw ethnic fighting in East Gonja) up to the relative political stability of the present with local government reform and promises of improved recognition and representation. The sections of empirical data comprise highly compressed and reworked parts of previously published works that are based on different conceptual and theoretical framings (Stacey 2014; 2015; 2016).[13] Accordingly, this chapter provides new Wolfe-inspired interpretations of Nawuri history and struggle.

5   Categorizing Tradition 1930–57

In the 1930s the Nawuri were a minority in the area in which they lived. With other minorities in the Kpandai area, the Nanjuro and Nchrumbru, they shared a limited inclination to develop institutions of chieftaincy in the dispersed hamlets they populated prior to the introduction of indirect rule by the British colonial power.[14] The early 1930s, however, marked a turning point as the homelands of the three minority groups were incorporated into the newly demarcated East Gonja district in the Northern Territories of the Gold Coast. This was an element in the policy of indirect rule introduced by Guggisberg (Governor of the Gold Coast, 1919–28) which meant ruling through designated 'Native' institutions with what was to become the Native Authority system. In East Gonja, the chiefs and traditions of a much larger group, the Gonja, gained colonial recognition. This was based on a firm colonial belief in a traditional allegiance existing between the minority groups and Gonja overlords, and of a historical Gonja conquest over the area.[15] Subsequently, society was ethnically stratified with the Nawuri, Nanjuro, and Nchrumbru coming under the control of state-recognized Gonja chiefs. The policy of indirect rule through Native Authorities was convenient and cheap as it allowed large areas and scattered groups to be ruled effectively through select Africans who held extensive powers over land and people. It also required the presence of an

---

13   Empirical data are reused and reprinted with permission of *Journal of African History; African Studies Review*, and *Development and Change*.
14   Interview, Mbimgadong (see footnote 12), 18 December 2009.
15   NRG 8/2/198, report by Duncan-Johnstone on the Yapai conference, 6 May 1930.

absolute minimum of colonial staff, who defined procedures for the selection and appointment of new chiefs through dialogue with those already recognized by the colonial state (Bening 1999; Chanock 1991). A key objective for the colonial power was to separate what was understood as modern and secular political development from African socio-political organization, which itself was perceived as bounded and fixed. The policy was flawed in its conception, however, by assumptions of African fixity and the presumption that African social organization could be changed radically by meetings with colonial powers (Lund 2004; Spear 2003).

The Native Authority system was designed to ensure that the Northern Territories of the Gold Coast underwent a slower pace of economic development than that planned for the southern 'Colony' of the Gold Coast. Subsequently, in the area occupied by the minority groups, commercial farming, land sales, and cash-cropping were restricted. Both the British administering authority and the newly recognized, ethnically defined chiefs accordingly asserted politically convenient versions of the past that justified Gonja control in the present and at the same time dismissed all other versions as historical fictions (Mbowuru 2002; Ampiah 1991). Forthwith, a form of tributary mode of production governed land and people, with the state-recognized Gonja chiefs controlling land distribution and extracting a cut of agricultural production from the minority groups, who were mainly subsistence farmers. In turn, the recognized chiefs had the power to control land access and to distribute the extracted surplus as they saw fit. This facilitated the development of ethnically defined patron–client relations. Thereafter, the colonial power and privileged Gonja authority figures reconstructed social mechanisms and cultural meanings around resource distribution, so that different forms of tribute, rent, 'drink money', and labour were imbued with and legitimated in line with ancient Gonja customs and Nawuri traditional allegiance.

Ethnically defined contentions between the stratified groups surfaced soon after the imposition of the Native Authority system and demonstrate how radically the newly formed power relations had reshaped socio-political relationships. In 1932, for example, Nawuri protested their exclusion from the selection process for a new Gonja chief of Kpandai.[16] And in 1935 colonial officers voiced concern that segments of the minority groups were calling for secession from Gonja-controlled areas.[17] In 1943, Nawuri protested to the colonial administration that Gonja-led conscription drives, supposedly for World War II efforts,

---

16   NRG 4/2/1, correspondence from DC Krachi to CCNT, 26 Sept. 1932.
17   NRG 8/4/73, DC Salaga, Informal Diary, July 1935.

were misused as labour was diverted to the detriment of Nawuri farming livelihoods. In the following years, the power of the social field around tradition that had produced, and systematized, ethnically based inequalities led the Nawuri to construct their own unique institutions and power symbols. Hence, they developed institutions of chieftaincy like their colonially endorsed masters to resist Gonja domination and gain control over their own history and traditions. Agency vested in chieftaincy by the minority groups gained momentum with changes in formal state law, when new local government institutions in the form of District Councils and Local Councils replaced the Native Authority system in 1951. Although suffrage was introduced, one third of the new government institutions' membership was reserved for the recognized (Gonja) chiefs, who were to preside over the new councils, which also bore Gonja names.[18] In East Gonja the reform established the Alfai Local Council in Kpandai in 1951, which was one of twelve local councils under the new Gonja Volta District Council.[19] The minority groups had just one traditional representative on the Alfai Local Council and none at the district level. The local government reform triggered minority group mobilization with the elevation of a Nawuri, 'Nana Atorsah', as 'Nawuri-wura' (literally, Nawuri head-chief), and as 'Chief of the Nawuri Land'. This was a direct counter to Gonja influence over the new councils and aimed to ensure that minority groups had traditional representation there.[20]

In the early 1950s there were numerous skirmishes in Kpandai, ethnically based complaints, and protests of unfairness, prejudice, and discrimination against the local council. Nawuri subsequently refused to pay market stall fees in Kpandai, sent dozens of complaints to all levels of government that went unheeded, and eventually boycotted the local councils altogether (Stacey 2014). Their protests emphasized their own unique traditional titles, sacred rights, traditions, and histories in attempts to overturn the lack of representation and recognition. Written complaints were rife with colonially introduced nomenclature such as 'paramount chief', 'divisional area', 'native authority', 'traditional area', 'traditional council', 'customary rights', and 'native land rights'. And their protests highlighted numerous traditions, customs, deities, fetishes, and ancient rites defined in ethnically exclusive terms. They asserted fundamental

---

18   NRG 4/7/1, letter from CCNT Norton-James to the Chief Secretary, Ministry of Local Government, Accra, 21 November 1950.
19   The name 'Alfai' is the Gonja term, literally 'Home of Muslims'. The local council system was abolished by President Kwame Nkrumah, who centralized power in the early years after independence and removed chiefs' powers.
20   NRG 8/2/210, letter from Nawuri elders to DC Salaga, 14 October 1951.

differences between their ways and those of their ostensibly 'traditional' overlords by describing divergences in settlement patterns, languages, dances, and clothes, and utilized the Akan prefix *Nana* (denoting a revered elder) to affirm a southern heritage which the 'northern' Gonja did not have.[21] Indeed, the Nawuri did all they could in accordance with ideals of civil disobedience to affirm and establish a separate past. They also constructed imaginary worlds to define themselves as unique, and, by so doing, to appeal to the ideas and values recognized by the British under the Native System of rule.[22]

The local contentions sparked by the outright dismissal of Nawuri claims to their own history quickly reached the attention of global institutions. This was because Kpandai and the East Gonja district were situated in the UN-administered territory of Togoland, and the UN Trusteeship Council had a responsibility to monitor the status of rights of the population living there. More broadly, the trusteeship system oversaw the thorny issue of whether Togoland, which at the time was divided into British and French territories, should eventually be unified, or integrated into existing British and French colonial territories. Significantly, the UN trusteeship mandate stated that any future status of Togoland (either unified or integrated) must pay full regards to the wishes of the whole Togoland population and respect their native status.[23] This meant that the UN Trusteeship Council monitoring the area had an obligation to ensure the British administering authority protected the *native rights* of all the minority groups living there.[24] Consequently, Nawuri developed a language of rights, ideas, and symbols to promote their own *native status* and appealed to the UN Trusteeship system to recognize that British policy dismissed these very rights, which the mandate held in high regard. As such, Nawuri highlighted how the British administering authority had dismissed any ideas that the group could have a history and traditions of their own, thus unjustly excluding Nawuri from representation on the local council and on

---

21 NRG 8/3/184, 'UN Visiting Mission Annual Report for Northern Togoland 1952'.
22 Interview, Mbimgadong (see footnote 12), 18 December 2009.
23 Britain outwardly committed to neutrality, as expected by the UN Trusteeship Council, but pushed nevertheless for integration. See Amenumey (1989), 80.
24 The debate over unification and integration was known as the so-called Togoland Question and became pressing through the 1950s as two of the largest Gold Coast political parties, the southern-based Convention People's Party (CPP), and the Northern Peoples Party (NPP), in the Northern Territories of the Gold Coast, both pushed for independence and integration of British Togoland into a future Ghana.

UN-supported institutions, which were otherwise designed to ensure local consultation and protection of local native rights.[25]

Nawuri gained the attention of the UN Trusteeship system by sending alarmist telegrams such as 'Intimidation and human torture being administered'[26] and 'Inhuman atrocities being inflicted on peoples'.[27] They developed social justice and humanitarian dimensions of 'tradition' and emphasized 'modern' characteristics of their traditional cultural institutions. Their aims were to legitimate their claims to ancient homelands, gain political representation in modern institutions, and ensure recognition of their native status by appealing to the language of rights promoted by the UN Trusteeship system. The newly proclaimed 'Nana Atorsah Agyeman, Head Chief of the Nawuris, Kpandai', wrote protests to the Trusteeship Council in 1951 and 1952 which were rebuffed on the grounds that the group did not represent the whole area and that their 'traditional allegiance' was to the Gonja (UNBISNET 1951; 1952). And in December, 1952, the Nawuri dissident J. Mbimgadong (later Nana Obimpeh I, Balaiwura, see Figure 7.1) spoke to the UN in New York on behalf of a delegation supporting the unification of Togoland, and accentuating the persistent undermining of Nawuri native status and history.[28]

> We are unduly suppressed [and] not allowed to speak [and are] subjected to severe punishment [because men] have been brought over to Northern Togoland and are made chiefs superceding our own chiefs. We hope that this Committee being made up of sympathetic people – people who are really humanitarian – [will ensure] a humanitarian measure will be taken [which is] satisfactory to the needs of the people.[29]

Other appeals pointed out the uniqueness of Nawuri and that the UN was 'dedicated to peace, law, order, justice and fair play among the nations irrespective of size, race, or strength' while the British administering authority had

---

25   The institutions were the Enlarged Joint Togoland Consultative Commission (EJTCC), and the Joint Togoland Council (JTC). That Nawuri persistently emphasized notions of inclusiveness and justice contrasts with a dominant historiographical perspective that the meeting of European and Africans resulted mainly in authoritarian institutions of customary authority. See for example Mamdani 1996.
26   NRG 8/22/27, telegram from Secretary of Togoland Congress to Ministry of Defense and External Affairs, 31 July 1953.
27   NRG 8/22/27, anonymous telegram to GA Salaga, 1 August 1953.
28   Interview with J. K. Mbimgadong, Kpandai, 22 December 2009.
29   NRG 8/22/27, speech by Ijemple (J. K) Mbimgadong, Representative of Joint Togoland Congress to the UN Fourth Committee, 19 December 1952.

undermined the 'basic guarantees, securities, rights and protections granted to the people ... under the UN Charter'.[30] Hence, the situation conditioned the minority groups to justify their own claims to native status with references to the ideals and ideas of the UN system itself. The influence of the UN system on Nawuri mobilization around tradition is moreover evident in that the campaign which attempted to rewrite history was non-violent at this juncture because it endeavoured to appeal to the well-publicized ideals of the powerful UN system. Overall, then, we see how the power of tradition influenced the actions, ideas, language, and organization of competing local, colonial, and global institutions, none of whom, incidentally, cast any doubt on the role tradition had played and should play in determining socio-political organization. This is clear from some correspondence below, where Nawuri campaigners emphasize how the British administering authority has negated sacred traditions:

> [I]s there any wors[e] injury to a tribe whose dialect, customs and culture are not identical to each other, [to force] that tribe in his own God-Given-Land to subjugate entirely to [another] tribe, who is in no way superior in anything to that of the aborigines [?] [A]nd for the Administering Authority [to keep silent] over our repeated petitions and resolutions. [This] is a serious challenge to our integrity, which is not the least expected from a representative of such a Great Empire whose democracy the whole British Subjects are proud of [sic].[31]

Other petitions stressed that Great Britain and France, in 'classic colonial style through suppression, oppression, [and a] reign of terror [had contradicted] the sacred, international, legal, and moral duties they have assumed'.[32] After several years of protests, countless complaints, and investigations including a UN-instigated inquiry in 1955, the minority groups finally managed to gain the right to *traditional* representation on the local council. However, the outcome was a pyrrhic victory because the position was conditional on the approval of Gonja chiefs, so the move provided for a new mechanism for Gonja to assert

---

30   NRG 8/22/27, 'Petition submitted by the Togoland Congress, including the natural rulers and various political parties', undated.
31   NRG 8/2/210, petition from the Paramount Chief of Kpandai and 13 others to the Trusteeship Council, the governor, and 12 other administering authority institutions, 1 February 1954.
32   NRG 8/22/27, 'Petition submitted by the Togoland Congress, including the natural rulers and various political parties', undated.

authority over the Nawuri. In brief, the 'solution' reproduced the social field of ethnically defined inequality and the narrative of a need to protect ancient tribal allegiances (Stacey 2014).[33] This is evident in the conclusion to a colonial investigation into the Nawuri complaints:

> The Nawuris have gone to such pains to distort historical fact in order to try and build up claim to dominance in the local Alfai council (sic). That their case has been shown to be fictitious does not disprove the forces of tradition.[34]

So, the British administering authority dismissed Nawuri claims and affirmed that their chiefs were false and that the group had no traditions or history of their own. For assurance, strict instructions were sent that, forthwith, colonial officials should address the proclaimed Nawuri Paramount Chief Nana Atorsah by lay name only, and that official correspondence should label the man in terms such as 'self-elected' leader, a 'self-styled chief', and 'person describing himself as a Head Chief'.[35]

The dialectic between the colonial denial of Nawuri agency and history, and the social mobilization and development of Nawuri chiefs exemplifies how cultural change developed under 'variable, but also highly determinate circumstances' which at different times both provided for and limited the creativity and resistance of the emerging group in 'varied circumstances [in which the social group] shape, adapt, or jettison their cultural understandings or, alternatively, find themselves blocked in doing so' (Wolf 2010, xxiii). We also see how structural power orchestrated the social field, with Nawuri adopting the nomenclature of their oppressors and contributing to the production of a contested field of action around tradition that became a key marker of social organization, with previous, fluid socio-political relations giving way to mutually exclusive, ethnically defined categories.

---

33 NRG 8/2/212, file note from GA Salaga to Dixon, undated. The compiler assumed the Gonja version of history was correct but wrote the related file is 'in effect little more than an index with notes of the files in question and cannot claimed [sic] to be a complete or fully authoritative record of the subject'.

34 Dixon, para. 66, 1955.

35 NRG 8/2/22, letter from CRO to Ass. GA Salaga, 10 December 1952. NRG 8/2/21, letter from CCNT to Permanent Secretary, Ministry of Local Government, 22 February1952. NRG 8/2/212, letter from CRO to GA Damongo, 30 November 1955. The process of eliding Nawuri from history as an autonomous group is also evident in a 1960 map of Ghanaian ethnic groups, where the group does not appear, despite the naming of many other, numerically smaller ethnic groups.

On independence in March 1957, the Nawuri did not experience any changes in the fields of power that defined them as unequal both in law and practice. In the perspective of the unintended effects of structural power, however, the minority group did succeed in creating locally legitimate and popular traditional institutions that took advantage of the ambiguities that developed as result of colonial power vesting its agency in tradition. Informally, Nawuri chiefs, for example, gained substantial ability to influence local affairs even though the formal avenues were closed off, and the group's instrumentalization of tradition enabled the development of a group identity, collective ethnic expression, and the assertion of local discourses around rights and justice. Thereby, translocal relationships enabled the development and mobilization of a local language of rights to come to terms with political upheaval, but which itself was conditioned by the norms and ideas of more powerful institutions that from the start had defined the group as unequal.

6 New Politics and Stalled Ambitions 1968–1976

This section outlines the continuation of the Nawuri struggle for the recognition of their traditional authorities, as exemplified by a complex dispute over the appointment of the chief of Kpandai, and which spanned about a decade of political change and upheaval in Ghana from the late 1960s. The struggle reflects the continuation of Nawuri resistance to the constraints imposed by ethnically defined chief-based rule, their efforts to affirm their own constructions of cultural relations, and how their articulations were conditioned by broader power relations and the continuation of discursive assertions that denied their claims. The struggle shows therefore that, as a continuation of the colonial period, the use of tradition by Ghanaian governments after independence categorized the Nawuri as a group without agency, and, ultimately, still without traditions and a history of their own.

The so-called 'Kanankulai skin affair' was a dispute which on the surface concerned whether the subject group, Nawuri, should have a say in the selection of their immediate traditional overlord, the Gonja chief of Kpandai. It emerged in Kpandai, East Gonja, in 1968 after the death of the incumbent chief. It caused a good deal of disruption in East Gonja over the following decade and the warring parties never agreed on any lasting solution.[36] The

---

36 *Kanankulaiwura*: literally, Chief Eater of Meat Lumps. Interview with J. Mbimgadong, Kpandai, 23 July 2009. The 'skin', or in southern Ghana the 'stool', symbolize a social group, ancestry, leadership, or attachment to land.

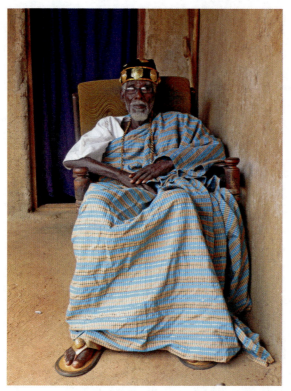

FIGURE 7.1   Balaiwura, Obimpeh J. Mbimgadong I, 2009.
SOURCE: AUTHOR

dispute became a Gordian knot as it spread from the local level to embrace key movements in Ghana's political development through the decade, including the transition from one-party rule to a return to multi-party politics. As such, its unravelling provides insights into state formation continuities amidst radical political change at the centre. In February 1966, for example, the country experienced a coup led by the military and the National Liberation Council (NLC). This overthrew the one-party state and the Convention Peoples Party (CPP) under President Kwame Nkrumah. Following the coup, the NLC lifted a ban imposed by the CPP on political party formation. A new constitution was written, and the country returned to parliamentarianism with multiparty elections held in August 1969. These were won by Kofi Busia and the Progress Party, but in January 1972, the country was rocked again as Busia himself was ousted in a second coup, again driven by the NLC. The NLC subsequently morphed into the Supreme Military Council (SMC), withdrew the 1969 constitution, and halted the democratic experiment (Boafo-Arthur 2001; Biswal 1992).

Military rule continued until 1979, when, in June, the SMC itself was ousted in a third coup, this one led by Flight Lieutenant J. J. Rawlings and the Armed Forces Revolutionary Council (AFRC), which proceeded to introduce another constitution.[37]

The considerable changes at the political centre reverberated at the local level and shaped the dispute in Kpandai. An unravelling of the struggle thus provides key insights into processes of continuity and change concerning structural power and local agency through a decade of political upheaval. Specifically, it tells of how colonially supported powers and discursive constructions of relationships between traditional and modern institutions impacted on local democratization and limited the manoeuvrability of the historically marginalized Nawuri, at the same time as conditioning their mobilization. We see therefore how structural power conditions the social field of action through discourse, laws, and practice to permit and support some kinds of socio-cultural organization while simultaneously limiting and outlawing the formation of others.

The dispute commenced with the death of the Gonja Chief of Kpandai in February 1968. Nawuri leaders claimed they had a historical right of inclusion in the decision making for a successor and objected when a candidate was put forward by senior Gonja chiefs without their consultation. The initial objections were based on a history of animosities between Nawuri and the proposed candidate's family. Despite the framing of the dispute as purely 'traditional' by government, there were many material dimensions as well, because the position enjoyed central positions in local government institutions with the authority to decide on, and influence, a range of resource-distributing mechanisms. These included job positions, agricultural extension services, the awarding of contracts, tendering and procurements, the ability to set land rents, taxes, levies, and rates (for example for marriages and funerals), the granting of building permission, hunting licenses, and the right to rule on the punishment of offenders charged with breaching chiefs' jurisdictions. Thereby, the position of Chief of Kpandai was critical to upholding a form of tributary mode of production and the structuring of a situation, where agriculture was based overwhelmingly on subsistence, where ethnically defined elites extracted a cut of the surplus in the name of customary homage, and where the development of land markets was controlled (at least officially) to keep 'traditional' authority intact.

---

[37] For an overview of political events at the centre, see Owusu, 1989; Biswal, 1992; Boafo-Arthur, 2001.

Nawuri resentment against the candidate and his family stretched back to at least 1964, with complaints of extortion, nepotism, and the appropriation of public goods for private gain, all of which were possible because of the family's alleged dominance over local government in Kpandai at the time. Still, the proposed candidate was elevated to be Chief of Kpandai with the backing of the highest Gonja figure, the Gonja Paramount Chief. In turn, Nawuri argued for respect of the democratic principles behind their traditions and lobbied for another Gonja candidate. In efforts to resolve a brewing stand-off, public servants adopted the ontology of colonial administration and the idea that traditions and customs were clearly identifiable and fixed, accordingly ruling that Nawuri had no right in the matter of selecting the chief because of their traditional allegiances to Gonja overlords (Dixon 1955). In effect, this ruling reproduced the social field of action where Gonja traditional institutions were fundamentally unaccountable to Nawuri and outside the reach of secular government and any emerging democratization objectives.

In defiance, Nawuri initiated a traditional ceremony of their own and appointed their preferred candidate. This took advantage of uncertainties and disagreements between different state officials as to what the correct tradition was, and it succeeded in creating divides between rival Gonja sub-groups. Power vested in tradition was thereby evident as different social, political, and cultural configurations were inadvertently drawn into affirming and negating various versions of the past to justify access to resources and positions in the present, and in the belief that it was possible to solve the dispute with a correct identification of past practices. With this, it was universally accepted that fixed understandings of tradition were *the* means to rationalize society and increase the coherence of otherwise fluid social actions. Conversely, there is no evidence that points to any actors airing misgivings about how agency vested in traditional laws and practice itself only served to fuel contention and the production of competing understandings. This failure to problematize the meanings and roles assigned to tradition in modern political institution building points, therefore, to the ability of structural power to orchestrate the social setting. This is also evident as 'traditional affairs' – as codified in Ghanaian law at the time (and continuing up to the present) – means that any matters related to the appointment of chiefs are off-limits to non-traditional actors such as civil administrators, public servants, and officials.

As such, tradition was something one had to argue with, but which one could not so easily argue about. To recall, this demarcation between ostensibly 'modern' and 'traditional' affairs was institutionalized by the British colonial power to ensure social stability. The discursive and practical separation was retracted on Ghana's independence in 1957 by Nkrumah, with the politicization of the appointments and removals of chiefs. After Nkrumah's overthrow, however, the demarcation was established anew in the 1969 constitution (Stacey 2014). In practice, this confirmation enabled influential actors to accumulate power by positioning themselves as exclusive experts in local traditional affairs to influence local politics. And at the same time, the same influential actors used access and influence over modern political institutions to ensure their traditional interests were protected there, and to ward off interference in traditional matters by 'outsider' public servants. As a continuation of the colonial period, therefore, the reintroduction of the separation of modern and traditional affairs in 1969 was inherently flawed, because it failed to recognize that agency vested in one version of 'tradition' while closing off all others was in fact a product of modern political decision making and amounted to convenient, politically constructed intervention.

With the lifting of the ban on political parties in May 1969, the protagonists aligned along party lines for elections in Kpandai, with Nawuri and supporters canvassing for the National Alliance of Liberals (NAL), and their opponents for the pro-chief Progress Party. Nawuri strength and support for the Gonja chief they appointed was reflected in the NAL winning the constituency with the Nawuri dissident Joseph K. E. Mbimgadong as MP. Still, the chieftaincy dispute dragged on until November 1970, when the sudden death of the Nawuri-supported chief resulted in his opponent gaining the seat as Chief of Kpandai. The new Prime Minister, Busia, was informed that the dispute was now solved and that 'the Nawuris were in no way connected with the case[sic]' (NRG 8/2/171). In that way, the role of Nawuri in the affairs of Gonja traditional politics was systematically omitted from the official view. This was despite the Nawuri-supported Gonja candidate ruling in Kpandai throughout the dispute, successfully challenging the decisions of state institutions, undertaking different customary tasks, and enjoying substantial local support. Formally, however, Nawuri continued to have limited influence over the rules of the polity they lived in, and were excluded from positions of traditional authority. In this way, the state recognized Gonja traditional institutions, which were created by former governments, enjoyed a productive path trajectory, and continued to enjoy the ability to influence the decisions of local government and once more to define traditional affairs in their favour (Weir 2006). The state-recognized Gonja traditional institutions continued to enjoy the ability to affirm traditions in their favour, through which power was drawn and from which rivals were excluded, but which also conditioned the social mobilization of opponents. Legitimacy vested in versions of 'tradition' upheld ethnically defined sovereignty and dismissed other histories as false.

7 Democratization and Exclusion 1990–2020

The Nawuri continued their struggle to rewrite local history and gain recognition of their chiefs as Ghana experienced broader processes of political stability and democratization. The root causes of structural inequality as based on assertions of tradition in formal state law that negated Nawuri agency sparked land-related ethnic fighting between Gonja and Nawuri in the Kpandai area in 1991, and claimed at least 19 lives.[38] The conflict resulted in the ousting of the incumbent Gonja chief of Kpandai, the seizure of Gonja land and houses by Nawuri combatants, and the emergence of competing groups of Nawuri traditional leaders who jostled to take charge of the town and gain control over land. Following the ethnic fighting, a government report, the so-called Ampiah Report ('Report of the committee of inquiry into the Gonja, Nawuri, and Nanjuros dispute to Flt. Lt. Jerry John Rawlings Head of State and Chairman of the Provisional National Defence Council') recommended that Nawuri chiefs gain formal recognition to erase ethnically defined inequality, but this and other pro-Nawuri recommendations in the report did not materialize in practice (Ampiah 1991; Stacey 2015).

In the years following the conflict an internal Nawuri dispute developed over the selection processes for Nawuri chiefs. A central point of contention here was (and remains) control over land in the town centre and rights to sell plots of land for development. One faction comprises supporters of a proclaimed Nawuri 'Paramount Chief' who wishes to seek reconciliation with the Gonja and return their property seized in the 1991 conflict. An opposing anti-Gonja group of Nawuri hold control over land in the centre of Kpandai town and reject Gonja claims to the area outright. Thus the most recent era of intra- and inter-ethnic conflict reflects an underlying shift bought about by the inability of Gonja to continue a tributary mode of production based on the extraction of surplus from Nawuri, to a capitalist mode of production where 'traditional' Nawuri groups compete to define rights to land in order to sell, profit from, and establish new power relationships, and where capital derived from land enables the remaking of claims to authority based on tradition.

Ghana transitioned to democratic rule in 1992 with a new constitution and multi-party presidential and parliamentary elections in 1996. Still, the structural divide between recognized and non-recognized traditional authorities has continued in subtler and more blurred forms. This is because, as a

---

38 The north of Ghana experienced a series of ethnic conflicts in the late 1980s to mid-1990s. See Jönsson 2007; Tonah 2007.

continuation of colonial policy and the trajectory of state law since, the 1992 Republic of Ghana Constitution formally separated chieftaincy affairs from modern, formal political development. Party political involvement in matters of chieftaincy was proscribed (as it was in the 1969 constitution), chiefs were barred from canvassing on party political platforms, and traditional institutions gained constitutional protection. For Nawuri, the legal set-up means that their calls for recognition of their chiefs are directed to Gonja traditional institutions.

Today, interactions between state officials and different Nawuri traditional authorities are pragmatic and influenced by state officials' need to develop productive relations with the powerful but non-recognized local chiefs. On the one hand, state officials need to access powerful Nawuri traditional actors to facilitate local development and increase state legitimacy. But on the other, they are wary not to get drawn into the ever-present debates about Nawuri native status and questions of who the 'correct' chief is. As such, public recognition by a state official of one Nawuri chief or other always risks allegations of undermining the status of others and inciting protest (Stacey 2015). As a senior local government official in Kpandai put it: 'we have to constantly massage all the chiefs so as not to upset anyone' (Interview: 12 December 2009). Nevertheless, the historical dispute resurfaced with the demarcation of a new district and the creation of a new district assembly in Kpandai as an element of democratic local government reform in 2008, with Nawuri hoping to gain traditional representation on the new council (Stacey 2015). Yet the constitutional principle of separating modern and traditional affairs means that, formally, the Kpandai area is still under the traditional authority of the Gonja Traditional Council and the administrative demarcation of the new district's boundary is not to undermine any Gonja traditional jurisdictions (Brobbey 2008). Meanwhile, the position of Gonja Chief of Kpandai has not been occupied in Kpandai since the 1991 conflict.

Thus the discursive power of tradition continues and has in many ways eclipsed the political, administrative and democratic developments as it structures the situation by defining what is, and what is not, possible for different groups and actors. The Nawuri are unable to gain traditional representation on the new district assembly because they were not recognized as chiefs and the institution with the mandate to bestow recognition – the Gonja Traditional Council – refused to provide formal recognition to them. Further, and following the first local elections in the new district in 2008, the historical experiences of Nawuri exclusion resurfaced because their relatively low numbers translated into limited representation based on ballot box logic. Accordingly Nawuri interpreted local government reform as reproducing their ethnic exclusion.

In turn, public servants and state officials became increasingly embroiled in the historical contentions around tradition and found it almost impossible to maintain neutrality. In the first years of the new local government the district assembly executive therefore chose not to involve any of the competing Nawuri chiefs directly in assembly affairs, and decided, in the name of protecting public order, not to allow speeches by the warring chiefs at cutting of the sod ceremonies (a respected tradition) so as to avoid accusations that all land-related developments involved one chief or another's contested land claims.

Yet at the same time the vying chiefs instrumentalized almost any interaction with the district assembly executive to claim recognition over opponents, or to accuse public officials of bias. Accordingly, while public officials endeavoured to stay on the right side of competing Nawuri chiefs and outside the contentious field of tradition, traditional actors instrumentalized social interactions to claim traditional status and gain influence enabling them to control and distribute land. Tradition continued, therefore, as a discursive point which defined a contentious social field of action to both include and exclude groups and to organize social settings. Indeed, the situation in the new district resembled Dennis Austin's astute description of the political situation in Ghana over 50 years ago where: 'tradition became a bottomless well of uncertain practice from which endless arguments could be drawn to justify whatever was thought desirable in current practice' (Austin 1964: 34). Today, to try and avoid the contentious arena around tradition, the assembly executive highlights the Nawuri chiefs' secular credentials – their knowledge of the locality, political experience, networking skills, ability to cooperate, and developmental ambitions. In a novel way, therefore, officials have come to recognize Nawuri chiefs without admitting recognition of their traditional credentials. All the while, however, discourses of tradition are reproduced in numerous ways through public reverence paid to the chiefs and meanings vested in Nawuri customs through ceremonies, everyday social practices, relations, behaviours, and displays. Social interactions between Nawuri chiefs and state officials have also shaped new unequal social categories within the Nawuri themselves: Some actors have gained influence over local government decision making and the ability to position themselves as land custodians and actors whom the assembly must consult to access land for development. In turn, this has led to Nawuri fragmentation, with outbreaks of violence, skirmishes, lengthy land-related litigation between different sub-groups, public arguments about the credentials of different traditional leaders, and accusations against state officials who 'meddle' in traditional affairs. In Kpandai today, contending Nawuri traditional actors continue, therefore, to debate who should rightfully be recognized and who should not, and to make claims accordingly. This is not directed towards gaining the ability to extract labour and agricultural surplus, as it was in the past, but towards control over land in the centre of town, where prices are increasing, the population is growing, and there are new gains to be made from assertions of traditional authority. A key part of the contention around the control of land is the continuation of efforts to rewrite the colonially-initiated versions of local tradition and history that underpin Nawuri exclusion. As such, all Nawuri sub-groups continue to experience the exclusionary effects of structural power because, from the state's perspective, they remain unrecognized traditional authorities. As we saw in the opening vignette, the conjuncture of historical exclusion and demands for recognition continue to drive the production of Nawuri chieftaincy and traditions as socio-cultural institutions with unique customs, symbols, and norms. Communities develop leadership around chieftaincy because, since the colonial period, formal state law has vested agency in tradition and traditional institutions. Hence, unique traditions are created to affirm what a group stands for and to what it lays claim.

8 Conclusion

The chapter builds on Wolf's understanding of structural power as both organizing and orchestrating social and political settings, as structuring fields of action, as influencing manifestations of agency, and as enabling and limiting the direction and articulations of societal organization. To understand the workings of structural power the chapter investigated the vesting of agency in tradition and its influence on social organization in law and practice, and processes of exclusion in East Gonja from about 1930 to the present. The ability of structural power to define and orchestrate social settings meant that Nawuri established their own chiefs and asserted their own histories in their struggles against state law that recognized others and defined the group as unequal and without its own history. The production of Nawuri cultural-political institutions around chieftaincy with an emphasis on native status relates directly to translocal forces and the group's historical meetings and contentions with institutions and organizations that extended well beyond their immediate ethnographic context, but nevertheless impacted heavily on their personal sphere and on meanings that people knew as authentic and defined as their own (Neveling and Steur 2018, 2; Gledhill 2005). Initially, the vesting of agency in particular versions of tradition by the British administering authority created ethnically defined inequality, with privileged groups enjoying the ability to extract rent, tribute, and labour, and control the distribution of land. This process endeavoured to fix colonial ideas of a tributary mode of production as based in the ancient past, but for Nawuri it was experienced as a radical narrowing of their ability to shape the polity in which they lived and 'the direction in which the play [could] go' (Wolf 1959, 173). The Nawuri struggle for recognition and the making of their own chiefs therefore exemplifies culture as a series of processes, social actions, interactions, and confrontations with power and the 'ambiguities of inherited forms [and] new evaluations of valencies of them [and where] new forms more expressive of their interests [are established] to create wholly new forms to answer changed circumstances' (Wolf 1982, 387). Accordingly, Nawuri institutionalized essentialist ideas of identity and culture as a group-in-the-making and as organized around chiefs. The emerging group also experienced internal division as conditioned by their meetings with broader forces in 'historically changing, imperfectly bounded, multiple and branching social alignments' (Wolf 1982, 387). As such, Nawuri fragmentation in recent decades and the production of sub-groups with opposing cultures around chieftaincy exemplify processes of differentiation arising from political change that has bought about crisis and disrupted objectives to establish group coherence, common history, and stability. As such, experiences of crisis have impacted on the socio-cultural and organizational situation (Ghani 1995). The production of cultural characteristics as an open and unfinished process serves multiple purposes including defining the group, establishing historical significance, institutions of leadership, and relations with ancestors and the spiritual world. These are efforts to use tradition and history to establish certainty amidst indeterminacy and as people experience disruptions bought about by political developments (Procter 2004; McGee and Warms 2013). The Nawuri struggle shows, then, how 'the people who claim history as their own and the people to whom history has been denied emerge as participants in the same historical trajectory' (Wolf 1982). This plays out as the group forms through struggle to make sense of and gain control over a social field of action that *demands* they gain recognition to thrive. But, at the same time, the social field of action provides legitimacy for a much broader system of rule that has long defined the Nawuri as unequal, and which means that recognition as an autonomous group with their own history and traditions is unattainable (Rabasa 2005).

References

Amenumey, Divin Edem Kobla. 1989. *The Ewe Unification Movement, a Political History*. Accra.

Ampiah, A.K.B. 1991. "Report of the Committee of Inquiry into the Gonja, Nawuri and Nanjuros Dispute to Flt. Lt. Jerry John Rawlings Head of State and Chairman of the Provisional National Defence Council". Accra: Government Printers.

Austin, Dennis. 1964. *Politics in Ghana 1946–1960.* Oxford University Press, Great Britain.

Barrett, Stanley, R., Sean Stokholm, and Jeanette Burke. 2001. "The Idea of Power and the Power of Ideas: A Review Essay". *American Anthropologist* 103 (2): 468–180.

Bening, R. Bagulo. 1999. *Ghana: Regional Boundaries and National Integration.* Ghana Universities Press.

Biswal, Tapan. 1992. *Ghana: Political and Constitutional Developments.* New Delhi: Northern Book Centre.

Boafo-Arthur, Kwame. 2001. "Chieftaincy and Politics in Ghana Since 1982." *West Africa Review* 3 (1). www.africaknowledgeproject.org.

Bourdieu, Pierre 1993. *The Field of Cultural Production: Essays on Art and Literature.* New York: Columbia University Press.

Brobbey Stephen Alan. 2008. *The Law of Chieftaincy in Ghana.* Advanced Legal Publications, Accra, Ghana.

Chanock, Martin. 1991. "A Peculiar Sharpness: An Essay on Property in the History of Customary Law in Colonial Africa". *The Journal of African History* 32 (1): 65–88.

Dixon, J. 1955. "Dixon Commission of Enquiry; Report by Mr. J. Dixon, Administrative Officer, Class I, On Representations made to the Trusteeship Council of the United Nations Organisation Concerning the Status of the Nawuris and Nanjuros within the Togoland area of the Gonja district". British Colonial Administration.

Foucault, Michel 1982. "The Subject and Power". *Critical Inquiry* 8 (4): 777–795.

Ghani, Ahraf. 1995. "Writing a History of Power: An Examination of Eric R. Wolf's Anthropological Quest". In *Articulating Hidden Histories: Exploring the Influence of Eric R. Wolf.* Edited by Jane Schneider, and Rayna Rapp, 31–48. Berkeley: Univ. of California Press.

Gledhill, John. 2005. "Some Histories are more Possible than Others: Structural Power, Big Pictures and the Goal of Explanation in the Anthropology of Eric Wolf". *Critique of Anthropology* 25 (1): 37–57.

Hall, Derek, Philip Hirsch, and Tania M. Li. 2011. "Introduction to Powers of Exclusion: Land Dilemmas in Southeast Asia". *In Powers of Exclusion: Land Dilemmas in Southeast Asia.* Singapore and Honolulu: National University of Singapore Press/ University of Hawaii Press, 1–27.

Heyman, Josiah, McC. 2003. "The Inverse of Power". *Anthropological Theory* 3 (2):139–156.

Jönsson, Julia. 2007. "The Overwhelming Minority: Traditional Leadership and Ethnic Conflict in Ghana's Northern Region". CRISE Working Paper 30. University of Oxford, UK.

Lund, Christian, ed. 2007. *Twilight Institutions; Public Authority and Local Politics in Africa*. Blackwell, UK.

Lund, Christian. 2004. "This Situation is Incongruous in the Extreme: The History of Land Policies in the Upper Regions of Ghana". Working Paper 46, Sahel-Sudan Environmental Research Initiative (SEREIN).

Mamdani, Mahmood. 1996. *Citizen and Subject: Contemporary Africa and the Legacy of late Colonialism*. Princeton.

Mbowura, Cletus Kwaku. 2002. "Nawuri-Gonja Relations 1913–1994". m.Phil Thesis, University of Ghana, Legon (unpublished).

McGee, R. Jon and Richard L. Warms, eds. 2013. *Theory in Social and Cultural Anthopology: An Encyclopedia*. Sage Publications, Inc.

Moore, Sally Falk. 1978. *Law as Process: An Anthropological Approach*. International African Institute, LIT, James Currey.

Neveling, Patrick, and Luisa Steur. 2018. "Introduction: Marxian Anthropology Resurgent". *Focaal – Journal of Global and Historical Anthropology* 82: 1–15.

Nuijten, M.C.M. 2003. *Power, Community and the State: The Political Anthropology of Organisation in Mexico*. London and Sterling, VA: Pluto Press.

Owusu, Maxwell. 1989. "Rebellion, Revolution and Tradition: Reinterpreting Coups In Ghana". *Comparative Studies in Society and History* 31 (2): 372–397.

Portis-Winner, Irene. 2006. "Eric Wolf: A Semiotic Exploration of Power". *Sign Systems Studies* 34 (2): 339–356.

Procter, James. 2004. *Stuart Hall*. Routledge Critical Thinkers.

Rabasa, José. 2005. "On the History of the History of Peoples Without History". *Humboldt Journal of Social Relations* 29 (1): 204–222.

Ribot, Jesse C., and Nancy L. Peluso. 2009. "A Theory of Access". *Rural Sociology* 68 (2): 153–181.

Russell, Bertrand. 1938. *Power: A New Social Analysis*. George Allen & Unwin, Great Britain.

Schneider, Jane, and Peter Schneider. 2004. "Mafia, Antimafia, and the Plural Cultures of Sicily". *Current Anthropology* 46 (4): 501–520.

Smith, Gavin. 2018. "Elusive Relations". *Current Anthropology* 59 (1): 247–267.

Spear, Thomas. 2003. "Neo-Traditionalism and the Limits of Invention in British Colonial Africa". *Journal of African History* 44: 3–27.

Stacey, Paul. 2016. "Rethinking the Making and Unmaking of Traditional and Statutory Institutions in Post-Nkrumah Ghana". *African Studies Review* 59 (2): 209–230.

Stacey, Paul. 2015. " Structure and the Limits of Recognition and Representation in Ghana". *Development and Change* 46 (1): 25–47.

Stacey, Paul. 2014. "'The Chiefs, Elders, and People Have for Many Years Suffered Untold Hardships': Protests by Coalitions of the Excluded in British Northern Togoland, UN Trusteeship Territory, 1950–57". *The Journal of African History* 55 (3): 423–444.

Stacey, Paul. 2012. "Struggles for the Attainment of Public Authority in the Gold Coast and Ghana: Competing Logics of State Formation and Local Politics in East Gonja 1930–2010". PhD dissertation (Unpublished). International Development Studies, Roskilde University, Denmark.

Thompson E.P.1982. *The Making of the English Working Class*. Penguin Books, Great Britain.

Tilly, Charles. 2005. *Identities, Boundaries and Social Ties*. Paradigm Publishers, Boulder, London. USA.

Tonah, Steve, ed. 2007. *Ethnicity, Conflicts and Consensus in Ghana*. Woeli Publishing, Accra, Ghana.

UNBISNET 1951. United Nations Bibliographic Information System. "401 (IX) Petition from the people of Nanjuro and Nawuri in the Kpandai area to UN (T/Pet.6/215)".

UNBISNET 1952. United Nations Bibliographic Information System. "630 (XI) Petition from Nana Atorsah Agyeman, Head Chief of the Nawuris, Kpandai T/Pet. 6/315). Concerning Togoland under British administration".

Weber, Max. 1978. *Economy and Society: An Outline of Interpretative Sociology*. Berkeley, CA: University of California Press.

Weir, Margaret. 2006. "When Does Politics Create Policy? The Organizational Politics of Change." In *Rethinking Political Institutions: The Art of the State*, edited by Ian Shapiro, Stephen Skowronek, and Daniel Galvin, 171–86. New York: New York University Press.

Wolf, Eric R. 2010. *Europe and the People Without History*. University of California Press.

Wolf, Eric. R. 2001. *Pathways of power: Building an Anthropology of the Modern World*. Berkeley: Univ. of California Press.

Wolf, Eric. R. 1999. *Envisioning Power: Ideologies of Dominance and Crisis*. Berkeley: University of California Press.

Wolf, Eric R. 1990. "Distinguished Lecture: Facing Power – Old Insights, New Questions". *American Anthropologist* New Series 92 (3): 586–596.

Wolf, Eric. R. 1982. *Europe and the People Without History*. University of California Press.

Wolf, E. 1959. *Sons of the Shaking Earth: The People of Mexico and Guatemala*. Chicago: University of Chicago Press.

Primary Sources

Northern Region of Ghana Public Records, Tamale, Northern Region, Ghana

NRG 4/2/1 'Kpandai Affairs' 1931–32

NRG 4/7/1 'Government Legislation' 1937–52

NRG 8/2/22 'An Essay on the Traditional Native-Authority in Urban Administration in W/Africa'1929–30

NRG 8/2/171 'Instigation of Kanankulaiwura' 1968-71

NRG 8/2/198 'Gonja Native Affairs' 1930–74

NRG 8/2/210 'Nawuri and Nanjuro (N.T.S) Under United Nations Trusteeship' 1951–54
NRG 8/2/212 'Local Authority Police Force' 1955–70
NRG 8/3/184 'Togoland Report' 1958–53 (sic)
NRG 8/4/73 'Informal Diary- Salaga' 1935–38
NRG 8/22/27 'The Ewe and Togoland Unification Problem' 1952–54

CHAPTER 8

Persistent Connections and Exclusions in Mozambique: From Colonial Anxieties to Contemporary Discourses about the Environment

Raquel Rodrigues Machaqueiro

1   Introduction: Climate Change and Forests in the Global South

Climate change has been considered the most important threat to humankind and the planet. Although decision-makers from more than 150 countries have been discussing possible solutions to this problem since at least 1992, no comprehensive agreement on effective measures to reduce the concentration of greenhouse gases in the atmosphere has been reached. Perhaps because of the difficult changes that such measures would entail – such as phasing out fossil fuels, and radically changing Western patterns of production and consumption – ruling groups in the industrialized world have increasingly focused their attention on the potential of forestry and land sectors in countries of the Global South. Given that, according to some estimates, deforestation is responsible for around 20 percent of global emissions (Parker et al 2009), the idea that avoiding deforestation in these countries can offset carbon emissions from industrialized countries became very popular – not just amongst these decision-makers, but also amongst environmentalists and development practitioners.

The assumption that carbon emissions[1] could be significantly reduced by certain interventions in forests of the Global South has, however, been criticized by many scholars who have denounced such interventions as constituting a new form of colonialism (McAfee 2017), for creating regimes of 'carbonised exclusion' precluding communities' access to forest resources (Asiyanbi 2016), and for promoting processes of capitalist 'accumulation by

---

1   Although carbon dioxide is just one of several greenhouse gases, carbon stands for all of them. The process of equating all greenhouse gases to carbon was part of the creation of emissions-trading mechanisms, but it is not exempt from controversies. For more on this, see MacKenzie 2009.

decarbonization (Bumpus and Liverman 2008). Building upon some of these critiques, this chapter will, however, provide a multi-level and historical analysis of the assumptions inherent in, as well as the implications of, these interventions as they are conceived within an international policy-making arena, and then locally implemented. The urgency to solve the problem of climate change has increasingly propelled policy solutions that involve forests and the land sector in the Global South. Under this logic, the World Bank has been promoting a series of initiatives in Mozambique intended to reduce this country's carbon emissions by preventing deforestation. For the Bank's officials, deforestation in Mozambique is caused by rural (and poor) populations' 'unsustainable' practices of slash-and-burn and charcoal production – all of which ought to be prevented with conservation agriculture, intensification of cashew production, and an industrial plantation of eucalyptus. These types of interventions in the Global South have been criticized for constituting forms of colonialism that create regimes of exclusion and sustain processes of capitalist accumulation.

Drawing on Wolf's scholarship, and interweaving data from ethnographic research in Mozambique with information collected during archival research on Portuguese colonial practices in the forestry sector, the chapter explores the continuous (yet historically differentiated) interconnections between a larger capitalist system and the 'people to whom history has been denied' (Wolf 1982, 23). It provides a multi-level and historical analysis of the political implications of these interventions as they are conceived internationally, and implemented and experienced locally. The chapter interweaves a critical analysis of the mode of production around carbon as a new commodity with histories of conservation agriculture, and modes of production of older commodities such as cashew and cellulose for paper production. The aim is to analyse current discourses about climate change and the environment to substantiate an argument that such discourses have legitimized a new political economy responsible for the perpetuation of forms of capitalist accumulation and the creation of new and diverse forms of local exclusion in Mozambique. The chapter then provides different examples from Mozambique of historical and contemporary extractivism, again on the rise in global political economies, which typically renders local forms of agricultural production invisible and negates the agency of small-scale farmers.

2 Creating a New Commodity: The International Policy-Making Arena

The use of forests to reduce emissions was introduced early in the political negotiations to tackle climate change – held under the United Nations Framework Convention for Climate Change (UNFCCC) – but always rejected. This rejection was related to technical issues concerning the accounting of reduced emissions, the permanence of those reductions, and the fear that, by using forests to reduce emissions, countries would not devote enough effort to reducing emissions in other sectors (Fogel 2005). Responsible authorities in African countries, however, were as much concerned about social and environmental impacts known from prior experiences of programmes led by Western countries in the management of African landscapes that all too closely resembled colonial enterprises of timber exploitation and cash-crop plantations.

Despite these concerns, after 2005 industrialized countries were able to push forward the creation of a global carbon market through a new mechanism of reducing emissions by simply avoiding deforestation: since forests are carbon sinks – meaning that they act like giant storages tanks – emissions could be reduced just by keeping forests intact. This mechanism, called REDD + (Reduced Emissions from Deforestation and forest Degradation, with the '+' sign standing for the enhancement of carbon sinks) meant, in practice, that countries in the Global South would be paid to maintain their forests, thus generating carbon offsets – a new commodity – and compensating for pollution by industrialized countries.

The first REDD + projects were marked by serious conflicts when forests were fenced and closed to local populations, who lost access to forested areas on which they depended for food and other important resources (Asiyanbi 2016; Chomba et al. 2016; Mahanty et al. 2012). However, even when projects abandoned the fences and sought to engage local communities, practitioners still faced the same problems affecting other forest-based development projects: financial, technical, and human resource requirements, dependence on donors, inability to address the drivers of deforestation, conflicts over ownership rights, weak local governance, and rule enforcement (Lund et al. 2017, 132). Ultimately, the implementation of REDD + projects was challenged by the disjuncture between local modes of production and a global capitalist system with investments in the creation of new forms of capital accumulation.

Wolf defined a mode of production as a 'specific, historically occurring set of social relations through which labour is deployed to wrest energy from nature by means of tools, skills, organizations, and knowledge' and identified three main modes: kin-ordered, tributary, and capitalist (Wolf 1982, 75–6). Although the capitalist mode of production became dominant, it was not exclusive, hence the utility of the concept of mode of production: it can 'reveal the changing ways in which one mode, capitalism, interacted with other modes to achieve its present dominance' (Wolf 1982, 76). Unlike the other modes of production, the capitalist mode is defined by three features: capitalists detain the means of production; labourers, deprived of the means of production, are forced to sell their labour to capitalists; and the extraction of surplus is intended to accumulate additional capital (Wolf 1982, 78).

The creation of carbon offsets as a new commodity – although justified with environmental reasons – follows from a capitalist logic, since not only does the trading of offsets generate profit, but more importantly, the production of carbon offsets in countries of the Global South enables companies from industrialized countries to continue polluting as usual – and therefore, continuing to accumulate capital. Many of the problems faced during the implementation of REDD + projects had to do, therefore, with the ways in which the capitalist mode of production of these projects interacted with and came to dominate different local modes of production. Ultimately, the difficulties experienced demanded change in the relationship between local and capital modes of production, which shifted the scale of operation from 'project-based' into what practitioners termed a 'jurisdictional level' – to include an entire province, state, or even country (Wunder et al. 2020).

This shift in scale expanded the scope of the interventions in the forests of the Global South: any type of land-related activity considered to have the potential to reduce emissions (either directly or indirectly) could thereby be included under the REDD + umbrella. Concomitantly, this transformation was followed by a progressive erasure of this acronym, and its replacement by other expressions such as 'sustainable forest management' 'rural development', or 'landscape approach'. If such discursive changes have allowed the continuity of certain intervention practices (Lund et al. 2017), they have also enabled a new political economy justified by the fight against climate change. As such, while commodities that have historically connected the Global south to international markets (such as timber and cash crops) continue to be part of this political economy, a new carbon-based commodity with powerful effects has emerged. This new commodity – carbon offsets, or simply the idea of reducing emissions in the forest and land sectors – has thus authorized new forms of transnational intervention in the Global South with far-reaching consequences for local organization.

3 Connecting Mozambique to Global Climate Change

The process of REDD+ implementation in Mozambique offers a compelling example of this new political economy. Although considered a country highly vulnerable to the effects of climate change (Ministry of Foreign Affairs, 2019), rather than a culprit in the current situation, Mozambique is being called upon by leaders of the developed world to shoulder the efforts to reduce emissions through its forests. With that purpose, the World Bank has been funding the country since 2008 to support the creation of a framework for REDD+'s implementation. Despite the disbursement of a significant amount of money,[2] in 2014 there was not a single REDD+ project in the country or plans to implement one. Rather, government officials and World Bank officers gradually dropped the acronym, talking instead about the need to change the modes of production of subsistence farmers and reform the forestry sector – all of which would supposedly lead to a reduction in the country's emissions.

During a public event held in Maputo in March 2016, several authorities, members of various NGOs, business representatives, and academics discussed the events of the 2015 Paris meeting and its much-celebrated 'Paris Agreement'. The event was inaugurated by the Minister of the Environment, who expressed the official position of the country: the Agreement was not as ambitious as Mozambican authorities would like it to be, but it was still an important achievement in the fight against climate change. Since Mozambique is already suffering from its impacts (namely floods in the north and droughts in the south), the Minister concluded that the country must do its part in fighting climate change, and that the reform of the forestry sector would be Mozambique's contribution to reducing emissions.[3] This reform included the protection of some tree species (particularly affected by demands from the Chinese markets) but, more importantly, the implementation of a vast programme targeting forests and the rural sector in general – especially in the province of Zambézia (see Figure 8.1).

This programme was referred to as a 'landscape approach' and was justified by authorities and World Bank officials by the need to have a more comprehensive approach to the rural sector, promoting both the 'rural development' of poor areas like the Zambézia province, and the reduction of emissions. This dual goal would therefore be achieved through the implementation of REDD+

---

2 In 2012 Mozambique was awarded $200,000 to prepare its Readiness Preparation Proposal, and in 2014 entered into an additional grant agreement of $3.6 million to prepare for REDD +. See Legal Agreements in https://www.forestcarbonpartnership.org/country/mozambique.
3 Fieldnotes, 23 March 2016.

but, more importantly, through the development of other activities such as the promotion of conservation agriculture, the intensification of specific cash crops, and a large-scale plantation of eucalyptus.

FIGURE 8.1   Map of Mozambique with Zambézia area, adapted by the author.
SOURCE: UNITED NATIONS DATABASE

Underwriting these plans was an old environmental narrative according to which the main deforestation drivers are poor peasants' unsustainable practices of slash and burn, and charcoal production (Skutsch and Turnhout 2020). World Bank officers were particularly adamant in singling out these problems, to the point of having forced the redrafting of an official document on the national strategy to implement REDD+, to emphasize these drivers while omitting others. Thus, if the old document identified multiple drivers of deforestation, including commercial large-scale agriculture, urbanization, or mining, the new one only briefly mentioned these, highlighting instead the role of shifting agriculture and charcoal production.[4] Under this rationale, the solutions to tackle these two culprits involved ending farmers' mobility as well as their traditional methods of charcoal production – all to be achieved through conservation agriculture, the promotion of cash crops, and eucalyptus plantations. Conservation agriculture would render fire and the rotation of cultures unnecessary; cash crops would undermine farmers' mobility and increase their productivity; and the eucalyptus plantations would provide a sustainable source of wood for charcoal production – all the while achieving rural development. If conservation agriculture and cashew production were not exactly new endeavours in Mozambique, the eucalyptus plantation – which was part of a major investment by a Portuguese pulp and paper company, partially funded by the International Finance Corporation[5] – was presented as a new enterprise with great potential for the development of the rural world.

Government officials and members of the World Bank talked about these initiatives with great enthusiasm, noting their potential to modernize Mozambican agriculture by integrating it in global markets and promote economic development, while also tackling climate change. However, this enthusiasm constituted a major disjuncture in the face of a long history of past attempts at promoting these same initiatives, all of them failing to either change traditional agricultural practices or generate development – here understood as the improvement of lives through the application of practices that increase production and stimulate economic growth.[6] In fact, these initiatives only seemed to add to a persistent history of exclusion as experienced by small-scale and poor Mozambican farmers.

---

4 See República de Moçambique n/d and 2016.
5 The International Finance Corporation is a member of the World Bank Group that promotes the development of the private sector in poor countries.
6 While this is how development is understood by development agencies, NGOs, and donor countries, this chapter takes a critical approach to this perspective and concomitant interventions (see Escobar 1995; Rist 1997).

4 Conservation Agriculture: A Long History of Failed Repetitions

According to the World Bank, shifting agriculture is the most important driver of deforestation in Mozambique, "responsible for more than 65 percent of forest cover loss throughout the country between 2000–2013" (World Bank and República de Moçambique n/d, 2). In fact, this mantra was constantly repeated by World Bank officers working in the country:

> Here, it's several small farmers doing that [deforesting] as a survival strategy. They do the mobile system because … well, because that's the way they have always done it, and there's no support to do it in any other way. Changing that will be very difficult. (…) [But] if we want to reduce deforestation, you can forget everything, just do one thing: agriculture! (…) If you don't change the agriculture, then forget about it. If we can't really enhance the productivity of small farmers, and with Mozambique's birth rate, there's no way.
> Maputo, 29 March 2016[7]

Implicit in this perspective, and as expressed by Arnaldo[8] (one of the World Bank managers for Mozambique), is the assumption that Mozambican farmers have no history, since their modes of production simply replicate *what has always been done*, and at the same time, their form of agricultural production has no real value to society because it is inherently destructive. The solution is thus, conservation agriculture – even if implementing it can be very difficult, as Arnaldo recognized. In fact, despite the many years during which different development organizations have tried to implement conservation agriculture in Mozambique (and other African countries, for that matter), none was successful at sustaining this practice over the long run (Giller et al. 2009). Yet, Arnaldo and some governmental officers presented this initiative as a new one, expressing excitement at its expected outcomes.

The Food and Agriculture Organization (FAO) defines conservation agriculture as a farming system that promotes maintenance of a permanent soil cover, minimum soil disturbance (i.e., no tillage), and diversification of plant species; claiming that this method promotes biodiversity, water conservation, and reduced greenhouse gas emissions due to lower energy inputs, improved nutrient use efficiency, and lower release of carbon from soils (FAO 2017).

---

7 All conversations with government authorities and World Bank officials were held in Portuguese. Translations were made by the author.
8 All names are pseudonyms.

Before concerns over global climate change came to dominate development interventions in countries of the Global South, conservation agriculture was already part of development agencies' and NGOs' toolkit to tackle poverty and low agricultural yields. Mozambique was no exception to this logic, having hosted several conservation agriculture projects led by European and North American NGOs (Silici et al. 2015, 35–7) – especially after the end of the civil war that followed the country's independence from Portugal.

Despite the claimed benefits of conservation agriculture (which now include the reduction of carbon emissions) by FAO and some NGOs, the results have been disappointing. In fact, some scholars have provided empirical evidence demonstrating low adoption rates by farmers – and even reduced yields – due to high labour and input requirements, as well as risk aversion (Giller et al. 2009; Silici et al. 2015). According to these same scholars, conservation agriculture practices are knowledge-intensive, requiring a continuous process of learning and experimenting that marginalized and poor farmers cannot risk trying. Moreover, it demands increased labour (often falling on women's shoulders) and expensive inputs (such as herbicides and improved seeds) that farmers simply cannot afford once NGOs stop supporting them. It is thus not surprising that Mozambican farmers resist implementing these practices to the chagrin of some of my interlocutors, like Fabian, working for a French NGO involved in the efforts to implement conservation agriculture in Zambézia:

> [Farmers] produce corn and manioc for three, four years, depending on the soils, and then leave ... The fertility of the soils is very weak ... so they go out and deforest another hectare – and that is how they are deforesting at an incredible rhythm ... They are deforesting as much as 14 thousand hectares a year, and it is 95 percent subsistence agriculture. That's it ... The only solution is conservation agriculture. To try and maintain the fertility of the soils ... [But] farmers are not big fans ... they hardly change their practices ... They don't like risk, and since we're talking about subsistence agriculture, the risks are even higher.
> Maputo, 3 March 2016

While Fabian acknowledged the reasons for Mozambican farmers' aversion to risk – if crops fail, farmers face famine – and Arnaldo recognized how difficult it is to change farming practices, neither could he explain why conservation agriculture is still pushed on Mozambican farmers despite a history of past failures. Arnaldo even denied such a history, arguing instead that, if there were failures in the past, these were due to projects being too small and not having a market approach that could sustain the farmers at a scale beyond subsistence farming.[9]

Their trust in conservation agriculture as a panacea for deforestation and low agricultural productivity was, in many ways, like the reliance of Portuguese colonial authorities on scientific agriculture – often going against traditional practices of Mozambican farmers. At that time, low agricultural yields were seen as technical and not political problems, to be addressed through technical solutions that often disregarded locally specific ecological conditions, and farmers' practices intended to reduce the risks of farming (Isaacman 1996, 69). One of those practices was precisely shifting agriculture – equally deplored by colonial authorities – which constituted a strategy of risk diversification against historical patterns of erratic rainfall and chronic drought (Lubkemann 2008, 126). Significantly, all attempts made in the past to bind Mozambican peasants to fixed locations – from the colonial *aldeamentos*, to the post-independence communal villages – failed dramatically, leading to situations of crisis and famine (Lubkemann 2008, 211; Yañez Casal 1996). History has thus proven that the mobility of Mozambican farmers is not just a necessary risk aversion strategy perfectly adapted to local ecological circumstances, but also a strategy that allowed farmers to maintain possession over their means of production.[10] Although some scholars have argued that conservation agriculture cannot be taken as a universal panacea (Knowler and Bradshaw 2007), development agencies and international NGOs continue to promote it as if no other alternatives existed (Giller et al. 2009) – and the more so, since the reduction of greenhouse gas emissions has become one of the main goals to be achieved through conservation agriculture.

5 Slash and Burn: Reproducing Colonial Anxieties

The idea that traditional farming practices are responsible for Mozambique's emissions is reinforced by authorities' anxieties regarding the use of fire. While historically fire has been a crucial tool to clear fields, improve soil fertility, and control certain pests and weeds (Isaacman 1972, 64–5), for authorities and World Bank officers, it is the main culprit with responsibility for deforestation. In their view, fire is not only unacceptable for causing deforestation, but also for generating carbon emissions. Their anxieties over the use of fire echo, with

---

9   Interview 29 March 2016.
10 Colonial authorities sought to control Mozambicans' labour process, undermining their relative autonomy as small farmers (Isaacman 1996: 38, 48).

remarkable similarities, colonial concerns about the irreversible loss of forests and important timber resources by fire.

In a 1950 publication from the former Portuguese Ministry of Colonies, engineer Esteves de Sousa wrote about the "balance" between forest communities and the environment in Mozambique, considering "the fearsome African fires" as the most important agent of destruction to such a balance (Sousa 1950). However, there was an important difference between understandings of this imbalance among white settlers and the 'indigenous'. While the former destroyed the forest to create 'agricultural enterprises' (which, even if technically inadequate and doomed to failure, should still be praised), the latter's objective was a 'rudimentary' agriculture, with constant moving from one plot to the next once the first one was exhausted. For this forest engineer, fire had a predominant role not just in the destruction of forests, but also in the degradation of soils, disruption of weather patterns, and lack of productivity (1950, 10). He stated, 'Only those who have witnessed one of these immense fires can appreciate its destructive power' (1950, 11) – as such, he suggested, heavy fines should be implemented to prevent the use of fire to clear fields for agriculture (1950, 15). Perhaps more to the point is the report of a 1948 forestry mission to Mozambique, also published by the Portuguese Ministry of Colonies. Its author explained:

> The negro man, still numbed by centuries of intellectual apathy, solves his banal problems ... in the simplest way ... When thinking about his nourishing needs, he marked a plot in the forest ... and set it on fire, which finally came to kill those giants [the trees], often centuries old. For four or five years he repeats the plantation of sorghum ... until, once [he has] exhausted the fertility of the soil ... he looks for another plot in the forest where to set, once again, his meagre agriculture. It is through this process, primitive but infallible, that the most beautiful forests of this territory have become ... true graveyards of the best forest and flora specimens.
> JUNTA DAS MISSÕES 1948, 28–30

However, the author noted, the same detrimental practices were carried out when local farmers were 'asked' to prepare fields for cash crops such as cotton and wheat, also causing the destruction of Mozambique's forests on a yet-larger scale (Junta das Missões 1948, 31). Setting aside the extraordinary racism of this excerpt and the fact that Mozambicans were never 'asked' but instead forced (often violently) to plant cotton (Isaacman 1996), the deforestation caused by cotton plantations (and other cash crops) was never a matter of great concern for colonial authorities. Both authors cited here recognized (and lamented) the large-scale deforestation caused by industrial agriculture; however, its productivity – in the context of a colonial enterprise – justified the environmental destruction. This form of agriculture, operated under a capitalist system of production, was intended to turn Mozambique into a specialized producer of important raw materials, such as cotton, generating damning consequences for Mozambican communities and households (Wolf 1982, 310) – including famine and death (Isaacman 1996, 150–70). This capitalist mode of production was, therefore, praised against the 'primitive' and 'rudimentary' subsistence agriculture practised by Mozambican peasants. As such, the development of the capitalist mode of production depended not only on rendering local forms of agriculture obsolete, but of neglecting the agency of local producers and the social organization that went with it to chastise them into sedentary cash crop farming for export markets.

Similarly, World Bank officers blame slash and burn practices of poor farmers for the current levels of deforestation, neglecting to acknowledge the effects of industrial activities (such as large-scale agriculture and mining), the expansion of urban areas, and the increasing demand for high-quality timber by Chinese markets. In fact, it is very hard to find studies connecting Mozambique's deforestation with mining activities or urban expansion. Even if some studies recognize the direct and indirect effects of mining activities on forest cover (Sitoe et al. 2012, 19),[11] they do not quantify the scale of deforestation caused by it. Considering that just the province of Tete holds an estimated 23 billion tons of coal reserves, and a projected area of extraction of 6 million hectares, with at least 1,400 households (who will need to be relocated),[12] it is hard to imagine that this area will remain mostly forested. And yet, most of the time, documents prepared by authorities and the World Bank relegate mining to a footnote, or consider it to have a limited impact. In the same way, although demand for timber has been causing devastating effects in Mozambican forests (MacKenzie 2006; Ekman et al. 2013) – a situation constantly denounced by local media[13] – it is not considered 'deforestation' but rather, 'degradation', which does not seem to concern authorities and the World Bank as much as 'deforestation'.[14] In this specific case, this reduced level of concern might also

---

11 An indirect effect, for instance, is the deforestation caused by people relocated from the mining areas.
12 See Environmental Justice Atlas: https://ejatlas.org/conflict/resettlements-for-mining-projects-in-tete-province.
13 See newspapers *Canal de Moçambique* March 23 (Mulungo 2016), and *Savana* March 25 (Senda 2016), and TV news reports on STV April 1, 2016.
14 In the definitions used by FAO and the UNFCCC, deforestation entails clear-cutting and a complete shift in land use.

be due to the involvement of high-level governmental officials in this trade – a situation also denounced by the local media and mentioned by some people during fieldwork.[15]

Significantly, illegal logging, mining, and industrial agriculture are all part of complex networks of international trade and global capitalism processes related to highly demanded commodities, involving many different stakeholders, across many countries. This renders almost any local policy, social movement, or social organization to end deforestation ineffective, if not powerless. This is because actions against increased immersion into the global capitalism system, even if involving widespread deforestation, are framed as outright detrimental for the development of country – just consider the possibilities of retaliation by powerful companies such as the Brazilian Vale, or the British Rio Tinto (both involved in coal mining in Mozambique), or by Chinese officials. In this context of increasing pressure to open up the country to diverse forms of extractivism and the benefits that follow for the select few, it is not surprising that slash and burn or charcoal production continue to be arraigned as the main culprits in deforestation: both can be addressed locally (even if ineffectively), and both are constitutive elements of an 'environmental narrative' (Skutsch and Turnhout 2020) that became hegemonic within the development world (Crewe and Harrison 1998, 11). Thus, for the World Bank and national authorities, fighting deforestation and reducing emissions boils down to one thing: banning the use of fire among poor farmers, negating any potential benefits of this form of agricultural production, and pushing for sedentarization.

6   Trendy Cashew: Continuing to Ignore History

Another strategy pursued by the World Bank and government officials to counter the mobility of farmers was the promotion of cashew production. The idea was that once cashews became profitable, farmers would necessarily stay on their plots to take care of their trees instead of roaming into the forest to open new plots. According to an official from the Ministry of Agriculture,

> the cashew is very valuable here in Mozambique and normally, people conserve it … [S]o the goal of the project is to create this border [around the plots] with cashew plantations, because conservation happens

---

15   Fieldnotes 20–21 April 2016.

automatically ... By incentivizing [the cashew], they will reduce the areas to explore for firewood and charcoal.

Maputo, 10 July 2014

Fabian agreed with this assumption, explaining the strategy implemented among farmers in Zambézia:

[T]he price of the cashew is too low in comparison to that of Tanzania.... That is why, in the past twenty years, the production has not increased, unlike in the rest of the world ... Our idea ... was to pay more to those farmers who elect conservation agriculture ... And the Bank liked this idea a lot because it's trendy ... And also, the increase in the production scale is necessary in order to find an international buyer for the cashew – all at a better price.

Maputo, 3 March 2016

The assumptions behind this plan ignored the complicated history of cashew production in Mozambique, and the fact that low productivity has nothing to do with farmers' unwillingness to take care of cashew trees, but, rather, with difficult weather conditions, the very long war that affected the country (Penvenne 2015, 219–221), the interconnection of the crop with international markets, and the domestic policies ruling this sector. In fact, cashews are cherished by Mozambicans for being truly national, almost a 'national symbol' – unlike other cash crops promoted by colonial authorities such as cotton (Pitcher 2002, 225).

In the early 1970s Mozambique was 'the world's largest combined producer of raw and processed cashew nuts, contributing around 40 percent of global production in the peak years of the early 1970s' (Penvenne 2015, 217). Although cashew processing was protected by both colonial authorities and the independent Mozambican government, during the 1990s authorities liberalized the whole sector. This decision followed a *suggestion* by the World Bank, which actively promoted the liberalization of whole agricultural sectors across the Global South, together with the withdrawal of input support from state institutions.[16] According to Bank officials, the sector had a problem of low production and profitability due to all the protectionist measures applied to cashew processing. The government then lowered the tariffs on the export of raw

---

16   The word 'suggested' is rhetoric, since the World Bank threatened Mozambican authorities with refusal to restructure the country's debt or renew its credits if they did not reduce the tariffs on the export of raw cashew nuts (Penvenne 2015: 224).

cashews, which increased sales but broke the vertical integration that characterized the sector. Within two years of the liberalization, most of the cashew processing units were closed, thousands of jobs were lost, and prices failed to increase contrary to predictions by the World Bank (Pitcher 2002, 227–9). If the Mozambican cashew production was already in dire straits due to weather and war conditions, and fierce competition from other markets, after the measures imposed by the World Bank the sector was almost destroyed – hitting poor farmers and workers from processing units the hardest.

The fact that in 2015 World Bank officials were, once again, suggesting measures to incentivize cashew production was ironic, if not downright insulting. Even if the sector could certainly benefit from new cashew orchards, increased productivity would still face a weakened processing industry, as well as 'oligopolistic practices' that continue to keep the raw nut prices very low (Pitcher 2002, 229).[17] Cashew production has recovered significantly since the 1990s, but it is mostly led by small producers, and is far from the levels reached during the 1970s (Penvenne 2015, 229).

By insisting on cashew production as a solution to rural poverty or, more recently, as a deterrence to shifting agriculture, World Bank and government officials only demonstrate their ignorance of both the importance of cashews in Mozambique's domestic economy as part of the farmers' strategies to tackle risk and achieve some level of food security,[18] and the history of wrong policies that almost destroyed the sector. Their enthusiasm for cashew production demonstrated, once again, how some government and World Bank officials conceive Mozambique as disconnected from a capitalist world economy, in which over time, some regions are central and strategic – as Mozambique once was – only to become auxiliary, occupying marginal positions later (Wolf 1982, 353). Like the history of conservation agriculture and eucalyptus plantation (next section), tracing the plight of cashew production in Mozambique also demonstrates how 'new' ideas around agricultural production furthered historical processes of excluding small-scale land users. To increase production to the market scale targeted by the World Bank, the national processing industry would need significant investment,[19] and the government would have to

---

17 According to Pitcher, the problem is that the government liberalized trade without liberalizing the wholesale traders allowing them to keep prices low. The reason is that these traders include companies that have historically supported the government (2002: 231).
18 Which includes consuming cashews in the face of food shortages.
19 The landscape approach program mentions the launching of a cashew-processing unit with an installed transformation capacity of 5,000 tons of raw cashew nut, employing 600 workers, but during interviews this unit was never mentioned (UT-REDD/MITADER 2015: 20).

enforce policies to counter the low prices of raw cashew nuts maintained by other international actors.[20] None of these are part of the 'landscape approach' proposed by the Bank and the government to promote 'rural development'.

7 Eucalyptus Plantation: Reliving Colonial Dreams

The main element of the 'landscape approach', however, was a scheme for a large plantation of eucalyptus led by a Portuguese paper company. The plantation was not exactly a new endeavour, since for several years other private companies have developed, similar projects[21] – but this one was being presented as an integral part of a governmental programme targeting 'rural development'. Through this programme, Mozambican authorities gave the Portuguese company two concessions with more than 300,000 hectares, across the provinces of Zambézia and Manica. Although the company recognized that not all this area would be planted – since it also contains an estimated 25,000 households – the goal was to occupy a total of two thirds with eucalyptus trees.[22]

In a governmental document describing the several interventions planned for the forestry sector, this plantation was presented as a large investment, partially funded by the International Finance Corporation, intended to reduce the country's emissions, as well as provide employment opportunities for local communities (amongst other benefits offered by the Portuguese company), and to source charcoal production. The idea was to increase the productivity and economic growth of poor rural areas, while also helping tackle climate change:

> The vision is to take a landscape of *low productivity* such as the current mosaic of slash and burn agriculture, *degraded lands*, and forests, and turn it into a *highly productive landscape*, creating prosperity that will subsequently be shared by all those living within the landscape.
> UT-REDD/MITADER 2015, 67[23]

---

20 Namely, by India. Given its dominant role in the raw cashew nut market, Indian traders can pretty much define the price they are willing to pay Mozambican producers (Penvenne 2015: 225).
21 The Norwegian company Green Resources, for instance, has several monoculture plantations in Nampula, Niassa and Zambézia.
22 Interview with the director of the company, fieldnotes March 2016.
23 Emphasis added.

These same promises of development and improvement of *degraded lands* through eucalyptus plantation were made during a workshop organized by the government and the World Bank in Quelimane, the capital of Zambézia. During that event, a representative of the Portuguese company noted that only around 60 percent of the total area would be planted, that the customary rights of the local populations would be respected, and that the goal was to improve the food security and the annual income of the families living in the area.

The project would entail a mosaic structure interspersing areas operated directly by the company, and others under the responsibility of Mozambican farmers, who would sell back to the company the timber harvested. As described by Wolf, the development of capitalist agriculture leads to the creation of 'factories in the field' and the growth of small-scale specialized producers whose operations are dictated by cash-product markets – precisely what the company was proposing; other farmers, stripped of their means of production, would have no recourse but to sell their labour power (Wolf 1982, 314). Indeed, this was a major concern for some of the participants in the workshop[24] (along with the possibility of forced displacements) – while the possibility of easy cash from selling the timber seemed appealing, the scenario of losing a family's source of food – the land – to eucalyptus plantation was very real.

Although other eucalyptus plantations in the country have been fraught with controversies – some of them leading to violent conflicts amongst disgruntled communities (Lexterra 2016) – the government and the World Bank were very keen on making this plantation the showcase for the whole 'landscape approach' in Zambézia.[25] The reason (besides the capital accumulation enabled by this investment) is that it offered a persuasive narrative about tackling climate change while promoting development. The plantation was presented as an instrument to preclude shifting agriculture (by fixing households to single tree plots), and a sustainable source for fuelwood and charcoal production, leading to a reduction in the country's emissions. Simultaneously, it would also promote rural development by providing jobs, increasing family income, and creating the conditions for the emergence of 'small entrepreneurs' – an important selling point at the workshop. Except for the most recent goal of reducing emissions, arguments about rural development were also used by colonial authorities to promote eucalyptus plantations in

---

24 Fieldnotes on the Zambézia Forum, 20–21 April 2016.
25 So much so, that it was the World Bank who invited the Portuguese company to include the plantation in the governmental strategy of emissions reductions – until then, the company was not aware of carbon offsets' generation through tree plantations. Interview with director of the company, fieldnotes March 2016.

Mozambique. In 1966, the 'Technical Commission for Economic Planning and Integration of the Mozambique Province' prepared a report about the forestry sector which suggested that local communities in Manica and Sofala should plant eucalyptus to supply themselves (and other communities) with firewood and timber. Additionally, the report continued, farmers should intensify such plantations to export the timber to South Africa and Rhodesia – all with the goal of 'avoiding the growing and centrifugal degradation of the natural vegetation surrounding urban centres' (Comissão Técnica 1966, 885). The concerns of colonial officials with the 'degradation of the natural vegetation' were not exactly environmental. Rather, their goal was to improve the economic profitability of the colony, which could be challenged if high-valued timber was being used by natives to supply their needs instead of being exported. Additionally, by incentivizing eucalyptus plantations, these officials were promoting a new commodity with significant economic potential.

Unsurprisingly, The World Bank and the Mozambican government were reliving colonial dreams of turning eucalyptus into a new cash crop, creating a new source of capital accumulation. The colonial logic underwriting the Portuguese company's decision to carry out such a significant investment in Mozambique was not even disguised. First, it followed from the impossibility of expanding the 120 thousand hectares the company already explores in Portugal (Lusa 2015).[26] The Portuguese authorities denied such an expansion, probably because this monoculture is becoming increasingly unpopular due to its water demands and, more recently, its high flammability – which fuelled the tragic fires of 2017 where more than 100 people lost their lives (Camargo and Castro 2018). Thus, the eucalyptus plantation constitutes the mere transference to a poor African country of what cannot be done in (the metropole) Europe – a common practice in a global capitalist system to avoid labour costs and environmental regulation. Second, the company also announced that it does not intend to produce paper in Mozambique but instead, to export cellulose to where paper production will take place – namely, Asian markets (Lusa 2015). In other words, as in all colonial enterprises, this company only intended to use Mozambican resources (i.e., land, water, and labour) to export a raw material, and not a transformed product. Once again, poor Mozambican peasants – those *without history* – were being drawn into a system that harnesses the world's resources to the cause of capital accumulation (Wolf 1982, 353).

---

26   Portugal is the country with the largest eucalyptus area in Europe and the fifth-largest worldwide, occupying 9 percent of the territory (www.ejatlas.org/conflict/eucalyptus-monoculture-and-common-lands-Portugal).

Many environmentalists across the world have denounced the argument that plantations of fast-growing species such as eucalyptus or pine can reduce carbon emissions as being deeply flawed, given the fact that these trees are ultimately meant to be cut down (The Oakland Institute 2014; WRM 2017). However, such critiques have not deterred the development of several industrial plantations throughout the Global South which, tragically, resemble prior colonial enterprises of forest management, marked by the systematic exploitation of labour and resources (Sodikoff 2012), violent encroachment, and land grabbing (Hughes 2006; Moore 2005). The repetition of these forms of violence and the stripping of poor peasants from their means of production has, ironically, been enabled by narratives about climate change. In these narratives, the land used for these monoculture plantations is always portrayed as idle, degraded, or unproductive, while the plantations themselves are presented as powerful instruments to reduce emissions, either because they will be used to produce biofuels (thus replacing fossil fuels), or because they will absorb a significant amount of emissions from the atmosphere – or both.[27]

8 Deforestation: A History of Persistent Connections and Exclusions

The long-standing narrative that portrays poor farmers in the Global South as carrying out less-productive and environmentally-damaging activities, resorting to 'primitive' methods of slash- and-burn and charcoal production (*'because that's the way they have always done it'*) has recently been re-enacted in the context of climate change policy-making. Taken at its face value, this narrative seems logical and valid: when scientists warn against the increasing level of greenhouse gases in the atmosphere, burning forested areas to develop agriculture, or using valuable forest resources to produce charcoal are understandably condemned. As such, efforts to reduce deforestation by replacing these practices with more-sustainable and less-polluting methods of production can only be praised. This is one way of understanding current World Bank interventions in Mozambique to implement REDD+ and a 'landscape approach' programme that also claims to promote "rural development".

However, as Wolf showed, things do not happen in isolation and this narrative needs to be contextualized not just historically, but, more importantly, in

---

[27] See https://newgenerationplantations.org/en/studytours/13; http://newforests.net/shared-value/; https://www.climatechangenews.com/2019/08/08/un-science-reports-show-biofuels-essential-climate-action/ or https://www.aidforafrica.org/member-charities/trees-for-the-future/ as examples of these narratives.

its wider connections to a global capitalist system. These brief histories of conservation agriculture, anxieties regarding slash and burn, cashew production and eucalyptus plantations exemplify the multiple processes of connecting Mozambique to global circuits of capital accumulation – ultimately promoting the disenfranchising and exclusion of small-scale land users. Indeed, there is an interconnectedness between a long history of forest and land-use management (including the promotion of capitalist forms of agricultural production) in the Global South, and the different 'encompassing systems' in which such management occurred (Wolf 1982, 23). In the past, modernity imperatives of efficiency and profitability – namely those tied to colonial systems of production – justified the imposition of an export-model agriculture and scientific forestry (Scott 1998). The purpose was to improve productivity, providing fiscal and commercial revenue, independently of the needs of native populations. In the process, native practices were deemed unproductive, 'rudimentary' or outright 'primitive', especially when fire was used to clear new plots of land. Reports prepared by colonial authorities about Mozambique clearly expressed this position.

The anxieties that natives' practices created amongst colonial authorities were not just related, however, to the environmental destruction perceived to be caused by fire – of greatest concern was the mobility of farmers enabled by such fire. It is not surprising, thus, that both Portuguese colonial authorities and the Mozambican post-independence government tried to preclude such mobility, confining peasants to specific areas. Even though shifting agriculture constitutes one of the most important risk-aversion strategies employed by farmers, current interventions in the Mozambican rural world emulate the goal of confining peasants to allocated places. Conservation agricultural schemes, featuring cashew and eucalyptus plantations, have been described by World Bank officials and Mozambican authorities as important tools of development and emissions reduction; but their underlying goal is to simultaneously hinder farmers' mobility. Once farmers are circumscribed to specific areas, the development of large-scale projects (whether in agriculture or mining) faces fewer obstacles.

At the same time, by considering shifting agriculture and charcoal production the main culprits responsible for deforestation in Mozambique, the scope of action is simplified and limited. In other words, if deforestation is caused by these practices, it can be addressed locally. This assumption facilitates the World Bank's culture of disbursement, and enables national authorities' access to much-needed funds, while both can claim to be doing something about climate change. However, and perhaps more importantly, this assumption also isolates the problem of deforestation from its complex connections to global circuits of capital accumulation, which means that while interventions remain focused on slash-and-burn or charcoal production, other industrial enterprises (such as mining, industrial agriculture, and illegal logging) can proceed without being challenged for the deforestation, exclusion, and marginalization (through forced displacements) that they cause.

By disconnecting deforestation from these global circuits of capital accumulation, forests in the Global South can be presented as in need of protection from local threats – namely, deforestation caused by local agents (that is, poor farmers) due to their lack of knowledge, of resources – and even, as some suggest, of active will to protect those forests. In current discourses about climate change, not only are these forests presented as being under threat and in need of protection, but they are also championed as a significant part (if not the whole) solution to the climatic problem.[28] In other words, the protection of these forests becomes necessary to save the planet from climate change.

9 Conclusion: Climate Change Discourses and the Emergence of a New Political Economy

Discourses about climate change and deforestation fail to explain why poor countries in the Global South are supposed to shoulder burdens in the efforts to fight climate change – in sacrificial proportions that are similar, if not superior, to those of industrialized countries – when their contribution to the accumulated concentration of greenhouse gases in the atmosphere is residual. In the case of Mozambique, its vulnerability to the impacts of climate change is far higher than any developed country – as seen recently, when Beira province was hit by the deadly cyclone Idai.[29] And yet, Mozambique (along with other poor countries) has been part of the efforts to tackle climate change, while excluded from the financial resources needed to remedy its impacts.[30]

---

28   See as examples: https://www.worldwildlife.org/initiatives/forests; https://www.iucn.org/resources/issues-briefs/forests-and-climate-change; http://www.fao.org/forestry/climatechange/53459/en/; https://www.rainforest-alliance.org/articles/relationship-between-deforestation-climate-change.

29   Idai hit Mozambique on 14 March 2019, killing more than 600 people and destroying more than 100,000 homes. Since then, the central part of Mozambique has been hit by three more tropical storms (Chalane, Eloise, and Ana) which have affected more than 300, 000 people. International funding for relief continues to fall short in the face of the increased demands. See https://reliefweb.int/report/mozambique/2-years-cyclone-idai-and-mozambique-has-already-faced-additional-3-cyclones.

30   Setting aside the bureaucracies faced by countries like Mozambique to access funds from the Green Climate Fund, the comparison between the money raised to rebuild Notre

By eliding the disproportionality of the efforts required from countries like Mozambique *vis-à-vis* their responsibility (or lack thereof) for the problem of climate change, and their vulnerability to its impacts, the industrialized world is also able to deflect difficult questions about their own efforts to reduce emissions. One such question could be why France is insisting on developing a natural gas project in Cabo Delgado, when the use of such gas will only increase the amount of greenhouse gases in the atmosphere – not to mention the extreme violence that has been generated around this project since 2017.[31]

More to the point, while Mozambican forests (and those of others) can compensate for the pollution generated in Europe and North America, industrialized countries will not be forced to make demanding changes in their production and consumption patterns. At the same time, these discourses about climate change legitimize colonialesque interventions in countries of the Global South, which include large-scale plantations and other industrial agriculture projects – none of which are identified as drivers of deforestation. In the same way that Portuguese colonial authorities considered the environmental destruction caused by cotton and other cash crops justified, World Bank officials and Mozambican authorities refuse to acknowledge the high levels of deforestation caused by eucalyptus plantations and other large-scale agricultural enterprises being developed in the same country[32] – these investments, too are as readily justified.

Discourses and assumptions about the role of forests in the Global South in tackling climate change have enabled the perpetuation of a capitalist system of accumulation based on both the extraction of older commodities, and a new political economy. Plantations of eucalyptus and other monocultures of fast-growing trees are already part of a global system of capitalist accumulation that includes other countries in the Global South. The same can be said about all the other components of the 'landscape approach' intended to preclude Mozambican peasants' mobility, such as conservation agriculture or cashew plantations – ultimately, all these components aim at either transforming

---

Dame ($1 billion) and the donations to Mozambique after Idai ($74 million) should be enough to illustrate this point. See https://www.nytimes.com/2019/04/20/world/africa/mozambique-cyclone.html.

31 The account of the violence generated around French Total's gas development falls outside the scope of this chapter. For more information, see Introduction to this volume.

32 One of such enterprises is ProSavana, a massive agricultural project to be developed in the Nacala corridor. The contestation to this controversial project reduced its initial area of implementation however, it continues to instill fears of land-grabbing and other forms of exclusion amongst rural populations. See Shankland and Gonçalves 2016 for more information.

these farmers into 'small-scale specialized producers' conditioned by the urges of global markets (Wolf 1982, 314) or stripping them of their means of production (of which land is the primary example). In sum, as in colonial times, Mozambique continues to be a source of important raw materials, land, and labour, while the country's immersion in the global political economy demands the denunciation and obligatory vanishing of alternative forms of local agricultural production. There is, however, a new political economy, with a new commodity, that expands this system of capitalist accumulation – that is, the claimed goal of tackling climate change by generating carbon offsets through emissions reductions. Even if the goal of 'development' still underlies some of the activities and interventions promoted by the World Bank (and other transnational organizations), the reduction of emissions is the ultimate justification for all of them. Conservation agriculture reduces emissions because it releases less carbon from soils while also preventing the use of fire and subsequent deforestation; cashew orchards reduce emissions because they prevent shifting agriculture; and eucalyptus plantations reduce emissions because the trees constitute carbon sinks, while also providing for a sustainable source of charcoal. A new carbon-based commodity thus emerges, either in the form of a quantifiable carbon offset – traded in carbon markets – or in a more abstract form that serves the purpose of authorizing specific activities that emerge by reorganizing labour relations.

This new political economy generates powerful effects, as it legitimizes interventions in the Global South that otherwise would be considered outright neo-colonial. Paraphrasing Wolf, the categories through which climate change ought to be perceived deny the existence of alternative categories, or, in this case, the existence of alternative interventions to tackle climate change (1982, 388). By understanding climate change as a mere problem of excessive carbon emissions – and not as the necessary outcome of an intensive global system of capitalist accumulation –solutions can thereby simply address those excessive emissions, notably by using forests in countries of the Global South to offset them. While understanding climate change through this lens exempts industrialized countries from their responsibilities in creating this problem, it also denies Mozambican farmers the agency to adapt to climate change impacts, preventing them from pursing their traditional risk-aversion practices. Local farming practices lose their ecological and socio-cultural significance and, instead, are deemed threats to the environment and enemies of the activists who seek to tackle climate change.

Simultaneously, current discourses about climate change and the role of forests in the Global South legitimize modes of production that sustain persistent practices of global capitalist accumulation (using land, natural resources, and labour) – which only exacerbate the problem of climate change – while producing new forms of exclusion. Mozambican peasants are excluded from deciding whether they want to make sacrifices to fight climate change (which include the risk of famine), from the processes through which their agricultural practices are defined (and then imposed upon them), and from the deals that ultimately seize their lands and livelihoods. And although Mozambican authorities are active agents in this process, the country is still excluded from accessing much needed resources that could help mitigate the impacts of climate change.

References

Asiyanbi, Adeniyi P. 2016. "A Political Ecology of REDD+: Property Rights, Militarised Protectionism, and Carbonised Exclusion in Cross River". *Geoforum* 77: 146–56.

Bumpus, Adam G., and Diana M. Liverman. 2008. "Accumulation by Decarbonization and the Governance of Carbon Offsets". *Economic Geography* 84 (2): 127–55.

Camargo, João, and Paulo Pimenta de Castro. 2018. *Portugal Em Chamas: Como Resgatar as Florestas*. Lisboa: Bertrand Editora.

Chomba, Susan, Juliet Kariuki, Jens Friis Lund, and Fergus Sinclair. 2016. "Roots of Inequity: How the Implementation of REDD+ Reinforces Past Injustices." *Land Use Policy* 50: 202–13.

Comissão Técnica de Planeamento e Integração Económica da Província de Moçambique. 1966. *III Plano de Fomento, Parte II, Relatórios Sectoriais, Volume I Agricultura e Silvicultura, Tomo VI Capítulos 18º e 19º*. Lisboa: Ministério do Ultramar.

Crewe, Emma, and Elizabeth Harrison. 1998. *Whose Development? An Ethnography of Aid*. London: Zed Books.

Ekman, Sigrid-Marianella Stensrud, Huang Wenbin, and Ercilio Langa. 2013. *Chinese Trade and Investment in the Mozambican Timber Industry A Case Study from Cabo Delgado Province*. Bogor, Indonesia: Center for International Forestry Research (CIFOR).

Escobar, Arturo. 1995. *Encountering Development: The Making and Unmaking of the Third World*. Princeton and Oxford: Princeton University Press.

FAO. 2017. "Conservation Agriculture." FAO – AG Dept factsheets. http://www.fao.org/publications/card/en/c/981ab2a0-f3c6-4de3-a058-f0df6658e69f/.

Fogel, Cathleen. 2005. "Biotic Carbon Sequestration and the Kyoto Protocol: The Construction of Global Knowledge by the Intergovernmental Panel on Climate Change". *International Environmental Agreements* 5: 191–210. https://doi.org/10.1007/s10784-005-1749-7.

Giller, Ken E., Ernst Witter, Marc Corbeels, and Pablo Tittonell. 2009. "Conservation Agriculture and Smallholder Farming in Africa: The Heretics' View". *Field Crops Research* 114: 23–34.

Hughes, David McDermott. 2006. *From Enslavement to Environmentalism: Politics on a Southern African Frontier*. Seattle and London: University of Washington Press.

Isaacman, Allen. 1972. *Mozambique: The Africanization of a European Institution – The Zambezi Prazos, 1750–1902*. Madison: The University of Wisconsin Press.

Isaacman, Allen. 1996. *Cotton Is the Mother of Poverty: Peasants, Work, and Rural Struggle in Colonial Mozambique, 1938–1961*. Portsmouth, London, Cape Town: Heinemann.

Junta das Missões Geográgicas e de Investigações Coloniais. 1948. *Missão Silvícola de Moçambique – Relato Dos Estudos Efectuados Nas Áreas de Chimoio, Mavita e Dombe, Referente Ao Período Dos Primeiros Seis Meses de Trabalho*. Lisboa: Ministério das Colónias – Junta de Investigações Coloniais.

Knowler, Duncan, and Ben Bradshaw. 2007. "Farmers' Adoption of Conservation Agriculture: A Review and Synthesis of Recent Research". *Food Policy* 32: 25–48. https://doi.org/10.1016/j.foodpol.2006.01.003.

Lexterra. 2016. "The Progress of Forest Plantations on the Farmers' Territories in the Nacala Corridor: The Case of Green Resources Moçambique". Livaningo, Justiça Ambiental, União Nacional dos Camponeses. https://wrm.org.uy/wp-content/uploads/2017/04/The_Progress_of_Forest_Plantations_on_the_Farmers_Territories_in_the_Nacala_Corridor_the_case_of_Green_Resources_Mocambique.pdf.

Lubkemann, Stephen C. 2008. *Culture in Chaos: An Anthropology of the Social Condition in War*. Chicago and London: The University of Chicago Press.

Lund, Jens Friis, Eliezeri Sungusia, Mathew Bukhi Mabele, and Andreas Scheba. 2017. "Promising Change, Delivering Continuity: REDD+ as Conservation Fad". *World Development* 89: 124–39.

Lusa, Agência. 2015. "Portucel lamenta ter de plantar eucaliptos em Moçambique em vez de Portugal". *Observador*. Accessed April 7, 2020. https://observador.pt/2015/09/08/portucel-lamenta-ter-de-plantar-eucaliptos-em-mocambique-em-vez-de-portugal/.

MacKenzie, Catherine. 2006. "Forest Governance in Zambézia, Mozambique: Chinese Takeaway! Final Report for FONGZA". Tanzania Forest Conservation Group. http://coastalforests.tfcg.org/pubs/GovernanceZambezia-MZQ.pdf.

MacKenzie, Donald. 2009. "Making Things the Same: Gases, Emission Rights and the Politics of Carbon Markets". *Organizations and Society* 34: 440–455. https://doi.org/10.1016/j.aos.2008.02.004.

Mahanty, Sango, Sarah Milne, Wolfram Dressler, and Colin Filer. 2012. "The Social Life of Forest Carbon: Property and Politics in the Production of a New Commodity." *Human Ecology*. https://doi.org/10.1007/s10745-012-9524-1.

McAfee, Kathleen. 2017. "Profits and Promises: Can Carbon Trading Save Forests and Aid Development?" In *The Carbon Fix: Forest Carbon, Social Justice, and Environmental Governance*, Stephanie Paladino and Shirley J. Fiske, 37–59. New York: Routledge.

Ministry of Foreign Affairs, Government of the Netherlands. 2019. "Climate Change Profile Mozambique". Ministry of Foreign Affairs. https://reliefweb.int/sites/relief web.int/files/resources/Mozambique_4.pdf.

Moçambique, República de. n/d. "Estratégia de Redução de Emissões Por Desmatamento e Degradação Florestal: Reduzir as Emissões de Carbono e a Pobreza Melhorando o Maneio Das Florestas". Ministério para Coordenação da Acção Ambiental MICOA.

Moçambique, República de. 2016. "Estratégia Nacional Para a Redução de Emissões de Desmatamento e Degradação Florestal, Conservação de Florestas e Aumento de Reservas de Carbono Através de Florestas (REDD+) 2016–2030". Ministério da Terra, Ambiente e Desenvolvimento Rural – MITADER.

Moore, Donald S. 2005. *Suffering for Territory: Race, Place, and Power in Zimbabwe*. Durham and London: Duke University Press.

Mulungo, André. 2016. "Operadores Florestais Acusam Governo de Falta de Vontade Para Acabar Com Exploração Ilegal." *Canal de Moçambique*, March 23, 2016.

Parker, Charlie, Andrew Mitchell, Mandar Trivedi, and Niki Mardas. 2009. *The Little REDD + Book: An Updated Guide to Governmental and Non-Governmental Proposals for Reducing Emissions from Deforestation and Degradation*. Global Canopy Programme. http://redd.unfccc.int/uploads/2_162_redd_20091201_gcp.pdf.

Penvenne, Jeanne Marie. 2015. *Women, Migration & the Cashew Economy in Southern Mozambique: 1945–1975*. Suffolk and New York: Boydell & Brewer, James Currey.

Pitcher, M. Anne. 2002. *Transforming Mozambique: The Politics of Privatization, 1975–2000*. Cambridge: Cambridge University Press.

Rist, Gilbert. 1997. *The History of Development: From Western Origins to Global Faith*. London: Zed Books.

Scott, James. 1998. *Seeing Like a State: How Certain Schemes to Improve the Human Condition Have Failed*. New Haven and London: Yale University Press.

Senda, Raul. 2016. "Abate Indiscriminado de Madeira Na Província Da Zambézia: Um Crime Antigo, Mas de Que Ninguém Se Dá Conta." *Savana*, March 25, 2016.

Shankland, Alex, and Euclides Gonçalves. 2016. "Imagining Agricultural Development in South–South Cooperation: The Contestation and Transformation of ProSAVANA". *World Development* 81: 35–46.

Sitoe, Almeida, Alda Salomão, and Sheila Wertz-Kanounnikoff. 2012. *The Context of REDD + in Mozambique*. Bogor, Indonesia: CIFOR. http://www.cifor.org/publicati ons/pdf_files/OccPapers/OP-79.pdf.

Silici, Laura, Calisto Bias, and Eunice Cavane. 2015. "Sustainable Agriculture for Small-Scale Farmers in Mozambique: A Scoping Report". IIED – International Institute for Environment and Development.

Skutsch, Margaret, and Esther Turnhout. 2020. "REDD +: If Communities Are the Solution, What Is the Problem?" *World Development* 130: 1–9. https://doi.org/10.1016/j.worlddev.2020.104942.So.

Sodikoff, Genese. 2012. *Forest and Labor in Madagascar – From Colonial Concession to Global Biosphere*. Bloomington & Indianapolis: Indiana University Press.

Sousa, Esteves de. 1950. *Considerações Acerca Do Equilíbrio Entre as Comunidades Florestais e o Ambiente Em Moçambique*. Lisboa: Ministério das Colónias – Junta de Investigações Coloniais.

The Oakland Institute. 2014. "The Darker Side of Green Plantation Forestry and Carbon Violence in Uganda: The Case of Green Resources' Forestry-Based Carbon Markets". The Oakland Institute. https://www.oaklandinstitute.org/sites/oaklandinstitute.org/files/Report_DarkerSideofGreen_lorez.pdf.

UT-REDD/MITADER. 2015. "FIP Forest Investment Program in Mozambique – Investment Plan First DRAFT Version 11/12/2015".

Wolf, Eric. 1982 (1997). *Europe and the People Without History*. Berkeley, Los Angeles, London: University of California Press.

World Bank, and República de Moçambique. n/d. "Zambezia Integrated Landscape Management Program: Towards a Sustainable Forest Management and Improved Livelihoods of Rural Communities". World Bank IBRD-IDA. http://documents.worldbank.org/curated/en/945201525957363451/pdf/WP-ZILMP-Brochure-Jan-11-PUBLIC.pdf.

WRM World Rainforest Movement. 2017. "The Paris Agreement on Climate Change: Promoting Tree Plantations and Reducing Forests to Tradable Carbon Stores | WRM in English". February 6, 2017. http://wrm.org.uy/articles-from-the-wrm-bulletin/viewpoint/the-paris-agreement-on-climate-change-promoting-tree-plantations-and-reducing-forests-to-tradable-carbon-stores/.

Wunder, Sven, Amy E. Duchelle, Claudio de Sassi, Erin O. Sills, Gabriela Simonet, and William D. Sunderlin. 2020. "REDD + in Theory and Practice: How Lessons from Local Projects Can Inform Jurisdictional Approaches." *Frontiers in Forests and Global Change* 3 (February): 1–17. https://doi.org/10.3389/ffgc.2020.00011.

Yañez Casal, Adolfo. 1996. *Antropologia e Desenvolvimento: As Aldeias Comunais de Moçambique*. Lisboa: Ministério da Ciência e Tecnologia Instituto de Investigação Científica Tropical.

CHAPTER 9

Chinese Indonesian Identity at Work: Political Exclusion and Division of Labour in Indonesia

Tirza van Bruggen

1   Introduction

Despite efforts to democratize and manage societal diversity (Schulte Nordholt and van Klinken 2007, 1; Eilenberg 2016, 139; Berenschot et al. 2017, 6), recent Indonesian governments have had limited success in including Chinese Indonesians in public life in Indonesian society. They continue to be excluded from positions of direct political leadership, from occupations in public administration, the military, and police force, and from places at public universities (Mackie 1991, 92; Aguilar 2001, 518; Purdey 2003, 426; Koning 2007; Kapoor and Arviriyatni 2014; Setijadi 2017). This chapter explores and explains historical and contemporary political and economic processes resulting in the overrepresentation of Chinese Indonesians in Indonesia in business, and their underrepresentation and social exclusion in politics – a deep-rooted phenomenon that continues in the post-Suharto era of democratization and liberal market reforms that began in 1998. In this chapter,[1] I revisit the question *why this is* and build on Wolf's (1982) pioneering observation that contemporary differentiation and inequality in societies is the result of changes in and various forms of global *and* local connectivity over time. I trace the persistent exclusion of Chinese Indonesians to a combination of the historical organization of Indonesia's labour force and the social reproduction of naturalizing boundaries, which discursively circumscribe social identities and define who is, and who is not, appropriate for certain jobs and positions through processes of othering.

Chinese Indonesians in Indonesia are 'commonly perceived as politically weak and economically strong' compared to *pribumi* – so-called 'indigenous' – Indonesians (Setijadi 2016a, 3). Many enjoy strong positions in Indonesia's commercial, financial, and industrial spheres but are excluded

---

[1] A version of this chapter forms part of the PhD dissertation 'Fluid and Fixed: Chinese Indonesian Identity at Work'. (Bruggen 2021).

from military, bureaucratic, and political positions (Mackie 1992, 41; Purdey 2005; 2006; Somers Heidhues 2017, 612–18). The most common fundamental explanation given for this identity-based differentiation and corresponding 'division of labour' is the unfolding of colonial history. James Rush (1988; 1990), Jamie Mackie (1988; 1991; 1992), and Alexander Claver (2014), amongst others, write extensively about the privileged economic role Chinese Indonesians played in colonial Indonesia and how this preconditioned the development of both their prominent identity and weak political position in contemporary society.

However, whereas such historical studies are right to point towards the role Western colonialism and global politics have had and continue to have in the development of contemporary identities and divisions of labour in Indonesian society, they also tend to lack an understanding of the complex role that local political and economic relationships, processes, and social practices have had and continue to have in these outcomes. As rightly argued by Wolf (1982, 4), ignoring these dimensions risks creating an understanding of dynamic and interconnected phenomena as if they were static and disconnected 'things'. Therefore, in this chapter, I investigate from multiple societal perspectives the interconnections between historical and contemporary global and local processes and the shaping of identities around the division of labour. First, I discuss what complex processes led to the invention of social discourses, a complex differentiation of skills, the development of material relations, and the establishment of occupational niches, which presently reinforce the consolidation of a communally constructed 'glass ceiling' on occupational mobility in Indonesia. Subsequently, I show how this in practice leads to the contemporary reproduction of a particular division of labour that separates the Chinese Indonesian identity group from others by categories of occupation, as they all have in one way or another become invested in their lived realities (Arendt 1958; Barth 1969; Wolf 1982, 23; Jenkins 1994; Tilly 1999, 8 and 139; Weyer 2007). Last, I reveal the current (trans)national political and economic forces that fuel the reproduction of those narratives and modes of exclusion that actively work to 'create' Chinese Indonesians and prevent their social mobility, acquisition of bureaucratic competence, and advancement in political careers (Barth 1969, 34; Wolf 1982; Tilly 1999; Setijadi 2017). The chapter demonstrates how the historical and social construction of the division of labour limits the availability of occupational choices for Chinese Indonesians, permeates the entire job allocation process, and denies political influence to a diverse group despite its significant contribution to the Indonesian economy. In a Wolfean perspective, the discussion and analysis builds on Eric R. Wolf's pioneering observation that contemporary social differentiation and inequality emerge from processes of global *and* local connectivity over time. Here, I demonstrate that the trajectory of history organizes social relations in Indonesia and 'shapes the [contemporary] social field of action so as to render some kinds of behaviour possible, while making others less possible or impossible' (Wolf 1990, 587). Specifically, we see how the contemporary division of labour influences the making and knowledge about social categories and vice versa, and constitutes what Wolf terms a 'totality of interconnected processes', with the whole process of job allocation based on, and reproducing, an intricate trans-local organization of social relations.

To do so, I elaborate on the concept 'division of labour' and show how it is embedded in the wider social processes of constructing identities and structuring of power inequalities. This asserts that the practice of job allocation in Indonesian societies rests not on colonial history alone, nor on individual-by-individual experience or choice. Rather, the organization of the labour force results from a historically conditioned process of 'unequal selection and unequal selectedness' (Bourdieu and Passeron 1990, 72), and which is consolidated at the intersection where job allocation processes interconnect with ongoing global *and* local processes of identity differentiation.

2   Methods and Data

My analysis in this chapter is based on fieldwork in Semarang, conducted in 2013 (three months), 2017 (two months), and 2018 (five months). Semarang is a medium-sized city[2] on the northern coast of Indonesia's most populated island, Java, and is the capital of the province of Central Java. During my time there, I collected data through observation, participation, the gathering of (historical) documents, and by carrying out 80 semi-structured interviews with a wide range of informants. These included business entrepreneurs, government officials – including customs, tax, and land officials – and politicians, lawyers, notaries, teachers, historians, journalists, NGO workers, and students. Data collection focused on uncovering key elements in the reproduction of Chinese Indonesian identity and corresponding categorical inequality. To conform with the expressed wishes of (most of) my informants, all names are pseudonyms.

---

2   With over 1.8 million residents in the urban area in 2019. See: https://populationstat.com/indonesia/semarang.

3 Division of Labour: Interconnecting Occupation and Identity

Division of labour – the organized separation of occupations in a socio-economic system – is a phenomenon as old as 'society' itself. In fact, Adam Smith (2007 [1776], 19; see also Polanyi 2001, 46) suggested it was a necessary consequence of the very existence of human nature – of man's 'propensity to barter, truck and exchange one thing for another'.[3] As such, Smith (2007) postulated that the entire existence of markets was predicated on an advanced division of labour – as the result of the natural processes of commercialization (Hann and Hart 2011 25). However, whereas Smith (2007) believed that a division of labour in terms of occupational specialization and trade would increase wealth for society as a whole, for Marx it was studied as part of the wider processes of political economy and reflected a concern 'with *how* wealth was generated in production, with the role of *classes* in the genesis of this wealth, and with the role of the state in relation to the different classes' (Wolf 1982, 19–20).

According to Marx, the unequal division of tasks and rewards in the process of production defines systemic inequality between social classes, which continues to exist unless a revolution takes place (Ultee, Arts, and Flap 2009, 309–10; Eriksen 2010a, 156–8; 2010b, 10–-11). His main scholarly contribution is widely considered to concern the fact that he posited a relational and systemic view of the division of labour, rather than viewing it as a consequence of self-interested human nature (Wolf 1982, 19–23; Polanyi 2001, 46). Max Weber, however, while agreeing with Marx that social classes could be viewed as delineated by economic power, also considered his approach as too exclusively focused on people's material circumstances. As such, he acknowledged that (dis)advantaged positioning in life was the result of wider relations of power, including but not restricted to relations of economic power (Ultee, Arts, and Flap 2009, 309–10; Eriksen 2010a, 156–8; 2010b, 10–11).

According to Weber, different criteria besides income levels combine to organize labour and positions of power in the context of everyday life, including notions of prestige, stature, education, intellect, religion, belonging, ability, and influence. Therefore, Weber prefers to speak of a person's social position more broadly and in terms of their *social status* rather than in terms of *class* – as defined by Marx (Eriksen 2010b, 10–11). It is these unequal relations of power, Weber asserts, that invoke the practice of 'social closure' – meaning that those

---

3 This notion would later yield the concept of the 'Homo Economicus' – i.e., 'Economic Man' (Polanyi 2001 [1944], 46).

advantaged in life exclude those that are less advantaged from occupational advancement and, in doing so, create observed patterns of organizational and job segmentation (Tilly 1999, 133–4; see also Tomaskovic-Devey 1995, 29).

These scholarly exchanges of views gradually led social scientists to understand the division of labour as inherently relational, rather than based on individual merit, and as resulting from existing and categorical differences in power. Polanyi (2001), for example, writes that the division of labour 'springs from [power] differences inherent in the facts of sex, geography, and individual endowment'. A frequently studied example is gendered division of labour, the hierarchical stratification of occupations between men and women, with men excluding women from occupational mobility. However, Tilly (1999, 134) argues that whilst this view rightly turns to categorical rather than individual discrimination in terms of job allocation and rewards, the relation is not causal (see also Wolf 1982, 9). As such, 'it describes a situation in which a single bargain sets rewards for work', rather than considering the historical processes and root causes that lay the foundation for such categorical inequalities to emerge (Tilly 1999, 134; see also Wolf 1982).

Drawing on Weber and Marx, Tilly (1999, 135; see also Bourdieu and Passeron 1990, 72) suggests that, on closer observation, a division of labour derives not merely from sorting at the hiring gate or pay table. Nor does it result straightforwardly from satisfying a personnel officer's predilections in terms of making categorizing decisions about who [what kind of people] should get which [types of] jobs (Jenkins 1994, 206). As such, a division of labour is about much more than the segregation of occupations, rewards, and other categorical differences. This is because it concerns complex relations of power that are inherent to society and are part of a grander processual mechanism that serves to reproduce social order itself. Therefore, division of labour is now more commonly understood to bring into play not only the influence of categories (of knowledge) on the labour market and vice-versa, but the whole of society and all its institutions. It is in this perspective that this chapter approaches the societal division of labour in Indonesia in line with Wolf as 'a totality of interconnected processes' (Wolf 1982, 2; see also Hann and Hart 2011, 51).

Hence, whereas the term occupation is widely understood to simply mean 'paid work' and defined as 'that which someone chooses to do to secure a livelihood', on closer observation, people's 'choice' of jobs operates within the strict limits of its social context (Jenkins 1994, 205). Granted, in most modern societies, there is indeed an element of election involved in the assumption of an occupation. However, occupational choices made by individuals are shaped by personal backgrounds and biographies, as well as by domestic and family structures, institutional and organizational contexts, and interconnected processes of history and identification (Wright 2016, 5; see also Bourdieu and Passeron 1990, 72). This means that the process of job allocation – from early training on to recruitment and promotion – rests not simply on colonial institutional-structural legacies or levels of individual-by-individual competences and experience, but on the intricate and ongoing processes of the (trans)local organization of social relations (Jenkins 1994, 205; Tilly 1999, 135; see also Wolf 1982).

From this perspective, a division of labour is an ongoing process of 'unequal selection and unequal selectedness' (Bourdieu and Passeron 1990, 72), with both managers, workers, and so forth, devising or borrowing beliefs and practices that support it (Douglas 1986; Tilly 1999, 135–138). By directing occupational 'choice', it brings about a convergence between people's self-image and aspirations with their public image and outcomes, as 'gatekeepers of one sort or another' within society, like the education system and labour market, 'play a crucial role in validating (or not) occupational aspirations' (Jenkins 1994, 205). On this Bielby and Baron (1986, 790; see also Bourdieu and Passeron 1990, 72) point out that 'if jobs are almost perfect[ly] segregated by [for example] sex, authority hierarchies and career ladders are likely to be segregated as well'. As such, division of labour is a process that results *in* as well as *from* a power imbalance in the social stratification of occupations in a particular societal context – understood by Wolf (1982, 3) as a 'bundle of relationships', rather than a fixed 'thing'.

In sum, building on the argument put forward by Wolf (1982, 23), I argue that to understand how and why the contemporary division of labour in Indonesian society results in exclusion of Chinese Indonesians from occupations in public service, we need to start by tracing the history of political, mercantile, and capitalist development in Indonesia and follow how these processes affected the 'local' population. This demands an understanding of how 'historical legacies of colonial rule, power struggles, legislative changes after independence and the like' established labour market dynamics (Lund 2008, 3). Moreover, it demands that we understand the historical interpretations of idioms and practices that are central to the contemporary process of dividing labour. I proceed now to discuss what Indonesian history tells us about the construction of a Chinese Indonesian identity vis-à-vis 'the rest' in terms of occupational specialization and differentiation.

4   Peoples with History: Dividing Labour in the Netherlands Indies

In southern parts of China subsistence was secured with relative difficulty. This led people to migrate to and conduct long-distance maritime trade with much of Southeast Asia long before any European 'discovery' of Indonesia.[4] As such, this diverse group of migrants do not constitute a 'people without history' (Suryadinata 1985; Lembong 2008, 48; Claver 2014, 140; see also Wolf 1982). Through long-standing experience in overseas trade, the Chinese emigrants to Indonesia acquired a high degree of commercial sophistication, as well as knowledge of the lands they traded and settled in, and of the people with whom they traded. This meant that by the time the Dutch United East Indian Company (VOC)[5] landed on the shores of Java, it was advantageous for the Dutch to cooperate with accomplished Chinese traders. This was to the detriment of local traders who partook in small-scale inland trade (Claver 2014, 140; Geschiere 2009, 15).

As a result, foreign merchants over time came to dominate Java's commercial activities. At first, these developments simply forced most local Javanese into roles of production – predominantly farming – as they were unable to accumulate capital, gain business experience, or build trade networks. In other words, they could not compete as traders (Mackie 1991; Kathiritamby-Wells 1993, 130–132; Stuart-Fox 2003, 93; Claver 2014, 142). However, as the power of the VOC advanced on Java over the seventeenth century, and after a series of military confrontations with local rulers, the occupational divide was more actively reinforced. The local population was forced to abandon trade in the region's most important products and experienced a gradual elimination from all Javanese trade (Claver 2014, 143).

Having firmly established its power, the VOC, on one hand, was resolved to respect local law and cultures as much as possible. However, on the other hand, it became clear that 'what they did not respect and given their ambitions *could* not respect, were local economic and political relationships' – especially in the form of trade networks and martial alliances (Lev 1985, 58). Therefore, since the VOC relied heavily on the services of the Chinese, they administratively separated the Chinese from local – Javanese – communities to restrict the latter's opportunities to form alliances and their effectiveness as intermediaries in trade (Lev 1985, 58; Claver 2014, 143). This administrative trend would be cultivated further under the development of what Lev (1985, 58) terms the 'colony proper' in the nineteenth century – when the government of the Netherlands took power and possession in Java from the VOC and established the Netherlands East-Indies (Dutch East Indies) at the end of the eighteenth century.

---

4 See also Wolf (1982, 3).
5 Short for the original Dutch name of the Dutch United East Indian Company; Vereenigde Oostindische Compagnie.

Much like the VOC, the principal interest of the government of the Dutch East Indies was exploitation by means of the expeditious extraction of agricultural commodities. In practice, this implied the strict separation of communities according to occupational specializations. In fact, the very logic behind the intricate administrative systems of *indirect rule*[6] and *legal pluralism*[7] in the Dutch East Indies was to equip each different community with the institutions needed to play their appointed roles (Lev 1985, 55; Eller 2016, 236). In this apparatus, those referred to by the legal category of *'inlanders'* – the 'local' population – mainly fulfilled the roles of farmers, tenants, and labourers dedicated to the cultivation of agricultural resources. As such, they literally formed the backbone of the Dutch East Indies economy. Those falling under the category *'Foreign Orientals'*, were in the main Chinese, who continued to fill the occupations of traders, merchants, moneylenders, and low-grade civil servants. Lastly, the category consisting of *'Europeans'* occupied high positions in administration and commerce (Mackie 1991; Claver 2014, 139). In a Wolfean perspective, we see therefore how the establishing of a capitalist mode of production and the related increasing interdependence between a global power in the form of the VOC/Government of the Dutch East Indies and Chinese traders, demanded and reproduced a division of labour defined along social and ethnic categories with their own forms of economic organization, expectations, and level of rights.

However, it is important that we realize that these colonial distinctions were not rigidly applied (Mackie 1991, 84; see also Rush 1983, 54; Claver 2014, 139). Some locals worked as traders and large numbers of Chinese started out in much less desirable jobs, such as *koelies*, millers, dockworkers, and artisans. Nevertheless, under these administratively structured conditions, a significant number of Chinese did indeed end up working as traders and moneylenders, as there were few appealing alternatives and choices. In fact, Claver (2014, 18) writes, whereas the Chinese population only amounted to approximately 1 per cent of the entire population on Java in the nineteenth century, in the busy port towns of Java's northern coast[8] Chinese traders outnumbered indigenous traders. This demonstrates that there was indeed already a distinction and correlation between different Chinese (Indonesian) and local, identities and occupations, resulting from a process of adjustment and adaptation to

---

6 In which the colonists employ locally established authorities to participate in the governance of the colony (Eller 2016, 236).
7 Defined as 'a situation in which two or more legal systems coexist in the same social field' (Merry 1988, 870).
8 Referred to in Bahasa Indonesia as *Pasisir*.

structural and evolving political and economic conditions (Mackie 1991, 84; Claver 2014, 139).

5 Dividing Labour in Indonesia

By the end of the nineteenth century, the colonial government had become uneasy about increasing immigration from China to Indonesia and the growing influence of the Chinese in the colonial economy. As such, Chinese experienced hostility and suspicion expressed in public accusations of exploiting and mistreating the *inlander* population, and were forced out of big business operations and denied access to substantial capital (Mackie 1991, 84–6; Claver 2014, 133). Moreover, the disintegration of the longstanding relationship deprived many Chinese of what little political power they had accumulated. Chinese were now subordinated more directly to the formal administrative apparatus of the Dutch East Indies as the relationship to the colonial government became more oppositional than collaborative (Rush 1983, 64). Under these circumstances, Mackie (1991, 84–8) writes that only a handful of large Chinese entrepreneurs survived. By the 1920s, most could no longer compete with their Dutch rivals and were forced to make their way in occupational roles and positions that today are considered typically characteristic for Chinese, such as (petty) traders, moneylenders, commodity dealers, and retail operators (Mackie 1991, 84).

For the next few decades, covering the Great Depression, the Japanese occupation in World War II, and the struggle for independence, the Chinese who chose to stay in Indonesia[9] adapted to drastically changing economic circumstances by starting up new small-scale industries such as textiles, food processing, or cigarette and soap production. During most of this time, any opportunity for occupational mobility remained effectively closed by the continuing economic and political dominance of Dutch enterprises. Yet, as the economic power of the Dutch started to wane and Indonesia was declared independent, some wealthier Chinese entrepreneurs started to take their places. However, they did not gain dramatically from this short-lived window of opportunity as the new Indonesian government, now led predominantly by Javanese, decided to nationalize all remaining Dutch businesses as part of a diplomatic offensive at the end of the 1950s (Mackie 1991, 89; Erman 2007, 179; Schulte Nordholt 2008, 15; Claver 2014, 349).

---

9 Many emigrated to Singapore or to China (Somers Heidhues 2012).

During these decades, Chinese also experienced increasing political vulnerability with widespread violations, personal attacks, and destruction of property on Java during the Japanese occupation and the struggle for independence. On the one hand, Chinese were targeted because of associations with the colonial regime and accused of continuing collaboration with the Dutch both during the Indonesian Nationalist Awakening and throughout the struggle for independence. On this point, Somers Heidhues (2012, 382) writes that 'Indonesian nationalist lore associated them [the Chinese] with colonialism' and, in extension, of not supporting the idea of an independent Indonesia (see also Purdey 2006). On the other hand, however, those who were identified as Chinese but were now citizens of the new Indonesian nation were also targeted because they were viewed as foreigners and traitors who did not truly belong and who were quite possibly more loyal to and sympathetic with the political agenda of their 'original homeland' – China.[10] Therefore, the Chinese in Indonesia were considered a potential danger on many fronts to the precarious Indonesian nation (Aguilar 2001; Vickers 2005, 98; Chalmers 2006, 62–8; Somers Heidhues 2012, 381–3).

This general hostility to the Chinese, who were also viewed as wielding substantial economic power, meant they had limited political support and influence (Ricklefs 1981, 226). It shows that Chinese Indonesian access to political power continued to be affected by colonial discourses associated with a specific Chinese identity (Purdey 2006, 13). In fact, at this time, only President Sukarno and the Indonesian Communist Party (PKI) felt inclined to shield Chinese Indonesians from some of the worst violence, a show of solidarity aimed at strengthening bilateral relations with China (Mackie 1991, 90). Moreover, as the Indonesian economy was deteriorating in the late 1950s, President Sukarno increasingly sided with China in the heat of the Cold War, whilst the PKI was gaining a foothold domestically.

Alarmed by this increasing foreign influence of China in Indonesian affairs, Indonesian military leaders sought to counter the leftist hold on Indonesian politics. This eventually led to a violent struggle for power that would bring about the fall of President Sukarno's regime in 1965 (Ricklefs 1981, 236–7; Purdey 2006, 10; Schulte Nordholt 2008, 15). As a result, between the mid- and late 1960s, the new Indonesian President, Suharto, systematically eradicated communism in Indonesia, simply by brutally annihilating anyone under suspicion as a communist sympathizer: 'Whole quarters and villages were left empty by

---

10 This image, however, of a single, foreign, and disloyal Chinese community was and remains misleading (Somers Heidhues 2012, 384).

the executions', Vickers (2005, 157) writes. In fact, Suharto found legitimation of his power in defining an internal enemy in the communists, whom he could demoralize, dehumanize, and hold accountable for the existing political and economic crisis. As such, for the next thirty-three years, Suharto's New Order regime cultivated a perception of Chinese Indonesian participation in politics as a potential *'Trojan horse'*. Chinese Indonesians were actively depicted as a threat to national security and as a force capable of establishing communism in Indonesia at any given moment, or one which would help establish foreign Chinese influence in Indonesia's domestic politics and economy (Smith 2003; Herlijanto 2017, 2).

Accordingly, Chinese Indonesians were again excluded from any public form of participation and representation in Indonesian politics. They were effectively banned from occupations in public services, including the military, and had only limited access to higher education especially (Purdey 2003, 426; Lindsey 2005, 56). At the same time, however, they were encouraged to remain active in specified areas of the economy, to keep it going, 'whilst Suharto enjoyed lucrative and often high-profile business deals with wealthy Chinese Indonesians' (Purdey 2003, 426). According to Studwell (2007, 44; see also Chalmers 2006, 67; Schulte Nordholt 2008, 23–31) this was mainly because Chinese Indonesian entrepreneurs were less of a threat to his political power than Javanese business interests. Near the end, Mackie (1991, 90) writes that a great many Chinese Indonesian entrepreneurs were prospering financially from patronage relationships that came to characterize New Order Indonesia. Some would even grow extraordinarily rich in an intimate alliance with the new political elite.

Eventually, President Suharto was forced to resign in 1998, after years of economic decline and amidst months of ensuing economic crisis in Asia. This led to decreasing political legitimacy and increasing political instability, massive student protests, violence, and bloodshed. During this time, Chinese Indonesian 'wealth' was amongst the chief targets of the ensuing violence, and this was widely covered by international media (Chalmers 2006, 263–6; Purdey 2006, 23–4). Because of all this, Indonesia was politically as well as economically severely weakened at the end of the New Order, becoming dependent on foreign aid. Under pressure from necessary international donors, such as the World Bank, Indonesia endeavoured to decentralize, democratize, implement good governance, establish the rule of law, and carry through neo-liberal reforms. Moreover, eager to prove their commitment to the social norms of the international community, they attempted to demonstrate their commitment to human rights (Vickers 2005, 210; Schulte Nordholt 2008, 113–47; Setijadi 2016b, 826). As a result, all Indonesian citizens gradually received equal rights to vote, run for office, speak freely, and work in public service (Lindsey 2005; Chalmers 2006; Purdey 2003; 2006; Schulte Nordholt 2008; Winarta 2008).

In sum, what I have demonstrated here is that colonially invented stigmas and identities were effectively reproduced throughout Indonesian history and reinforced through practices supporting a strict division of labour and patronage relationships. Therefore, whereas many Javanese were still mainly farmers during the New Order, other Javanese had come to represent the bureaucracy and political elite, whilst Chinese Indonesians had remained largely confined to working in the private sector – as small- or large-scale entrepreneurs, bankers, importers, and exporters, et cetera. In other words, long-standing lack of access to political power, ability and judgement amongst the Chinese in Indonesia has been caused by the very nature and reproduction of Indonesia's (trans)local history (Arendt 1958, 8). I now turn to the local level and discuss, first, how internalized and ongoing social discourses, material relations, and practices of occupational differentiation are continued presently in relation to the drawing of boundaries between Chinese Indonesian vis-à-vis Javanese identities. Secondly, I consider how (trans)national political and economic forces currently reinforce the reproduction of active processes of exclusion of Chinese Indonesians from career opportunities in public service, even though work and educational opportunities are now formally equal for all citizens.

6 The Glass Ceiling: Family Traditions, Business and Identity

'The Chinese have the economy here [in Indonesia]', Doddy – an entrepreneur and 'heir' to his family's tannery – replied, when I asked him why most Chinese Indonesians still appear to choose a life in business over politics. 'This is because working hard and taking over your family business is an important part of Chinese Indonesian culture', he said. 'And', he added, 'it is because our parents know that if you want to have a good life in Indonesia, you need to have your own business and be your own boss'. (Interview 50, 6 April 2018, Figure 9.1).

Whereas the Chinese in Indonesia under colonialism and after demonstrably came to be defined by their weakness in terms of political participation, they have also gradually developed a steadfast discursive reputation as economically privileged, ambitious, and entrepreneurial, for dominating the Indonesian economy, and for having unparalleled success in establishing and running business enterprises (Mackie 1992, 41; Dieleman 2007, 37; Setijadi 2017, 4). It is 'generally agreed that the Chinese immigrants and their descendants were (and still are) not only hard-working and thrifty, but a hardy, self-reliant,

FIGURE 9.1   Chinese-Indonesian shopkeeper.
An elderly Chinese Indonesian woman working in her family business in Chinatown in Semarang, Indonesia
SOURCE: AUTHOR

and above all, a risk-taking lot' and that this explains overseas Chinese business success (Mackie 1992, 41; see also Wu 1983, 113).

The existence and persistence of these views is confirmed by the results from the Indonesian National Survey Project (INSP), carried out in 2016, which also found that 68.1 per cent of all respondents believed that 'Chinese Indonesians have a natural talent for making money',[11] that 60.1 per cent believed 'Chinese Indonesians are usually at least middle-class',[12] and where 59.8 per cent thought 'Chinese Indonesians are more likely to be wealthy than the pribumi'[13] (Setijadi 2017). As such, Chinese Indonesians are traditionally viewed as natural-born entrepreneurs who are almost guaranteed economic success: 'It is the authentic soul of the Chinese people to trade everywhere and anywhere', Yohanes – a local archaeologist – said to me on this: 'They can sell anything' (Interview 22, 12 February 2018).

It appears that because of this belief, many Chinese in Indonesia continue to choose the perceived certainty of success in a career in the private – business – sector over that of a less obvious and more precarious career in public service. The belief is that securing safety and prosperity – a 'good life' – depends overwhelmingly on an innate ability to be successful in business – to 'sell things'. However, as we can observe, these career choices are not solely influenced by the existence of this naturalizing discourse on Chinese Indonesian identity. Rather, they are also deeply embedded in the continuation of everyday *practices* of job training and home education, conditioned by corresponding identifying notions of separate 'cultural traditions'. On this, Mentari – a customs official at Semarang's port – said to me:

> In my line of work, I see that most of the custom officials are Javanese and most of the importers Chinese. This is because of culture. Indonesians learn from their parents and in public schools – they are indoctrinated – that they have to become *ambtenaren* [i.e. civil servants] and become officers. This comes from colonialism, when only noble and rich families could become *ambtenaren*. The biggest dream of any Indonesian is to become President. The Chinese are also indoctrinated by their parents, who send them to private schools and universities, to go into business.

---

[11] Only 11.4 percent of the respondents actively disagreed, whilst 20.6 percent were undecided (Setijadi 2017, 6).

[12] Only 16 percent of the respondents actively disagreed, whilst 23.9 percent were undecided (Setijadi 2017, 6).

[13] Only 18.1 percent of the respondents actively disagreed, whilst 22.2 percent were undecided (Setijadi 2017, 6).

> This is also a matter of responsibility to your parents: to take over the family business ... Javanese people, they take secure jobs and live quiet lives. They are not as adventurous as the Chinese. Indonesian people prefer to stay close to home.
> Interview 28, 20 February 2018

In other words, whilst the general practice in Indonesia is that the Javanese are taught by their parents to aspire to a career as a government official and to dream of – one day – becoming President; it is also a longstanding Chinese Indonesian 'cultural tradition' to actively encourage and educate children to go into business – preferably the family business – to secure economic interests, social status, and material relations. As such, occupational aspirations and opportunities are directed at Chinese Indonesians from within the family as well as outside of it from a young age. This shows how the forces that historically and discursively have conditioned the social field of action both through laws and practice continue in new and familiar guises and act as conduits which shape future socio-economic organization, individualization processes, and trajectories around the (ethnic) division of labour – while, in turn, discouraging the shaping of alternative trajectories.

When he was seven years old, Doddy first told his parents that he wanted to become a professional football athlete. He ended up arguing with them about this for the next ten years – until he finally moved to The Netherlands to study business management in college. Doddy explained to me that this was not only because his parents were aware that discrimination is still a problem in professional Indonesian football – especially if you want to play for the national team – but also because they simply expected him to become a businessman. Since his infancy, Doddy's parents had planned for him to take over the family's tannery business someday, as his father, grandfather, and even great-grandfather had done before him. Therefore, this was where Doddy had to work every day and from a young age – before and after school. This was so that he could learn everything there was to know about the ins and outs of running a business, he continued, particularly the tannery. 'This is because it is still very common [for Chinese Indonesian businesses], that they go from father to son' (Interview 50, 6 April 2018).

Hence, I observe here that, to a greater or lesser extent, 'dynastic' plans, family business traditions, developed skill and values, established material relations, and corresponding notions of their own identity have long played a part in reproducing the discourse, status, and practices of 'Chinese Indonesian business entrepreneurship' in Indonesia – from early training on (Stewart 2003;

2013; Verver and Koning 2017). Jonny Herwibawa – the co-owner and manager of a company that wholesales pharmaceutics – also effectively illustrates this:

> We have had this business from a long time ago. It started as a small family pharmacy and only recently grew towards a wholesale business – in 2014. My grandfather started the business, in Pasar Johar near the centre of the city. When the business really started to grow [after 1998], my father invested some money in this land in [the middle of an outlying industrial area] He didn't know for sure that one of the children would take over the business. He expected it, of course, but he also wanted an investment. So, when I first took over the business, with my brother, we wanted to modernize it with technology, and we used the land to build the warehouse and to become a wholesale business.

When I asked why they decided to transition to a wholesale business, instead of continuing the local pharmacy, Jonny answered;

> Actually, at first my parents refused it. They wanted to continue the business in the traditional way, like it always worked. But there is a lot of competition and in order to survive in this business and grow, you have to be good and continuously improve and update your system.

When I asked him if he could name his greatest competitors now, Jonny answered, 'Most distribution businesses are owned by Chinese, like us, and like ours theirs are usually family businesses'. When I asked him why this was so,, he replied:

> The influence of family is very important in the business, because how you run the business and value your staff is based on trust. Every company has its own culture and way of working and only a few people can know everything there is to know about the business.
> Interview 52, 7 April 2018

This shows how social discourses establish a shared understanding of Chinese Indonesian and Javanese culture, and shape socially acceptable avenues along which people develop skills, acquire social status, pursue material interests within the established organization of society in terms of social occupations, and reproduce divisions of labour within Indonesian social categories. In brief, discourses around social mobility structure career opportunities, decision-making paradigms and, in extension, their eventual occupational 'choice' – by depressing or encouraging aspirations (Jenkins 1994, 206; Verver and Koning 2017, 639).

This is also demonstrated when looking at family and community bonds, which are embedded in the larger social register of 'identity groups' and bounded by established categorizing moralities, discourses, and behavioural norms that are demonstrably relevant to the reproduction of society's division of labour (Stewart 2003, 385). This phenomenon is frequently referred to as a 'glass ceiling' as a metaphor for socially structured, subconscious and frequently unintentional obstacles, such as the existence of biological or socio-cultural analogical mechanisms that condition a group's mobility and advancement (or lack thereof) in the labour market (Douglas 1986; Townsend 1997, 6; Tilly 1999, 139; Weyer 2007, 483). In short, identifying yourself and being identified as Chinese Indonesian means to adhere subconsciously to those behavioural norms and social practices that discursively circumscribe the categorical group to which you belong (Brubaker 2002, 166).

7   A Trojan Horse: 'Foreign' Interference, Political Exclusion, and Identity

Despite the above findings, it would be misleading to conclude that the straggling participation of Chinese Indonesians in Indonesian public service and shaping of occupational aspirations results solely from their reproduction of practices, perceived identification of cultural traditions, and behavioural norms in Indonesian society. Whilst we were having a cup of coffee and discussing the reason why most Chinese Indonesians go into business, Bondan replied: 'Most of us [Chinese Indonesians] do not go into politics … It is useless to go into politics'. On my questioning why this was the case, Bondan replied:

> Because at the end of the day, you lose anyway. I have a keen desire to go into politics, but I just don't know how. I don't have a good chance. Working in a government office is still hard, you have to take a test and even now they [the Javanese] have a different view of the Chinese in politics because of our stereotype, and they conduct nepotism in government offices.
> Interview 59, 16 April 2018

Hence, the tendency amongst Chinese Indonesians to work in the private sector is not just born out of internalized ideas about 'who [what types of people] should get which kind of jobs', but inevitably also out of cultivated contextual notions about who [specifically] should *not* get certain jobs (Jenkins 1994, 206). In other words, it results from discourses and practices that underpin the active exclusion of Chinese Indonesians from occupations in the public sector. When discussing to what extent Chinese Indonesians now have a chance to become successful in politics with one of the largest entrepreneurs in Semarang, called Prayitno Salim, he answered me straightforwardly: 'I have one friend who is [also] Chinese and in a political party and he says that they will say: 'As long as you are not Chinese, you will be chosen' (Interview 12, 7 September 2017). Similarly, Paul Candrautama – the owner of a local music school – said: 'Here, they say 'democracy, democracy', but we [Chinese Indonesians] cannot be politically active and still have to watch what we say' (Interview 54, 13 April 2018)

We can indeed observe that active processes of 'social closure' (Tilly 1999, 133; see also Weber 1968 [1921]) continue to inhibit Chinese Indonesians from gaining bureaucratic competence and advancing themselves in politics in Indonesia. And, at the same time, the process enforces an ethnically defined and societally produced Chinese Indonesian ethnic predisposition to go into business. In doing so, the division of labour between the Chinese Indonesians and the 'local' Indonesians is reproduced, as is an ethnically defined capitalist mode of production that is not only an expression of the economic domain, but which continues to shape, and be shaped by, the historical role of Chinese Indonesians in relation to the state and the political sphere.

At present, the most frequently discussed example of active exclusion of a Chinese Indonesian from politics is the contentious case of Governor Basuki Tjahaja Purnama, popularly known as 'Ahok', of Jakarta. Ahok became Governor of Jakarta by default in 2014, by directly succeeding Joko 'Jokowi' Widodo after he had been elected President. Even before, but especially after taking office, Ahok was subject to frequent racist comments questioning whether it was appropriate or even acceptable for a Chinese Indonesian to hold a position of direct political leadership in Indonesia (Setijadi 2017, 2–3). In 2016, circumstances deteriorated further as Ahok was accused of having committed blasphemy – by quoting and (mis)interpreting the Quran. Large masses of people mobilized against him in the streets of Jakarta and in 2017 he was sentenced to two years in prison on these blasphemy charges – rendering him, amongst other setbacks, unable to finish his term as Governor (Holmes 2016; Lamb 2017).

Whilst there is ample debate over whether Ahok's conviction was mainly racially charged,[14] the result of growing religious radicalism, or social inequality in Indonesia, or all these, it has in any case rekindled questions over the

---

14   I observed this at a Roundtable Discussion organized by the Embassy of Indonesia in Denmark and held at Aarhus University on 20 March 2017. The discussion was organized

extent to which Chinese Indonesians are still excluded from Indonesian public service – particularly in politics. When discussing this with Mentari – why Ahok was both convicted of blasphemy and not (re)elected for the position of Governor of Jakarta in 2017 – he shrugged dismissively and said: 'Every group wants to be ruled by its own and the *pribumi*[15] are the majority here. Since the end of the reformation [1998–2004], the President is directly elected and so are the governors or heads of regions. So, people choose their own … Many people that vote say: 'We don't need clever people to rule us, just someone who understands". (Interview 28, 20 February 2018)

The Indonesian National Survey Project (INSP), conducted in 2016, clearly established that, on average, most Indonesians (64.4 percent) would indeed be uncomfortable with having a Chinese Indonesian as their political leader. Secondly, 41.9 percent of the respondents agreed with the statement that 'Chinese Indonesians have too much influence in Indonesian politics already'. Lastly, 47.6 percent of those questioned agreed with the statement that this partly is because 'Chinese Indonesians may still harbour loyalty towards China' – against only 17.9 percent of the respondents explicitly disagreeing with this (Setijadi 2017, 7–10). On this, Setijadi (2017, 8) writes that Indonesia's 'dark historical legacy of assimilation and the associated suspicions of Chinese Indonesians as agents of communist China in the late 1960s' appear to continue to feed into the fear of the Chinese Indonesians as 'others' and politically too close to China.

Hence, whereas the transnational relation between Indonesia and China gradually normalized after 1998 (Suryadinata 2008, 13), it appears that the social, political, and economic antagonisms of the past, and the anti-Chinese discourse that was cultivated by the New Order regime are continuing, along with fears that China plans to take over decision-making power in Indonesia using the Chinese Indonesians as a 'Trojan horse' (Setijadi 2016b, 834). Accordingly, the increasingly close relation between Indonesia and China in recent years has led to concerns in Indonesia about growing Chinese investment, a 'flood' of immigrating Chinese workers, and to worries about developments in the South China Sea. These issues have come to dominate the public discourse about the role of China in Indonesia (Herlijanto 2017, 2–4).

---

around the theme 'The good society: experiences from Indonesia and Denmark'. During this meeting, the participants discussed, among other topics, whether Ahok's prosecution was the result of religious intolerance, social inequality, or race.

15 The Bahasa Indonesia, particularly Javanese, term used to refer to the original 'local' Indonesian population as opposed to 'foreigners', 'immigrants', or 'aliens', terms which include the Chinese Indonesians.

'These joint ventures between the government and Chinese from mainland China give fire to the 'Chinese issue' [in Indonesia]', Tawakal – an entrepreneur[16] and art enthusiast – sighed, when I asked him how he felt about increasing investments from China in Indonesia: 'It is very dangerous if not handled well', he continued. 'The trains, malls, roads … many of them … electricity plants … They are big projects taken on by big Chinese companies. They also bring their own labourers to Indonesia. This puts pressure on the local Chinese, the Indonesian Chinese'. (Interview 6, 17 August 2017) The Indonesian National Survey Project (INSP) also pointed out that almost half of those questioned believe that China's growing political power will affect Indonesia negatively. Though most believe that Chinese investments in Indonesia should be allowed, 54.9 percent believe this should 'only be in some cases', whilst 25.2 percent believe it should never be allowed at all. Moreover, 26.6 percent of those questioned believe Chinese workers should not be allowed to work in Indonesia, 19.9 percent expressed the view this should only be allowed if they are highly skilled, and 50.2 percent shared the view that it should only be allowed in very limited numbers (Herlijanto 2017).

Hence, though there appears to be some level of tolerance for Chinese investments in Indonesia, political and economic influence from China in Indonesia – especially when it concerns the labour market in terms of job security and direct political leadership – still appears to be considered a potential 'security risk' (Suryadinata 2008, 13–14; Herlijanto 2017, 11). Widespread reports, circulating especially on social media, suggesting that millions of Chinese workers are overwhelming the Indonesian labour market in the wake of growing Chinese investment in Indonesia have led to the waxing of already existing anti-Chinese sentiments. This is the case even though most of these reports appear to be false and have been rejected by Indonesia's Minister of Manpower Harif in 2016 – he claimed that the number of recently arrived Chinese migrant workers did not exceed 21,000 (Herlijanto 2017, 5).

'It hurts almost every national industry', Yayak Tri – a restaurateur – explained to me. 'Our President [Joko 'Jokowi' Widodo] works with a lot of Chinese companies from China. These companies demand that they can bring at least a percentage of the workers. This results in jealousy and as a result, we [Chinese Indonesians] also get into trouble' (Interview 14, 2 February 2018). Controversially, the public Indonesian figure Bachtiar Nasir, who is the leader

---

[16] Of all my informants, Tawakal was the only one who did not want to discuss the type of business he engages in – for reasons unspecified.

of a powerful Indonesian Islamist organization,[17] gave voice to this concern in a contentious interview given in 2017. Namely, he stated publicly that 'the [Indonesian] state should ensure that it does not sell Indonesia to foreigners, especially the Chinese', and that when it comes to fighting social inequality, the economic power and role of the Chinese Indonesians cannot be denied (Allard and Da Costa 2017).

In other words, established categorical inequalities run deep in Indonesia, even as they lack legal recognition due to changing political conditions (Tilly 1999, 124). Whereas Chinese Indonesian citizens now formally have equal rights, (trans)national political and economic forces in combination with myriad local practices demonstrably work to reinforce the 'local' reproduction of processes of exclusion of Chinese Indonesians from political advancement (Lindsey 2005; Chalmers 2006; Purdey 2003; 2006; Schulte Nordholt 2008; Winarta 2008). Namely, they affect the Indonesian society in such a way that the protection of individual as well as common political and economic interests coincide with the reconstructions of identities, through the maintenance of boundaries between them in terms of occupations. This leads to the reproduction of the historically conditioned division of labour, in which the process of job allocation coincides with the organization of categorical identities and the unequal relations of power between them.

8 Conclusion

The chapter set out to explore why Chinese Indonesians are not able to establish themselves in occupations in public service and politics, and are still excluded in the context of Indonesia's ongoing process of democratization in a post-colonial and post-author/itarian period of governance. Building on work by Wolf (1982), it argues that this issue is defined, first, by the reality that is also put forward by Salemink and Rasmussen (2016, 8): that our present state of being emerges from a shared historical trajectory and that, therefore, to be 'post' something does not necessarily mean being 'past' it. The start of democratization is hardly the definitive end of inequality and processes of exclusion (Lund 2016, 1204). Second, we see that social phenomena related to the Chinese Indonesian exclusion cannot be comprehended in isolation from the extensive and complex social context in which they take place (Wolf 1982).

---

17   This stands for National Movement to Safeguard the Fatwas of the Indonesian Ulemas Council (GNPF-MUI).

Here, we see how the historical and discursive forming of Chinese Indonesians conditions an ethnically defined role for them in a capitalist mode of production, and in turn conditions political possibilities, shapes livelihoods, and the division of labour vis-a-vis other population groups and as an expression of broader power relations.

Whereas Indonesia gradually reformed its system of governance and established legal equality for all its citizens after the fall of its authoritarian New Order regime in 1998, this chapter demonstrates that, when it comes to dividing labour, this change in governance system "combines with the institutional debris of the past" (Lund 2016, 1204). First, historical legacies of political, mercantile, and capitalist development established a diverse social system of identity inequality based on, amongst others, 'occupational differentiation and articulation in the marketplace' (Barth 1969, 34; see also Wolf 1982, 23; Lund 2008, 3). Secondly, 'false' interpretations of historical idioms and practices impinge on contemporary divisions of labour and so reproduce this social system of identity inequality by reconstructing the Chinese Indonesian identity – versus 'the rest' – in terms of occupation.

Hence, history interacts with the organization of the Indonesian labour market by conditioning social reality through the adoption of discourses and practices stipulating who [what kind of people] should get which [types of] jobs (Jenkins 1994, 206). Power relations configure people with self-images and public images through social discourses and practices and, in doing so, depress or encourage occupational aspirations and affect outcomes (Jenkins 1994, 206; Verver and Koning 2017, 639). As part of this process, history defines the division of labour in Indonesia by segregating contemporary career ladders according to identities – from early training on to recruitment and promotion. Moreover, historical and discursive conditioning produce political rationalities that lead to the active practice of excluding Chinese Indonesians from public service and politics, while transnational political and economic forces transform the 'local' context in which the division of labour occurs. This reminds us that law is not a tool for social engineering – the introduction of legal equality does not guarantee social equality (Moore 1973, 719). Rather, the systemic division of labour in Indonesia follows historically produced lines of inequality in combination with the effects of locally established and opportunistic organizational logics, and the impacts of transnational political and economic power (Wolf 1982; Stacey, this volume). As such, the exclusion of Chinese Indonesians from advancement in a career in public service and politics is still widespread and expected to continue, with Chinese Indonesians continuing to work mainly in the private sector – particularly as entrepreneurs – while experiencing a general exclusion from politics.

References

Aguilar, Filomeno V. 2001. "Citizenship, Inheritance, and the Indigenizing of "Orang Chinese" in Indonesia." *East Asia Cultures Critique* 9 (3): 501–533.

Allard, Tom, and Agustinus Beo Da Costa. 2017. Exclusive – Indonesian Islamist leader says ethnic Chinese wealth is next target. Online: Reuters.

Arendt, Hannah. 1958. *The origins of totalitarianism*. New York: Meridian Books.

Barth, Frederik. 1969. "Introduction." In *Ethnic groups and boundaries the social organization*, edited by Frederik Barth. Boston: Little, Brown and Company.

Berenschot, Ward, Gerry van Klinken, and Laurens Bakker. 2017. "Introduction: Citizenship and Democratization in Postcolonial Southeast Asia." In *Citizenship and Democratization in Postcolonial Southeast Asia*, edited by Ward Berenschot, Gerry van Klinken and Laurens Bakker. Leiden: Brill.

Bielby, William T., and James N. Baron. 1986. "Men and Women at Work: Sex Segregation and Statistical Discrimination." *American Journal of Sociology* 91: 759–799.

Bourdieu, Pierre, and Jean Claude Passeron. 1990. *Reproduction in education, society, and culture*. Sage Publications Ltd.

Brubaker, Rogers. 2002. "Ethnicity without groups." *European Journal of Sociology* 43 (2): 163–189.

Bruggen, T.J. 2021. "Fluid and Fixed: Chinese Indonesian Identity at Work". PhD Dissertation, University of Copenhagen.

Chalmers, Ian. 2006. *Indonesia: an Introduction to Contemporary Traditions*. Oxford University Press.

Claver, Alexander. 2014. *Dutch Commerce and Chinese Merchants in Java: Colonial Relationships in Trade and Finance, 1800–1942*. Leiden and Boston: Brill.

Dieleman, Marleen. 2007. "How Chinese are Entrepreneurial Strategies of Ethnic Chinese Business Groups in Southeast Asia." Leiden University.

Douglas, Mary. 1986. *How Institutions Think*: Syracuse University Press.

Eilenberg, Michael. 2016. "A State of Fragmentation: Enacting Sovereignty and Citizenship at the Edge of the Indonesian State." *Development and Change* 47 (6): 1338–1360.

Eller, Jack David. 2016. *Cultural Anthropology: Global Forces, Local Lives*. 3 ed. London: Routledge.

Eriksen, Thomas Hylland. 2010a. *Ethnicity and nationalism: Anthropological Perspectives*. 3 ed. New York and London: Pluto Press.

Eriksen, Thomas Hylland. 2010b. *Small Places, Large Issues: An Introduction to Social and Cultural Anthropology*. 3 ed. New York and London: Pluto Press.

Erman, Erwiza. 2007. "Deregulation of the tin trade and creation of a local Shadow State: A Bangka case study." In *Renegotiating Boundaries: Local Politics in Post-Suharto*

Indonesia. Edited by Henk Schulte Nordholt and Gerry van Klinken, 177–202. Leiden: KITLV Press.

Geschiere, Peter. 2009. *The Perils of Belonging: Autochtony, Citizenship, and Exclusion in Africa and Europe*. University of Chicago Press.

Hann, Chris, and Keith Hart. 2011. *Economic Anthropology*. New York: Wiley & Sons.

Herlijanto, Johannes. 2017. "Public Perceptions of China in Indonesia: the Indonesia National Survey." *ISEAS Perspective* 89.

Holmes, Oliver. 2016. Jakarta's violent identity crisis: behind the vilification of Chinese Indonesians. Online: The Guardian.

Jenkins, Richard. 1994. "Rethinking Ethnicity: Identity, categorization and power." *Ethnic and Racial Studies* 17 (2): 197–223.

Kapoor, Kanupriya, and Anastasia Arvirianty. 2014. A first for Indonesia, ethnic Chinese leader takes charge in the capital. Online: Reuters.

Kathiritamby-Wells, J. 1993. "Restraints on the development of merchant capitalism in Southeast Asia before 1800." In *Southeast Asia in the early modern era. Trade, power and belief.*, edited by A. Reid. Ithaca: Cornell University Press.

Koning, Juliette. 2007. "Chineseness and Chinese Indonesian Business Practices: A Generational and Discursive Enquiry." *East Asia* 24: 129–152.

Lamb, Kate. 2017. Jakarta Governor Ahok sentenced to two years in prison for blasphemy. Online: The Guardian.

Lembong, Eddie. 2008. "Indonesian Government Policies and the Ethnic Chinese: Some Recent Developments." In *Ethnic Chinese in Contemporary Indonesia*, edited by Leo Suryadinata. Singapore: ISEAS Publications.

Lev, Daniel S. 1985. "Colonial Law and the Genesis of the Indonesian State." *Indonesia* 40: 57–74.

Lindsey, Tim. 2005. "Reconstituting the Ethnic Chinese in Post-Soeharto Indonesia: Law, Racial Discrimination, and Reform." In *Chinese Indonesians: Remembering, Distorting, and Forgetting*, edited by Tim Lindsey and Helen Pausacker. Singapore: ISEAS Publications.

Lund, Christian. 2008. *Local Politics and the Dynamics of Property in Africa*. Cambridge University Press.

Lund, Christian. 2016. "Rule and Rupture: State Formation through the Production of Property and Citizenship." *Development and Change* 47 (6): 1199–1228.

Mackie, Jamie. 1991. "Towkays and Tycoons: The Chinese in Indonesian Economic Life in the 1920s and 1980s." *Indonesia*: 83–96.

Mackie, Jamie. 1992. "Overseas Chinese Entrepreneurship." *Asian-Pacific Economic Literature* 6 (1): 41–64.

Merry, Sally Engle. 1988. "Legal Pluralism." *Law and Society Review* 22 (5): 869–896.

Moore, Sally Falk. 1973. "Law and Social Change: The Semi-Autonomous Social Field as an Appropriate Subject of Study." *Law and Society Review* 7 (4): 719–746.

Polanyi, Karl. 2001 [1944]. *The Great Transformation: The Political and Economic Origins of Our Time*. Boston: Beacon Press.

Purdey, Jemma. 2003. "Political Change Reopening the Asimilasi vs Integrasi Debate: Ethnic Chinese Identity in Post-Suharto Indonesia." *Asian Ethnicity* 4 (3): 421–437.

Purdey, Jemma. 2006. *Anti-Chinese Violence in Indonesia, 1996–1999*. Hawaii: University of Hawaii Press.

Ricklefs, M.C. 1981. *A History of Modern Indonesia*. London: Macmillan.

Rush, James R. 1983. "Social Control and Influence in Nineteenth Century Indonesia: Opium Farms and the Chinese of Java." *Indonesia* 35: 53–64.

Rush, James R. 1990. *Opium to Java: Revenue Faromg and Chinese Enterprise in Colonial Indonesia, 1860-1910*. Ithaca: Cornell University Press.

Salemink, Oscar, and Mattias Borg Rasmussen. 2016. "After dispossession: Ethnographic approaches to neoliberalization." *Focaal* 2016 (74): 3–12.

Schulte Nordholt, Henk. 2008. *Indonesie na Soeharto. Restauratie en Reformasi.* Amsterdam: Bert Bakker.

Schulte Nordholt, Henk., and Gerry van Klinken. 2007. (eds). *Renegotiating Boundaries: Local Politics in Post-Suharto Indonesia*. Leiden: KITLV Press.

Setijadi, Charlotte. 2016a. "Ethnic Chinese in Contemporary Indonesia: Changing Identity Politics and the Paradox of Sinification." *ISEAS Perspective* 2016 (12).

Setijadi, Charlotte. 2016b. "'A Beautiful Bridge': Chinese Indonesians Associations, Social Capital and Strategic Identification in a New Era of Chinese-Indonesia Relations." *Journal of Contemporary China* 25 (102): 822–835.

Setijadi, Charlotte. 2017. "Chinese Indonesians in the Eyes of the Pribumi Public." *ISEAS Perspective* 2017 (73).

Smith, Adam. 2007 [1776]. *The Wealth of Nations*. Cosimo, Inc.

Smith, Anthony L. 2003. From Latent Threat to Possible Partner: Indonesia's China Debate. Asia-Pacific Center for Security Studies.

Somers Heidhues, Mary. 2012. "Anti-Chinese Violence in Java during the Indonesian Revolution, 1945–149." *Journal of Genocide Research* 14 (3–4): 381–401.

Somers Heidhues, Mary. 2017. "Studying the Chinese in Indonesia: A Long Half-Centyry." *Sojourn: Journal of Social Issues in Southeast Asia* 32 (3): 601–633.

Stewart, Alex. 2003. "Help One Another, Use One Another: Toward an Anthropology of Family Business." *Entrepreneurship: Theory and Practice* 27 (4): 383–396.

Stewart, Alex. 2013. "The anthropology of family business: an imagined ideal." In *The SAGE handbook of family business*, edited by Leif Melin, Mattias Nordqvist and Pramodita Sharma. Sage Publications Ltd.

Stuart-Fox, Martin. 2003. *A short history of China and Southeast Asia. Tribute, trade and influence.* Crows Nest: Allen and Unwin.

Studwell, Joe. 2007. *Asian Godfathers: Money and Power in Hong Kong and Southeast Asia*. Grove Press.

Suryadinata, Leo. 1985. "Government Policies towards the Ethnic Chinese: A Comparison between Indonesia and Malaysia." *Southeast Asian Journal of Social Science* 13 (2): 15–28.

Suryadinata, Leo. 2008. "Chinese Indonesians in an Era of Globalization: Some Major Characteristics." In *Ethnic Chinese in Contemporary Indonesia*, edited by Leo Suryadinata, 1–16. Singapore: ISEAS Publications.

Tilly, Charles. 1999. *Durable Inequality*. University of California Press.

Tomaskovic-Devey, Donald. 1995. "Sex composition and gendered earnings inequality: A comparison of job and occupational models." In *Gender inequality at work*, edited by Jerry A. Jacoks. Thousand Oaks, California: Sage.

Townsend, B. 1997. "Breaking through the glass ceiling revisited." *Equal Opportunities International* 16 (5): 4–14.

Ultee, W.C., W.A. Arts, and H.D. Flap. 2009. *Sociologie: Vragen, Uitspraken, Bevindingen*. Martinus Nijhoff.

Verver, Michiel, and Juliette Koning. 2017. "Toward a Kinship Perspective on Entrepreneurship." *Entrepreneurship: Theory and Practice* 42 (4): 631–666.

Vickers, Adrian. 2005. *A History of Modern Indonesia*. Cambridge University Press.

Weber, Max. 1968 [1921]. *Economy and Society: An outline of Interpretive Sociology*. New York: Bedminster.

Weyer, Birgit. 2007. "Twenty years later: explaining the persistence of the glass ceiling for women leaders." *Women in Management Review* 22 (6): 482–496.

Winarta, Frans H. 2008. "No More Discrimination Against the Chinese." In *Ethnic Chinese in Contemporary Indonesia*, edited by Leo Suryadinata. Singapore: ISEAS Publications.

Wolf, Eric R. 1982. *Europe and the People Without History*. University of California Press.

Wolf, Eric R. 1990. "Distinguished Lecture: Facing Power – Old Insights, New Questions." *American Anthropologist* 92 (3): 586–596.

Wright, Tessa. 2016. *Gender and Sexuality in Male-Dominated Occupations: Women Working in Construction and Transport*. London: Palgrave Macmillan.

Wu, Yuan-Li. 1983. "Chinese Entrepreneurs in Southeast Asia." *American Economic Review* 73 (2): 112–117.

CHAPTER 10

Global Competition and Local Advantages: The Agency of Samoan Factory Youth in an Untold History of the Automotive Supply Chain

Masami Tsujita

1 Introduction

In August 2017, after 26 years of operation, a Japan-based multinational car parts supplier closed its export-oriented, labour-intensive manufacturing plant in Samoa, a small Pacific Island developing state. This closure was a direct result of an Australian government decision to stop subsidizing the automotive industry. It is a classic example of the flow-on effects of changes in globalized supply chains and illustrates how the neoliberal economy has undermined the circumstances of workers in peripheral economies. In this respect, low-paid workers in global factories are typically seen as passive victims of capitalistic exploitation who remain silent in the process of development. This chapter, however, offers an alternative perspective. Drawing on Wolf's perspective of the totality of interconnected processes that emphasizes the nature of global–local and core–periphery mutual interdependence, it offers a case study that explores the roles factory workers have played in the context of seemingly irresistible forces of multinational operations in the cut-throat competition of the automotive industry. This suggests that global factory employment was a valuable opportunity that helped young workers become active agents of change in their life trajectories in the internationally interconnected webs of capitalist development. Critical studies of multinational corporations and supply chains have contributed significantly to a deeper understanding of the underlying mechanism that widens inequalities in wealth and power and perpetuates the international division of labour. Studies based particularly on structuralist and political economic approaches typically depict workers in global factories as passive victims of capitalistic exploitation who remain silent in development processes (Fernandez-Kelley 1983; Elson and Pearson 2011; Siegel, Pyun, and Cheon 2019; Lim 1983; Fuentes and Ehrenreich 1983). On the other hand, ethnographic studies of factory workers in developing countries have examined relationships between factory employment and everyday lives of workers (Chang, 2008; Louie, 2001; Ngai, 2005; Ong, 1987; Zhang, 2014). These studies

© MASAMI TSUJITA, 2023 | DOI:10.1163/9789004527928_011

acknowledge grassroots agency among factory workers but focus on changes at microeconomic levels, often overlooking the active participation of workers in the larger-scale dynamics. Accordingly, 40 years after Eric R. Wolf's book *Europe and the People without History* (EPWH), it remains common for studies of microcosms to lack macro perspectives and theory. Global factory workers are still viewed repeatedly as "people without history" in the accounts of international development (Buckley 2018; Selwyn 2017). Inspired by EPWH, this chapter consequently explores the agency of factory workers in the context of neoliberal-driven global competition and interdependent transformation in the small Pacific Island state of Samoa.

The study is built on the case of young factory workers in a Japanese-owned car parts manufacturing plant called Yazaki Electrical Distribution System Samoa (YES), located in Samoa. YES was an independent subsidiary of Yazaki Corporation, a Japan-based multinational car parts supplier that operated in Samoa from 1991 to 2017. This plant was initially established in Australia and later shifted to Samoa in the wake of Australia's neoliberal industrial policies that encouraged the outsourcing of labour-intensive car parts overseas. YES was the largest private employer in Samoa and employed a total number of over 60,000 local workers during the 26 years of its operation. This illustrates YES's key role in job creation in the country whose total population is approximately 195,000. The factory, however, ceased operation in 2017 due to the Australian government's decision to stop subsidizing the car manufacturing industry, which led to the closure of the Toyota Australia assembly plant in Melbourne, YES's sole client since 2007.

The closure of YES illustrates how a decision made in the context of global market competition by a core economy negatively affected development of a peripheral economy. It is also a classic case of multinationals that shift their operational sites for profit maximization while exploiting workers in developing countries as seemingly disposable commodities. In these terms, factory workers can be seen as powerless victims of the multinational's profit-seeking operation, which undermines their situation and promotes inequality in wealth between dominating core and subordinate peripheral economies. This chapter presents an alternative insight that emphasizes how worker agency is exercised, even in the cut-throat competition of the global automotive industry where factory workers in developing countries are often seen as powerless. The empirical investigation of this process seeks to contribute to the validity of Wolf's totalizing analysis in furthering the understanding of the effects of neoliberal-driven capitalist networks represented by supply chains on development on the ground and relationships to local socio-cultural organization. As such, it employs Wolf's insights on the totality of interconnected processes;

that socio-cultural facts mediate the structural manifestations of seemingly unequal power relations in ways that transcend the boundaries between macro and micro contexts. It explores ways in which young Samoans have agency, even in their typical situation as low-paid workers employed in a global factory in a country on the periphery of the global political economy. Empirical data was collected primarily through direct observations at the factory where I worked as part of the management team for six years from 2010 to 2016.

2 A Totality of Interconnected Development Processes

Wolf's central assertion in EPWH is:

> [T]he world of humankind constitutes a manifold, a totality of interconnected processes, and inquiries that disassemble this totality into bits and then fail to reassemble it falsify reality.
> WOLF 1982, 3

He contends that a holistic, interdisciplinary approach that looks at the human world as a multidimensional, interconnected entity is needed to properly understand the effects of global development processes like European expansion on a microcosm. His perspective emphasizes the context of structural power relations in their totality and challenges the commonly employed dualism that divides the human world into two separate, static entities – core and periphery, global and local, and macro and micro – with little consideration of their mutual interrelationships and interdependencies. The concept of core–periphery duality, for instance, was developed by Andre Gunder Frank in the early 1960s in response to the modernization theory and elaborated further by Immanuel Wallerstein. Their dependency school of thought sought to understand 'the development of underdevelopment' examining the exploitative relationships between the two entities. While Wolf acknowledges the theoretical advances made by Frank and Wallerstein, he points out the shortcomings of their 'one-way' analyses that focused on the ways in which the core subjugates the periphery but omitted to examine different ways in which micro-populations in the periphery respond to the core's activities (Wolf 1982, 23). In such analyses, the effects of capitalist development on the ground remained unclear and the peoples on the periphery appeared monotonously as passive victims. To fill these gaps, Wolf asserts the necessity of a perspective to explore the totality and mutually interdependent nature of the core–periphery relationships. EPWH acknowledges such mutuality even in colonial relationships.

For example, some colonized populations drawn into mercantile activities suffered dire consequences while other became active participants in the fur trade and the slave trade for their own advancement. Their participation, at the same time, helped shape the course of colonial expansion. Furthermore, Wolf's perspective on the diversity of such interactions and outcomes in their totality challenges the conventional approach that separates local and global as two independent spheres of human activity. He argues rather that local and global are inseparable, interconnected spaces. Local worlds are often dominated by global and transnational development processes, but people adapt these processes flexibly by retaining old ways and adopting the new. They transform their ways as they go along (Wolf 2010, x), so that the global becomes evident in the local over time. EPWH illustrated the global–local interconnections and why the global process must be studied in local contexts.

Similarly, Wolf emphasizes the importance of integrating macro-micro forces in theoretical analyses, asserting the need to bridge theoretical constructs of global power relations, which explain determining features of capitalism and structural powers, and empirical micro-population data collected through ethnographical investigation and direct observations. He points out the risk of inductive reasoning commonly employed particularly in functionalist anthropology, which tends to generate a theoretical construct about society and culture based primarily on micro-social ethnography. Due mainly to the limited scope of information and observations, such studies are often unable to examine larger dynamics and fail to contextualize the micro-populations studied within the macrocosm. Macroscopic study, on the other hand, repeatedly overlooks the diversity of micro-populations, mistakenly interpreting them as culturally, politically, geographically, and historically comparable entities. In such studies, questions such as how locals resist external forces or how they adapt mercantile transformations remain unanswered. Consequently, both micro and macro approaches view local populations as isolated from global processes and not an agency of capitalist transformation – in order words, people without history. Wolf therefore deems it necessary to merge micro-macro studies.

> Theoretically informed history and historically informed theory must be joined together to account for populations specifiable in time and space, both as outcomes of significant processes and as their carriers (1982, 21).

With these insights, Wolf rewrote the history of European expansion and breathed life into people previously depicted as people without agency. European expansion was not independent processes of populations, but rather the consequences of globally and locally interconnected and interdependent events that occurred simultaneously within and between colonizers and colonized peoples. People of colonies were no longer voiceless, passive victims of colonialism but became active agents in the multidimensional transformations that happened in conjunction with the expansion of capitalism. EPWH is not only an anthropological and historiographical milestone, but also a respected model of study in and across any disciplines to understand the totality of global development processes and their effects on micro-populations.

This chapter draws on Wolf's insights into the interconnectedness of global and local power relations in its analysis of the impact of the operation of multinational corporations on local workers and their responses. It draws on EPWH and has two somewhat overlapping goals. First, it explores the interconnected and mutually interdependent nature of development forces between core and periphery as well as global and local from the standpoint of factory workers in a developing country. More specifically, it illustrates how neoliberal regimes adopted by developed countries can impact, intentionally or unintentionally, on the operation of a multinational enterprise and the livelihood of its workers. Secondly, it emphasizes the agency of a grassroots population in global processes and explores the roles young Samoan factory workers have played in the context of seemingly irresistible forces of multinational operations in the highly competitive automotive industry. It concludes by suggesting that global factory employment, from the worker's perspective, provided Samoan youth with a valuable opportunity to become active agents of change, despite their limited power imposed by their own life trajectories within the context of the global neoliberal-driven economic system. Ultimately, the chapter hopes to contribute the validity of Wolf's perspectives on the totality of interconnected processes in studies of contemporary development.

3 The Automotive Supply Chain

To contextualize the history of YES, a Japanese-owned car parts manufacturing plant, in the larger economic context, one must understand the automotive supply chain, which represents the globally interconnected and mutually interdependent nature of today's economic development processes. The automotive industry operates on economies of scale due to the nature of technologically intensive processes and products, as well as a substantial degree of specialization in component production. Consequently, the industry today has become progressively internationalized and underpinned by globally dispersed car parts industries and their internationally connected supply chains.

Factories assembling cars are located in countries with large domestic markets or in countries that provide good logistics for regional export while component production for individual car models has been shifted to many countries (Pursell 2001, 4). However, as a growing number of emergent economies can now produce cars at low cost with a satisfactory level of quality, the automotive industry has become ever-increasingly competitive worldwide (Holweg 2008). The competition among car parts suppliers has also reinforced the competitiveness of their respective clients. In other words, the success of carmakers relies heavily on wisely managing supply chains and enhancing supplier performance (Cox 1999, 168). Global competition is no longer only between carmakers but between their supply chains who must deliver 'a product and service to the right place at the right time at the lowest price' (Li et al. 2006, 107). Consumers, on the other hand, increasingly demand a wide range of car models and options. This has made the automotive supply chain more complex, competitive, mutually interdependent, and difficult to manage.

As the technology of car manufacturing advances, components and features used in a vehicle have multiplied. Today's vehicles contain thousands of parts supplied by thousands of different firms and manufactured across the globe. To build a single vehicle, for example, Toyota Motor Company (hereafter Toyota), uses an average of more than 30,000 component pieces provided by about 580 parts suppliers (Toyota Motors Corporation 2016; Kito, Brintrup, and New 2014). These parts suppliers are divided into different tiers, forming a supply chain pyramid. First-tier suppliers supply components and materials directly to carmakers. They procure subcomponents from second-tier suppliers who procure subcomponents from third-tier suppliers, and thus supply chains continue to the original provider of raw materials. Top world carmakers like Toyota have an extended supply chain with a hierarchy of four to five tiers. Some top first-tier suppliers are themselves large multinational firms with complex global operations with their own supply chains (US Department of Commerce 2016). Denso, one of the top first-tier suppliers of Toyota, for instance, has 5,600 second-tier suppliers across 38 countries and regions (Denso Corporation 2018). These supply chain pyramids are built upon trust as vehicle assembly depends on the availability of quality components supplied on time by lower tier suppliers (Waters 2006, 397). A defective product or supply shortage at any tier could stop carmakers' production lines and might cost more than USD$22,000 per minute on average (Sustained Quality 2018). Therefore, carmakers must maintain tightly forged supply chains with highly reliable, trustworthy suppliers in order to survive (Cox 1999, 168).

The competitiveness of automotive industry suppliers is usually measured by their performance on quality, cost, and delivery (QCD). The QCD measurement was developed originally in the UK automotive industry to improve the production management of carmakers. This widely used measurement helps to assess and improve manufacturing performance for products and production processes. In the automotive industry, quality is based on the 'product's ability to match a specification' and measured by the defect rate, or the quantity of defective units per million in supplied products. The quality requirements for some electrical components such as wiring harnesses are stricter than other car parts as they are directly related to safety features like air bags, steering control, and braking systems (Wei 2012, 5). Cost, on the other hand, is measured by total expenses required to produce a product, including the cost of direct labour, raw materials, and production overheads such as electricity and water, administration, meals, transportation, security, and insurance. Lastly, the measurement of delivery is straightforward as it is based on the supplier's adherence to the delivery schedule. It can be measured scientifically by the ratio of the quantity of failed and incorrect deliveries over the quantity of scheduled deliveries. Each carmaker sets its own QCD goals and requirements as simultaneous achievement of QCD is foremost in producing highly credible new products ahead of competitors (Amasaka 2004). Thus, each supplier must establish an innovative and reliable production system to meet the specific QCD requirements of its customers.

Meeting QCD requirements, however, has become more challenging since just-in-time delivery became the global norm in car manufacturing in the 1980s. The just-in-time system, also known as the lean production system, is a demand-based production management strategy established by Toyota to eliminate waste and produce a higher quality product with a shorter lead time at lower cost. This requires all suppliers in the supply chain to deliver only 'what is needed, when it is needed, and in the amount needed' (Toyota Motor Corporation 2016). Receiving only what is needed allows customers, either carmakers or parts suppliers in an upper tier in the supply chain, to keep their inventory level low. Such waste elimination not only saves cost and space but also reduces the risk of components becoming obsolete as vehicle designs change. Furthermore, receiving products on time helps maintain the production pace and avoid stoppages and unnecessary waits. In short, the just-in-time system improves and stabilizes production quality and efficiency. It does, however, make it extremely difficult for parts suppliers to meet the QCD requirements and deliver exact quantities on very tight schedules with the minimized production costs needed to maintain their competitiveness (Wiring Harness News 2020).

In the early 1990s, the idea of supplier parks emerged to create an effective environment for the just-in-time delivery and demand-driven logistics process

(Reichhart and Holweg 2006). This shifted the location of first-tier suppliers of assembly plants within the distance of one-day delivery range to car assembly plants (Cox 1999; Sako 2009). The first supplier park was established in Spain in 1992 (Reichhart and Holweg 2006, 4). Despite this trend, some Australian car parts suppliers took advantage of the neoliberal policies of the late 1980s that deregulated trade barriers and allowed outsourcing parts assemblies to overseas locations with cheaper labour. Yazaki Australia, a first-tier supplier of Toyota Australia and second-tier supplier of General Motors Australia, shifted its parts assembly plants to Samoa, over 5,000 kilometres away from the automotive supplier parks in Australia, in 1999. The necessity of long-distance shipment from Samoa to Australia made just-in-time delivery particularly challenging for Yazaki Samoa but, as will be shown, this created an opportunity among factory workers to take advantage of the challenge and to increase their bargaining power.

4   Relocation of the Factory from Australia to Samoa

The Yazaki Corporation, the mother company of YES, was established in 1941 and headquartered in Tokyo. It has 143 subsidiaries across 45 countries, operating at 487 sites with a global workforce of over 249,000 (Yazaki Corporation 2016a). The company develops and manufactures various automotive components, but Yazaki's core business has been the automotive wiring harness, for which it has the largest world share. An automotive wiring harness is a bundle of wires and data circuits that run through a vehicle, integrating electric circuits and multiple systems. It distributes power and relays information to various electrical components, functioning similarly to the essential nervous system of human body (Yazaki Corporation 2016a). A large harness is made of more than 500 cables and circuits bound together by clamps, cable ties, tubes, or sleeves with insulated tape on an assembly board by hand, and then attached to different branches. Bundling of harnesses with these materials not only protects cables but also facilitates installation on the carmaker's production line (Kobayashi, Hirano, and Higashi 2013, 305). These manual assembly processes are labour-intensive but are the most flexible and cost-effective way to accommodate a large range of part numbers, vehicle models, and options with specific requirements. Harness production has, in fact, become increasingly complex due to the changes in vehicles' functionality, including in-vehicle infotainment systems and advanced driver assistance systems (Trommnau et al. 2019; Wiring Harness News 2020). For these reasons, the harness assembly is difficult to automate even though most vehicle manufacturing today is highly automated.

Minimizing labour cost, therefore, is crucial for harness makers like Yazaki to remain competitive in the cut-throat car parts industry. Yazaki established its first overseas manufacturing plant in Thailand in 1962 and later shifted most of its harness manufacturing operations to less-industrialized countries to take advantage of low wages. In 1965, Yazaki set up an office in Melbourne, Australia and, in 1976, expanded its operational scope to support the growing demands in the automotive manufacturing industry in Australia. Australia has a long history of automotive manufacturing established through protectionist policies since early 1900. Domestic carmakers were protected from global competition by limited quotas and high tariffs on imported vehicles and components (Clibborn, Lansbury, and Wright 2017; Stanford 2017). Furthermore, the local content programme, started in 1948, set a requirement that was as high as 85 percent of the value of a car to be assembled domestically. Such policies stimulated the establishment of the car parts manufacturing industry in Australia. By the end of the 1970s, automotive manufacturing had become the largest industry in Australia's manufacturing sector. In this context, Yazaki headquarters decided to build two assembly plants in Melbourne and Adelaide in South Australia, to supply wiring harnesses for domestic carmakers as well as for the markets in the South East Asia, the United States, and Europe (Australian Arrow Pty. Ltd. n.d.).

However, the Australian federal labour government (1983–1991), led by Bob Hawke, initiated substantial reform in the manufacturing sector and pursued a liberal approach to make it more internationally competitive. In 1984, as part of the reform, the Motor Industrial Plan, also known as Button Plan after the Industry Minister Senator John Button, reduced tariff protection and eliminated import quotas on vehicles and car parts. The overarching aim of this plan was to unwind, according to Button, the 'culture of protection' within the automotive industry (Leigh 2002, 499) and strengthen the industry's international competitiveness. The Button Plan not only achieved its initial objectives but also induced car parts suppliers like Yazaki to outsource their labour-intensive products outside Australia to curb the high costs of domestic labour. In 1986, the Yazaki headquarters first shifted the automated section of harness manufacturing to Auckland, New Zealand and imported the products back to Australia under reduced trade restrictions. A few years later, the headquarters shifted the remaining labour-intensive section of the manufacturing to a country close to Australia but kept the electronic research and development section in Melbourne (Thomas 1993).

The government of Samoa, at that time, was struggling to recover from consecutive economic crises. In the 1980s, its economy was highly dependent on a narrow range of income sources including overseas remittances, foreign development aid, subsistence farming and fishing, commercial agriculture, fisheries and forestry, and small-scale tourism. The small manufacturing sector, which accounted for less than 15 percent of GDP, produced import replacement items like cigarettes and beer mainly for the small domestic markets (The World Bank 1991, 319). The country faced major macro imbalances due primarily to a decline in major export items such as copra, cocoa, and bananas as well as a rapid expansion of public sector expenditures. In the mid-1980s, the government implemented some significant changes to improve export competitiveness, including imposing high import duties, devaluing the national currency, and fixing the exchange rate. Prior to the introduction of these measures, the government had experimented with socialist approaches to development. As the then incoming Prime Minister Tuilaepa Sailele Malielegaoi, explained the situation:

> When our party came to power in 1983, the country was broke, the economy was poor, inflation was high, imported food stuffs were short, the business community was frustrated with the tender system and foreign reserves were limited. Foreign banks refused to lend to Samoa because of its poor loan repayment record. The new government needed to take action to steer the country out of the poor economic status at that time.
> Interview, 10 October 2005, cited in KERSLAKE 2007, 123

However, agricultural exports still suffered from fluctuating market prices, declining demand, and poor product quality, while fixed exchange rates affected domestic production incentives (The World Bank 1991, 320). In the late 1980s the government adopted the economic reform policies known internationally as structural adjustment and recommended by Samoa's major multilateral donors, including the World Bank and Asia Development Bank (ADB). Structural adjustment aimed to adjust the country's economic system to improve its global competitiveness and reduce its balance of payments (ADB 1999, 100). One of the key objectives was to attract foreign investment and assure export markets (Fairbairn 1993, 246). This period coincided with news that a Japanese company in Australia was planning to relocate a labour-extensive plant.

Yazaki screened potential sites and ruled out Papua New Guinea due to its political instability and Solomon Islands for the prevalence there of malaria. Other Pacific states like Kiribati and Tonga were too small in terms of a labour pool (Thomas 1993). Ultimately, Indonesia, Fiji, and Samoa were shortlisted. Indonesia offered the cheapest labour pool while Fiji offered the best logistics. Nevertheless, Yazaki chose Samoa for its political stability and the positive, enthusiastic approach of its government (Sasabe 1994, 50). Prior to the 2021 political unrest triggered by a national election that replaced the ruling party of nearly 40 years, Samoa had been known as the most politically stable country in the region compared to other Pacific Island states, where civil conflicts and military coups have become more frequent. Tofilau Eti Alesana was Samoa's Prime Minister at the time that news of the Yazaki opportunity became known, and he and his Cabinet acted quickly, offering generous incentives to entice the Japanese company to relocate in Samoa (Yazaki Corporation 2016b; Feagaimaali'i-Luamanu 2017). Yazaki was offered various tax exemptions for 15 years, free lease of government land, and construction of a large factory building (8,100 square metres) at a cost of USD$2.5 million, in addition to a moderate-sized, cheap, and non-unionized labour pool (Aiavao 1992, 51; Sasabe 1994, 50). At the time, the minimum wage in Australia was AUD$10–17 (USD$7.20–12.30) per hour, whereas in Samoa, it was only SAT$1 (USD$0.38) per hour (Malua 2009, 118). In addition to high labour costs, Australia's automotive industry was highly unionized, industrial relations were sometimes tense, and Yazaki Australia was facing union disputes at its Melbourne plant (Fraenkel 1998, 52). In contrast, Samoa had experienced only one three-month labour strike by public servants in 1981 since a Public Service Association was established in 1969, and the private sector was stable. In short, tax exemptions, government support, and a low-cost non-unionized labour force made Samoa the strongest competitor.

In 1991, Yazaki established a subsidiary of Yazaki Australia in Samoa. In the following year, the company started its full operation, with 1,327 employees working at three different locations while they awaited the completion of the promised factory building in Vaitele (Yazaki Corporation 2016a). During this period, Samoa continued to face economic setbacks. Cyclone Val in 1990 and Cyclone Ofa in 1991 devastated infrastructure and much of the agriculture sector. A taro-leaf blight in 1993 led to the collapse of Samoa's leading export product. The demand for wage employment intensified and made Yazaki's recruitment of factory workers very easy. According to a production manager, 'a single radio advertisement in Apia caused a deluge of as many as 1,500 applicants, so recruitment now is by word of mouth' (Thomas 1993). From 1992 to 1994, the company continually expanded the scope of its operations, but at the same time the Yazaki management struggled with product quality and the industrial disciplining of its factory operators. Similarly, the workers themselves struggled to adjust to unfamiliar industrial culture conditions, particularly long working hours and low pay rates. In 1993, about 200 workers went on strike, marching on Parliament to protest their working conditions (Thomas 1993). It was the first industrial strike in Samoan history. Prime Minister

Alesana denounced the strike as a foreign influence that left people in countries like New Zealand without jobs (Samoa Observer 1993). He explained:

> The company did not persuade the government to allow it to operate in Samoa. It was us who asked Yazaki to come in ... If you are Samoan and love your country, return to work.
> SASABE 1994, 54

Some government officials worried that Samoa might lose its reputation as a place with no industrial disputes, but Yazaki had no problem quickly replacing all the protesters and continued operations without major disruptions. In 1994, the pre-assembly process, undertaken in the Auckland factory, was shifted to Samoa to start the full assembly process. In 1995, the factory became an independent subsidiary of Yazaki Corporation Asia and Oceania Group and was renamed Yazaki Electric Distribution System Samoa or YES. YES gradually increased the number of employees to meet expanded production volume from its three clients: Toyota, Holden (formerly General Motors-Holden), and Mitsubishi – all in Australia. Between 1991 and 2007, the company employed an average of 2,200 workers per year, with a peak of 3,500 workers in 1996. However, in mid-2007, YES reduced the number of employees, due in part to the global financial crisis. The company also lost some buyers, so Toyota Australia became its sole remaining client. After 2012, employees usually numbered around 800. Despite this decline, YES remained the largest private sector employer in Samoa. According to YES's human resources office, the last employee identification number issued for a wageworker was 66,302, meaning the company had hired at least that many people in its history. This illustrates YES's significant contribution to job creation during its 26-year period in Samoa, a country whose total population was approximately 195,000 when the factory closed in 2017. At that time, YES had 740 Samoan workers, three Japanese expatriates from Yazaki headquarters, one Filipino expatriate from Yazaki Philippines, and two locally hired Japanese staff in the translation section. About 60 percent, or 450, of the employees were shop-floor operators who worked on the assembly line to build wiring harnesses. These operators were young, with an average age of 20–23. The majority had left school before the age of 14 or 15. Traditionally, the gender ratio for the assembly lines was 90–95 percent women to 5–10 percent men. In later years, however, men increasingly engaged in manual processes on the assembly lines. As a result, the gender ratio among shop-floor operators became more equal over time, with a ratio of 65 percent women to 35 percent men when the company closed in Samoa. This change may reflect an increased demand for wage employment among Samoan male youth who, in rural households, usually did unpaid farming and fishing. Manual assembly work, once perceived as a "female" job, gradually became a gender-neutral employment opportunity.

5 Working Conditions

A normal workday at YES began with a three-minute "radio exercise", a common practice in factories in Japan, to limber up workers before work to prevent accidents. The company's regular operation hours were from 7:30 a.m. to 5 p.m. (Monday through Thursday) and 7:30 a.m. to 2:10 p.m. on Fridays. Workers had a 20-minute morning tea break and a 40-minute staggered lunch break. A free lunch valued at SAT$2.30 (USD$0.90) was provided daily. Shop-floor operators worked in a poorly ventilated concrete and corrugated iron factory building that was both hot and humid, with an average temperature of approximately 30–35 degrees Celsius. They were required to stand and assemble wires on the conveyor line all day while production leaders shouted at them to work faster to meet targeted quota. They were also often fully expected to work overtime until 8 or 9 p.m., thus extending working hours to 11–12 hours a day.

Starting pay rates at YES were based on discussions between the company and the government of Samoa as low production costs were the key reasons Yazaki shifted to Samoa. Low wages were another complaint among operators, however. During the last five years of YES, the starting rate for shop-floor operators was SAT$2.30 (USD$0.90) per hour, or about SAT$4,800 (USD$1,930) per year, with an annual pay increase of SAT$0.10 (USD$0.04) per hour. Given the low wages and arduous working conditions, an operator's job at YES was low in the occupational hierarchy in status-conscious Samoa. YES operators were sometimes taunted by village peers who looked down on factory work and regarded teaching, nursing, and office work as more prestigious (Grevel-Lameko 2000; Tsujita 2002). Some operators, uncomfortable with the reputation of their factory jobs, commuted in regular clothes and changed into the operator's light blue uniform when they reached the factory. One operator shared mixed feelings regarding her employment, saying, 'I like my job, but I don't want my children to work at the factory. I want my daughter to go to college and become a teacher because although pay is not so good, it's a good job'. Others compared themselves positively to their unemployed village peers and looked more favourably at their employment. One explained 'I feel proud of working at Yazaki because I've heard some ministers at the Parliament meeting were thanking Yazaki for its contributions to Samoa. They said if there isn't Yazaki, where will those youth find jobs?'

Socializing opportunities at YES were also viewed positively and cited by most employees interviewed as the best part of working for YES. On assembly lines, workmates bonded as friends, chatted, and joked behind the line leaders' backs, and sometimes burst into song. In addition, company events provided operators with opportunities to interact socially and bond with each other. For many young operators, working at YES was their first time ever away from the strict oversight of their families or from supervised communal work organized by villages. They were free to meet people from other villages and church communities. Many of them found a boyfriend, girlfriend, or future spouse in the factory. In fact, five out of seven production department managers met their spouses in the factory. For young operators, YES was an ideal place to develop friendships without parental interference. For all employees, regardless of age and position, YES was a unique place of socialization where hundreds of people from different villages interacted and shared the factory space for long hours, thereby forging a village-like communal bond. Such bonds and social incentives usually outweighed employee grievances about the workplace and encouraged them to continue working.

YES management gradually increased the number of social events held inside and outside the factory premise. All YES employees and managers, divided into four groups, competed in different games at the annual day-long sports day held at a public stadium in town. Many employees enjoyed playing ping-pong and Samoan chess in YES's recreational areas during breaks. Christmas celebration included the lighting of a giant Christmas tree on the shopfloor, Samoan dances, Christmas carols, and skits as well as photos with a jumbo decorative Santa. The end-of-year ceremony began with a thank-you speech by the vice-president, followed by prizes for perfect attendance, best production line of the year, and best operators of the year. All workers received a premium gift with the company logo (e.g., a watch, umbrella, or water bottle) and a special lunch box. In addition to these annual events, special ceremonies helped to mark company anniversaries and celebrate company accomplishments, such as zero customer complaints or the Best Supplier Award from Toyota Australia. Through these social events, employees developed friendships beyond those with their immediate fellow workers on assembly lines.

6   YES Production Line and Quality Control

YES shop-floor operators were at the bottom of the company's organizational structure and had the most unsatisfactory working conditions, but they were not necessarily passive victims exploited by the profit-driven operation of a multinational corporation. Because shop-floor operators were indispensable core manpower on whom the YES QCD performance depended, workers gained leverage over the company to change its operational policies in their favour. On the shopfloor, harness manufacturing processes were divided roughly into three sections: pre, sub, and final assembly. The pre-assembly section cut wires to the required length, stripped them and crimped the designated terminals using special wire-cutting machines. The cut and crimped wires were inspected and stored at mini stores located between pre and sub assembly lines. In the sub-assembly section, the crimped wires were inserted into designated respective connector housings by hand and assembled into sub-modules for final assembly. At the heart of the production process, in the final assembly section, manually assembled sub-modules of wires prepared in the previous section into a harness on a special board were placed on the conveyor line. The sub-modules of wires were laid on the board according to the assembly drawing, bound together with corrugated tubes, sleeves, sockets, and other accessories and wrapped by insulated tape, to be built into a harness. The conveyor line for big harnesses consisted of 18 to 20 assembly boards with one to two operators stationed at each board. The operators completed their respective sequences according to the process standard designed by the production engineering team. Usually, each operator was tasked to complete five to ten processes within the production 'takt' time, which refers to the speed with which a product must be produced to meet customer demand. After the assembly process, a harness was subject to electrical and visual inspections to ensure perfect functionality and quality before delivery.

Due to the dominance of manual processes, maintaining stable product quality and high production efficiency was critical. At YES, the pre-assembly was the only automated section where one operator was allocated per machine. Although sub-assembly processes at some Yazaki plants were automated, manual labour was more cost-effective at YES for simple processes that could be carried out by low-paid workers. The performance of pre- and sub-assembly operators was monitored by the achievement of target quantity per hour as well as by the number of defective harnesses produced. Quality control for sub-assembly processes was especially critical since the insertion of wires into incorrect connector housings (which insulate and encapsulates contacts) could cause defects affecting the fundamental function of the automotive harness: to provide a stable electrical connection between vehicle components when the vehicle is in use (Trommnau et al. 2019, 388). Automotive functionality errors typically caused production downtime and had adverse impacts on supplier competitiveness. At YES, however, insertion errors at the sub-assembly stage occurred almost daily due largely to high absenteeism among shop-floor operators. In the absence of designated operators, substitute operators frequently made mistakes. Operator absenteeism was even more serious in the final assembly process, where line balancing directly affected production quality and efficiency.

Line balancing involves balancing the workload of every operator at every workstation on the same conveyor line so that all the operators complete their tasks within an exact given takt time. When the line is perfectly balanced, no operator is either overloaded or left idle, even for a second (Wiring Harness News 2020). The concept of line balancing is rooted in Toyota's just-in-time system and enables manufacturers to improve production quality and efficiency to meet the customer requirement for the QCD. Line balancing also helps develop 'level production', another concept of Toyota's production system that stabilizes the production pace and ensures quality. Nevertheless, line balancing was extremely difficult at YES due to the high absenteeism of the operators. The daily attendance rate of the shop-floor operators was around 90 percent on average; on some days it was as low as 80 percent. In the pre- and sub-assembly sections, tasks were done individually, and a substitute operator trained for similar tasks or machines could easily fill in; one substitute for an absent operator. In the final assembly, however, the substitute process was complicated because of the need to balance available labour along each production line. At YES, each operator on the conveyor line was trained to operate three stations from her/his workstation to cover the absence of operators on the same assembly line. This method doubled the workload of operators who also covered another's tasks. Overloaded operators who were unable to complete the two sets of processes within the takt time often stopped the conveyor line to catch up. This typically resulted in production delays that were a direct result of absenteeism.

Production delays were commonly covered by overtime although this increased labour costs by providing transportation and additional meals. In some cases, products that were not ready for scheduled fortnightly shipments were air freighted to Australia. In the worst-case scenario, a management member would hand-carry products to Yazaki Australia for delivery. In such cases, although the extra costs exceeded the shipment budget and increased labour charge, YES prioritized customer demand and adhered firmly to delivery schedules. Meeting the just-in-time delivery was highly complex for YES given the remote location of Samoa from the customer in Australia, as well as material suppliers in Japan and Thailand. Geographical distance and infrequent shipment made YES's production lead time 14 days, compared to the common lead time of one day or less observed by other first-tier suppliers near Melbourne. This meant YES had to work harder to improve quality and maintain its overall performance on QCD, which was negatively impacted by the high rate of absenteeism. The overloaded operators raced against time, creating a situation in which more mistakes could occur. Any mistake in a production process could jeopardize the functionality of the harness and damage the company's reputation. Effective ways to overcome risks to quality maintenance were needed. When measures to encourage workers with social events proved insufficient, the company had to change its operational policies. In the following sections, policy changes that helped operators meet personal and cultural obligations will be discussed.

7 Global Competition and Local Advantages: Rehiring

YES's high absenteeism was due partly to a high turnover rate among shop-floor operators. More than half of the shop-floor operators left the factory within their first year of employment; over 75 percent within three years, and only 10 percent worked at YES for longer than ten years. Initially, YES had a strict policy that forbade rehiring to discourage trained operators from resigning. Eventually, in the context of the Samoan labour market, YES changed its rehiring policy and gave operators more flexible work choices. The high turnover rate frustrated Japanese managers who wondered why young workers in Samoa gave up their jobs so easily, given very limited competing employment opportunities. A Samoan manager explained two main reasons. First, their weekly earnings from YES were not high enough to be essential to the family's survival. Compared to low-wage developing countries in Southeast Asia, such as Philippines or Vietnam, the cost of living in Samoa is high. Few goods are manufactured locally, most are imported and subject to duties and value-added tax. Therefore, a minimum wage supplements a household income but does not cover all its necessities. Most households rely on several economic strategies to get by – including wages, remittances from relatives overseas, and semi-subsistence farming on customary land, or fishing. Thus, the level of operators' commitment to YES employment was low. Secondly, daily life in Samoa is full of unexpected communal demands including funerals, church hall openings, village clean-ups, hosting visitors, or looking after a sick grandmother or a sister's baby. Young adults are expected to give priority to work for family, church, and village activities. In this cultural context, the labour of young adults is an important household resource, and their services are often considered more important than the minimum wage they earn from the factory. Therefore, operators left YES when more important life events came up. This was also the main reason for high absenteeism among operators.

The company needed to modify its recruitment policy to cope with the intermittent commitment of young Samoan workers and retain an adequate number of operators. Ultimately, a production manager convinced the top management that rehiring trained operators would increase production efficiency by reducing the period needed for training. The company provided a one-month training for new operators which included modules on Yazaki corporate philosophy, YES rules, manufacturing processes and techniques, and Japan-based work ethics. Rehiring former operators reduced the needed time for training from one month to one week, just long enough to refresh the skills and techniques they had acquired previously. Rehiring helped the company recruit enough operations-ready manpower to meet customer demands on time. The rehiring system, at the same time, allowed young workers to move in and out of the factory according to their circumstances and needs for immediate cash. First-time operators generally had high expectations of earning much-needed cash income, but often quit when they encountered hardships, were scolded by line leaders, became disappointed by low pay, or found they were needed at a family event. Later, after boredom at home, an unsuccessful job search, the need for cash, or missing the camaraderie of the factory, they would return to YES. In most cases, they waited for the company to call for the return of former operators. When these operators reapplied, YES rarely checked the circumstances under which they had left the job. Within a day or two, they were generally rehired. The company did not limit the number of times an operator could be rehired, so some were rehired more than five times.

This rehiring system was adopted to secure operations-ready manpower, but it also increased the turnover rate among operators and lowered attendance. YES's strict attendance policy required a supervisor's approval for a leave of absence at least one day in advance. Those who failed to show up for work for three days without approval faced termination. These rigorous rules were based on the company's time-sensitive production system. Because a shortage of operators not only caused delays but also affected the quality of the products, production leaders repeatedly reminded workers of the attendance policy. Operators were aware of the policy, but many were terminated for disobeying it. On average, 75 percent of the operators who left YES were terminated rather than having resigned; and in 2016, 70 percent of those terminated had broken the three-day absentee rule. This suggests that most operators were not worried about termination. For some operators, dismissal was preferred over resignation because resignation required tedious processes, including an exit interview and the return of ID cards and uniforms. Those terminated knew that operators previously terminated could return to work, except when their dismissal was due to misconduct (such as stealing company tools). They also knew that, in practice, the company did not check the reasons for termination thoroughly and often even rehired those who had been terminated for stealing. Knowing that return was an option made it easier for workers to quit when they were dissatisfied with their working conditions or had other priorities. In this context, the rehiring system provided operators with increased bargaining power with their employer and quitting YES became a common strategy whereby workers could give priority to their own interests.

YES reluctantly permitted the rehiring of operators, making an adjustment in the Samoan context to maintain its production efficiency as a competitive supplier in the global automotive market. As noted previously, harness production required intensive manual labour, and so YES had to retain a core number of operators to meet the supply schedule clients demanded. By 2011–12, it had become more difficult to hold the required number of operators due to the growth in Samoa's private sector, particularly in wholesale and retail trade, which created more low-skilled jobs for local youth (MCIL 2013). This trend narrowed YES's options and forced them to adjust the rehiring policy. Although options were limited by low pay and difficult working conditions, YES operators were able to expand and exercise their options, which put pressure on the company to adopt more flexible hiring policies. In short, young workers became active agents in influencing and ultimately reshaping company policy and the conditions under which production took place. This illustrates Wolf's emphasis on the need to contextualize the interconnectedness, mutual interdependency, and power dynamics in local–global capitalist relationships, in this case forged between a substantial multinational company and its otherwise low-wage workers with extremely limited rights to influence working conditions.

8 Global Competition and Local Advantages: Cultural Obligation

Another example of worker agency is evident from their manipulation of the 'pass-out' system. Until recently, except for small stores located within villages, nearly all businesses and services in both public and private sectors in Samoa closed at 5 p.m. on weekdays and 12 noon on Saturday. Sunday is strictly observed by most Samoans as a day of rest and religious observances. At YES, this meant workers often needed a break during working hours to run errands, pay bills, do banking, or go shopping. Leaving a workplace for personal errands is not uncommon in Samoa, but was not acceptable to YES, whose primary mission was to reduce production time and increase production efficiency. However, a pass-out system, which allowed employees to do errands during operation hours rather than taking leave, was adopted in the early years of the company as a strategy to reduce absenteeism. In later years, when the company had 500–600 shop-floor operators, roughly 100 operators, or one fifth of the total per day, used this pass-out system and were absent from the assembly line for varying lengths of time. Because it affected negatively both the demands to balance labour on production lines and ensure product quality, decreasing the number of workers using the pass-out system became a leading concern for YES management, especially when Toyota Australia adopted ISO9000, a set of international standards on quality management and quality assurance that increased product quality requirements for all suppliers.

Operators had numerous reasons to leave the factory compound during working hours, but securing small loans was the most common errand. Borrowing money has become customary in Samoa as its people have become more dependent on cash incomes since the 1960s, and unexpected social obligations are now met with gifts or contributions of cash rather than traditional goods, as in the past. A national financial survey of 2015 found that nearly half of the adult population have borrowed money from formal or informal services (Central Bank of Samoa 2015, 32). Since saving is rarely practised, when there is an urgent need, people commonly either borrow money from a friend or a moneylender, request an advance on wages from their employer, or ask overseas family members to send money. Overseas remittances account for around 20 percent of Samoa's GDP and approximately half the population receive remittances on a regular basis. Survey data show that 70 percent of the remittance receivers use the money for daily needs (Central Bank of Samoa 2015). People also borrow money for asset purchases, house renovations, or obligatory contributions to big life-cycle events. Extended family members are expected to contribute to these life-cycle events, including funerals, weddings, chiefly title bestowals or church-related activities. These sociocultural obligations typically require taking out loans. Although YES operators took out loans for a variety of reasons, the majority did so to assist their parents or families with the above-mentioned financial obligations or for special occasions such as Mother's Day, Father's Day, Children's Day, or birthdays. Some workers borrowed so often that 80 to 90 percent or more of their pay went to loan repayments. Some even received SAT$0 net pay. Despite challenges, the ability to take out loans was a benefit and being able to help one's parents financially was a key reason for joining YES.

Many YES operators used their pass-outs to collect remittances or apply for loans from public financial institutions such as Samoa National Provident Funds (SNPF), the Development Bank of Samoa, or private microcredit firms. Commercial banks in Samoa generally do not provide microcredit (Moustafa and Kumar 2016, 20–21). SNPF is a compulsory saving scheme to which both employer and employee contribute a minimum of 10 percent of gross income to the member's account. All SNPF members can access up to 50 percent of their contributions. SNPF loans, however, were often insufficient to meet the financial needs of young workers with limited years of work and contributions. Some of them had already borrowed the maximum amount while others were behind on payments. Like other low-income earners, YES operators rarely qualified for a loan from the formal banking sector (Moustafa and Kumar 2016, 21). Requirements for a small loan of SAT$200 to SAT$1,000 at private microcredit firms was simple. A borrower must be employed for at least six months and receive her/his pay through a bank account. A bank statement, latest pay slip, a confirmation letter of employment, photo ID, and one guarantor with employment are required. These required documents must be sighted and verified by loan officers. As YES operators often served as guarantors for each other's loans, more than one operator at a time left the assembly line to facilitate the loan process. Usually, a borrower can receive cash or a cheque for the requested amount in less than half an hour at a fixed interest rate of approximately 20 percent. So, when operators had to obtain money for a purpose, they requested a pass-out – with which they could return to the factory within one or two hours – and many of them used the opportunity for shopping, other errands, or to enjoy a break from the assembly line. Although the approval of the pass-out indicated a return time, some did not return for the rest of the day, knowing they had been marked present in the morning and would still be entitled to a monthly perfect attendance award of SAT$100 or promotion based on their attendance.

To counteract the high pass-out rate, YES management designated Friday as a short workday so workers could do personal errands or apply for loans after work. Operation hours were modified to 8.5 hours on Mondays to Thursdays and 6 hours on Friday, with operators finishing at 2:10 p.m. Despite this concession, workers continued to request pass-outs during the week – mainly because Fridays were crowded in town and queues for loans and shopping often long, especially before holidays. Therefore, to facilitate loans, the company invited a private financial firm to set up a loan-processing desk within the YES compound on Wednesdays. The loan desk was technically open only during lunch hours, but borrowers were often still waiting after their lunch hours. As a result, although pass-outs continued, the attendance of operators improved on Wednesdays. YES also negotiated with financial institutions to deduct loan repayments directly from their payroll rather than from personal bank accounts. This assisted repayments to financial institutions who were then more willing to accept loan application from low-income casual wage workers like YES operators. With this system, even operators who had recently joined YES were able to apply for a small loan. Accordingly, for the sake of QCD achievement, the company had to accommodate the needs of operators as based in their local socio-cultural and economic practices, and to modify regulations and policies. In this respect, YES operators were not passive victims of the multinational operation, but active agents who were able to take advantage of labour-intensive operation and the time-sensitive production system for their own benefits. In turn, the production-related changes introduced by YES accommodated and enabled the furtherance of local socio-cultural traditions around economic transactions and obligations.

9 Conclusion

In August 2017, Yazaki ceased its 26 years of operations in Samoa because of the decline of the car manufacturing industry in Australia and its global supply chain. The closure of YES illustrates the flow-on effects of changes in transnational operations and the critique of the neoliberal strategies that undermines the situation of workers in peripheral economies. The history of YES, however, suggests exploitation may be in the eye of the beholder if the mutually interdependent nature of core–periphery relationships is considered. Wages were already very low before YES came to Samoa, and there were few opportunities to work for wages. The government of Samoa offered Yazaki Corporation tax breaks and the provision of premises, knowing that the low cost of a labour force was a key attraction for YES investment in Samoa. Within the Samoan context, YES was eventually forced to revise operation policies to accommodate the needs of operators, to maintain product quality and production efficiency, and to meet customer demands on QCD. The revised recruitment policy expanded young operators' options for work and increased their bargaining power with the employer because they knew the company depended on them. Factory employment, on the other hand, enhanced the ability of Samoan youth to help support their parents financially through wages and access to loans.

On 13 December 2017 the former Prime Minister Tuilaepa officially handed over the former YES building to new tenants. It marked the end of a chapter in Samoa's development history in which YES played an important role. Conversations with YES employees revealed that most were saddened by the factory closure and wished Samoa had more multinational factories like YES to provide wage employment, especially for rural youth like themselves. Such positive factors, voiced by a micro-population, complicate the critiques offered by macro studies that focus solely on the profit-oriented operations of multinational corporations searching for places to exploit cheap labour. For most employees, the closure of YES was the day they lost their employer and the workmates with whom they had established attachments. Even though YES offered only temporary employment for many operators, they were an essential element in the struggles and successes of this Japanese company in the pursuit of its profitable operation in Samoa and also in a highly competitive global market. These operators were the reason Yazaki shifted the labour-intensive factory from Australia to Samoa. They were the reason the company was able to maintain its QCD performance as the first-tier supplier despite the logistical disadvantages.

This chapter has used Wolfean perspectives on the totality of interconnected local–global processes to explore the mutually interdependent relationships between core and peripheral economies, customer and supplier, and localized factory and worker in the context of an automotive supply chain. The case study from Samoa highlights the analytical significance of investigating dynamics that emerge within specific local-level socio-cultural organization, and their impact on multinational operations and the organization of labour. The dynamic relationships between YES and its young Samoan workers highlight the agency of an otherwise marginalized labour force. Despite long hours, unpleasant working conditions and line leader pressure, their factory employment increased life choices and significantly reshaped production conditions, whilst also providing means to earn a cash income, build self-confidence, and seize opportunities that would otherwise be beyond their reach. In the context of Wolf's capitalist mode of production, the case exemplifies how global interconnectivity produces local differentiation, and how ideas based on optimizing capitalist development accommodate, and act to further, localized forms of socio-cultural organization. In turn, the development of local idiosyncrasies forged by meetings with global economic power feed into processes of uneven and contingent global capitalism (Neveling and Steur 2018). From these perspectives, we learn that young Samoan factory workers were not docile victims, but dynamic participants in the history of global capitalist transformations. For the workers, the multinational factory employment provided a valuable opportunity to help them become active agents of change in the trajectory of their own lives and development in the face of seemingly irresistible forces of globalized supply chain operations. Conversely, worker–factory interconnectedness enabled the reshaping and furtherance of pre-existing socio-cultural organization and economic obligations. In this light, the social impact of multinational factories like YES can be viewed more positively in studies of the political economy of developing countries. Wolf's perspective, transcending spatial boundaries, enhances the study of labour relationships in today's ever more tightly and widely connected human world, while also revealing the untold history of young Samoan workers.

References

Aiavao, Ulafala. 1992. "What Yazaki Means to the Samoans: Hiring for Wiring Brings Job Boom." *Island Business Pacific* 18 (10): 51–54.

Amasaka, Kakuro. 2004. "Development of 'Science TQM', A New Principle of Quality Management: Effectiveness of Strategic Stratified Task Team at Toyota." *International Journal of Production Research* 42 (17): 3691–3706.

Asian Development Bank. 1999. *Reforms in the Pacific: An Assessment of the Asian Development Bank's Assistance for Reform Programs in the Pacific*. Manila, Philippines: Asia Development Bank.

Australian Arrow Pty. Ltd. n.d. "Australian Arrow." LinkedIn. Accessed August 8, 2020. https://www.linkedin.com/company/australian-arrow.

Buckley, Peter J. 2018. *The Global Factory: Networkes Multinational Enterprises in the Modern Global Economy*. Chektenham, UK, Northamptom, MA: Edward Elgar Publishing.

Central Bank of Samoa. 2015. *Financial Services Demand Side Survey Samoa*. Apia, Samoa: Central Bank of Samoa.

Chang, Leslie T. 2008. *Factory Girls: From Village to City in a Changing China*. New York: Random House Publishing.

Clibborn, Stephen, Russell D. Lansbury, and Chris F. Wright. 2017. Who Will Make Our Cars? Global Lessons from the Demise of Australia's Auto Industry. Perspectives on Work. 21. 12.

Cox, Andrew. 1999. "Power, Value and Supply Chain Management." *Supply Chain Management: An International Journal* 4 (4): 167–75.

Denso Corporation. 2018. "Promoting CSR throughout the Supply Chain." Corporate Homepage. Accessed August 1, 2019. https://www.denso.com/global/en/csr/sociality-report/suppliers/procurement- policy/.

Elson, Diane, and Ruth Pearson. 2011. "The Subordination of Women and the Internationalization of Factory Production." In *The Women, Gender and Development Reader*, edited by Nalini Visvanathan, Lynn Duggan, Nan Wiegersma, and Laurie Nisonoff, 212–224. London New York: Zed Books.

Fairbairn, Te'o I J. 1993. "Samoa Mo Samoa: A Less Troubled Present?" *The Journal of Pacific History* 28 (2): 233–55.

Feagaimaali'i-Luamanu, Joyetter. 2017. "Samoa Bids Farewell to Yazaki." Samoa Observer. Apia, Samoa. Accessed August 26, 2017. https://www.samoaobserver.ws/category/article/ 19028.

Fernandez-Kelley, Maria Patricia. 1983. *For We Are Sold, I and My People: Women and Industry in Mexico's Frontier*. Albany: State University of New York Press.

Fraenkel, Jon. 1998. "Yazaki's Black Hole in Samoa-Australia Trade." *Islands Business* 24 (11): 52–53.

Fuentes, Annette, and Barbara Ehrenreich. 1983. *Women in the Global Factory*. Boston: Soth End Press.

Grevel-Lameko, Sally. 2000. "Multinational Employment, the Family Institution and the Status of Women in Samoa." MA thesis, University of the South Pacific.

Holweg, Matthias. 2008. "The Evolution of Competition in the Automotive Industry." In *Build To Order*, edited by G Perry and A Graves, 13–34. London: Springer.

Kerslake, Maria Talaitupu. 2007. "Maloafua: Structural Adjustment Programmes: The Case of Samoa." PhD dissertation, Massey University.

Kito, Tomomi, Alexandra Melike Brintrup, and Steve New. 2014. "The Structure of the Toyota Supply Network: An Empirical Analysis." Said Business School Research Papers WP2014-3, Available at SSRN: https://papers.ssrn.com/sol3/papers.cfm?abstract_id=2412512.

Kobayashi, Masakazu, Yoshiya Hirano, and Masatake Higashi. 2013. "Optimization of Assembly Processes of an Automobile Wire Harness." *Computer-Aided Design & Applications* 11 (3): 305–11.

Leigh, Andrew. 2002. "Trade Liberalisation and the Australian Labor Party." *Australian Journal of Politics and History* 48 (4): 487–508.

Li, Suhong, Bhanu Ragu-Nathanb, T.S. Ragu-Nathanb, and Raob S. Subba. 2006. "The Impact of Supplychain Management Practices on Competitive Advantage and Organizational Performance." *Omega* 34: 107–24.

Lim, Linda YC. 1983. "Capitalism, Imperialism, and Patriarchy: The Dilemma of Third World Women Workers in Multinational Factories." In *Women, Men, and the International Division of Labor*, edited by June Nash and Maria Patricia Fernandez-Kelley, 70–91. New York: State University of New York Press.

Louie, Miriam Ching Yoon. 2001. *Sweatshop Warriors: Immigrant Women Workers Take on the Global Factory*. Cambridge, MA: South End Press.

Malua, Margaret B. 2009. "Australia's WTO Trade-Policy Changes and the Future of a Samoan Car-Parts Investor." In *Trade and Poverty Reduction in the Asia-Pacific Region: Case Studies and Lessons from Low-Income Communities*, edited by A Stoler, J Redden, and L Jackson, 112–30. New York: Cambridge University Press.

Ministry of Commerce, Industry and Labour (MCIL). 2013. *Annuan Report*. Apia, Samoa: MCIL.

Moustafa, Ahmed, and Amit Kumar. 2016. Financial Services Sector Assessment for Samoa. Suva, Fiji: Pacific Financial Inclusion Programme 2016.

Neveling, Patrick, and Luisa Steur. 2018. "Introduction-Marxian Anthropology Resurgent." *Focaal* -Capitalism and Global Anthropology, Special Issue-Marxian Anthropology Resurgent: 1–15.

Ngai, Pun. 2005. *Made in China: Women Factory Workers in A Global Workplace*. Durham and London: Duke University Press.

Observer, Samoa. 1993. "Go Back to Work, P.M. Tells Strikers." *Samoa Observer*, August 1, 2019. https://www.samoaobserver.ws/category/samoa/14844.

Ong, Aihwa. 1987. *Spirit of Resistance and Capitalist Discipline: Factory Women in Malaysia*. Albany: State University of New York Press.

Pursell, Garry. 2001. *Australia's Experience with Local Content Programs in the Auto Industry: Lessons for India and Other Developing Countries*. Policy Research Working Paper, No. 2625. Washington: World Bank. Available at https://openknowledge.worldbank.org/ handle/10986/19604 License: CC BY 3.0 IGO.

Reichhart, Andreas, and Matthias Holweg. 2006. "What Is the Right Supplier Park for Your Supply Chain?" *Supply Chain Forum* 7 (1): 4–13.

Sako, Mari. 2009. "Outsourcing of Tasks and Outsourcing of Assets: Evidence of Automotive Supplier Parks in Brazil." In *Platforms, Markets, and Innovation*, edited by Annabelle Gawer, 251–272. Cheltenham and Northampton: Edward Elgar.

Sasabe, Mari. 1994. *Women & Work*. Suva, Fiji: Pacific Conference of Churches.

Selwyn, Benjamin. 2017. *The Struggle for Development*. Cambridge, UK, Malden, MA: Polity Press.

Siegel, Jordan, Lynn Pyun, and BY Cheon. 2019. "Multinational Firms, Labor Market Discrimination, and the Capture of Outsider's Advantage by Exploiting the Social Divide." *Administrative Science Quarterly* 64 (2): 370–97.

Stanford, Jim. 2017. "When an Auto Industry Disappears: Australia's Experience and Lessons for Canada." *Canadian Public Policy* 43 (S1): 1–18.

Sustained Quality. 2018. "Calculating Manufacturing Downtime Costs." Sustained Quality Group Homepage. Accessed August 1, 2019. http://www.sustained-quality.com/calculating-manufacturing-downtime-costs/.

Thomas, Tony. 1993. "Wiring Plant Get Settled in Samoa." The Australian Financial Review. 1993. https://www.afr.com/companies/wiring-plant-gets-settled-in-samoa-19931126-kasj9.

Toyota Motors Corporation. 2016. "How Many Parts Is Each Car Made Of?" Children's Question Room, Corporate Homepage. Accessed August 1, 2019. https://global.toyota/jp/ kids/faq/parts/001.html.

Trommnau, Jerome, Jens Kuhnle, Jorg Siegert, Robert Inderka, and Thomas Bauernhansl. 2019. "Overview of the State of the Art in the Production Process of Automotive Wire Harnesses, Current Research and Future Trends." Procedia, CIRP, vol. 81: 387–392.

Tsujita, Masami. 2002. "Becoming A Factory Girl: Young Samoan Women and A Japanese Factory." MA thesis, University of Hawai'i at Manoa.

US Department of Commerce. 2016. "2016 Top Markets Report Automotive Parts'." The International Trade Administration, The Deapartment Homepage. 2016. https://www.trade.gov/ topmarkets/pdf/autoparts.

Waters, Donald. 2006. *Operations Strategy*. London: Thomson Learning.

Wei, Wei. 2012. "Complexity Management of Vehicle Wiring Harnesses: An Optimized Model to Analyse Tradeoffs between Product and Manufacturing Costs." MA thesis, University of Windsor.

Wiring Harness News. 2020. "New Solutions Automate Wire Harness Production Line Balancing." Wiring Harness News. Accessed September 29, 2020. https://wiringharnessnews.com/article/new-solutions-automate-wire-harness-production-line-balancing/.

Wolf, Eric R. 1982. *Europe and the People without History*. Berkeley and Los Angeles: University of California Press.

Wolf, Eric R. 2010. *Europe and the People without History*. 3rd ed. Berkley, Los Angeles, London: University of California Press.

World Bank. 1991. "Pacific Island Economies: Toward Higher Growth in the 1990s." Washington: World Bank.

Yazaki Corporation. 2016a. "Global Network." Yazaki Corporation Homepage. Accessed September 20, 2020. https://www.yazaki-group.com/global/network/.

Yazaki Corporation. 2016b. "History of Yazaki Corporation."Yazaki Corporate Homepage. Accessed Septembefr 29, 2020. https://www.yazaki-group.com/global/pdf/history/g_018.pdf.

Zhang, Lu. 2014. *Inside China's Automobile Factories: The Politics of Labor and Worker Resistance*. New York: Cambridge University Press.

Index

Aborigines 15
abstraction 36, 46, 48
agency 1, 2, 2n.1, 4, 6, 10, 15, 16, 18, 22, 24, 25, 26, 28
   grassroots 255
agro industry 86
agro-industrial 105
aid industry 43
aldeamentos 210
aldeia(s) 125, 126, 128
Algeria 10, 17
alienation 36, 52
Andre Gunder Frank 256
Anthropocene 138
Anti-Politics Machine 41
Arab Spring 17
Armed Forces Revolutionary Council (AFRC) 189
Arundhati Roy 41
Australia 255
automotive industry 254, 255, 258, 259, 262, 264

Bachtiar Nasir 247
Bert J. Barickman 128
Black Lives Matter (BLM) 13
Bob Hawke 262
Boston Globe 60
bouradè 54
Bourdieu, Pierre 176, 178
Brisas del Frayle 86
Broad Reach Healthcare 60
Bruno Latour 113, 120, 139

Cali–Buenaventura railroad 95
capitalist expansion 5, 12, 13, 26, 60
Capitalocene 21
carbon
   as commodity 202, 204
   carbon emissions 201
cash crops 207
   coffee, tobacco, sugar 64
   cashew 213–215, 220
   charcoal 202, 213
   cocoa 157–58, 160

eucalyptus 131, 207, 216–218
Cauca Valley 86
Charles Tilly 6n.7, 232
China 10, 17, 27
Chinese Indonesian
   cultural tradition 242
   culture 243
   group identity 229
class
   and theory 11, 151
   consumer 16
   global perspective 155
   middle 162
   working 162
climate change
   mitigation 20
Climate change
   challenges 201
Cold War 9, 10, 11, 237
Colombian Institute for the Agrarian Reform 99
colonial subjects 59
Columbia University 64
Commodificatio 55
commodification 8, 21, 124 *See also* abstraction, privatization, valuation, alienation
   definition of 44
Commodification 37, 44
Commodities
   definition 39
commodity fetishism 119, 140
commodity relations 38
conservation agriculture 208
   critique of 209
   promotion of 210
Conservation agriculture 223
Convention Peoples Party (CPP) 188
Cooperatives of Associated Labour 104
core–periphery relationships 3, 5, 158, 254, 256
countermovement
   commodification 36, 38, 44
countermovements 41
Cuba 10, 17

cultural hybridity 115
Cyclone Ofa 264
Cyclone Val 264

David Graeber 113, 120
democratization theory 17
Denmark 14
dependency theory 117
development industry 42
  and capitalism 42
differentiation 135
Discovery Coast 113
dispossession 88, 130
division of labour 230, 232, 233
  conceptualisation of 231
Donald Trump
  shithole countries 18n.17
Dutch East Indies 234, 235, 236
Dutch United East Indian Company
  (VOC) 234

E. P. Thompson 11, 177
earthquake
  and NGOs 42
  Haiti 36
East Gonja 180
ejidos 93
empty lands 106
encomenderos 91
encomienda system 91
enganches 102
Enlarged Joint Togoland Consultative
  Commission 184n.25
environmental narrative 213
EPWH
  and migration 62
  critique of 3, 119
  influence of 4n.6
  originality of 1, 2, 8
  overview of 5
  reviews of 3n.3, 4, 8
  and cardinal research question 6, 22
Eric Hobsbawm 11
Eric Olin Wright 152
eucalyptus
  and World Bank 218
  controversy 217
Eurocentric 3, 141

European Union
  expansion 15

Farm Labour Program
  Puerto Rico 67
Fernando Sierra Berdecía 69
fetishism 112, 142
  definition of 120
  political ecology of 116
fictitious commodities 39
financialization 19
fixity 6, 9
  colonial understandings of 172, 180
Flight Lieutenant J. J. Rawlings 189, 192
Foucault, Michel 178

Garden State Association 71
George Floyd 13
Ghana
  and Nawuri 173
global connectivity. *See also* relational totality,
  interdependence
global interconnectedness. *See also* relational
  totality
Global South
  definition of 2n.1
Gold 158
Gonja chiefs
  power of 181
Gonja Traditional Council 193
Governor Basuki Tjahaja Purnama
  (Ahok) 245
Governor Guggisberg 180
Great Depression 64, 66
Greenland 14
Gurkha 14
Gypsy Question 14

hacendados 95
hacienda 92–95, 103
hacienda-ingenio 99
Hegelian perspective 19
historical amnesia 16, 117, 119, 133, 139
Historical amnesia 139
homo economicus 140
homogeneity
  understandings of 2
Hurricane Maria 59

INDEX

hurricane San Felipe 66
Hybridity 136
hybridizing frontiers 117

Immanuel Wallenstein 3n.2, 256
Indonesian Communist Party (PKI) 237
Indonesian National Survey Project
    (INSP) 241, 246, 247
Indonesian Nationalist Awakening 237
ingenios 97, 99, 101, 104
insurgent citizenship 138
interconnectedness 16

James Ferguson
    anti-politics machine 37
James Holsten
    differentiated citizenship 116
James Scott 21
Java 234
Jean Copans 159
Jean-Bertrand Aristide 49
Jean-Claude Duvalier 49
Jeremy Campbell 128n13, 138n.18
Jesús T. Piñero 69
Jones Act 65
Juan A. Giusti-Cordero 81
Julian Steward 63

koelies 235
Kofi Busia 188
Kpandai 180, 194
    and disputes 182
Krause, Monika 45
Kwame Nkrumah 182n.19, 188, 190

Labour Migration under Capitalism 63
landscape approach 204, 205
landscape interventions 89, 96
latifundas 92
LGBTQ 51
Li, Tania
    rendering technical 46

Margaret Thatcher 11
Marx
    and fixity 7
    and mode of production debate 7
    and power 178

Communist Manifesto 54
Marxist analysis 10
    challenges of 9
Marxist anthropology 6, 9, 12n.13
    challenges 6
Marxist framework 152
Max Weber 231
Media 13, 18, 19, 238, 247
mestiço 129, 140
mestizo 94
mestizos 93
Mexican *braceros* 66
Michael Taussig 3n.3, 113, 142
migration
    agency 62
    and agency 59
    and labour 59
    history of capitalism 14, 61
    Puerto Ricans 59
    to US 65
mode(s) of production 3, 5, 7, 8, 87, 92, 103,
        105, 118, 119, 124, 202–204
    Marx 7
        Dialectical 6
    capitalist 3, 5, 67, 90, 95, 101, 104, 151, 204,
        212, 235, 245, 249
    tributary 91, 181, 189
Mongol 15
mutual interdependence 254

National Liberation Council (NLC) 188
Native Authorities 180
Native Authority
    reform 182
native Indians 15
native rights 183
Nawuri
    protests 182
    traditional dance 175
neoliberal 258
neo-liberal 19
neoliberalism 11n.11, 17, 37, 40,
        132, 138–40
Netherlands East-Indies 234
New Deal 40, 64
    Bureau of Employment and
        Migration 68
New Dealers 66

New Order   238
    Indonesia   249
NGO   38n.1
    and society   41
NGO
    indicator species   17, 41
NGOS
    and Haiti   42
NGO-ization   41
NGOs
    and project management   47
Nkrumrah   190
noble savage   132
Northern Scandinavia   14
Northern Territories of the Gold Coast   180

Obama administration   59
Olin-Wright   158

palenques   92
Palestinians   15
Palmira   96
Panama Canal   95
Paris Agreement   205
Pataxó   114, 115, 130
patronage democracy   88, 105
Paulo Freire   53
peasant wars   40
Peasant Wars   17, 55
periphery–core. *See* core-periphery, and
    world system
Petras, James   42, 45
petty trade   157, 161
Polanyi   39
    division of labour   232
    labour power   39
    substance of society   39
Polanyi, Karl
    fictious commodities,
        countermovement   37
political ecology of fetishism   121, 142
Popular Democratic Party
    Puerto Rico   64
Portuguese Ministry of Colonies   211
post-Suharto era   228
precariatization   105
President Putin   15
pribumi   228
Prime Minister Alesana   265

privatization   36, 50
Privatization   48
Progress Party   188, 191
protests
    use of tradition   182
Puerto Rican migrants
    labour camps   78
Puerto Rican migration to US   71
Puerto Rico
    Dept. of Labour   70
    Farm Labour Programme   70
    Public Law 25   69
    Public Law 89   69
Puerto Rico Project   64

quality, cost, and delivery (QCD)   259

radical alterity   139
Raymond Williams   11
REDD\+   203, 204, 205n.2
REDD\+
    and Mozambique   205
reducciones   91
Regional Autonomous Corporation Valle del
    Cauca   97
    CVC   97
relational totality   8
resilient acclimatization   135, 143
Rexford G. Tugwell   66
Rhodes-Livingston Institute   64
Rockefeller Foundation   64, 96n.6
Rohingya   15
Ronald Reagan   11
Rosalind Morris   113
Russia   10, 15, 17, 30

Sally Falk Moore   178
Sami   14
scientific agriculture   210
Second World War   64 *See also* World War II
Sidney Mintz   31.3, 63, 64, 78, 81
slash and burn   202, 219
    colonial anxieties   210
    demonization of   210, 211
social closure   245
South China Sea   246
Southeast Asia   9, 234
Spanish-American War   59
statistical data

INDEX

critique of 161
structural adjustment programmes 11, 41
structure 18 *See also* agency
subjectivities 115
sugar 65, 98
Suharto 228, 237, 238, 251, 252
superstructure 7
Supreme Military Council (SMC) 188
surplus labour 105
Susanna Hecht 138n.19
Synchronic explanations 18

Terry Turner 120
Third World 9
timber 212
Tofilau Eti Alesana 264
traditions
    denial of 186, 191, 193
trapiche 92
trickle down 12
Truman Administration. *See* New Deal

Ukraine 15
UN General Assembly Declaration on the
    Rights of Indigenous Peoples 19
UN Trusteeship Council 174, 183
    complaints to 184
UN Trusteeship system 183
UN-administered territory of Togoland 183
United Nations Framework Convention for
    Climate Change (UNFCCC) 203
US Bureau of Employment and Migration
    (BEM) 67
US citizenship
    Puerto Ricans 65
US Congress 69
US Supreme Court 65
Uyghur 15

valuation 36, 50, 52
Value theory 120
Vietnam 10, 17
Vietnam War 9
violence
    concept of 123
VOC 234

Wagner-Peyser Act 68
Weber

social status 153, 231
Weber and Marx
    comparison 152
Weberian framework 152, 154
William Roseberry 81
Windrush 13
Wolf
    analytical deforestation 11
    and alienation 52
    and culture 172, 196
    and fetishism 119
    and historical materialism 143
    and legacy 4
    crisis and differentiation 118
    cultural change 186
    Cycles of Violence 18
    Envisioning Power 176n.5, 178n.10
    factories in the field 217
    fetishism 123
    field of action 68
    fields of power 59
    hybrid metabolism 117
    links to Vienna 10n.10
    Pathways of Power 61
    Peasant Wars in the Twentieth
        Century 10, 37
    power 119
    power of culture 177
    power, conceptualisation
        of 4, 176, 177
    relational totality 2n.1
    structural power 67, 179
    structure of the situation 63
    totality of interconnected processes 117,
        230, 256, 258
Wolf & Mintz
    The People of Puerto Rico 63–65,
        74, 76, 81
    critique of 59, 61, 74
working class
    in Africa? 159, 166
working conditions
    Yazaki 266
World Bank
    and Mozambique 202
    and Samoa 263
    cashew 220
    eucalyptus 222
world system 3n.2, 6, 117, 152

world systems
  theory   3, 117
World War II
  and labour   69, 118
  migration to US   66
  See also Second World war

Yazaki   261
  production line   268

Yazaki Electrical Distribution
    System Samoa
  YES   255
  YES   255, 258, 261, 265–276

zafra   96
Zambézia   205, 209
Zygmunt Bauman   152, 168
  and liquified modernity   151

Printed in the United States
by Baker & Taylor Publisher Services